OTHER TITLES OF INTEREST FROM ST. LUCIE PRESS

For more information about these titles call, fax or write:

St. Lucie Press
100 E. Linton Blvd., Suite 403B, Delray Beach, FL 33483
TEL (561) 274-9906 • FAX (561) 274-9927
E-MAIL information@slpress.com • WEB SITE http://www.slpress.com

S⁴

D1417509

WILDLIFE ISSUES
in a
CHANGING WORLD

Michael P. Moulton
James Sanderson

S^t_L

St. Lucie Press
Delray Beach, Florida

Phone: (561) 274-9906
Fax: (561) 274-9927
E-mail: information@slpress.com
Web site: http://www.slpress.com

S$_L^t$

Published by
St. Lucie Press
100 E. Linton Blvd., Suite 403B
Delray Beach, FL 33483

CONTENTS

PREFACE

In the spring of 1979, Dr. Larry D. Harris at the University of Florida created a class called Man and Wildlife Resources. In the fall of 1987, he changed the name to Wildlife Issues in a Changing World. Dr. Harris, a lifelong conservationist and co-founder of the Florida Greenways program, was frustrated because he felt he was "preaching to the choir" in his graduate-level classes. He needed a forum where he could reach many people at once regarding conservation of our natural resources. His solution was to create an undergraduate class called Wildlife Issues and open it up to anyone interested in wildlife and conservation. The class was moved from a small classroom to an auditorium.

In the fall semester of 1996, class enrollment reached 675 students, and more than 1800 students took the class that same year. Beginning in 1997, two classes per semester are planned and enrollment is expected to exceed 4000 students. Are students today more interested in wildlife issues? We suggest that most people, young and old, are interested in issues concerning wildlife.

When we began investigating general issues, we quickly discovered that some wildlife issue was covered in nearly every edition of every major newspaper. The problem was to make sense of all the separate and apparently isolated issues. Early in 1996, record numbers of dead or dying manatees (an endangered species) were turning up in southwest Florida. In New Mexico, the winter was unusually dry and bears were wandering into Albuquerque neighborhoods in search of food. In Chicago, a trial involving smuggled parrots was wrapping up. In Miami, Fly River turtles from Papua New Guinea were turning up in the pet trade. U.S. Fish and Wildlife Service officials arrested a footwear manufacturer for using endangered species skins from South America to make boots. In the North Atlantic, harp seal hunts resumed, and one of the greatest offshore fisheries was so badly overharvested it was closed. Walrus had been hunted to extinction there 250 years ago.

Several remaining monarch butterfly populations died as the result of a freak snowfall in the mountains outside Mexico City. In China, tiger penises were sold as aphrodisiacs. In Kenya, only ten dugongs remain. While the U.S. Fish and Wildlife Service tries to protect 11 endangered piping plovers by poisoning some of the more than 5000 gulls that feast on the plovers' eggs and young, the Human Society of the United States tries to protect the gulls. In Zaire and Rwanda, gorilla habitat was under immense pressure from refugees. In Cameroon, forestry practices produced an unexpected benefit for bush meat hunters. Estimates are that three gorillas and three chimpanzees are consumed for food each day. Wildlife issues, some humorous and some sad, were with us wherever we went.

When early humans depended on animals for food, there were rarely any wildlife issues. The only issues probably concerned ownership of the kill. Today, wildlife is threatened for many reasons. Often wildlife populations cannot regenerate, and the survival of many species depends on active protection.

Issues arise when at least two people disagree. A wildlife issue arises when two or more people disagree over some aspect involving wildlife. Here, we urge that resolution of the issue must occur proactively. That is, resolving an issue does not include a default option. Issues must be decided upon and a course of action followed, and changed if necessary. In no instance is doing nothing an option.

We urge readers to take a historical perspective and use the scientific method to resolve wildlife issues. That is, we discourage participants from basing their decisions on "belief," however common such belief is. For instance, one often hears statements such as "there are more manatees in Florida today than when Columbus arrived." A counterargument is that there are more warm-water refugia provided by nuclear power plants than when the Spanish arrived, and so there are more manatees now than ever. The scientific method requires testable hypotheses to decide issues. Neither of these previous statements is testable today.

With all the national laws and international agreements protecting wildlife, it's a wonder there are any wildlife issues at all. It seems like the number of wildlife laws has grown in proportion to the number of wildlife issues. Protection laws and agreements generally are a response to wildlife issues and do not foresee them. For instance, the African Elephant Protection Act passed by Congress and signed by the president of the United States became law well after Africa had lost most of its elephants. Other laws appear to serve local research projects. The Endangered Species Act has "teeth" because it provides for stiff penalties, but the act can be circumvented by filing a "take permit," which is often granted. Another law protects wild horses and burros and demands that their habitat be managed in a natural way. However, because horses and burros are introduced species, they are generally harmful to the very habitat that must also be protected. Humans can enact laws but they cannot change the laws of nature, however stiff the penalties are made.

No number of laws will protect wildlife species, just as no number of parks and reserves will save all species. Worldwide habitat destruction is continuing, and the developed world continues to consume vast quantities of global resources. Introduced species are homogenizing the world, creating widespread problems. Can we address these issues and resolve them? In our last chapter, we present several novel solutions that have been developed and applied with success.

During a recent trip to Papua New Guinea, a group of foreign tourists urged their native guide to break off discussions with the logging companies. "Preserve your forests and wildlife," they told him. "Do not sacrifice them for money." He responded by saying his people wanted access to modern healthcare, schools for their children, and to motorboats and fuel. "You would put us in zoos and stare at us," he said. Then he asked a critical question that silenced the tourists: "Will you pay me for my trees and wildlife to save them?" He knew they would not.

People all over the world want nothing more than a better life for themselves and their families. Somehow we must redefine our quest for a better life. A better life, a high-quality life, means living with nature, not apart from nature. As the Papua New Guinea guide said, "You can try to explain conservation to my people, but they will not understand. They were born conservationists and their lives depend on conserving their resources. They do not understand how one could act otherwise." Certainly, issues depend on one's perspective.

Although most people will never see mountain gorillas in the wild, we are certain that most people favor protecting them through preserves and laws. By understanding some of the worldwide wildlife issues we discuss, we hope that readers will gain a better understanding of issues in their own backyard as well as others'. As educators, we believe that one way to resolve wildlife issues is through understanding and not emotion. Quality of life is synonymous with living as a part of nature and accepting wildlife for what it is. It is a depressing thought to imagine living in a world without free-roaming gorillas, elephants, or manatees. Therefore, we are prepared to deal with and resolve difficult wildlife issues and make hard choices. With greater appreciation for wildlife issues, our readers will gain the confidence to deal with them.

The growing use of the World Wide Web has enabled users to explore globally wildlife issues most never knew existed. We have included exercises designed to expand our readers' horizon so as to broaden their perspective and encourage their own thinking. Since we could not cover all wildlife issues in this text, other issues are explored in the exercises. Certainly, there is as yet no substitute for a good library, and we frequently suggest that readers seek one out for further exploration of issues we discuss. The act of discovery yields reward in and of itself.

ACKNOWLEDGMENTS

We wish to thank Dr. Larry D. Harris for creating the Wildlife Issues class and for enthusiastically encouraging this book.

Mike Moulton wishes to thank Becky, Rachel, and Linda for support and encouragement and access to the computer. He also thanks Deborah M. Epperson, Drs. Jon D. Johnson, John M. Davis, Susan K. Jacobson, and Mel Sunquist for stimulating conversation about various wildlife issues.

Jim Sanderson wishes to thank his spouse, Joan Morrison, for support and encouragement. He also thanks Manuel Molles, University of New Mexico, and his son Anders for additional research material. Dr. Estaban Sarmiento and Dr. Dieter Steklis added much to the discussion of gorillas. Dr. Katie Sieving also provoked several interesting wildlife issue discussions.

We also reserve special thanks for our friends at St. Lucie Press. Dennis Buda provided us the opportunity to organize our thoughts and present them to others. Our editor, Ms. Sandy Pearlman, deserves thanks for all the hard work she did—and made us do—to make our efforts a reality. That picture of the medicinal shop in China is perfect, Sandy.

ABOUT THE AUTHORS

Michael P. Moulton is an Associate Professor of Wildlife Ecology and Conservation at the University of Florida. He spent his undergraduate years at the University of Colorado and later received his Ph.D. from the University of Tennessee. His principal area of research deals with introduced species of birds.

Jim Sanderson is currently working for the Biological Resources Division of the U.S. Geological Survey and is a Visiting Professor at the University of Florida. He received his Ph.D. from the University of New Mexico in 1976. An avid traveler, Dr. Sanderson has collected and synthesized wildlife issues from around the world. His interests include quantitative ecology, community ecology, and landscape ecology.

INTRODUCTION

With increasing frequency, we hear and read about mysterious decreases in or disappearances of living organisms. Often these organisms are reptiles, fish, birds, or mammals—what people commonly call wildlife. This book addresses current wildlife issues. Exactly what does the term *wildlife* mean and what do we mean when we suggest there is an *issue* at stake? For the purposes of this book, we will accept the definition of "issue" as given in *Webster's New Collegiate Dictionary*: an issue is "a matter in dispute between two or more parties, a point of debate or controversy." Certainly "two or more parties" refers to two or more humans. Thus, without two or more humans involved, there can be no issue.

What does the term wildlife mean? Basically, all living wild animals are wildlife. We will spend much time discussing this catchall term. For instance, are elephants in a highly managed African park really wildlife? Are zoo animals wildlife? Are insects wildlife? How about bacteria? Humans create parks for endangered species. Do we create parks for endangered or rare malaria-causing tsetse flies? The term wildlife is often synonymous with benign wildlife. That is, animals are wildlife as long as they pose no direct threat to humans. When something poses a direct threat to humans, it becomes something other than wildlife, such as a pest or disease-causing agent that must be searched out and destroyed. We generally do not deliberately seek out and destroy a wildlife species. Thus, wildlife is a relative term with respect to human experience.

WILDLIFE ISSUES

The phrase *wildlife issue* is by definition a wildlife controversy that pits at least two and usually more human participants against one another over a problem relating to wildlife. Nearly everyone in North America is familiar with timber harvesting in the Pacific Northwest and the need to preserve northern spotted owl (*Strix occidentalis*) habitat. This is clearly a wildlife issue involving the continued harvesting of timber in forests that are essential habitat for the northern spotted owl. Some humans derive material gain from harvesting timber. Others want to have spotted owls around for their viewing pleasure or perhaps want to look at forested hillsides and resent the harvesting of timber on public lands.

Other wildlife issues are equally controversial. The manatee is a large endangered aquatic mammal that lives in Florida's streams, rivers, and lakes. Many boaters consider manatees to be nothing more than "speed bumps" and fail to exercise appropriate caution to avoid collisions with them. Many manatees show linear scars on their backs from boat propellers. Are manatees worth saving or are they doomed because they are an inconvenience to boaters? As with any issue, there are strong proponents on both sides. Each side frequently offers arguments to try to sway those who are neutral or undecided. For instance, a boating industry spokesperson suggested that increased manatee deaths were the result of there being more manatees than the environment can support. Statements such as "there are more manatees now than when Columbus was here" are offered as evidence.

Many wildlife issues span a broader context, where wildlife is a subset of a broader issue. For example, it has been suggested that the human-altered hydrological cycle in Everglades National Park is responsible for declining wading bird populations. Because much water is diverted to nearby human population centers such as Miami, the issue of water in the Everglades becomes a wildlife issue insofar as it impacts wildlife populations. Certainly, there is an issue here. Human control of water resources directly impacts the Everglades landscape and hence its living organisms, including wildlife.

In many areas of the United States, raccoon populations are increasing. An injured raccoon found by a sympathetic human is often taken to a wildlife rehabilitation center where it is treated and released. Yet raccoon populations are increasing because of a lack of predators that keep raccoon populations in check. Raccoon themselves are predators of birds' eggs and chicks, and in some areas raccoons now consume a large percentage of gopher tortoise eggs. Often, the raccoon does not wait for the tortoise to lay the eggs but rather scoops them out of the living tortoise, killing it. Alligators lose eggs to raccoons. In towns and rural areas everywhere, raccoons raid garbage cans, and their populations are increasing. When the population density becomes too high, rabies outbreaks are common and spread rapidly throughout the regional population. Humans are susceptible to rabies, and thus an issue is raised. Should humans indeed act as predators of raccoons, keeping their populations in check? Should humans shoot raccoons on sight? Should wildlife rehabilitation centers treat raccoons or euthanize them? Indeed, are raccoons really wildlife or a human-adapted nuisance that is no longer wild?

Some wildlife issues seem bizarre or almost unbelievable. For example, on February 17, 1994, the *Gainesville Sun* reported, "Toke a toad, go to jail." A California couple was arrested on charges of possessing the illegal chemical bufotenine, obtained from a toad (*Bufo alvarius*). The toad apparently secretes a venom from a gland on its back. When smoked, users say it produces a high that eclipses the psychedelic properties of LSD. Laws against the use of bufotenine date back to the 1960s.

As reported in the *Gainesville Sun* on July 12, 1994, "A chemical used for greener lawns is killing fish, birds, otters" and is contaminating drinking water. According to the article, a certain chemical had caused ten documented massive fish kills in Florida. The chemical is a pesticide used to control microscopic worms that are especially dangerous to golf course turf. In May, the chemical had been applied on 100 acres, and thousands of fish turned up dead in a nearby canal after a heavy rain. The U.S. Golf Association studied the chemical, and the association's research director issued a statement to the public that there was no threat to groundwater. The study did not look at runoff however, which the state of Florida says caused ten other incidents of fish, bird, and otter kills. The company that makes the lawn chemical wants to cooperate with Florida, but golf courses are major customers for the chemical. Surely there is a testable hypothesis somewhere here. What is it?

"Locust threaten continent's food" was yet another wildlife issue. Swarms of 3-inch-long desert locusts capable of devouring 100 tons of vegetation per day were eating their way across Africa. The locust infestation posed a serious threat to the food supply. Some 250 locust species cause formidable problems for agricultural crops. Is it the locust or the intensity of agriculture that is the problem here?

How about this attention-grabber from the January 13, 1994 *St. Petersburg Times*: "Caterpillar kills 5 in Brazil." A venomous, hairy species of caterpillar whose sting causes burns and internal bleeding killed five people in Brazil. The latest victim was 57 years old and the cause of death was officially "death by caterpillar sting." The fire caterpillar (*Lonomia obliqua*) can grow to three inches, is green, and is covered with a dense mat of fine hairs. The hairs act like hypodermic needles which, when contacted, inject a venom that interferes with coagulation of the blood. Rapid deforestation and the disappearance of predators appear to have led to an increased presence of the stinging caterpillars near towns and cities in Brazil's southernmost state, Rio Grande do Sul.

What is the basis for deciding whether an issue exists? Issues are human constructs and would not be issues if humans were not involved. That is, the basis of all issues lies in the different perceptions or beliefs among humans. Two humans with identical beliefs would never have any issues to decide. They would simply agree on a certain course of action and proceed. This is equivalent to suggesting that a person has never had a disagreement or difference with anyone else—and we all know how probable that is!

Consider the following example. Nearshore commercial fishing in Florida using gill nets was a profitable enterprise. Indeed, many people who had enjoyed recreational fishing blamed the great success of nearshore commercial fishing for depleting fish stocks. In 1994, Florida voters passed an amendment to the state constitution banning commercial netting of fish with gill nets within 3 miles on the Atlantic coast and within 9 miles on the Gulf coast. On July 1, 1995, the amendment became law. How did this issue arise?

Recreational fishing in Florida is one of the state's top tourist attractions. Evidently fishermen (and fisherwomen) had noticed a decline in the number and size of fish caught for several years. Numerous causes, such as pollution, commercial gill netting, development of beachfront hotels, and global warming, were discussed in the press and on local radio shows. Notice that recreational fishing was not considered to be a cause for concern. This is because the recreational fishing industry was behind the campaign in the first place. After months of debate, the presumed cause was identified—commercial gill netting. Once a cause was found, it could be targeted for solution. The recreational fishing industry had to convince voters statewide to pass a law prohibiting gill netting.

A grass roots campaign was organized statewide, and recreational and weekend fishermen were armed with petitions. Over 400,000 signatures were collected—enough to place a proposed amendment on the statewide ballot during the general election. The amendment passed, and Governor Lawton Chiles threatened to call out the National Guard to enforce the net ban. The grass roots campaign succeeded. People from all professions who enjoyed fishing took the day off—to go fishing!

Of course, there were two sides to this issue. The opposition consisted of commercial fishing interests that had difficulty getting organized. Their arguments progressed in stages. Initially, they denied there were fewer fish. How could commercial fishing alone deplete huge fish stocks? Surely, this was impossible. This was the denial phase. Such statements as "there is no data to support the conclusion that stocks are depleted," "natural fluctuations in fish populations occur all the time," and even "we don't believe you" appeared in the media. When these arguments failed to reverse the general opinion, the campaign moved to phase two—acceptance of "facts" without supporting "data." The commercial interests accepted that fish stocks were reduced but continued to deny responsibility.

When the grass roots petition drive spread throughout Florida towns and cities, the third and final phase—total confusion—set in and the opposition faltered. A statement typical of this phase was, "Now what will we do if we are unable to make a living fishing?" Note that this statement is no longer a wildlife issue. The wildlife issue would be decided in the voting booth. Lawmakers at the state level could now endlessly debate the commercial fishing business. Commercial fishing companies failed to grasp the widespread interest in sport fishing. Indeed, had they decided to help increase fish stocks through alternative stocking programs or to simply move further offshore, they might have saved the day. Today, gill netting is illegal within the offshore distances set by law. Curiously, these limits are beyond where recreationists with boats most often fish. The number and size of the fish have not yet increased.

THE PROBLEM WITH "BELIEF"

Notice the role of "beliefs" on both sides of the Florida fishing issue. One side "believed" fishing stocks were being depleted by commercial fishing interests. The opposing side "believed" it was not responsible and that some other factor was causing the decline. Note also that commercial interests did not blame recreational fishing businesses. In the absence of good, solid scientific data, these "beliefs" became the foundation for an open public debate based not on fact but on faith (Lakatos 1978).

At one time, people believed the earth was flat. Ptolemy, the greatest scientist of his time, believed the earth was the center of the universe and the sun and all heavenly bodies revolved around the earth. This belief persisted for 1500 years, until Copernicus whispered to his friends that the sun was the body around which all planets, including earth, revolved and that he had accumulated scientific data to support this conclusion. Copernicus died before seeing his disciples held up to public ridicule by the church. Belief is a powerful force.

Belief is not a medieval practice. Early in the 20th century, passenger pigeons formed flocks that darkened the sky and blocked out the sun for hours at a time. Who would have believed the few bird-watchers who foresaw the demise and eventual complete extinction of the ubiquitous pigeon? Philosopher Imre Lakatos (1978) reminds us that "no degree of commitment to beliefs makes them knowledge." What then is the difference between accepted knowledge and belief? Even Copernicus's view of the solar system was changed by

Kepler and Kepler's by Newton. Were these views beliefs or scientific facts? How does a series of facts lead to a theory that permits predictions which can be tested?

One goal of this book is to help you sort out the issues that will be independent of people's beliefs. A trend or pattern may exist even if no one believes it and may not exist even if everyone believes it. The solution to this conundrum is to always use the scientific method to decide an issue.

RESOLVING ISSUES

There is often more than one way to resolve an issue. We might, for instance, want to decide an issue on the basis of economics. Cattle grazing on public lands is a wildlife issue because cattle frequently destroy habitat that could otherwise be used by deer and elk. The Bureau of Land Management is responsible for collecting grazing fees paid by ranchers to use public lands. Currently this fee is approximately $1.85 a head per month. That is, a rancher with grazing rights pays $1.85 per cow or bull per month for the right to graze these cattle. Suppose the Wilderness Society or the Nature Conservancy would be willing to pay $2.00 per head per month to the U.S. government to keep a like number of cattle off public lands. Economically it would be a good business decision by the government to accept the higher offer.

Sadly, some issues resolve themselves before humans can decide to act responsibly. The passenger pigeon became extinct before laws could be enacted to protect it. The Carolina parakeet left us similarly, its joyous melody denied to us before our forebearers could introduce a law and bring it to a vote. The scientific method is supposed to prevent such atrocities as extinction from happening without the majority of the voting public deciding that extinction is an acceptable alternative instead of deciding by default.

THE SCIENTIFIC METHOD

The scientific method works in a series of steps. First, a pattern or trend is observed. This could correspond to our belief that a trend exists, for instance. An explanation is offered as to why the trend or pattern exists. We are led to the creation of a scientific hypothesis. Predictions are made based upon the hypothesis. Finally, tests of the predictions are conducted using controlled laboratory experiments or statistical tests. If a prediction fails, we can return to the creation of a new hypothesis from which to make predictions. If a prediction is true, then we draw the indicated conclusion.

Unfortunately, when dealing with emotional issues, hypotheses are not clearly stated or are untestable. For instance, someone might suggest that there are more manatees now than when Columbus arrived in the New World. This statement is untestable, and the scientific method cannot be used to prove or disprove it. The most important characteristic of hypotheses is that they must be mutually exclusive alternatives. In other words, two opposing hypotheses must span the space of all possibilities and lead to opposite conclusions. One hypothesis is referred to as the null hypothesis, or no difference hypothesis, and is labeled H_0. The opposing hypothesis, labeled H_1, is called the alternative hypothesis and states that there is a difference. Some examples will help clarify these hypotheses:

H_0   There is no difference in frog abundance between areas where frog harvesting is allowed versus protected areas.

H_1   There is a difference in frog abundance between the two areas.

Another example is:

H_0   Agricultural practices in the Everglades Agricultural District have no effect on concentrations of phosphorus in the water.

H_1   Agricultural practices in the Everglades Agricultural District alter the phosphorus concentration in the water leaving the district.

Notice that in both cases, one of the two hypotheses must be correct. This is not the case for hypotheses that are not mutually exclusive, such as:

H_0   The boss's new car is a Ford.

H_1   The boss's new car is a Chevy.

TESTING HYPOTHESES WITH EXPERIMENTS

Experiments are powerful ways to test hypotheses. In an experiment, one: (1) applies some treatment and (2) compares the effects of the treatment on some variable that could be influenced by the treatment to the effects on the variable when the treatment is not applied. A controlled experiment requires a *control* and a series of *experimental treatments* or manipulations. In ecology, control plots are simply plots of ground, for instance, that do not receive the treatment. The aim is, of course, to see what happens if the treatments were not applied. We also need to specify some variable of interest that the experimental treatments might influence. There is no point in measuring variables that are: (1) not likely to be affected by the experimental treatment or (2) not measurable.

For example, if you were interested in comparing the effects of a new fuel on the performance of your car, there is no sense in checking your tire pressure before the new fuel is used and then after the new fuel has been tried. A better measure of performance would be mileage or acceleration.

Now recall our first pair of hypotheses above which dealt with frogs. A prediction of our hypothesis is that frog hunters reduce populations of frogs in areas where frogs are hunted. We could survey areas where frogs are hunted to see if their numbers are reduced each evening, but this would really show nothing because other factors might be involved. For instance, wading birds eat frogs, as do fish, so the frog count might go down anyway. Similarly, the frog population might go up because frogs invaded the area when the bigger hunted frogs were killed out.

For these reasons, we need to do a controlled experiment. We could establish ten replicates of two experimental plots, say 3 m^2 on a side (called a quadrat), and survey the quadrats for frogs. In ten of the quadrats, there will be no frog hunting. In the other ten quadrats, hunting of frogs will be allowed. The quadrats will be chosen randomly along the shoreline of a lake where frogs are hunted.

On successive mornings after an evening of hunting, we will catch and release as many frogs as we can from the 20 quadrats, making certain not to release frogs into any of the other quadrats. Ideally, the survey would be done simultaneously in all the quadrats and for the same length of time in each quadrat. We will count every frog caught in each quadrat. Note that it would be unlikely that we could catch every frog in every quadrat, nor is it essential to do so.

After ten successive evenings, we could compare the number of frogs in each quadrat. However, what is important is not the number of frogs in each quadrat but the change in the number of frogs in each quadrat. For instance, let's say that in one of the unhunted quadrats, the number of frogs went from 20 down to 10 over the course of 10 days. In one of the hunted quadrats, the number of frogs might have increased from 15 to 30. However, it is important to compare all the quadrats simultaneously. We could sum up all the frogs caught in the unhunted quadrats each day and compare the change to that found in the hunted quadrats. The changes can be compared statistically.

If there was a decrease in the number of frogs over the course of our study in both sets of quadrats, and the difference in the two decreases was large, then we could conclude that hunting negatively impacted the frog population. If there was a slight increase in the unhunted quadrats and a slight decrease in the hunted quadrats, however, the difference might not be significant, and we would be led to conclude that hunting did not impact the frog population. The important parameter is the difference in the changes in population in each set of quadrats and not the absolute number of frogs.

Now consider the second set of hypotheses above:

H₀   Agricultural practices in the Everglades Agricultural District have no effect on concentrations of phosphorus in the water.

H₁   Agricultural practices in the Everglades Agricultural District alter the phosphorus concentration in the water leaving the district.

Here we have a problem setting up a controlled experiment because we cannot specify any kind of control. That is, we have no way of comparing test plots to plots where nothing was done. Certainly, we could measure the phosphorus concentration in the water exiting the Everglades Agricultural District, but the result would not tell us anything about whether the level of phosphorus is higher or lower because of agricultural practices. Furthermore, we would be unlikely to pinpoint the source of the phosphorus because of all the other inputs to the water supply. Unfortunately, in most wildlife issues, we face a similar situation: we cannot set up a controlled experiment. The scale is simply too grand. What we end up doing is collecting a great deal of circumstantial evidence. Remember, however, that even though the evidence is circumstantial, it is still evidence!

The value of the scientific method is that often new tests are generated that lead to the prediction of novel facts, and one well-formed sequence of experiments can lead to volumes of new information. Of course, there are always errors associated with experiments and hypothesis testing. These errors are referred to as *Type I* or *Type II* errors. To understand these errors, we need to understand how hypotheses are tested. The probability used to reject the null hypothesis is called the *significance level* and is denoted by α. The significance level is chosen before any experiments are done. Typically, $\alpha = 5\%$ is used in ecological experiments. The value of the test statistic is called the *critical value* and is found in a table of whatever statistical procedure we are using.

A *Type I* error occurs when the null hypothesis is rejected when it is in fact true. That is, suppose the null hypothesis H_0 is true and we reject it based on the value of α. We have made a Type I error. Now suppose H_0 is false. If we accept H_0, then a *Type II* error has occurred. The only way to minimize both types of errors is to have many replications of the experiment. Table 1.1 summarizes the two types of errors.

Throughout this book, we will use the scientific method to evaluate wildlife issues. We will approach these issues as scientists, as biologists and ecologists,

TABLE 1.1   The Two Kinds of Errors in Statistical Hypothesis Testing

	H_0 is true	H_0 is false
H_0 is rejected	Type I	No error
H_0 is accepted	No error	Type II

and not as environmentalists or activists. We will take positions based on science and not belief, no matter how widespread such beliefs are. Our focus will be current threats to wildlife around the world. We will use the World Wide Web to explore wildlife issues globally, from the clubbing of harp seals in Canada to the introduction of exotic birds in Hawaii, the creation of parks in Africa, and the consumption of tiger bones in Asia. To understand current wildlife issues, we must understand and appreciate the origin and distribution of global biodiversity and threats to this diversity, wildlife ecology, and wildlife conservation in a world dominated by humans. You will learn that nothing less than the survival of our own species is at stake.

USING THE WORLD WIDE WEB

Exploring for information on the World Wide Web is both interesting and informative—as well as addictive. Many people are familiar with electronic mail, or e-mail. The days of using surface mail to send information are rapidly coming to an end. Certainly solid objects must be sent from one point to another using a medium other than electrons. We cannot yet beam anything anywhere. However, when only information needs to be communicated, e-mail, and not so-called snail mail, is the method of choice. Sending information and receiving information sent from someone else via the Internet has become commonplace. The next logical step on the Information Superhighway is information proliferation. Information made available by users of the Internet for users of the Internet is as accessible as your patience will allow.

Many users of the Internet have what is called a World Wide Web address, or Web address for short. Using one of the popular Internet browsing tools such as Gopher, Lynx, Mosaic, or Netscape, a user can access anyone's Web pages—worldwide and at the speed that information can travel the Internet. Thus, an online user anywhere on earth can access information from anywhere else on earth nearly instantly. Information available on the Web is generally put there by people who want the information to be disseminated. What is impressive is the amount of information on the Web. Simply put, the amount of freely accessible information on the Web is staggering, and information continues to be added daily. Web sites get updated and new Web sites are added by the minute across the world. There is almost no limit to what kind and how much information can exist on the Web. Each and every computer user could potentially have hundreds of megabytes of information on his or her personal Web site just waiting to be explored by an unknown user on another continent. No one really knows where all this will lead us, except that the changes that are occurring are occurring more frequently and more rapidly than ever before. Today is the age of information proliferation. Free information via the Internet is brought to you virtually anywhere you are and customized to make it easy to use. The only problem is finding the information you want. Information mining is an acquired skill. The more time you spend, the more skilled you will become.

The Internet browsing tools display both text and graphics with ease. Many Web site owners have customized their Web page to use graphics, text, and sound, and some are interactive. A Web page is created or written in HyperText Markup Language (HTML) and has a Uniform Resource Locator (URL) address. HyperText Transfer Protocol (HTTP) is the set of rules that computers use to send HTML documents over the Net. Thus, the University of Florida has a home page located at the Internet address

http://www.ufl.edu

When a home page is displayed, there are usually places where the user can point to select new addresses to access. These addresses are linked via the Internet and are not usually on the same storage device. Thus, one can think of the Web quite literally as an electronic, interconnected information network. The usual way of presenting choices is in a menu format that lists what is available and allows the user to select from various choices. The choices can be other addresses at other sites. Thus, the Web is highly distributed geographically.

The World Wide Web is the fruition of a project begun in 1990 at CERN, the European Particle Physics Laboratory in Switzerland. HTML and HTTP protocols, conventions, and standards are defined and supported there. CERN's home page can be found at

http://info.cern.ch/hypertext/WWW/TheProject.html

Access to information on the World Wide Web is gained by using one of the popular Web browsers. Mosaic was developed at the National Center for Supercomputing Applications at the University of Illinois. Netscape Communications Corporation, founded by several members of the original Mosaic team, also produces a popular Web browser called Netscape. Presuming you have access to the Web through one of the tools, typing either Mosaic or Netscape brings up a home page. Netscape offers an array of search engines to help you locate and access information on the Web. For instance, there are at least a dozen search engines that do keyword searches. Alta Vista is a search engine produced by Digital Equipment Corporation that is particularly effective, but others are also useful and generally find different Web addresses for the same keyword.

Search engines such as Alta Vista create an index using a software "spider" to visit all Web sites. They run night and day. The Alta Vista spider visits 2.5 million pages a day. The index in April 1996 was 30 gigabytes. There were an estimated 21 million pages and 10 billion words. The Alta Vista search engine was handling two million search requests a day back in December 1995. In February 1996, it was processing four million a day.

The amount and quality of information on the World Wide Web vary enormously. Most information on the Web is put forth in good faith. However, misinformation can also be found on the Web. For instance, in the summer of 1996, one of the authors (JGS) planned a visit to eastern Zaire to investigate an isolated group of gorillas living on a remote mountaintop. Using the net browser Netscape and the search engine Alta Vista, he typed in the name of the mountain and did a keyword search worldwide. In a few minutes, up came the name of the mountain in Zaire that was to be explored. An Australian had written an article about the region, including the mountain, and put his article on the Web for all to see. He reported that the forest surrounding the mountain had been completely destroyed, and all wildlife on the mountain had been eaten by Rwandan refugees spilling into Zaire from their war-torn country. This was blatant misinformation. Thus, suffice it to say that all information should be cross-checked for authenticity and accuracy.

One way to do a search is to bring up a Web browser such as Netscape, invoke a search engine such as Alta Vista, and do a keyword search. Then you briefly explore the list of the top ten keyword matches. At the bottom of the page are usually many more listings that match some or all of your keywords. For instance, suppose we type in the two words *harp seal* and see what comes up. Information on the musical instrument, the harp, is interesting. Also, the state seal of Alabama might be of interest, but it is not really a wildlife issue. Further exploration reveals information about harp seals. We now begin exploring the information network, descending down fruitful paths and blind alleys. The *back up* feature allows you to drop "bread crumbs" along the path so you can back out gracefully if necessary. Another useful tool is the *bookmark* feature, which allows storage of important addresses that survive after you log off.

Printing and copying whole Web pages is also easy. Indeed, one way to create a Web page is to find one you like on the World Wide Web, copy the entire page, and then modify it to fit your needs. Pictures can be scanned in and stored in a number of different formats. Your images will then be accessible by any popular Web browser when you link them through your page. Thus, creating your own Web page is relatively easy. Some Web pages contain copyrighted information, and these copyrights should be respected. By protecting others' right to own information, your own right to own will be protected.

The popularity of the Web is astounding, and no one can say where it will lead. One thing we can say is that there is a universe of information available on the Web. Combined with a local library, the problem we must deal with today is not a lack of information but a veritable flood of information. Managing the information, making sense of it, and summarizing it from disparate sources requires persistence and patience.

You are never alone on the Web. According to a 1995 survey by the Georgia Institute of Technology, there were an estimated 20 to 40 million users of the Web. The number of users was growing at the rate of 10% per month. The average age of all users was about 35. The previous survey showed that the average user was 28. Of these users, 15.5% were female and 82% were male; the rest did not report their sex. Of U.S. users, 36% had a college degree, 18.8% had a master's degree, and 4.06% had a doctoral degree. The average user's income was $69,000 a year. The survey found that 50.3% of the users were married and 45.7% were single; the rest did not report. Fully 31.3% of the users on the Internet had used the Internet for less than 6 months, and 19.0% had used the Internet for 6 to 12 months. An amazing 70% browse the Web once a day, and 50% spend two to six hours a week on the Web.

What all of this means is that the popularity of the Web is growing dramatically. New users are older, which means that most young people are already users. The average user is well paid and highly educated. Users are obviously gaining new information from the Web or they would not spend so much time browsing. In short, this means that if you are not "virtual," you are missing out on an adventure in learning. We will use the Web to explore information space just as we would a library to explore printed information. Hopefully, you will realize that you too should add to the information on the Web. Not only will we synthesize information, but we will create new information. New information should find its place on the Web. One night, a spider will crawl your Web site and explore your information and assimilate it. Across the globe, someone, somewhere, for whatever reason, will run a search and your site may well show up. No one knows where information is taking us. Changes are occurring faster and across a broader horizon. All we can do is surf high on the information wave and ride it for what it is worth. The alternative is to be left behind in an information desert.

EXERCISES

1.1 On April 5, 1996, the *Tampa Tribune* reported that a tourist attraction in Florida had offered "to adopt a huge rogue sea lion and four of his buddies who have been condemned to die for decimating the salmon population in the state of Washington while the fish try to make it to spawning grounds." Comment on this statement and suggest how we, as scientists, can contribute to understanding the issues at stake.

1.2 Practice using several search engines on the World Wide Web to locate some interesting Web sites. Start by typing in "crested caracara" and see what comes up. Next try "gorilla." Explain, in your own words, how to use the Web.

1.3 Using the World Wide Web, search for the phrase "animal damage control" and compile a list of interesting sites. What animals are becoming a nuisance? What makes an animal a nuisance?

1.4 Stamp collectors often assemble interesting stamps from across the world. One of the authors collects bird stamps, for instance. Using the World Wide Web, locate a source for wildlife stamps.

1.5 Repeat the previous exercise for coins. Make a list of coins that have wildlife on them.

LITERATURE CITED

Lakatos, Imre. 1978. Falsification and the methodology of scientific research programmes. *in* Worrall, J. and G. Currie (Eds.). *The Methodology of Scientific Research Programmes,* Volume I. Cambridge University Press, Cambridge.

WILDLIFE LAWS

2

Wildlife issues affect all of us nearly every day. Not a day passes without some wildlife issue confronting us. Perhaps it is a road-killed squirrel that we drive past and hardly notice or the endangered bald eagle we see circling above in the afternoon. The small stream we cross during our evening walk may have a locally endemic fish in it. The nest box we put out for birds attracts raccoons. The hamburger we have at a fast-food restaurant may have come from beef cattle raised in the American West on public land. The fuel we use in our vehicle may have come from oil pumped from a Papua New Guinea rain forest. The fact is, wildlife issues surround us. Sometimes we simply ignore them. Other times we are gripped by them, such as when three whales were stranded in ice-bound waters of the Arctic a few years ago.

CHRONOLOGY OF IMPORTANT LAWS

To understand wildlife laws, it is necessary to understand the recent history of how and why those laws came into being. A chronology of historic developments can be found on the Web site of the U.S. Fish and Wildlife Service. Beginning in 1900 with the Lacey Act, the chronology is a fascinating look at the history of wildlife law because these laws were passed by Congress in response to critical wildlife needs. For instance, in 1935 it was recognized that foreign commerce in illegally taken wildlife was becoming a serious threat to wildlife populations in the United States. The Lacey Act was then expanded to include a prohibition against such commerce. A shortened chronology of the more important wildlife laws is included here.

1900—The Lacey Act was enacted as the first federal law protecting game. It prohibited the interstate shipment of illegally taken wildlife as well as the

15

importation of injurious species (i.e., those species that might cause humans harm).

1913—The Federal Migratory Bird Law became effective and the first migratory bird hunting regulations were adopted on October 1.

1913—The United States signed the Migratory Bird Treaty with Great Britain (for Canada), recognizing migratory birds as an international resource.

1918—The Migratory Bird Treaty Act became law, making it unlawful to take, possess, buy, sell, purchase, or barter any migratory bird, including feathers, parts, nests, or eggs.

1926—The Black Bass Act became law, making it illegal to transport across state boundaries for the purpose of commerce black bass taken, purchased, or sold in violation of state law.

1934—The Migratory Bird Hunting Stamp Act became law, requiring all waterfowl hunters age 16 and over to possess a "Duck Stamp."

1935—The Lacey Act was expanded to prohibit foreign commerce in illegally taken wildlife.

1936—The United States signed the Migratory Bird Treaty with Mexico.

1940—The Bald Eagle Protection Act became law. The act prohibited a variety of activities involving the species, making it illegal to import, export, take, sell, purchase, or barter.

1962—The Bald Eagle Protection Act became the Bald and Golden Eagle Protection Act and extended protection to golden eagles.

1970—The Endangered Species Conservation Act of 1969 became effective, prohibiting the importation of into the United States species "threatened with extinction worldwide," except as specifically allowed for zoological and scientific purposes and propagation in captivity. The act amended the Black Bass Act to prohibit interstate and foreign commerce in fish taken in violation of foreign law, a provision that the Lacey Act had made in 1935 for wildlife. It also amended the Lacey Act so that its prohibition on interstate and foreign commerce applied not only to wild birds and mammals, but to reptiles, mollusks, amphibians, and crustaceans. This amendment was made in an effort aimed primarily at protecting the American alligator. (There is now an alligator hunting season in Florida.)

1971—The Airborne Hunting Act was signed into law, prohibiting the use of aircraft to hunt or harass wildlife.

1972—The United States signed the Migratory Bird Treaty with Japan. The Migratory Bird Treaty with Mexico was amended to protect additional species, including birds of prey.

The Marine Mammal Protection Act of 1972 became law, establishing a moratorium on the taking and importing of marine mammals, such as polar bears, sea otters, dugongs, walrus, manatees, whales, porpoise, seals, and sea lions.

The Eagle Protection Act was amended to increase penalties from $500 or six months imprisonment to $5000 or one year and to add the provision that a second conviction was punishable by a $10,000 fine or two years imprisonment, or both. In addition, the amendment allowed for informants to be rewarded one-half of the fine, not to exceed $2500.

1973—The Endangered Species Act of 1973 became law, recognizing that "endangered species of wildlife and plants are of aesthetic, ecological, educational, historical, recreational, and scientific value to the Nation and its people." The act expanded the scope of prohibited activities to include not only importation but exportation, taking, possession, and other activities involving illegally acquired species, as well as interstate or foreign commercial activities. It implemented protection for a new "threatened" category—species likely to become in danger of extinction.

1975—The Convention on International Trade in Endangered Species of Wild Fauna and Flora (CITES) entered into force, regulating the importation, exportation, and re-exportation of species listed in its three appendices (Hemley 1994).

1976—The United States signed the Migratory Bird Treaty with the Union of Soviet Socialist Republics.

1981—The Black Bass and Lacey Acts were repealed and replaced by the Lacey Act Amendments of 1981. A comprehensive statute, the Lacey Act Amendments restored protection for migratory birds, removed from the act in 1969, and initiated protection for plants. The Lacey Act Amendments increased penalties and included a felony punishment scheme to target commercial violators and international traffickers, with fines of up to $20,000 or five years imprisonment, or both.

1982—The Endangered Species Act was amended to include a plant-taking prohibition on federal lands and a new exception allowing the inadvertent noncommercial transshipment through the United States of endangered fish or wildlife.

1988—The African Elephant Conservation Act became law, providing additional protection for the species, whose numbers had declined by 50% in the last decade. The Lacey Act was amended to include, among other things, felony provisions for commercial guiding violations.

1992—The Wild Bird Conservation Act of 1992 was signed into law to address problems with international trade of wild-caught birds, which contributes both to the decline of the species and to unacceptably high mortality rates.

According to Lund (1980), American wildlife policy from the colonial period to the turn of the 20th century was based on "taking" as its goal. Steep declines in wildlife from the northeast through Florida had occurred. When the Pilgrims arrived, they were amazed at the abundance of deer and turkey. Yet by 1900, deer had disappeared from the east. Turkey and beaver were hunted out. Those who traveled by rail thousands of miles west were "never out of sight of a dead buffalo, and never in sight of a live one" (Matthiessen 1964). The passenger pigeon and the Eskimo curlew, whose numbers staggered the imagination, were hunted down relentlessly and wiped out forever.

Commercial exploitation 100 years ago decimated many species. Millions of buffalo were shot just so their tongues could be shipped back east in new refrigerated railroad cars. Elk were common across the Great Plains of America, although they had been driven west. The last wild elk in New York was killed in 1845 (Day 1949). Fifteen years later, the last moose was gone from New York as well. They were soon killed out, and what was left retreated to the mountains. Today, we think of elk as occupying the Rocky Mountains and other similar regions. Humans drove them there. Men's hats were made of beaver skins, and ladies' fashions demanded plumes from millions of Florida's wading birds. In fact, wading birds were killed during the breeding season for a few feathers from the backs of the birds. The carcasses were left to rot. Spring shooting of waterfowl in Rhode Island was outlawed in 1846. Even as early as 1864, Idaho had a closed season on buffalo. Enforcement was impossible, however. Waterfowl were especially hard hit. Bag limits were unknown. At the same time, the U.S. population was growing—from 17 million in 1840 to 23 million in 1850 and 32 million in 1860. Imagine the view seen by Colonel R.I. Dodge along the Arkansas River in Colorado back in 1871, when his patrol, over the course of six days and nights, was among a herd of buffalo he estimated "contained no fewer than 4 million head" (Trefethen 1975). "At times they pressed before us in such numbers as to delay the progress of our column, and often a belligerent bull would lower and shake his craggy head at us when we passed him a few feet distant."

In 1865, the national buffalo kill was about one million head. By 1875, Kansas and Colorado closed buffalo hunting. There were none left anyway. In 1881, buffalo hunters had, quite literally, killed themselves out of business. By 1890, a small herd of mountain buffalo were the sole survivors of the tens of millions of buffalo that had roamed the great grasslands of the United States. Perhaps the saddest chapter in U.S. history was closed—a carnage Americans must accept as part of their history.

Market hunters used cannons to kill thousands of ducks—at night. Sporting games were held to see who could kill the most ducks with a single shot—81 dead, 46 crippled—from a double-barreled, four-gauge shotgun—a mighty stroke for humans (Wheeler 1947). Shooting 50 or more at once with this gun was easy. The carnage was massive and largely out of sight. No species was immune. The speed of the pronghorn antelope was no match for a bullet at 400 yards.

The belief was that wildlife resources were unlimited and the harvests could continue forever. They did not. Wildlife populations fell and species became extinct. Toward the turn of the century, sportsmen began to question commercial harvesting of wildlife resources. Indeed, it was sport hunting that pushed through the founding of wildlife agencies and specified how these agencies would be funded. Laws were passed to improve wildlife populations. The demand for sport hunting rescued wildlife across America from total destruction. Predators, however, would have to wait for their saviors. Predator control programs were designed to wipe out predators completely and they did. Full-time government hunters were assigned the job of hunting down and shooting predators or poisoning them.

In summary, early America wildlife laws permitted the cruelest form of complete exploitation. State laws were formulated by sportsmen to protect certain species considered game animals. At the turn of the century, American wildlife stocks were at their lowest level. Federal wildlife laws were first established to work cooperatively with the states to support the sport laws. The aesthetic value of wildlife was still not recognized. Today, we realize that many wildlife themes interact in the United States as well as other parts of the world. Butterflies do not attract hunters but rather collectors. Global commerce is accepted as commonplace. Wildlife laws must be agreed upon among nations. U.S. trade sanctions against China for illegally importing tiger parts from India could be used as a corrective measure. Today, wildlife issues take place on the global stage for all to see. While residents of northern Florida reject as outlandish the reintroduction of the secretive panther where it once was common,

donors from across the United States support research into why lion populations in Africa are crashing. Predators are okay, but only in someone else's
backyard it seems.

DEFINITIONS

Today, there are many laws that protect all kinds of wildlife. A summary is
provided later in this chapter. Indeed, there are so many laws that protect
wildlife that it is surprising there are any wildlife issues at all. And yet, wildlife
issues are surfacing more and more rapidly. There are laws that govern our air
and water quality, laws that govern policy in our national forests, laws that
protect elephants and migratory birds, and laws that protect threatened and
endangered species. There is a law protecting Antarctica and one that prevents
shooting animals from an airplane. To understand these laws and where they
come from, several terms need to be defined.

- **Misdemeanor**—An offense of lesser gravity than a felony, for which
  punishment may be a fine or imprisonment in a local rather than a state
  institution.
- **Felony**—Any of several crimes such as murder, rape, or burglary considered more serious than a misdemeanor and punishable by a more
  stringent sentence.
- **Civil law**—The body of law dealing with the rights of private citizens
  in a particular state or nation as distinguished from criminal law, military law, and international law.
- **Criminal law**—Pertaining to the administration of penal law as distinguished from civil law.
- **Standing**—To have standing means that you are a "proper party to request adjudication" of a particular issue (Littell 1992).

Wildlife law has four main goals according to Lund (1980). First and fore-
most to our predecessors, laws facilitated the sustained harvest of wildlife.
Wildlife management became a bean counter's paradise. Second, wildlife laws
can be formulated to control human behavior. For instance, the use of weapons
could be controlled through wildlife laws. Third, special groups can be favored
by wildlife laws. Wildlife could be treated as a form of wealth so that special
groups would be favored for protecting or providing habitat for wildlife. Lastly,
wildlife laws protect wildlife.

Bounties have always played an interesting role in wildlife laws because a
bounty is a reward for the hunter but, on the other hand, a cost to the govern-

ment in most cases. The government would have preferred to pay nothing to the hunters for services rendered. Thus, the bounty hunter's wits were matched against the government as lawmaker and bounty payer. Early on in U.S. history, bounty hunters aided farmers and settlers.

By placing a bounty on an animal's head, government was encouraging hunters to eliminate the animal. Hunters, however, would have preferred a more sustained yield approach to collecting bounties. Thus, when a hunter could ensure exclusivity to an area containing wolves, he would take only young wolves and male wolves, fully realizing that the females could provide a sustained bounty income. To ensure the killing of breeding females, bounties had to be increased.

Different counties sometimes paid different bounties. Hunters then shot wolves in one place and transported them to the county that paid the most. The local legislature moved to require that animals be killed in the county. Hunters acted swiftly by catching animals, transporting them to the appropriate county, and killing them locally. Long ago, New York City developed a thriving trade in wolves' ears when the government required proof of a wolf kill but did not want the body delivered. For panthers and foxes, however, the body had to be delivered. Stale wolf heads were always suspect because hunters would ship them to the highest payoff areas; thus, local paymasters were required to make sure the heads were "green."

At first, the highest bounties were paid on panthers. Wolves were more valuable than bears and wildcats, such as bobcats. In Virginia, the bounty for wolves and panthers was a license to kill a hog. Thus, very few dead panthers and wolves were recorded in Virginia; however, neighboring states had seemingly enormous populations. Ethical or aesthetic wildlife laws were not even dreamed of 200 years ago. No one would have been able to foresee that in a little under 150 years, North America would require laws to protect wildlife.

U.S. customs law prohibits the importation of most wild bird feathers, mounted birds, and skins. Most migratory birds are protected by international treaties. Just because something is for sale in another country does not make it legal for a U.S. citizen to purchase it. Many live birds and animals can be imported but must be quarantined in U.S. Department of Agriculture Animal Import Centers or quarantine stations for 30 days after entry.

Taking is a specific term used in laws regarding plants and animals. Taking refers to harassing, harming, pursuing, hunting, shooting, wounding, trapping, killing, capturing, and collecting species of plants or animals. So-called take permits are available from the federal government. For instance, a large windmill electricity generation project in Wyoming was required to apply for a take permit when researchers discovered that the location of the windmills was also a flyway for migratory birds, especially birds of prey such as eagles. Thus, the project was required to file for a take permit, requesting permission to "take" no more than a certain number of bald and golden eagles.

Injurious wildlife is wildlife that can cause harm. Animals such as fruit bats, mongooses, walking catfish, and Java sparrows cannot be imported into the United States because they have been declared harmful to people, animals, plants, or the environment and are thus injurious. These creatures need not be rare or endangered. Some states even have laws preventing the introduction of nonnative species.

Wildlife trophies other than marine mammals or threatened, endangered, or CITES Appendix I species lawfully taken by U.S. residents in the United States, Canada, or Mexico can be imported or exported for personal use.

UNITED STATES CODE

The United States Code (U.S.C.) is comprised of 50 titles that contain the laws by which the United States functions. Some of these titles are as follows:

> **Title 1   General Provisions**
> **Title 2   The Congress**
> **Title 3   The President**
> **Title 4   Flag, Seal, Seat of Government, and the States**
> ...
>
> **Title 16 Conservation**
> ...
>
> **Title 18 Crimes and Criminal Procedure**
> ...
>
> **Title 27 Intoxicating Liquors**
> ...
>
> **Title 50 War and National Defense**

Title 16 contains laws referring to conservation:

Chapter 1   National Parks, Military Parks, Monuments, and Seashores
Chapter 1A   Historic Sites, Buildings, Objects, and Antiquities
Chapter 1B   Archaeological Resources Protection
Chapter 2   National Forests
Chapter 3   Forests; Forest Service; Reforestation; Management
Chapter 3A   Unemployment Relief Through Performance of Useful Public Work (omitted or repealed)

INTERNATIONAL CONVENTIONS AND AGREEMENTS

In addition to the U.S. Code, there are also many treaties and international agreements. Many of the above laws refer to these international agreements and specify that the U.S. government will provide "assistance in the development and management of programs in that country which the Secretary [of the Interior] determines to be necessary or useful for the conservation of any endangered or threatened species." In other words, the U.S. government will actively seek partnerships in encouraging the protection of certain species beyond the borders of the United States. Some of these treaties and agreements as are follows:

- Agreement on the Conservation of Polar Bears of 1973
- Antarctic Treaty of 1959
- Convention Concerning the Conservation of Migratory Birds and Their Environment of 1976
- Convention Concerning the Protection of the World Cultural and Natural Heritage of 1972
- Convention for the Conservation of Antarctic Seals of 1972
- Convention for the Establishment of an Inter-American Tropical Tuna Commission of 1949
- Convention for the Preservation of the Halibut Fishery of the Northwest Pacific Ocean and Bering Sea of 1953
- Convention for the Protection of Migratory Birds of 1916
- Convention for the Protection of Migratory Birds and Birds in Danger of Extinction, and Their Environment of 1972
- Convention for the Protection of Migratory Birds and Game Mammals of 1936
- Convention for the Protection, Preservation, and Extension of the Sockeye Salmon of the Fraser River System of 1930
- Convention for the Regulation of Whaling of 1931
- Convention on Fishing and Conservation of the Living Resources of the High Seas of 1958
- Convention on International Trade in Endangered Species of Wild Fauna and Flora of 1973 (CITES)
- Convention on Nature Protection and Wildlife Preservation in the Western Hemisphere of 1940
- Convention on the Conservation of Antarctic Marine Living Resources of 1980
- Convention on the Territorial Sea and Contiguous Zone of 1958
- Declaration of the United Nations Conference on the Human Environment of 1972
- Interim Convention on Conservation of North Pacific Fur Seals of 1957
- International Convention for the High Seas Fisheries of the North Pacific Ocean of 1952
- International Convention for the Northwest Atlantic Fisheries of 1949

- International Convention for the Regulation of Whaling of 1946
- Treaty for the Preservation and Protection of Fur Seals of 1911
- Treaty with the Yakimas of 1855

The Convention on International Trade in Endangered Species of Wild Fauna and Flora of 1973 (CITES) is one of the most famous international conventions. Many U.S. laws refer to CITES and pledge the support of the United States to support CITES-listed species through international cooperation.

Convention on International Trade in Endangered Species of Wild Fauna and Flora

A conference in Washington, D.C. in early 1973 led to the signing of the Convention on International Trade in Endangered Species of Wild Fauna and Flora on March 3, 1973. CITES is a multinational agreement among 131 nations (as of January 1996) that attempts to regulate trade in specific plants and animals to prevent their excessive exploitation. Scientific authorities in each country are designated to issue permits to control the taking of listed species. National laws also protect CITES-listed species. In the United States, the African Elephant Conservation Act, the Eagle Protection Act, the Endangered Species Act, the Lacey Act, the Marine Mammal Protection Act, and the Migratory Bird Treaty Act are domestic laws that cover many species, including, but not limited to, CITES-listed species.

CITES listings include some 30,000 plants and over 2500 animal species. Listed in Appendix I of CITES are species threatened with extinction that are or might one day be affected by trade. Export and import permits are required for CITES-listed species. Appendix II of CITES includes species that are not threatened with extinction yet, but soon might be if trade in those species is not controlled. For instance, animal parts are often used as medicinal treatments or as aphrodisiacs. Ground-up antlers are used to treat certain illnesses. American black bears are listed in Appendix II because their gallbladders look like any other bear gallbladder and Asians use bear gallbladders for medicinal purposes. Appendix III contains a list of species that individual nations wish to protect within their borders. To prevent international trade in those species, a certificate of origin is required.

CITES is an agreement among nations (a list of signators to CITES is provided in the appendix to this chapter) and is not a law. Therefore, no fines or jail sentences apply. However, with proper certification, animals and plants can be confiscated and repatriated. Section 1532 Definitions in paragraph (4) refers specifically to the term "Convention," which means the Convention on

International Trade in Endangered Species of Wild Fauna and Flora. Section 1537 of the Endangered Species Act commits the United States to support CITES financially and encourages the secretary of the interior to assist other countries in support of their species protection programs.

EXAMPLES OF U.S. CODES

To better understand U.S. wildlife codes, let's take a closer look at some of the acts. For instance, Congress decided to do something about protecting coral reefs and enacted 16 U.S.C., Chapter 25A—Crown of Thorns Starfish. This will help us understand what Congress does when the American people decide to pass a law to protect a species or to protect a species from other species. Unless otherwise noted, all acts are 16 U.S.C.

Chapter 25A. Crown of Thorns Starfish

§ 1211. Congressional Statement of Purpose
§ 1212. Investigation and Control of Crown of Thorns Starfish
§ 1213. Authorization of Appropriations

§ 1211. Congressional Statement of Purpose

For the purpose of conserving and protecting coral reef resources of the tropical islands of interest and concern to the United States in the Pacific and safeguarding critical island areas from possible erosion and to safeguard future recreational and esthetic uses of Pacific coral reefs, the Secretary of Commerce and the Secretary of the Smithsonian Institution are authorized to cooperate with and provide assistance to the governments of the State of Hawaii, the territories and possessions of the United States, including Guam and American Samoa, the Trust Territory of the Pacific Islands, and other island possessions of the United States, in the study and control of the seastar "Crown of Thorns" (*Acanthaster planci*).

§ 1212. Investigation and Control of Crown of Thorns Starfish

In carrying out the purposes of this chapter, the Secretary of Commerce and the Secretary of the Smithsonian Institution are authorized—

(1) to conduct such studies, research, and investigations, as they deem desirable to determine the causes of the population increase of

the Crown of Thorns, their effects on corals and coral reefs, and the stability and regeneration of reefs following predation;

(2) to monitor areas where the Crown of Thorns may be increasing in numbers and to determine future needs for control;

(3) to develop improved methods of control and to carry out programs of control in areas where these are deemed necessary; and

(4) to take such other actions as deemed desirable to gain an understanding of the ecology and control of the seastar "Crown of Thorns."

§ 1213. Authorization of Appropriations

For the purpose of carrying out the provisions of this chapter, there is authorized to be appropriated for the period commencing on September 26, 1970, and ending June 30, 1975, an amount not to exceed $4,500,000.

Unlike the Crown of Thorns, which Congress was trying to control, African elephant populations were being decimated all across Africa in the 1980s when Congress decided to act. The African Elephant Conservation Act of 1988 was passed to help protect and conserve African elephants. The act makes it illegal to import raw ivory such as elephant tusks from any country other than an African country that contains any part of the range of African elephants. If an African country prohibits exportation of raw or worked ivory, then importation of that ivory into the United States is prohibited. Exporting African ivory from the United States is also prohibited. If the ivory is derived from illegal sources, importation of the ivory is illegal, even if the country allows exportation. However, on June 9, 1989, the United States established a moratorium on all ivory imports from all countries, including Asian countries, except where elephant trophy hunting is permitted and also for certain ivory antiques.

Chapter 62. African Elephant Conservation Act of 1988

§ 4201. Statement of Purpose

The purpose of this chapter is to perpetuate healthy populations of African elephants. The Congress finds the following:

(1) Elephant populations in Africa have declined at an alarming rate since the mid-1970's.

(2) The large illegal trade in African elephant ivory is the major cause of this decline and threatens the continued existence of the African elephant.

(3) The African elephant is listed as threatened under the Endangered Species Act of 1973 (16 U.S.C. 1531 et seq.) and its continued existence will be further jeopardized if this decline is not reversed.

(4) Because African elephant ivory is indistinguishable from Asian elephant ivory, there is a need to ensure that the trade in African elephant ivory does not further endanger the Asian elephant, which is listed as endangered under section 4 of the Endangered Species Act of 1973 (16 U.S.C. 1533) and under Appendix I of CITES.

(5) In response to the significant illegal trade in African elephant ivory, the parties to CITES established the CITES Ivory Control System to curtail the illegal trade and to encourage African countries to manage, conserve, and protect their African elephant populations.

(6) The CITES Ivory Control System entered into force recently and should be allowed to continue in force for a reasonable period of time to assess its effectiveness in curtailing the illegal trade in African elephant ivory.

(7) Although some African countries have effective African elephant conservation programs, many do not have sufficient resources to properly manage, conserve, and protect their elephant populations.

(8) The United States, as a party to CITES and a large market for worked ivory, shares responsibility for supporting and implementing measures to stop the illegal trade in African elephant ivory and to provide for the conservation of the African elephant.

(9) There is no evidence that sport hunting is part of the poaching that contributes to the illegal trade in African elephant ivory, and there is evidence that the proper utilization of well-managed elephant populations provides an important source of funding for African elephant conservation programs.

§ 4203. Statement of Policy

It is the policy of the United States—

(1) to assist in the conservation and protection of the African elephant by supporting the conservation programs of African countries and the CITES Secretariat; and

(2) to provide financial resources for those programs.

§ 4211. Provision of Assistance

(a) In general—The Secretary may provide financial assistance under this subchapter from the African Elephant Conservation Fund for approved projects for research, conservation, management, or protection of African elephants.

(b) Project proposal—Any African government agency responsible for African elephant conservation and protection, the CITES Secretariat, and any organization or individual with experience in African elephant conservation may submit to the Secretary a project proposal under this section. Each such proposal shall contain—

(1) the name of the person responsible for conducting the project;

(2) a succinct statement of the need for and purposes of the project;

(3) a description of the qualifications of the individuals who will be conducting the project;

(4) an estimate of the funds and time required to complete the project;

(5) evidence of support of the project by governmental entities of countries within which the project will be conducted, if such support may be important for the success of the project; and

(6) any other information the Secretary considers to be necessary or appropriate for evaluating the eligibility of the project for funding under this chapter.

(c) Project review and approval—The Secretary shall review each project proposal to determine if it meets the criteria set forth in subsection (d) of this section and otherwise merits assistance under this chapter. Not later than six months after receiving a project proposal, and subject to the availability of funds, the Secretary shall approve or disapprove the proposal and provide written notification to the person who submitted the proposal and to each country within which the project is proposed to be conducted.

(d) Criteria for approval—The Secretary may approve a project under this section if the project will enhance programs for African elephant research, conservation, management, or protection by—

(1) developing in a usable form sound scientific information on African elephant habitat condition and carrying capacity, total elephant numbers and population trends, or annual reproduction and mortality; or

(2) assisting efforts—

(A) to ensure that any taking of African elephants in the country is effectively controlled and monitored;

(B) to implement conservation programs to provide for healthy, sustainable African elephant populations; or

(C) to enhance compliance with the CITES Ivory Control System.

(e) Project reporting—Each entity that receives assistance under this section shall provide such periodic reports to the Director of the United States Fish and Wildlife Service as the Director considers relevant and appropriate. Each report shall include all information requested by the Director for evaluating the progress and success of the project.

§ 4223. Prohibited Acts

Except as provided in section 4222(e) of this title, it is unlawful for any person—

(1) to import raw ivory from any country other than an ivory producing country;

(2) to export raw ivory from the United States;

(3) to import raw or worked ivory that was exported from an ivory producing country in violation of that country's laws or of the CITES Ivory Control System;

(4) to import worked ivory, other than personal effects, from any country unless that country has certified that such ivory was derived from legal sources; or

(5) to import raw or worked ivory from a country for which a moratorium is in effect under section 4222 of this title.

§ 4224. Penalties and Enforcement

(a) Criminal violations—Whoever knowingly violates section 4223 of this title shall, upon conviction, be fined under title 18 or imprisoned for not more than one year, or both.

(b) Civil violations—Whoever violates section 4223 of this title may be assessed a civil penalty by the Secretary of not more than $5,000 for each such violation.

(c) Procedures for assessment of civil penalty—Proceedings for the assessment of a civil penalty under this section shall be conducted in accordance with the procedures provided for in section 1540(a) of this title.

(d) Use of penalties—Subject to appropriations, penalties collected under this section may be used by the Secretary of the Treasury to pay rewards under section 4225 of this title and, to the extent not used to pay such rewards, shall be deposited by the Secretary of the Treasury into the Fund.

(e) Enforcement—The Secretary, the Secretary of the Treasury, and the Secretary of the department in which the Coast Guard is operating shall enforce this subchapter in the same manner such Secretaries carry out enforcement activities under section 1540(e) of this title. Section 1540(c) of this title shall apply to actions arising under this subchapter.

§ 4225. Rewards

(a) In general—Upon the recommendation of the Secretary, the Secretary of the Treasury may pay a reward to any person who furnishes information which leads to a civil penalty or a criminal conviction under this chapter.

(b) Amount—The amount of a reward under this section shall be equal to not more than one-half of any criminal or civil penalty or fine with respect to which the reward is paid, or $25,000, whichever is less.

(c) Limitation on eligibility—An officer or employee of the United States or of any State or local government who furnishes information or renders service in the performance of his or her official duties shall not be eligible for a reward under this section.

Example—While visiting Tanzania, you notice a particularly attractive elephant's foot wastepaper basket. Your offer to purchase the basket for five dollars is accepted. So generous is your offer that the astounded merchant throws in a tiny hand-carved elephant of poor quality made, he says, from bone. He also throws in an old document that says something about CITES. You pack up your purchases and return home. At the airport, you are one of only a handful of people to have their luggage inspected. The customs official reads the yellowed document and ushers you aside as he points out that the carving is not bone but ivory. You are charged with violating the African Elephant Conservation Act.

Penalties—A misdemeanor carries a $5000 fine for an individual. Felony convictions carry a $100,000 fine and up to one year in jail for individuals. Organizations can be fined up to $200,000.

7 U.S.C. Chapter 54. Transporting, Sale, and Handling of Certain Animals

This is the so-called Animal Welfare Act of 1966 (1970, 1976) which deals with interstate transportation and commercial transactions involving animal species. The act outlaws animal fights, although gamebird fights are outlawed only where state law has precedence.

Chapter 30. Wild Free-Roaming Horses and Burros Act of 1971

President Eisenhower signed the first federal law written to protect wild horses and burros. The Wild Free-Roaming Horses and Burros Act of 1971 and as amended in 1978 provides for the protection from various forms of cruelty and the capture and killing of wild horses which live on federally owned public land (Cooper 1987). Specifically, unbranded and unclaimed horses and burros on public lands of the United States were protected as "living symbols of the historic and pioneer spirit of the West." The act applies to all lands administered by the Forest Service and the Bureau of Land Management.

The act is not limitless, however. It describes the range of the animals as "the amount of land necessary to sustain an existing herd or herds of wild free-roaming horses and burros, which does not exceed their known territorial limits." The act also denies any authority "to relocate wild free-roaming horses or burros to areas of public lands where they do not presently exist." If an overpopulation exists, under the 1978 amendment, the secretary of the interior can "immediately remove excess animals." However, the act also states that protected horses and burros are to "be considered...an integral part of the natural system of the public lands." Since horses and burros are both nonnative introduced species, one has to wonder how a "natural" ecological balance is to be preserved and maintained. Furthermore, it seems equally impossible to maintain a "thriving natural ecological balance" and a "multiple-use relationship," as the act suggests (Bean 1983).

Example—On your vacation to Nevada, you attend a wild horse auction. The horses are up for adoption, and you choose five of them. As you are loading them into your trailer, a sheriff walks up and asks to see your letter from the secretary of the interior that permits you to adopt five horses. You are arrested when you cannot produce the letter. You can, under the act, only adopt four horses.

Penalties—Violators are subject to a $2000 fine and one year in prison.

Chapter 9. Fish and Wildlife Service

In 1971, Congress amended the Fish and Wildlife Act of 1956 by adding the so-called Airborne Hunting Act. Section 742j-1 makes it unlawful to harass or take wildlife from aircraft except when protecting wildlife, livestock, and human health and safety as authorized by a federal- or state-issued license or permit. Permits have been issued in Alaska to allow the shooting of wolves from aircraft to protect other wildlife such as moose and caribou.

Example—You are a passenger in your friend's airplane and are out for a day of leisure flying. The pilot decides to get a closer look at some elk. He circles and flies directly over their heads, scattering them. Unknowingly, your friend has violated the Airborne Hunting Act. It is unlawful for anyone to knowingly participate in using an aircraft to "harass any bird, fish, or animal."

Penalties—Violators are subject to a $5000 fine, one year in prison, or both. In addition, hunters can forfeit their guns and aircraft, as well as the birds, fish, or animals they shoot.

Chapter 44. Antarctic Conservation Act

To protect the unique fauna and flora of Antarctica, this act makes it illegal for any U.S. citizen to carry, deliver, export, import, possess, receive, sell, take, or transport any native wildlife from Antarctica or any plant from specially protected areas in Antarctica. The act also expressly prohibits introduction of any animal or plant not indigenous to Antarctica.

Penalties—The amount of the civil penalty shall not exceed $5000 for each violation unless the prohibited act was knowingly committed, in which case the amount of the civil penalty shall not exceed $10,000 for each violation. A criminal offense is punishable by a fine of $10,000 or imprisonment for not more than one year, or both.

Chapter 5A. Protection and Conservation of Wildlife

Subchapter I. Game, Fur-Bearing Animals, and Fish

This act, which is often referred to as the Lacey Act of 1900 (1948, 1949, 1960, 1969, 1981), ensures that fish and wildlife shipped to the United States receive humane and healthful treatment. It also designates wildlife that is potentially harmful to humans and prevents its importation. Under the Lacey Act, importing, exporting, transporting, selling, receiving, acquiring, or buying any fish, wildlife, or plant that was taken, transported, or possessed illegally under state, federal, tribal, or foreign law is a federal offense. The United States can and does prohibit the export of certain species and can also ban the importation of certain species.

The Lacey Act is often used to prosecute smugglers of illegally taken fish and wildlife, including birds and reptiles. In 1981, amendments were passed that strengthen federal laws and broaden federal participation to states and foreign governments with respect to enforcement.

Example—In an effort to stock your home aquarium, you visit a local pet store that sells tropical fish. Many of the fish are new and different to you, and you purchase several of the more colorful ones. The fish are loaded into a plastic bag and put into a cardboard box for transport. Your receipt says you purchased "tropical guppies." On the way to your car, a U.S. Fish and Wildlife Service agent notices the box and asks you to show off your purchase. The agent quickly identifies the fish as rare and endangered tropical species from Papua New Guinea coastal waters. You are charged with violating the Lacey Act because you have purchased fish that are prohibited from export from Papua New Guinea.

Penalties—Individuals convicted of violating the Lacey Act can be sentenced to up to $100,000 and one year in jail for misdemeanors. Fines of up to $250,000 and five years in jail can be imposed for felony convictions. Businesses can be fined up to $250,000 and $500,000 for misdemeanors and felonies, respectively. Illegal wildlife, fish, and plants as well as vehicles, airplanes, boats, and other equipment used during the crime can be confiscated by the government.

Subchapter II. Protection of Bald and Golden Eagles Act of 1940 (1959, 1962, 1972)

This act was amended to include golden eagles as well and is now known as the Bald and Golden Eagle Protection Act. To import, export, or take bald or golden eagles or to sell, purchase, or barter their parts or products made from them, including their nests or eggs, is illegal. Furthermore, pursuing, shooting, poisoning, wounding, killing, capturing, trapping, collecting, molesting, or disturbing eagles is also illegal.

Exceptions—Permits can be granted for scientific or exhibition use or for traditional and cultural use by Native Americans. For instance, the Hopi Indians of Arizona use golden eagles in ceremonies. No permits can be issued for commercial or barter activities.

Example—In Anchorage, Alaska, bald eagles are ubiquitous. During a visit to a local park, you find a bald eagle tail feather. Apparently, the feather has molted (i.e., it has been replaced naturally by another feather). You stick the feather in your hatband, where it is prominently displayed. A local person offers to purchase the feather for five dollars and you sell it. The person turns out to be a police officer working undercover and places you under arrest for selling a bald eagle part.

Penalties—Fines of up to $100,000 for individuals and $200,000 for organizations and one year in jail are possible for misdemeanors. Fines of up to $250,000 and $500,000 for individuals and organizations, respectively, can result from felony convictions.

Chapter 35. Endangered Species Act of 1966, 1969, 1973, and 1988

The Endangered Species Act (ESA) is probably the most widely recognized law protecting plants and animals in the United States. The act was amended and signed into law on December 28, 1973 by President Richard M. Nixon. The ESA is the law that is used to designate threatened and endangered species of plants and wildlife. The term *endangered species* means that a plant or animal is listed by regulation as being "in danger of extinction." A *threatened species* is a plant or animal that is likely to become extinct within the foreseeable future. More than 1000 plants and animals are listed as endangered or threatened. The courts have consistently upheld the ESA despite legislative and administrative attempts to weaken it (Easter-Pilcher 1996).

The ESA prohibits importing, exporting, and taking endangered species in the United States. Taking is prohibited in U.S. territorial and international waters. In addition, carrying, delivering, possessing, selling, shipping, and transporting endangered species unlawfully taken in the United States, its territorial waters, and international waters is prohibited. Interstate and international commerce in endangered species is also punishable by law. Despite the vague definitions of endangered and threatened, the ESA continues to be a powerful law (Bean 1983, Wilcove et al. 1993).

Example—During a trip to Arizona, you notice an interesting cactus. Rather than dig up the cactus for later identification, you decide instead to take a flower. You insert the flower into your plant press book and return to the university museum to identify the curious cactus. The curator of the museum notices the flower and immediately calls state law enforcement officials. You are arrested for violating the ESA, having harmed an endangered species of cactus. If you are convicted, your car, shovel, notebooks, boots, and plant press with specimens can be confiscated.

Penalties—The ESA is considered to be a law "with teeth" (Kohm 1991). Violators can be fined up to $100,000 and can serve up to one year in jail. Organizations can be fined up to $250,000. Items used during the crime can be confiscated.

Chapter 31. Marine Mammal Protection Act of 1972 (1973, 1976)

In 1972, the United States halted the harvesting and importation of marine mammals such as dugongs and manatees, polar bears, porpoises, all seals, sea lions, sea otters, walruses, and whales and any of their parts such as tusks, bones, and hides. The law specifically prohibits individuals or groups of individuals from importing any marine mammal or marine mammal product into the United States and from taking any marine mammal in international waters or waters or lands under U.S. jurisdiction.

Additionally, the Marine Mammal Protection Act makes it illegal to use any U.S. port or harbor for any purpose connected with the taking or importation of marine mammals. It is also unlawful for any individual to possess parts or products of marine mammals. Thus, offering for sale, purchasing, selling, or transporting any marine mammal, including parts or products, is illegal.

Exceptions—Alaskan Native Americans such as Aleuts, Eskimos, and Indians residing in Alaska are permitted subsistence use of marine mammals. Subsistence uses include the taking of marine mammals such as walruses and whales for human consumption and the making of native handicrafts and products. The secretaries of the interior and commerce can grant permits for purposes that support scientific research or public displays such as zoo exhibits. With a permit, exportation of handicrafts and products for scientific or display purposes is not prohibited provided a "Certificate of Origin" accompanies the product.

Example—You are casually walking along a northern California beach when you come across a young sea otter with a fish line wrapped around its body. The twine has cut into the skin in places. Realizing the small sea otter can be saved, you decide to bring the animal to a nearby veterinarian. By putting the sea otter in your car, you have violated the Marine Mammal Protection Act and are subject to the following penalties.

Penalties—A fine of up to $100,000 and one year in jail are possible for individuals in violation of the act. Organizations can be fined up to $200,000. Additionally, all cargo can be seized from transport vessels such as airplanes, ships, or other means of transport.

Chapter 7. Protection of Migratory Game and Insectivorous Birds

This act provides protection for migratory birds. It is unlawful to pursue, hunt, shoot, poison, wound, kill, capture, possess, buy, sell, trap, collect, or barter any migratory bird, including feathers or parts, nests, eggs, or migratory bird products. The act is based on treaties with Great Britain, Mexico, and Japan and puts restrictions on specific birds covered under the act.

Exceptions—The U.S. Fish and Wildlife Service establishes bird hunting regulations and during hunting season allows for the taking of ducks, geese, doves, rails, woodcocks, and other species. Other permits may be granted for scientific research.

Example—As an avid bird-watcher, you pride yourself on knowing the local birds, their calls, and their habits. One day while birding, you find on the forest floor the nest of a Wilson's warbler. You correctly identify the nest for your companions and then stuff it into a plastic bag for later examination at home. By taking the nest, you have violated the Migratory Bird Treaty Act and are subject to the full penalties under the law. Suppose, for instance, that on the way home, you see a road-killed hummingbird and put it in your car to give to a museum. Again, you are in violation of the Migratory Bird Treaty Act unless you have a permit that allows you to collect.

Penalties—Individuals and organizations can be fined up to $5000 and $10,000, respectively, and can receive six months in prison for misdemeanor violations. For felony violations, individuals and organizations can be fined up to $250,000 and $500,000, respectively, and receive up to two years in jail.

Chapter 69. Wild Exotic Bird Conservation Act of 1992

This act prohibits the import of all CITES-listed birds into the United States except for those species included in an approved list either by country of origin or approved captive breeding facilities or for wild-caught birds. For wild-caught approved birds, a plan that provides for the conservation of the species and its habitat is required. The act also established the Exotic Bird Conservation Fund, which is funded by fines and penalties and is to be used to assist exotic bird conservation projects in their native countries.

Penalties—Civil violators can be fined up to $25,000. Criminal violations call for a fine specified in Title 18 and a jail term of not more than two years.

The international regulation of the trade in plant and animal products is an enormous undertaking. Certainly, finding a six-foot elephant's tusk is easy compared to examining a bottle of pills that contain ground-up tiger bones. Crates of snakes are imported every day into the United States. Discovering which are listed species, and therefore protected, and which are common is a formidable task for customs agents. Unfortunately, the profit from one successful theft can easily make up for ten intercepted shipments. The rich nations are by far the largest importers of rare and exotic plants and animals. Whales are still consumed at sushi bars in Asia. In the final analysis, each individual must decide what is right and what is wrong. Just because something is not prohibited by law does not make it right. Even when a "Certificate of Authenticity" is available, it is difficult to tell the difference between an authentic certificate and a fraud. Would you be prepared to discuss the situation with a customs agent representing the U.S. government?

Sometimes the situation in foreign countries is horrific, yet almost nothing can be done. While in Namibia, one of the authors (JGS) was offered two cheetah cubs for $2.50 each. The farmer (a rancher in our terms) said that if the cubs were not purchased, they would be drowned. Cheetahs are, of course, an endangered species under the ESA. Their international trade is strictly prohibited. Healthy cheetah populations still exist in Namibia, and the cat is considered vermin to farmers.

A trip down the Congo River through Zaire in Central Africa is the experience of a lifetime. The trip is, at best, arduous and brings to mind the phrase "survival test." Along the way, local people canoe out to the steamship and sell food such as bananas and various other fruits, bread, fish, and animals. Often the animals are alive and bound with twine. During one trip, a canoeist offered two live young chimpanzees for sale as food. Of course, chimpanzees are endangered. Needless to say, cash is an even rarer commodity in remote parts of Africa. Although the author refused to purchase the chimpanzees, another local passenger bought both. During the trip, the chimps were fed fruit and kept in a grass basket typical of the region. The small male was eaten first, while his sister whimpered inside her basket. Later that week, the basket contained a small forest antelope. Local enforcement of international law in certain parts of the world is impossible, and sometimes the situation seems hopeless.

Other U.S. Codes also specify many useful wildlife laws, including the following:

- Classification and Multiple Use Act of 1964, 1976, 43 U.S.C.
- Clean Air Act of 1970, 1980, 42 U.S.C.
- Clean Water Act of 1981, 33 U.S.C.
- Comprehensive Environmental Response, Compensation, and Liability Act of 1980, 42 U.S.C.
- Federal Environmental Pesticide Control Act of 1981, 7 U.S.C.
- Federal Fruit Fly and Tick Act of 1938 and 1942, 7 U.S.C.
- Federal Land Policy and Management Act of 1976, 1981, 43 U.S.C.
- Federal Noxious Weed Act of 1974, 1976, 7 U.S.C.
- Fishermen's Protection Act of 1967, 1981, 22 U.S.C.
- Intervention of the High Seas Act of 1976, 33 U.S.C.

- Mineral Leasing Act of 1976, 1981, 30 U.S.C.
- Mineral Leasing Act for Acquired Lands of 1976, 30 U.S.C.
- National Environmental Policy Act of 1976, 42 U.S.C.
- Outer Continental Shelf Lands Act of 1953, 1976, 1981, 43 U.S.C.
- Plant Pest Act of 1976, 7 U.S.C.
- Resource Conservation and Recovery Act of 1976, 1981, 42 U.S.C.
- River and Harbor Act of 1899, 1976, 33 U.S.C.
- Submerged Lands Act of 1976, 43 U.S.C.
- Tariff Act of 1930, 1976, 19 U.S.C.
- Tariff Act of 1962, 1976, 19 U.S.C.
- Tariff Classification Act of 1976, 19 U.S.C.
- Taylor Grazing Act of 1976, 1981, 43 U.S.C.
- Walrus Protection Act (omitted from 16 U.S.C. as obsolete)
- Wilson Original Package Act of 1976, 1980, 27 U.S.C.

U.S. FISH AND WILDLIFE SERVICE
DIVISION OF LAW ENFORCEMENT

The U.S. Fish and Wildlife Service (USFWS) Division of Law Enforcement is charged with upholding the laws and acts of the United States and making certain that the laws are obeyed by U.S. citizens and their entities, such as corporations, and any foreign citizens in the United States. The USFWS protects fish, wildlife, and plants through a wide variety of law enforcement techniques, including:

- Surveillance of areas where priority wildlife and fishery resources are concentrated. To protect the dwindling numbers of ducks and geese, the USFWS routinely creates task forces during the waterfowl season in many states.
- Inspection of shipments entering or leaving the United States at designated ports, border ports, and special ports; investigation of known and suspected violations; and distribution of information about federal wildlife regulations and their enforcement.
- Submission of evidence of violations to regional solicitors of the Department of the Interior or U.S. attorneys for consideration of civil penalties or criminal prosecution.

The objectives of the USFWS Division of Law Enforcement are to enforce the Lacey Act, Migratory Bird Treaty Act, Migratory Bird Hunting and Conservation Stamp Act, Eagle Protection Act, Endangered Species Act, Airborne

Hunting Act, Marine Mammal Protection Act, Convention on International Trade in Endangered Species of Wild Fauna and Flora, National Wildlife Refuge System Administration Act, Antarctic Conservation Act, Archaeological Resources Protection Act, Wild Bird Conservation Act, and the African Elephant Conservation Act. The Division of Law Enforcement is also charged with uncovering major commercial activity involving illegal trade of protected wildlife and wildlife products. When appropriate, the division also issues permits.

The USFWS is also charged with enhancing legitimate use and enjoyment of migratory birds and other wildlife and with keeping U.S. citizens informed of various federal laws and regulations relating to the protection of fish, wildlife, and plants.

The USFWS maintains a Branch of Special Operations comprised of eight special agents who are assigned full-time undercover duties and an Intelligence Section that is composed of one intelligence research specialist. The special agents employ highly sophisticated and innovative investigative techniques to uncover and document large-scale violations involving the illegal taking, importing, and/or commercialization of wildlife. We will see examples of their successes in subsequent chapters. The intelligence research specialist provides analytical and strategic intelligence to personnel within the Branch of Special Operations and to field agents located throughout the country.

The duties and responsibilities of the branch have taken on heightened importance due to the ever-increasing difficulty of detecting wildlife crime through more conventional methods and enforcement activities. Today, wildlife violations are often clandestine in nature, committed by organized and sophisticated persons and groups, and are complex in terms of the conspiracies and fraud associated with them and the worldwide arena in which they take place. While such undercover operations are time consuming and potentially dangerous, they nevertheless are very effective in combating significant and ongoing exploitation of wildlife resources and in deterring such activities.

In addition, wildlife inspectors monitor and assist in halting illegal trade. The USFWS employs approximately 85 uniformed wildlife inspectors. These inspectors work with U.S. Customs and Department of Agriculture inspectors to provide expertise in wildlife law and species identification. In addition to scrutinizing the legality of accompanying permits, wildlife inspectors conduct physical inspections, targeting repeat offenders and checking shipments on a random basis. Inspectors give priority to processing importation of live wildlife.

The Division of Law Enforcement of the USFWS has been particularly effective (or has chosen to prosecute only the most egregious cases).

	1992	*1993*	*1994*	*Total*
Cases brought to trial	75	64	123	262
Indictments	103	88	150	341
Sentences	97	82	138	317
Not guilty verdicts	6	6	11	23

ANIMAL RIGHTS GROUPS

Animals do not have standing; therefore, they must be represented by a group that does have standing. Sometimes the Sierra Club or the Wilderness Society represents forests or species. Dr. Albert Schweitzer, perhaps the greatest humanitarian to ever live, held a belief that life, all life, was sacred. In his world-famous hospital in Gabon, Dr. Schweitzer treated people and animals, and he won a Nobel Prize for his outstanding work. Animal rights groups also believe in the sanctity of all life. European animal rights groups are especially active, for instance. Animal testing labs, fox hunts, chicken factories, and kennel clubs have been their targets. Of course, not all animal rights groups are forthright about their concerns. Wildlife issues have a way of exciting people into actions they would not otherwise take.

A report issued by Direct Action for Animal Liberation summarizes recent actions taken against those perceived to have violated the sanctity of life. Many actions occur each month. Some highlights are given here. In January 1994, the Animal Liberation Front (ALF) smashed 17 animal abusers' windows. A horse was rescued from its owner, who was taken to court for abuse. The owners of a hunt club in the United Kingdom received a fake parcel bomb. The Hunt Retribution Squad planted three land mines at a horse racing club. A U.K. group called the Justice Department (JD) sent a hoax parcel bomb to a hunt club. In February 1994, an incendiary device was dropped through a mailbox at a leather boot factory. The ALF claimed to have freed, in separate incidents, 3 sheep, 158 hens, and 10 dogs. The JD sent a boot manufacturer an incendiary device. The ALF sabotaged a meat factory in April 1994. At Northeast Surrey College, the ALF freed more than 200 animals, including 15 rabbits, 52 guinea pigs, 58 hamsters, and more than 90 rats. The cages were smashed and the rooms were flooded. A bomb exploded at a pig company, injuring one man. No group claimed responsibility. Two incendiary devices caused severe damage to a boot factory in Cambridge, U.K. The Animal Rights Militia took credit.

In Finland, a fur store had its windows smashed and locks glued by the ALF. In Germany, nine fur shops were stink bombed by Autonome Tierschutzerinnen. In March 1994, 2500 worms and maggots were freed from anglers. In Frankfurt, Germany, the local McDonald's, Burger King, and Wienerwald toilets were blocked. In Northern Ireland, the local McDonald's had its windows smashed by the ALF. The ALF also sabotaged a fur shop in Norway. A Norwegian-registered outlaw whaling ship was scuttled and the engine room flooded. The Sea Shepard Conservation Society took credit for sinking a second outlaw whaler. A chicken breeding company in Scotland was targeted with a letter bomb by the JD. In Sweden, Animal Avengers sabotaged more than a dozen fur shops.

APPENDIX : CITES PARTICIPATING NATIONS AS OF JANUARY 1996

Nation	Signature date	Nation	Signature date
Afghanistan	January 28, 1986	Congo	May 1, 1983
Algeria	February 21, 1984	Costa Rica	September 28, 1975
Argentina	April 8, 1981	Cote d'Ivoire	February 19, 1995
Australia	October 27, 1976	Cuba	July 19, 1990
Austria	April 27, 1982	Cyprus	July 1, 1975
Bahamas	September 18, 1979	Czech Republic	January 1, 1993
Bangladesh	February 18, 1982	Denmark	October 24, 1977
Barbados	March 9, 1993	Djibouti	May 7, 1992
Belarus	November 8, 1995	Dominica	November 2, 1995
Belgium	January 1, 1984	Dominican	March 17, 1987
Belize	September 21, 1981	Republic	
Benin	May 28, 1984	Ecuador	July 1, 1975
Bolivia	October 4, 1979	Egypt	April 4, 1978
Botswana	February 12, 1978	El Salvador	July 29, 1987
Brazil	November 4, 1975	Equatorial	June 8, 1992
Brunei	August 20, 1990	Guinea	
Bulgaria	April 16, 1991	Eritrea	January 22, 1995
Burkina Faso	January 15, 1990	Estonia	October 20, 1992
Burundi	November 6, 1988	Ethiopia	July 4, 1989
Cameroon	September 3, 1981	Finland	August 8, 1976
Canada	July 9, 1975	France	August 9, 1978
Central African	November 25, 1980	Gabon	May 15, 1989
Republic		Gambia	November 24, 1977
Chad	May 3, 1989	Germany	June 20, 1976
Chile	July 1, 1975	Ghana	February 12, 1976
China	April 8, 1981	Greece	January 6, 1993
Colombia	November 29, 1981	Guatemala	February 5, 1980
Comoros	February 21, 1995	Guinea	December 20, 1981

Nation	Signature date	Nation	Signature date
Guinea-Bissau	August 14, 1990	Poland	March 12, 1990
Guyana	August 25, 1977	Portugal	March 11, 1981
Honduras	June 13, 1985	Romania	November 16, 1994
Hungary	August 29, 1985	Russian	December 8, 1976
India	October 18, 1976	Federation	
Indonesia	March 28, 1979	Rwanda	January 18, 1981
Iran	November 1, 1976	Saint Kitts and	May 15, 1994
Israel	March 17, 1980	Nevis	
Italy	December 31, 1979	Saint Lucia	March 15, 1983
Japan	November 4, 1980	Saint Vincent	February 28, 1989
Jordan	March 14, 1979	and the	
Kenya	March 13, 1979	Grenadines	
Korea,	October 7, 1993	Senegal	November 3, 1977
Republic of		Seychelles	May 9, 1977
Liberia	June 9, 1981	Sierra Leone	January 26, 1995
Liechtenstein	February 28, 1980	Singapore	February 28, 1987
Luxembourg	March 12, 1984	Slovak Republic	January 1, 1993
Madagascar	November 18, 1975	Somalia	March 2, 1986
Malawi	May 6, 1982	South Africa	October 13, 1975
Malaysia	January 18, 1978	Spain	August 28, 1986
Mali	October 16, 1994	Sri Lanka	August 2, 1979
Malta	July 16, 1989	Sudan	January 24, 1983
Mauritius	July 27, 1975	Suriname	February 15, 1981
Mexico	September 30, 1991	Sweden	July 1, 1975
Monaco	July 1978	Switzerland	July 1, 1975
Mongolia	January 5, 1996	Tanzania	February 27, 1980
Morocco	January 14, 1976	Thailand	April 21, 1983
Mozambique	June 23, 1981	Togo	January 21, 1979
Namibia	March 18, 1991	Trinidad and	April 18, 1984
Nepal	September 16, 1975	Tobago	
Netherlands	July 18, 1984	Tunisia	July 1, 1975
New Zealand	August 8, 1989	Uganda	October 16, 1991
Nicaragua	November 4, 1977	United Arab	May 12, 1990
Niger	December 7, 1975	Emirates	
Nigeria	July 1, 1975	United Kingdom	October 31, 1976
Norway	October 25, 1976	United States	July 1, 1975
Pakistan	July 19, 1976	Uruguay	July 1, 1975
Panama	November 15, 1978	Vanuatu	October 15, 1989
Papua New	March 11, 1976	Venezuela	January 22, 1978
Guinea		Vietnam	April 20, 1994
Paraguay	February 13, 1977	Zaire	October 18, 1976
Peru	September 25, 1975	Zambia	February 22, 1981
Philippines	November 16, 1981	Zimbabwe	August 17, 1981

EXERCISES

2.1 Find examples of wildlife crimes and cite the laws that were violated during these crimes. How do the sentences meted out compare with the possible sentences the laws provide? Consider looking at http://www.fws.gov/~r9dle/div_le.html on the Internet.

2.2 Inspect http://www.law.cornell.edu/uscode. What exactly is the Migratory Bird Act?

2.3 The United States has many laws that protect wildlife. Find examples of laws from other countries that protect wildlife.

2.4 Despite all these laws, the list of threatened and endangered species continues to grow. Explain why this is so.

2.5 Use your favorite search engine to surf the World Wide Web for international agreements.

2.6 Are there laws preventing harmful bacteria or viruses from entering the United States?

2.7 Find a list of all CITES Appendix I, II, and III species. Compare the most recent lists with older lists. Are trends evident?

2.8 Make a list of threatened and endangered species included in the Endangered Species Act. Examine historical lists for trends. Based on a comparison, make predictions about possible additions to the list.

2.9 The Endangered Species Act of 1973 was reauthorized and strengthened in 1988. The updated version of the Endangered Species Act required all federal agencies to undertake programs for the conservation of endangered and threatened species and prohibited them from authorizing, funding, or carrying out any action that would jeopardize a listed species or destroy or modify its "critical habitat." For the first time, plants and all classes of invertebrates were eligible for protection, as they were under CITES. Assemble a list of threatened and endangered species of mammals, birds, reptiles, amphibians, fishes, snails, clams, crustaceans, insects, arachnids, and plants. How has this list changed since 1973?

2.10 How is "critical habitat" defined in the Endangered Species Act? What does the law say about habitats that are used only rarely or seasonally, such as ephemeral wetlands in South Dakota that are used by migratory waterfowl?

2.11 Update the actions by animal rights groups. What is happening in the United States? Try doing a search on "Animal Liberation Front."

2.12 Trace the history of animal rights groups. Are there any clear trends in the issues these groups raise? Start your search at http://www.envirolink.org/adn/alt.old or do a search on "Direct Action for Animal Liberation."

2.13 Investigate more thoroughly which animals were heavily exploited during the early history of the United States.

2.14 Is there a wildlife issue with the buffalo anymore?

2.15 Will we protect more wildlife more effectively by enacting laws, arresting more violators, and levying more and heavier fines? What is the most effective way to protect wildlife? Explain your position using examples.

LITERATURE CITED

Bean, M. 1983. *The Evolution of National Wildlife Law.* Praeger Publishers, New York.

Cooper, M.E. 1987. *An Introduction to Animal Law.* Harcourt Brace Jovanovich, New York.

Day, A. 1949. *North American Waterfowl.* Stackpole and Heck, New York.

Easter-Pilcher, A. 1996. Implementing the Endangered Species Act. *Bioscience* **46**(5):355–363.

Hemley, G. 1994. *International Wildlife Trade: A CITES Sourcebook.* Island Press, Washington, D.C.

Kohm, K.A. 1991. *Balancing on the Brink of Extinction.* Island Press, Washington, D.C.

Littell, R. 1992. *Endangered and Other Protected Species: Federal Law and Regulation.* The Bureau of National Affairs, Washington, D.C.

Lund, T.A. 1980. *American Wildlife Law.* University of California Press, Berkeley.

Matthiessen, P. 1964. *Wildlife in America.* Viking Press, New York.

Trefethen, J. 1975. *An American Crusade for Wildlife.* Winchester Press and the Boone and Crockett Club, New York.

Wheeler, C.E. 1947. *Duck Shooting Along the Atlantic Tidewater.* William Morrow, New York.

Wilcove, D.S., M. McMillan, and K.C. Winston. 1993. What exactly is an endangered species? An analysis of the U.S. endangered species list: 1985–1991. *Conservation Biology* **7**(1):87–93.

EXAMPLES OF WILDLIFE ISSUES

3

Why, with so many laws in place, are there any wildlife issues left to resolve? How is it that new wildlife issues arise nearly every day? There is no law that prevents habitat destruction, no act that prevents birds from escaping from aviaries, no decree against constructing new highways that fragment habitat, and almost no universally accepted laws that apply globally. In fact, the laws are difficult to enforce, and when enforced, many judges apply only a so-called slap on the wrist for most criminal violations. As long as there is wildlife, there will be wildlife issues to resolve.

Few articles grab the attention of newspaper and magazine readers as stories about wildlife issues do. How many of us have seen a picture of a wolf on the cover of a newspaper or magazine? Not a day passes without someone mentioning one wildlife issue or another. This chapter is a sampler of issues. Remember, an issue is created by at least two people with a difference of opinion. Few people would suggest, for instance, that we set aside a preserve to harbor the Ebola virus, but when it comes to wolves, the two sides are often far apart. From insects and parrots to the consumption of gorillas as food, wildlife issues demand our attention and often our emotions.

The United States is by far the world's largest importer of wildlife. Demand for exotic pets in the United States is astounding, and where there is demand, there will be supply. According to TRAFFIC–USA (1996), 10,000 to 12,000 live primates enter the United States each year and are used primarily for research. A staggering 100,000 to 200,000 live birds are imported each year; an estimated 50,000 are smuggled in. Even more lizards are imported, 1 to 2 million each year, in addition to some 3 to 4 million whole skins and 25 to 30 million manufactured goods. Who buys this stuff?

The United States imports 200 to 250 million ornamental fish each year. The majority come from fish farms in Southeast Asia. Though little is known of the mollusk trade, some 10 to 15 million raw shells make it to the United States each year. Few mollusks are protected by any laws, national or international, so why should we care? Some 200,000 to 300,000 live corals make it to the United States as well. World trade in the above species is enormous. For instance, some 50 million manufactured reptile products are imported worldwide each year. Many species are poached for international trade. Certain special lizards and snakes are traded in the hundreds of thousands, presumably to end up as pets, many of which get flushed down toilets.

The Endangered Species Act of 1973, the Convention on International Trade in Endangered Species (CITES), and the Lacey Act of 1900 and its subsequent amendments have all been used recently to stop international trade in rare insects. Recently, the U.S. Justice Department successfully prosecuted professional butterfly collectors running international businesses. The U.S. Fish and Wildlife Service (USFWS) Division of Law Enforcement has put on notice all potential collectors of living organisms, from plants to animals. Collecting listed species, even insects, is against the law; violators will be prosecuted under the law and, if found guilty, can be fined and sent to prison.

SAMPLE WILDLIFE ISSUES

Butterflies

Williams (1996) reported that Stanford University's Center for Conservation Biology and its climate-controlled laboratory were used by a criminal to raise butterflies and their food plants. Oddly, no one reported the fact that some of the butterflies were threatened or endangered species. When one of the guilty men was apprehended in his home, federal agents seized 2375 specimens worth more than $300,000. Some 14 butterfly species were threatened and endangered under the Endangered Species Act. Another poacher connected to the case was found guilty of smuggling more than 30,000 Mexican butterflies, moths, and beetles. Another two poachers were also found guilty. The investigating team believed that with sufficient resources, hundreds of other collectors could have been indicted. Instead, as Williams reported, the U.S. District Court served 57 grand jury subpoenas and offered poachers the option of forfeiting the specimens in lieu of further criminal action. The U.S. government's conviction rate for wildlife violations is a whopping 94%, which would indicate that only the most flagrant cases are prosecuted. Most potential cases are not prosecuted.

Sometimes wildlife issues never get decided in a court of law. The migration of the monarch butterfly (*Danaus plexippus*) is one of nature's most spectacular events. According to Brower (1995), the monarch's overwintering colonies rank as one of the great biological wonders of the world. Unfortunately, there are only 12 such colonies. Human population growth and deforestation in the Oyamel fir forest enclaves threaten the colonies. Also, increasing use of herbicides across North America kills both larval and adult food resources. Monarchs co-evolved with milkweed (*Asclepias syriaca*), a toxic plant. The reduced area of the fir forest (40,000 to 50,000 ha) and patchy distribution make the forest more vulnerable to deforestation pressures than any other type of forest in Mexico. The monarchs survive from September to March in these forests.

The migratory and overwintering biology of the eastern monarch has become, in Brower's words, "an endangered biological phenomenon." Overwintering occurs in Mexico. The monarchs then migrate northward into the United States at the end of March and early April. They lay their eggs on southern milkweeds and then die. The eggs hatch, and eventually the monarchs fly further north to southern Canada, laying eggs and then dying along the migration route. After the first spring and two or three subsequent summer generations, the monarchs enter reproductive diapause and begin migrating to their respective overwintering sites.

During December 1995, heavy snow fell in five of the monarch butterfly sanctuaries in the rugged mountains of Michoacan State, west of Mexico City. Millions of butterflies overwinter in the mountains, where cold weather is rare. However, snowfall in 1992 killed an estimated 80% of the wintering butterflies, and the monarchs had not recovered from that episode before the most recent snows hit. What is the wildlife issue here? Surely, something can be done to protect the butterflies.

Perhaps the issue is climate change in the form of global warming. Global warming does not imply that the earth will uniformly warm. One of the critical hypotheses of global warming is that there will be increasing variability in the earth's climate. That is, while global average temperatures rise, climate variability will increase. Whereas snow in the monarch refuges might have occurred once every 25 years, snow will likely occur more frequently while generally higher temperatures will occur throughout the year, particularly during summer. If the monarch population is unable to recover in favorable years, perhaps these mountain populations are doomed. Thus, the issue might be larger in scope than turtles versus tires or ranchers versus wolves. The issue at stake addresses a more fundamental question: Will humans be able to accommodate other species' requirements or will they continue to garner more of the earth's finite resources for their own benefit and leave less and less for all other species?

In Papua New Guinea, native villagers sell tropical insects for cash. Endemic birdwing butterflies are among the most beautiful and prized collectibles in the butterfly world. Some birdwing butterflies being sold have been on the CITES list since 1977. Insects such as giant walking sticks are collected from the wild and sold to exporters. At a time when habitat loss through forest clearing and agricultural schemes is occurring elsewhere in the world, this seems like a ludicrous strategy.

Certainly insects have enormous reproductive capacity. Conservation requirements for vertebrates are much different than requirements for insects and other invertebrates. Parks and reserves are established mainly to protect vertebrates. Papua New Guinea is rich in unique birds, insects, and plants. Several large reserves may not be the answer in Papua New Guinea. Perhaps many smaller reserves would serve the needs of conservation better. Also, insect ranching might best serve the needs of butterfly conservation.

Parrots

On January 4, 1996, the *Chicago Tribune* and *USA Today* reported that Tony Silva intended to plead guilty to federal charges of conspiring to smuggle protected parrots into the United States. On January 29, he pleaded guilty to violating wildlife protection and customs laws and filing a false income tax return. A co-defendant in the case against Silva turned government witness and was sentenced to 3 years probation, 6 months home detention, and 300 hours of community service, in addition to a $10,000 fine and $200 in court fees. One conspirator remains a fugitive. Silva's sentencing was delayed because he has asked the court to reverse his guilty plea.

For the world-renowned parrot expert and his mother, such charges were unthinkable a decade ago. But that was before USFWS investigators began a probe code-named Operation Renegade 6 years ago that culminated in 35 convictions. The guilty party was a world expert on rare birds, especially rare and endangered parrots. At 35, he was already at the top of his field as the curator of birds at Loro Parque in the Canary Islands, which has one of the finest collections of parrots in the world. Today, there is but one male Spix macaw in the wild left on earth. The curator had convinced private owners of Spix macaws to establish a captive breeding program. As a result of his efforts, the captive population has tripled to 37, and these will be the founders of the next generation that will hopefully be released in the wild.

The author of two popular coffee table books on parrots, Silva was in demand as a speaker and was an outspoken advocate for bird protection. However, an avalanche of criminal evidence against him would have been released had his case gone to trial. He and his mother are charged with smuggling into the United States $1.3 million worth of rare birds, including blue-throated conures, Lilacine Amazons, African grey parrots, and red-vented cockatoos. Some 180 hyacinth macaws were also among the booty recovered. There are only a few thousand hyacinths left in the wilds of Bolivia, Brazil, and Paraguay. He had shipped some 30 hyacinths to a private collector and all died in transit. The live birds could have been worth $9000 apiece. Assistant Attorney General Lois Schiffer said, "These crimes threaten our endangered species and global biodiversity." His crimes carry penalties of up to $2.5 million in fines and 45 years in prison. His mother is also charged with possession of elephant tusks and with aiding her son in filing false income tax returns. She faces up to 50 years in prison.

Operation Renegade also netted Theodora Swanson, an animal keeper at the Playboy Mansion. She was sentenced to 37 months in prison for illegally smuggling eggs of threatened species from Australia to the United States. As of April 1996, 15 individuals received 186 months in prison (TRAFFIC–USA 1996) and Swanson was free pending an appeal of her sentence. William Wegner, the smuggling ringleader, received a $10,000 fine and a five-year prison sentence. Brian Bradley received 41 months in prison and three years probation for his participation in the smuggling ring. More than 800 Australian cockatoo eggs worth more than $1.5 million were illegally taken from the wild and smuggled into the United States. All cockatoos are protected by CITES.

In Central and South America, 16 species of macaws, large members of the parrot family, are found. Nine species of macaws, including the Spix macaw mentioned above, are endangered. Macaws are a poacher's favorite bird. They are intelligent, large, and colorful, and therefore, the pet trade demand for them is high. Guatemala's scarlet macaw is on the verge of extinction (Colclough 1996). Some 500 are estimated to remain in the wild. Habitat destruction, hunting, poaching, and taking of nestlings have contributed to their demise. While a chick can bring $300, an adult macaw, depending on the species, can be sold for $4000 outside the country. Smugglers, of course, pocket most of the money. A captive breeding program might be able to repopulate the forest, but unless habitat is saved, there will be no room for the scarlet macaw.

In 1990, some one-third of the 450,000 live birds imported into the United States were parrots. Japan, Belgium, the Netherlands, and Germany are also major importers of parrots. The vast majority of parrots sold on the import market are caught in the wild. In the 1980s, at least 50,000 parrots were smuggled into the United States each year. No one knows how many parrots died in transit and were never counted. Asian species come mainly from Indonesia, although Central and South America supply the bulk of the parrot trade.

Wolves

A picture of a wolf (*Canis lupus*) showing its teeth in a newspaper or magazine article is a real attention-grabber. This is no small feat because wolves tend to growl and growling does not fully expose the canines. Yawning and howling expose the canines, but a yawning wolf is not very threatening. On Wednesday, March 14, the *Tampa Tribune* printed an article on wolves in Yellowstone National Park. The headline in bold letters read, "a pack of trouble." The Montana Stockgrowers Association had apparently printed a pamphlet showing a wolf dressed as a Washington bureaucrat. It seems that the Montana ranchers did not fully appreciate that the Yellowstone wolves are part of the native wildlife. Of course, visitors and tourists have shown overwhelming support for the reintroduction of wolves. The thrill of seeing a wolf in the wild can be the highlight of a trip to Yellowstone National Park. Anyone can just walk up to Old Faithful and sit down on a bench to see it vent, but seeing a wolf is extremely rare and thus exciting.

Wolves roam widely and will kill rodents, deer, and elk, as well as sheep and cattle. When a local resident shot and killed one of the Yellowstone wolves that had left the park, he was fined $10,000 and sentenced to six months in prison. Local ranchers fear the worst for their livelihood. Perhaps as many as three million tourists visit Yellowstone each year, and most of them are on the lookout for wolves. The issue is clear. Should the U.S. government reintroduce wolves into Yellowstone National Park?

An editorial in the *Seattle Times* reported that "fears of ranchers outside the park...have not been realized." No livestock were killed in 1995 and only nine sheep were killed in the first half of 1996. Polls of visitors to Yellowstone National Park show that the public, by a significant margin, supports the reintroduction of the wolf.

Corals

Corals are marine animals of the invertebrate phylum Cnidaria. They are related to jellyfish and also sea anemones. Millions of individual coral, living in colonies, make up coral reefs. Coral reefs are known throughout the world for the variety of fish and other organisms that live in and around them. Reef-building corals are only found in warm tropical waters. Other corals do not form reefs. Although no species of coral is endangered, local reefs around the world have been severely damaged. The World Conservation Union (IUCN) considers all coral to be commercially threatened however, because if these reefs are commercially harvested, corals will become endangered. All reef-building corals are listed in Appendix II of CITES.

Reef-building corals are used commercially for a large variety of industrial uses, such as road construction, building material, bricks, and tile (TRAFFIC–USA 1996). Living corals are collected and sold for aquariums. Often coral is blasted loose with dynamite, and large sections of reef are destroyed. From 1989 to 1993, 12 million pieces of raw and 1.6 million pieces of live reef-building coral were reported in world trade. This figure is probably low, as domestic use of coral is not reported. The United States is the largest consumer of coral and imports over 90% of all commercial coral.

The origin of each piece of coral is difficult to determine and is generally not recorded. TRAFFIC–USA (1996) recommends that "it is best to refrain from buying *any* coral, whether for decoration, for your aquarium, or as jewelry." No one knows if yields are sustainable, and very few countries have any management plans for reefs.

Spiders

Many people dislike spiders (class Arachnid), and some find them offensive. Others, such as the authors, are fascinated by spiders and appreciate them for what they are. One spider family, tarantulas (Theraphosidae), is in demand by collectors (Fitzgerald 1989). Pet connoisseurs in the United States prize a Mexican tarantula, the red-kneed tarantula (*Brachypelma smithi*), because it is docile and beautiful. Although *B. smithi* is listed in CITIES Appendix II, many illegally make it into the United States each year. Almost all of them are wild-caught. They sold for about $12 in 1989. The species has a low reproductive rate. Attempts to monitor trade in spiders are almost impossible and the ban is not always enforced. Who would want a pet spider? Apparently, 30,000 people did in 1989.

Manatees

The West Indian manatee (*Trichehus manatus*) is an aquatic herbivore that seems to permit more children than adults to pet it. Indeed, the shy manatees of Silver Springs, Florida seem attracted to children frolicking in the clear water of the springs and often approach children to be stroked. When pursued, the manatee can swim faster than the best of swimmers. It is not unusual to hear residents of Florida claim that "there were more manatees 100 years ago than there are today" or "there are fewer manatees now than there ever were." Most manatees in Florida have motorboat scars on their backs. Researchers studying manatees recognize individuals by their unique scars. Recreational boaters have been successful in blocking attempts to establish speed limits in rivers with high manatee populations. Many see the manatees as putting a crimp in their recreational style.

During the first three months of 1996, 258 manatees died in Florida, 57 more than the total for all of 1995. Some 2639 manatees remain in Florida. News of the deaths reached around the world. As one newspaper suggested, "If the death rates continue, the population of manatees in this region [the western part of the state] could be wiped out by fall." Disease is a suggested killer, but pathologists were investigating each death. The manatee is listed as endangered. Although many residents were concerned, no large preserve has been set aside strictly for the manatees. The wildlife issue here is clear. If the manatee is endangered, why is there no large preserve for them where they will be protected from motorboats? Can a large reserve be set aside for this wide-ranging mammal? In 1995, a manatee named Chelsea showed up off Rhode Island and was airlifted back to Florida. During 1996, manatees have been sighted in Texas coastal waters. Are these dispersing individuals seeking out new territories or are they fleeing an overabundant Florida population?

Cockatoos

In August 1994, six people were indicted for smuggling into the United States cockatoo eggs obtained from the wilds of Australia. One suspect had 49 eggs hidden on his body, as reported in the *Daily News* on May 18, 1994. An adult cockatoo can sell for more than $12,000. Once the eggs pass customs, they are incubated, and the young are raised and then sold. Smuggling eggs has become a popular way of transporting species. The eggs can be kept in a vest close to the body and thus are very difficult to detect. The United States is the largest market for wild-caught birds. Seventeen people in Australia, New Zealand, and the United States were convicted and more convictions were expected. Smuggled species include the rose-breasted, Major Mitchell, red-tailed black, white-tailed black, greater sulphur crested, and slender-billed cockatoos. Of course, Australian cockatoos are protected by CITES.

Wildebeest

The European Economic Community (EEC) signed an agreement to import beef from Botswana, a landlocked semi-arid and desert country just north of South Africa. Botswana contains part of the Kalahari Desert, and water is scarce throughout the country except for the Okavango Delta in northern Botswana. During epidemics of hoof-and-mouth disease, the EEC refused to purchase beef from Botswana. The Department of Animal Health, a government agency, was given the task of devising a way to prevent hoof-and-mouth disease from contaminating the domestic stock. Since the rich and powerful owned the largest cattle ranches, something had to be done by the government. Hoof-and-mouth disease is carried by African cape buffalo and some species of antelope, and these carriers could presumably infect beef cattle, although it is not known whether this has actually happened. The government of Botswana decided that fences were the most effective means of segregating wild animal populations from cattle. There are, of course, two ways to consider the situation: either the fences serve to keep beef cattle in and wild animals out or, conversely, they serve to keep beef cattle out and wild animals in. The result was ultimately the same: a massive die-off among the wild herds occurred as a direct result of the fences (Owens and Owens 1984).

The cycle of rain and drought in the Kalahari, the great desert of southern Africa, ebbs and flows over time. In some years, the rains are good and the great herds of herbivores are nowhere to be found. Instead, the animals are scattered across the desert, following the rain clouds and feeding on the grasses. From 1974 to 1979 the rains had been generous, and great numbers of wildebeest (Figure 3.1), oryx (Figure 3.2), springbok, and eland penetrated deep into the desert. In 1979, the rains failed to come and the vegetation withered. The

FIGURE 3.1 Two hyenas capture and eat alive a wildebeest in Ngorongoro Crater National Park, Tanzania.

FIGURE 3.2 A water hole at Etosha National Park, Namibia. A giraffe, zebras, kudus, and oryx find water in the desert.

wildebeest knew, somehow, that they must head north or east to the only permanent water sources.

Slowly the wildebeest funneled north and east. Groups of tens became thousands, and thousands became tens of thousands. Some 90,000 strong plodded north, their heads hung low as the sun beat down on them. Dust rose from their hooves and turned the sky brown. They trekked for more than 300 miles, only to meet with the fences. They could smell the waters of Lake Xau, but they could not break through the fences. More than 100,000 wildebeest were forced to stumble along the fences, driven by instinct and the smell of water. Forage and shade were nonexistent. Now they could see the water, but their route was blocked by villages of herdsmen and their dogs. The last great die-off of Botswana's great herds had begun.

Some 87% of all wildebeest died. The herd of more than 100,000 animals was reduced to 13,000. Emaciated animals piled up along the fences. Some walked along, stumbled, rose, and fell again. Their chests heaving, they were unable to run when the dogs set upon them. Villagers stoned wildebeests to death. An almost surrealistic horror unfolded day by day, and the stench of death filled the air. The government of Botswana continues to erect fences today in compliance with the EEC's wishes to enjoy healthier beef cattle. One of the most powerful wildlife issues of our time was settled when the second largest migration of herbivores was wiped off the face of the planet within six months.

Sea Turtles

On Sunday, December 31, 1995, the headline "beach battle pits turtles vs. tires" appeared in the *Palm Beach Post.* The article reported that "Endangered sea turtles may push cars off Daytona's beach. But tourism would take a hit, the county fears." For thousands, perhaps tens of thousands of years, sea turtles have been nesting on Daytona Beach. Daytona is one of a few towns that still permits motorists and their vehicles on the beach, for a five dollar fee. The fee generates millions of dollars for the city, and local businesses thrive from the tourism. Businesspeople fear that a lawsuit filed on behalf of the sea turtles, if successful, would cause an economic disaster. An environmentalist claimed the county was "living in the Dark Ages."

As is typical of a wildlife issue, the different interest groups take sides and try to create an either/or issue. Either you are for business or against business. Either you are for the turtles or against the turtles. Maybe a different breed of tourist would show up during the sea turtle nesting and hatching season and would be willing to pay even more money to see young hatchling sea turtles make their way to the sea. Certainly vehicles would not be restricted from the entire beach. Perhaps the solution lies somewhere between the interests of the vested parties. In either case, the wildlife issue is clear: the Endangered Species Act of 1973 protects the sea turtle. By March 1996, county officials had submitted to the USFWS a conservation plan that specifically addressed the turtles' requirements. A federal judge postponed the trial, issued a temporary restraining order against nighttime driving and parking on county beaches, and imposed a protection area from the sea turtle nesting dunes to the beach. Is this an either/or issue?

On January 8, 1996, the *New York Times* reported that on December 29, 1995, the U.S. Court of International Trade issued an order against the Department of Commerce for "failure to bar shrimp imports into the U.S. from nations that are not implementing procedures to reduce sea turtle deaths." The judge cited the Department of Commerce for failing to carry out the Endangered Species Act, which requires the department to ban shrimp exports from all countries that do not have so-called "turtle excluder devices" on their nets.

On February 10, 1996, Reuters News Service reported that three people were caught stealing 372 endangered loggerhead sea turtle (*Caretta caretta*) eggs from their nests. The eggs are delicacies in local ethnic communities in southern Florida. An extraordinary Palm Beach police officer noticed a large cloth bag containing the eggs in the back seat of a car and was credited with the bust. One man received 2 years in jail and another 15 months for violating the Endangered Species Act.

Sharks

A recent advertisement in *American Health* magazine quoted an executive medical director: "Research on shark cartilage has been headline news, so more of my patients have been asking me about it. I've been impressed with the research, and Lane Labs, the maker of BeneFin (a trademark of Lane Labs–USA, Inc.), does more than anyone." The advertisement also quoted Dr. Lane, author of the book *Sharks Don't Get Cancer* and an authority on shark cartilage, who said "BeneFin is the most effective shark cartilage I have studied." Researchers agree that sharks do not get cancer. The claim is that if you eat their cartilage (i.e., if you take BeneFin), you won't get cancer either. Although clinical trials have only just begun, some 25,000 to 100,000 people have purchased and presumably taken shark cartilage. There is one certainty, however. Sharks are being killed indiscriminately. One small factory in Costa Rica harvests more than 111,000 large coastal sharks annually. The U.S. commercial shark fishery annual quota is 150,000 large coastal sharks.

The numbers from Costa Rica indicate intense fishing pressure (Dold 1996). Researchers suggest that the shark fishery will be decimated in a few years as some species require 30 years or more to reach sexual maturity and some have only one young every other year. In U.S. coastal waters, shark populations have declined 70 to 80% in the last two decades. Factory ships lay so-called "longlines" of hooks for a hundred miles and harvest anything that bites, including sea turtles and billed fish such as sailfish. There are virtually no controls beyond U.S. borders. Indeed, few people believe sharks should even be protected. Nevertheless, environmentalists convinced the CITES signatory nations to investigate and document the international trade in sharks. While scientific clinical tests of the efficacy of shark cartilage in cancer treatment will take years to complete, sharks will continue to be harvested for meat, fins, jaws, and cartilage. The fins remain the most valuable part of the shark. Asians in Hong Kong are willing to pay upwards of $20 per pound for the fins to turn them into shark fin soup.

Jellyfish

"Aggressive sea lice ambush swimmers," read the *Palm Beach Post* on April 17, 1996. Palm Beach County's famous beaches were the scene of reports from swimmers who were "covered with sea lice" and endured three to five days of itching, rashes, fever, hives, and general discomfort. Outbreaks are possible from March to August. The greatest infestation occurs in May, when the Gulf Stream is closest to the shore. Researchers believe that a microscopic juvenile jellyfish floating in the Gulf Stream causes the welts. As more people crowd the beaches, more cases are expected.

Alligators

There are many alligator (*Alligator mississippiensis*) farms where animals are raised for food and their skins sold. The wild population of alligators in Florida is estimated to be between one and two million animals. Alligators are legally hunted in Florida. So successful is protection of the American alligator that some alligators have become a nuisance. Residents who decide that an alligator has become a nuisance need only pick up the phone and call their local state game and fresh water fish representative. The nuisance alligator will be dispatched without charge. An alligator simply sunning itself on someone's lawn can be considered a nuisance. The definition of "nuisance" is left to the individual. One in three calls results in a removal. Figure 3.3 shows the number of

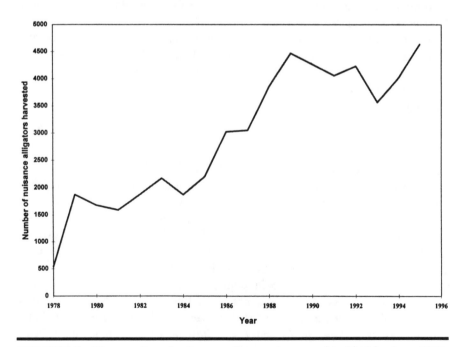

FIGURE 3.3 The number of nuisance alligators harvested in Florida since 1978.

nuisance alligators killed in Florida over the last 15 years. More nuisance alligators are killed each year than are killed during alligator hunting season.

Harp Seals

On December 18, 1995, Canadian Fisheries Minister Brian Tobin announced that seals were to blame for the 99% decline in cod in the North Atlantic. To stem the decline in one of the world's most productive fisheries, the Canadian government announced that the seal harvest would be expanded from 186,000 permits to 250,000 in 1996. From 1983 to 1994, approximately 57,000 seals were harvested every year. Primarily so-called young of the year (from ten days to several months old) are harvested by shooting or clubbing them.

The *Detroit News* wrote that Tobin estimated the seal population has more than doubled since the 1970s, to 4.8 million seals, and could reach 6 million by the year 2000 if no seal hunt is conducted. Tobin suggested the seals eat 6.9 million tons of fish and other prey in a year, including 1 billion cod, weighing 142,000 tons. The International Wildlife Coalition and the International Fund for Animal Welfare are among some 40 organizations that oppose the seal hunt. Since most Atlantic fishermen are out of work, the seal hunt provides them the opportunity to earn cash from the harvested seals. Seal penises sell for over $200 in oriental markets, for instance.

What is the wildlife issue? The Atlantic fishery has been decimated and many fisherman, especially those from Newfoundland, are out of work. Is the seal harvest the real issue? Certainly not. The heart of this issue lies in the Atlantic fishery. How can the scientific method be used to address this question?

Reptiles

According to a February 1, 1996 CITES Update, USFWS special agents served search warrants in Florida, New York, North Carolina, New Mexico, Indonesia, and the Netherlands against suspected smugglers of reptiles. As is so typical, USFWS agents were selected for their "expertise in wildlife import, export, smuggling, and illegal commercialization offenses." The international investigation involved suspected reptile smugglers operating in Australia, Indonesia, and the Netherlands. The United States is the world's largest importer of wildlife, and live exotic pets are in demand. In addition to frilled lizards (*Chlamydosaurus kingii*) from Indonesia, the Fly River turtle (*Carettochelys insculpta*), the green tree python (*Morelia viridis*), and two species of blue-tongued skinks (*Tiliqua gigas* and *T. multifasciata*) were among the species smuggled. All these reptiles are protected by law in their countries of origin, and hence their trade is strictly forbidden. However, the high demand for new and exotic specimens encourages smugglers to pursue wild-caught reptiles.

The investigation began in September 1994, when Netherlands police gathered information from Indonesia. Through an agreement known as the Mutual Legal Assistance Treaty, the United States and the Netherlands cooperate with each other in criminal matters. Indonesia is becoming a popular target for reptile smugglers. For instance, a firm owned by an Indonesian made over 1700 shipments totaling approximately 250,000 animals, mostly reptiles, to the United States. Shipping records were obtained by the International Primate Protection League using the Freedom of Information Act. An analysis of the firm's customers revealed many nationally known reptile dealers across the United States. Unfortunately, shipping records are not specific enough when it comes to reptiles, and generic names are often used for species that even an expert would have trouble identifying. The declared value of the reptiles was $2 million. Further analysis is underway.

Iguanas

Imagine standing before a federal judge and entering a felony guilty plea for "knowingly and unlawfully receiving, concealing, and facilitating the transportation of endangered Fiji banded iguanas (*Brachylophus fasciatus*)." That is exactly what Tom Crutchfield of Bushnell, Florida did. Since the Fiji banded iguana was protected by CITES, the Lacey Act, and the Endangered Species Act, the case was investigated by the USFWS and prosecuted by the U.S. attorney's office and the Environment and Natural Resources Division of the U.S. Department of Justice (U.S. Attorney's Office, Middle District of Florida, press release April 19, 1995).

On April 19, 1995, Mr. Crutchfield received five months in prison, five months home detention, two years supervised release, and a $3000 fine.

Rio Grande Silvery Minnow

The New Mexico Department of Game and Fish lifted the bag limit on most species of fish in the Rio Grande over a particular stretch of river in April 1996, the *Albuquerque Tribune* reported. The fish would likely become stranded when the spring irrigation diversion began. Agricultural lands along the river are irrigated in the spring, and stretches of the river are nearly dry. The Rio Grande silvery minnow remains a protected species, however. After Navajo Dam was built on the Rio Grande to control flooding and support spring irrigation, much changed along the Rio Grande, a unique riparian habitat that stretches longitudinally through New Mexico. Deep water in the dam is cold, and trout were introduced. Native squawfish soon disappeared, and snails were eaten by the trout and displaced by the cold water near the dam. New Mexico's beautiful cottonwood trees also suffered, as they require spring floods to set seed. Habitat alteration occurred, and nonnative species such as tamerisk invaded, destroying more wildlife habitat.

On April 19, 1996, The Associated Press reported that the endangered Rio Grande silvery minnow is threatened because the flow of the Rio Grande near Socorro, New Mexico has been diverted for irrigation projects. The USFWS, the press release claims, had informed the Middle Rio Grande Conservancy District that water diversion for agricultural crops, such as New Mexico's famous green chili peppers, would completely drain the Rio Grande for a stretch of 30 to 40 miles all the way to Elephant Butte Lake. The Rio Grande below the San Acacia diversion dam near Socorro supports 70% of the known populations of the Rio Grande silvery minnow.

The Middle Rio Grande Conservancy District has, in the past, steadfastly refused the USFWS's request to divert less water to support the endangered minnow. This is, of course, a violation of the Endangered Species Act because the act prohibits habitat destruction. The district claims it has a legal obligation to provide 461 farms along the river with adequate irrigation water. Yet no legal agreement between the state of New Mexico and local farmers can usurp federal law, including the Endangered Species Act.

A temporary solution recently agreed upon will be to release some water owned by the USFWS to support the minnow instead of directing the water to Bosque del Apache National Wildlife Refuge, where water is also needed. This will keep the minnows in water for 30 days while a long-term solution is negotiated.

Further north, the city of Albuquerque was considering whether to release "unused" water from its 1995 allotment from one of the many water diversion projects. Albuquerque would lose the water anyway. Albuquerque's water could then be redirected into a dry portion of the river about 12 miles north of Socorro. The water would help preserve the minnow population. The city has to pay for the water even if it is not used. At least for the month of May 1996, the minnows were safe. But how long can solutions such as these go on saving the minnows?

Semi-Tropical Insects

On April 30, 1996, the *Gainesville Sun* reported that millions of cockroaches, locusts, and grasshoppers had invaded the southern Iranian town of Baft, according to an Iranian official news agency report. After record rains fell in the preceding months, the insects swarmed the streets. Pesticides were being sprayed to combat the outbreak. The residual effects of the pesticides were not mentioned.

Why is this a wildlife issue? Normally, when large concentrations of insects "descend" on an area, large flocks of insectivorous birds "descend" upon the insects. No mention of birds appeared in the article. The work performed by the birds (that is, the consumption of insects) must now be done at great cost by humans using mechanical or chemical means. Are the insect outbreaks the problem or merely a symptom of a greater problem?

Australian Reptiles

The investigation by USFWS and Australian wildlife authorities started in Sydney and ended in a Wal-Mart store in Minnesota. On January 18, 1996, 40 reptiles, including rare and beautiful mountain dragons (*Amphibolurus diemensis*), geckos (*Gekkonidae* spp.), skinks (*Scinidae* spp.), and black-headed pythons (*Aspidites melanocephalus*), were smuggled via a courier flight to the United States. The lizards were kept in socks and pillowcases marked "fragile electronic equipment." Many of the reptiles perished in transit. Three days later in Tennessee, police dogs picked up the scent. The USFWS was notified, and the package was forwarded intact to its destination in Florida. Police then followed the package and its carrier to a private residence. The resident was confronted and quickly agreed to cooperate with federal officials. Another package was sent to a Wal-Mart store in Minnesota. When it arrived, store employees notified the USFWS, and $10,000 worth of dead reptiles were found. The investigation is still underway, and no arrests have been made yet. On February 6, 1996, the Australian Associated Press reported that a widely advertised "alternative pet" supplier in Minnesota and the role of courier service employees were being investigated.

Frog Gigging

About two tons of frogs were being taken from Big Cypress National Preserve in Florida every month, according to the page one headline of the *Miami Herald* on April 29, 1996. What the froggers, or giggers, as they are known, were doing was illegal according to the chief ranger of the preserve. One environmentalist referred to the taking of frogs as "amphibian clear-cutting." Moreover, two federally endangered species of frogs live in the preserve.

Giggers come from as far away as Georgia and Louisiana to get in on the bounty. During the month of March, a park service ranger counted 216 airboats being used to hunt frogs. On a routine check, one airboat operator caught 235 pounds, or about 1200 frogs, in one night. No one knows how many giggers there are or how many frogs are taken each season, let alone if listed species are taken. The frogs are systematically hunted at night with an airboat and a three-spiked jabbing stick called a gig. The airboat is driven slowly over the reeds to flatten them, and then the gigger circles back for the harvest. Using a flashlight, the gigger carefully scans the reeds for two eyes. When the eyes are seen, the gig is thrust forward, and the frog is impaled, lifted out of the water, and scraped into a plastic bucket strategically placed a gig's length away. The giggers are well practiced and deadly. Rarely does a frog escape.

European Birds

Studies in the Netherlands showed that acidic pollution is harming wild bird populations. Acid rain and other forms of acidic pollution leach calcium from the soil, which has led to a decrease in snail populations. With fewer snails to eat, birds have been getting less calcium in their diets. With less calcium, the birds' egg shells are thinner, and hence more porous, and many fail to hatch. Experiments performed by researchers confirmed that birds that were fed snails produced fewer defective eggs than birds that received fewer snails.

Kangaroo Rats

In March 1995, a California resident was introduced to the Endangered Species Act. A farmer wanted to plant part of his 700 acres of land with vegetables and market them in nearby Los Angeles. The land, however, was occupied by Tipton's kangaroo rats, a federally listed endangered species. When the farmer began plowing his fields, he was charged by the USFWS with not only killing an endangered species but also destroying its habitat. Under the Endangered Species Act, both killing and habitat destruction of endangered species are illegal.

Snail Darters

In 1978, the U.S. Supreme Court in *Tennessee Valley Authority v. Hill*, 437 U.S. 153, 184, rendered "the plain intent of Congress in enacting this [the Endangered Species Act] was to halt and reverse the trend towards species extinction, whatever the cost." The operation of the $100 million Tellico Dam across the Little Tennessee River was blocked by the snail darter, a small fish thought to be an endemic species.

The Tellico Dam was begun in 1967 by the Tennessee Valley Authority (TVA). When the project was 80% complete in 1973, a University of Tennessee ichthyologist discovered the snail darter, an unknown fish species. The snail darter was thought to exist only in the Little Tennessee River and was declared an endangered species under the newly enacted Endangered Species Act of 1973 (Littell 1992). A long court battle ensued, and in 1978 the Supreme Court affirmed an injunction against Tellico, thus halting the project as the dam was nearing completion. Congress was quick to act. It decided the snail darter was not worth saving and allowed the TVA to complete the project in 1979, creating a 33-mile reservoir and a 129-foot dam. Shortly thereafter, the snail darter was found in other rivers in Alabama, Georgia, and Tennessee. The same snail darter is no longer endangered but remains threatened.

In the *Hill* decision, the U.S. Supreme Court made clear that extinction of a species for any reason is not an acceptable alternative no matter how worthy the cause. Only Congress could circumvent the law, as it did in *Hill*. The intent of Congress in enacting the Endangered Species Act was to place the highest priority on endangered species, and Congress viewed the value of an endangered species as "incalculable." In *Hill,* the Court affirmed that Congress's command was "to halt and reverse the trend toward species extinction, whatever the cost." After the snail darter, time and again the Supreme Court has invoked precedence to block actions that threaten a species' survival. The snail darter case is one of the most famous in Supreme Court history, and it set the stage for the 1996 battles over the Endangered Species Act.

Pandas

In April 1991, *Time* magazine (Sachs 1991) reported on a visit to Quanzhou, China under the sponsorship of TRAFFIC–USA (Trade Records Analysis of Flora and Fauna in Commerce), a joint program of the World Wildlife Fund (WWF) and the World Conservation Union (IUCN). The panda (*Ailuropoda melanoleuca*) is one of the most widely recognized animals on earth. It is the symbol of the WWF. In 1991, an estimated 1000 remained in the wilds of China, their populations decimated by the disappearance of their bamboo hillside habitat. Without a $10,000 deposit, a panda skin that was for sale would not even be available for inspection. Perhaps a better deal was in the offing.

Soon the smugglers made their pitch—two live young pandas, chained together and ready to go, for only $112,000. The coast between Taiwan and mainland China was crowded with shops carrying on a multitude of businesses, including wildlife smuggling. Live Amur leopards (approximately 40 remain in the wild in 1996), gibbons, eagles, and golden monkeys were for sale. There were more Amur leopard skins available at $380 apiece than there were live animals in the wild, a tragic fact. Taxidermy shops were crowded with stuffed animals and birds. Although two panda smugglers were executed, the wildlife trade was brisk. As far as the WWF could tell, there was little or no enforcement of wildlife laws or international agreements.

Apparently, exotic pets are still status symbols, and pelts of rare animals are often hung in homes. People believe that eating elaborately prepared dishes featuring endangered animals carries mystical connotations of power. For example, if you eat a tiger's eye, your eyes will see like that of the tiger. Perhaps this explains why tiger penises are in demand (Figure 3.4). One has to wonder what you are supposed to do with it—sleep with it under your pillow, carry it around in your pocket, eat it, or just fondle it? Actually, the tiger penis is put into a bottle of table wine that is sipped during dinner. The sad fact is that China's wildlife and its unique biodiversity are on their way out. The panda will likely go extinct in the next 20 years. Is this a wildlife issue, and if so, what can we as individuals do about it? Are we willing to live in a world without pandas? Will we deny future generations the sight of living, wild pandas? Concern for species other than humans has a long way to go in Asia and especially China, where more than a billion people reside.

FIGURE 3.4 Display in a local shop in China.

Whales

A White House press release on February 9, 1996 confirmed that President Clinton had delivered a message to Congress aimed at curbing Japan's insatiable desire for whale meat under the Pelly Amendment. Japan continues to whale in the newly created Southern Ocean Whale Sanctuary in the Antarctic. This reserve circles the globe in the only part of the world where this is possible, the Antarctic. The sanctuary is 30 million square miles and was established in 1994 to protect whale populations. The Japanese government was the sole objector to the establishment of the sanctuary, and the Japanese continue to violate its boundary.

Japan's whaling is conducted under the guise of "taking whales for scientific purposes," which is a loophole in CITES. Japan announced its intention to kill 440 minke whales (*Balaenoptera acutorostrata*) in 1996 for "study." The catch ends up as high-priced sushi that sells for $200 a pound.

Kangaroos

Certain restaurants in Australia serve kangaroo. At Denekas Cafe Restaurant in Leederville, Western Australia, the chef's special recipe is "seared kangaroo." A 100-g kangaroo steak is brushed with olive oil and seared on an open grill until medium rare. The steak is served with beetroots and a sauce of parsnip and garlic. If the grilled dish is not to your liking, you can try the Asian stir-fried kangaroo.

Harvesting some species of kangaroos has become a way for farmers in Australia to earn extra cash and also protect their farms. The market for kangaroo meat and skin has developed in Australia and elsewhere. Kangaroo carcasses are inspected by authorities representing the state and territory and then sold to a processor. There are only a small number of so-called shooters and processors licensed to deal in kangaroos. In addition, there are penalties for killing kangaroos illegally.

Kangaroo harvesting does not occur in national parks or reserves (Caughley et al. 1987). A reported 95% of the harvested kangaroos are the eastern grey kangaroo (*Macropus giganteus*), the red kangaroo (*M. rufus*), and the western grey kangaroo (*M. fuliginosus*). Wallaroos (*M. robustus*) and whiptail wallabies (*M. parryi*) make up the bulk of the remaining 5% of the harvest.

Certainly there are alternatives to shooting kangaroos. Deterrents such as electric fences, noise cannons, and other methods can exclude kangaroos from selected areas. Contraceptives work, but only on kangaroos that can be treated. Quotas set by the Australian government ensure that the populations of the harvested kangaroos do not exceed established limits based on scientific recommendations. The Wildlife Protection Act of 1982 requires that management plans be in place and approved before harvesting is permitted.

Tropical Fish

On February 2, 1996, U.S. customs agents busted Scott Clark and confiscated his 1980 Chevy pickup. He won't need it for perhaps five years. At a border crossing from Mexico to the United States, customs agents discovered 36 tropical fish hidden in five plastic bags inside a converted gas tank on the pickup (TRAFFIC–USA 1996). The bags included garibaldi (*Hypsypops runicundus*), California's state marine fish. Although not listed as endangered or threatened, there is a three-year commercial moratorium in effect in Mexico and California.

Clark faces a penalty of five years in prison and a $100,000 fine. "Only 15 of the 36 fish were still alive when agents removed them from the leaking gas tank. Four more died from lack of oxygen and 11 garibaldi were taken to Sea World to recover" (TRAFFIC–USA 1996).

Bears

The demand for bear bile from South Korea, Japan, and Taiwan has had a detrimental effect on bear populations worldwide. Indeed, bear bile is more valuable than its weight in gold. In October 1991, a black bear was found dead in Riding Mountain National Park in Canada with only its gallbladder removed. International trade in animals and animal parts is regulated by CITES, but some countries such as Taiwan and South Korea are not signatories of the agreement. Moreover, CITES does not address bile taken from live bears.

Traditional Asian medicine claims that patients suffering from deafness, baldness, rheumatism, and numerous other ailments can be cured with a small dose of bear fat or meat, blood, bones, or bile, depending on the illness. Menus in restaurants often contain something from bears. In fact, bear gallbladders rank with rhino horn, ginseng, and deer musk as having a most powerful curative effect. Wildlife farms are a solution to the dilemma of taking animals from the wild, and in 1992 the Chinese were reported to have between 5000 and 8000 bears on bile-milking farms (Mills 1992). Asian bears are endangered.

On the last day of 1995, the *San Francisco Examiner* announced that on January 1, 1996 California would increase the penalties for illegal killing and selling of fish and wildlife to a maximum sentence of one year in jail and/or a $30,000 fine. Penalties were increased because a hunt club in northern California was killing bears and selling the parts to Korean counterparts.

The North American Bear Society reported that human garbage is one of the biggest threats to American black bears. Bears are opportunistic feeders and will eat garbage if given the opportunity. As bears lose their fear of humans, the result will be more nuisance bears that must be destroyed. Each spring in New Mexico, bears forage for food and water in the mountain communities east of Albuquerque. Dry winters and summers are hard on bears because their food supplies dwindle. Lack of quality food forces bears to search over wider areas, and this brings them into contact with humans. About 45 black bears live on the eastern slopes of the Sandia Mountains east of Albuquerque, New Mexico's largest city. The bears overturn barbecues, rummage through picnic sites, and search in open dumpsters for food. In 1989, 22 bears were captured in Albuquerque and returned to the mountains. Bear attacks on humans are rare in New Mexico; however, human attacks on bears are usually fatal. In 1995, two cubs were killed in a botched attempt to relocate them along with the sow as they were searching for food.

Elephants

On January 15, 1996, Chinese customs officials seized 1600 pounds of Asian ivory valued at about $840,000. Reuters News Service made the announcement on January 21, 1996. Finding the ivory was no easy task; 72 tusks had been cut up into 133 pieces and hidden in 22 bags of teak intended for a crafts company. China has expanded the investigation because of obvious smuggling. These 72 tusks from 36 elephants represent a substantial portion of the remaining population of some 150 to 300 wild Asian elephants. Considerably more elephants remain in Africa (Figure 3.5), but their populations have been dramatically reduced.

Saiga

Most people have never heard of the strange-looking saiga antelope (*Saiga tatarica*). Unfortunately, medicinal manufacturers in China and Hong have. TRAFFIC–USA (1995) reported that trade in saiga horns has reached unsustainable levels. The saiga is a tiny, horned antelope with a strange humped snout. The snout, however, is inconsequential compared to its tiny pointed horns. Saiga live in the steppes of Kazakhstan to Mongolia in three populations. The Mongolian herds once numbered in the thousands. Today, only an estimated 350 remain. The Kalmykia population is about 130,000, but that is about one-fifth the number in the 1970s, before the breakup of the Soviet Union. The number of saiga in Kazakhstan is estimated at one million.

FIGURE 3.5 A herd of elephants stop for a drink in a sand river in Ruaha National Park, Tanzania.

Because only males have horns, poaching occurs in one sex only. However, commercial harvesting takes place in both sexes. In Kazakhstan, about 500,000 saiga were harvested in some years. Kalmykia outlawed hunting of saiga in 1991; however, poaching takes about 12,500 animals each year. In short, all three populations are in danger of being wiped out. This is an example of an animal similar to the America buffalo in numbers. Its supply was thought to be inexhaustible. At present harvest rates, the last ones will end up in a museum.

TRAFFIC–USA (1996) reported that 44 metric tons of saiga horn was smuggled mainly into China, Japan, and South Korea in 1994. One metric ton is equivalent to about 5000 horns. The horns sold for about $30 per kilogram. At one small stall in China, the owner stated he could guarantee delivery of 6000 horns in a few days, which suggests that there are warehouses of horns in China that serve as distribution centers. While traditional Chinese shops were loaded with saiga horns, only 5 of 76 shops in Taipei had saiga horns for sale. Before the government ban in September 1994, saiga horns could be easily had. In Japan, only 6 of 110 shops sold saiga horns. In Malaysia, 35 of 39 Chinese shops sold saiga horns. Clearly, the Chinese believe that saiga horns cure something, and the Chinese make up fully one-fifth of the world's population. Can 1.1 billion people be wrong about the curative powers of this strange antelope?

Snakes and Frogs

On July 20, 1995, the U.S. Attorney's Office, Southern District, Miami reported that Manuel Frade was sentenced to six months in jail, three years probation, and a $1000 fine for smuggling boa constrictors and poison-arrow frogs into the United States from Venezuela. Customs officers at Miami International Airport found 14 boas and 300 frogs, along with 200 bird-eating spiders and six sacks containing 500 to 600 eggs, inside Frade's luggage. No one knows how many successful trips Frade had made. All the smuggled species were CITES listed and their street value was approximately $10,000.

Passenger Pigeons

Learning, understanding, and appreciating both sides of a wildlife issue are the first steps in resolving the issue. Resolution of the wildlife issue is the goal of all parties concerned. Back in the early 1800s, John James Audubon wrote about and painted the birds of North America. In his writings, he mentioned the passenger pigeon. Obviously, back when Audubon collected and painted birds, there were no wildlife laws. And why should there have been laws to protect wildlife? Wildlife was plentiful from the Atlantic to the Pacific. One day, Audubon attempted to count the number of passenger pigeons he observed migrating. "The air was literally filled with Pigeons; the light of noon-day was obscured as by an eclipse; the dung fell in spots, not unlike melting flakes of snow; and the continued buzz of wings had a tendency to lull my senses to repose." His estimate of the number of pigeons he saw that one day alone was "one billion, one hundred and fifteen million, one hundred and thirty-six thousand pigeons in one flock." Later, he commented that even though so many were killed, their numbers seemed not to be reduced. By 1914, the last passenger pigeon died in her cage, her species a victim of unmitigated greed and the vanity trade. The wildlife issue was resolved by default. One purpose of this book is to help resolve wildlife issues to prevent extinction by default.

Caimans

The following information was found on the USFWS World Wide Web site. On September 14, 1995, the USFWS's Albuquerque area office announced that the Tony Lama Boot Company of El Paso, Texas forfeited caiman lizard skins and boots valued at more than $1 million.

An investigation into illegal trade in exotic reptile skins resulted in the forfeiture, which included 907 pairs of caiman lizard cowboy boots and 2554 pairs of boot vamps (pieces used in the lower part of a boot, between the sole and the upper portion). In addition, a 15-count felony indictment for smuggling and violations of the Lacey Act (see Chapter 2) was returned by the grand jury in the Western District of Texas against two people who sold the skins to Tony Lama using fraudulent export permits.

"This is one of the largest forfeitures of protected animal parts ever undertaken by the U.S. Fish and Wildlife Service and the U.S. Attorney's Office," said Nancy Kaufman, regional director of the USFWS southwest region. "We trust the forfeiture and our prosecution of smugglers involved in this trade will send a message to anyone contemplating the idea of making money from trading in protected wildlife species."

The caiman (*Dracaena guianensis*) is an olive-brown lizard that inhabits the Amazon Basin of South America; it can grow up to 4.5 feet in length. Its lustrous skin is prized for cowboy boots, which retail for $700 to $1000. Four lizards are used to make one pair of boots. More than 13,800 caiman lizards were sacrificed for the skins sold to the Tony Lama Boot Company.

Because its populations are threatened by commercial trade, the caiman lizard is protected under CITES (see Chapter 2). As of January 1996, 131 countries were parties to CITES, a treaty that obligates signators to regulate international trade of plants and animals that could become extinct without this protection. Both the United States and Brazil are parties to CITES. Effective June 10, 1996, Saudi Arabia became a party.

Under CITES, member nations agree to control the import and export of plant and animal species listed by the convention. Species listed in Appendix II of CITES, including the caiman lizard, are not immediately threatened with extinction but may become so if trade in the species is not controlled. Countries may allow some commercial exportation of these species, but export permits are required.

The USFWS investigation into the illegal trade of exotic reptile skins used in the leather boot industry began in 1993. The illegal trade of caiman lizard skins was initially traced through a computer database that records wildlife imports and exports governed by CITES. Agents and wildlife inspectors discovered that U.S. CITES permits and Mexican export permits were being fraudulently acquired and illegally used for the worldwide movement of caiman lizard skins and products.

Fish Stocks

Looking out from a coastal beach, the ocean seems immense. The place we call "earth" should rightly be called "water" because the earth's surface is nearly 70% water. The average depth of the sea is about 3.8 km. If you were given the task of emptying the ocean of fish, you would probably conclude that this would be an impossible mission. Indeed, individual female fish lay thousands of eggs. How could you possibly catch all those fish? First, you would realize that you can only see about 50 feet into the water at most. If there were any waves at all, your vision would be completely obscured. The fish would be impossible to find. Even if you did locate fish, their evasive abilities are extraordinary. Your ability to move a net around underwater would be severely impaired. You would be better off dropping explosives into the water. Catching all the fish in a small lake seems impossible. Today, however, most of the world's fish stocks have been depleted to the point where they might never recover.

How could this have occurred? Coastal industrial development has led to increased pollution and runoff, destroying nearby coastal fisheries. The increasing use of technology to locate fish, the efficient use of many types of nets and longlines, and the increasing number of factory ships able to stay at sea longer have made year-round exploitation possible. According to Safina (1995), the worldwide catch of fish excluding aquaculture peaked in 1989 at 82 million metric tons. Since then, the catch trend has been negative, while the fishing effort has increased. Some of the world's best fishing areas have been depleted so badly that they have been closed to fishing altogether. Worldwide, only the Indian Ocean fisheries have yet to reach peak production, and this is because modern fishing methods have not been fully utilized yet. The Atlantic Ocean has been severely impacted. Sadly, the United Nations reported that an amazing 70% of the world's edible crustaceans, fish, and mollusks are in desperate need of managed conservation.

In every fishery, target species are not the only part of a catch. In the world's catch, one of every four creatures caught is "bycatch" or "bykill" and is "discarded" (Safina 1995). Discarded means that the remains of the creature are thrown overboard, since most likely it is dead by the time it is discovered. Discards are often fish that are too small to sell, sea turtles that are threatened or endangered, birds that are not protected, or sea mammals such as dolphins or otters. In 1990, high-seas drift nets alone accounted for 42 million animals that were discarded. Although the United Nations placed a global ban on the use of drift nets, Italy, France, and Ireland continue to use them.

HISTORICAL PERSPECTIVES ON WILDLIFE ISSUES

Taking a historical perspective on wildlife issues is invaluable. With some knowledge of history, how we got to where we are today is much clearer. Often the best solution to a problem is one that takes history into consideration. For instance, most people believe acid rain and the greenhouse effect are recent phenomena. At one time, 95% of western and central Europe was covered with forests; now only 20% remains. The last bear in the United Kingdom was killed back in the 1600s. Once China was 70% forested; a mere 5% remains today. North Americans typically forget that Asian and European civilizations have been around a very long time. Since the late 1700s, 75% of North America's forests have been cleared. How can we understand soil erosion, loss of wildlife habitat, desertification, salinization, siltation, dams, or industrial pollution without knowing the history of both human and naturally occurring events? We must learn from history, synthesize historical facts, and apply these facts as best we can today. Wildlife issues are really the symptoms of more insidious, widespread problems. By resolving wildlife issues in a timely and satisfactory manner, we will really be dealing with the much broader issues of environmental degradation and the loss of quality of life.

Ponting (1992) examined many societies beset with chronic environmental problems largely brought on by their own practices. To give a complete perspective on human history in one chapter, we would spend all but the last paragraph on hunter/gatherer groups of nomadic people. The last paragraph would then consider the history of humans for about the last 10,000 years, roughly the time when agriculture was first developed.

The first settlements of people took place as a result of agriculture in southwest Asia (Rzoska 1980), China, and Mesoamerica (Culbert 1973). These societies shared several attributes (Hughes 1973). For instance, farmers grew enough food to support a burgeoning class of nonproducing consumers such as priests, the military, and bureaucrats. Of course, agriculture involves a complete disruption of a natural ecosystem to make way for crops and livestock. Natural ecosystem functions are replaced with processes necessary to support people. For the first time in the history of the earth, humans were bending and twisting the environment to meet their needs.

The total population of the world 7000 years ago was a mere five million people. Just 2500 years ago, the population was 95 million. Agricultural systems and, in turn, technological developments throughout recent human history have allowed the population to explode to more than 5.5 billion. Pressure on natural ecological systems has increased. Ecosystem functions have been degraded and massive desertification has taken place, for instance. The all too brief histories of Easter Island, Mesopotamia, and Mesoamerica serve to illustrate what is in store for us in the future. Humans cannot simply continue to consume an increasing share of global resources while ignoring the consequences.

Because Easter Island is indeed an island, environmental problems were particularly acute because there was no place left for the inhabitants to go.

Easter Island therefore serves as an example for inhabitants of Island Earth. There is no place left to go. Furthermore, even the most casual observer can see that the moon and other planets are not better places to live. Wildlife issues of today are harbingers of greater problems later. How much later depends on the size of the human population and the resources necessary to sustain that population.

Easter Island

Easter Island is famous for its gigantic stone heads and its remoteness. The island is just 64 square miles in area, located 2000 miles west of South America and 1400 miles from the nearest habitable islands. One has to wonder how the ancient Polynesians found the island, much less colonized it, but they did. Located at 27 degrees south latitude, the climate is mild. Since the island is of volcanic origin, the soil is fertile.

Today, the giant stone heads have fallen and the island appears denuded. When first observed by Europeans, there was not a single plant higher than a shrub. Naturally, this raises an interesting question. How did people quarry, cut, and erect such large statues in so remote a place with few natural resources and little food? Did people go to the island just to erect stone heads, bring everything with them to stay for a while, and then leave when the task was finished? Hardly. Diamond (1995) related the human history of Easter Island. We cannot help but see the parallels to what is happening today.

On Easter Day, April 5, 1722, when a Dutch explorer sighted and named Easter Island, it appeared from a distance that the island was a desert. On closer inspection, it was a grassland with a few ferns and bushes. Because the grass was dried out, it appeared to be a desert. There were no birds, bats, land snails, or lizards. The inhabitants kept chickens for food. The islanders who rowed out to greet the visitors did so in flimsy canoes that filled with water and required constant bailing. Surely the direct descendents of the Polynesians, known worldwide for their seafaring abilities, could do better. Only a few canoes were found on the island. It would have been nearly impossible to do any serious offshore fishing in so pitiful a craft.

The islanders were apparently unaware of other human existence. The Dutch found some 200 stone statues that once stood on the hillside looking out to sea. Some 700 more statues were found in a quarry in various stages of development. However, it was clear that none had been worked on for a very long time. The quarry was about 6 miles from where the statues were erected, and many weighed more than 75 tons. Some in construction were four times as heavy and some 60 feet tall. How could the statues be moved such a distance? The resident islanders had not a clue. Without ropes, timber, or even wheels, the task would have been impossible. Moreover, resources were distributed around the island. The best soils were quite far from the quarries. Red capstone was found in a quarry different from that used for the statues. The best fishing was on yet a different coast. The Dutch explorers were astonished. Although they had traveled the world and made many new discoveries, nothing rivaled the mysteries of Easter Island.

Modern archeology is beginning to answer some of the mysteries. The inhabitants of Easter Island were definitely Polynesian, and their language places its roots at about 400 A.D. Radiocarbon dating has been used to establish the earliest settlement times to be around that date as well. Crops of taro, bananas, sweet potatoes, and sugar cane combined with chicken, fish, and marine mammal were standard table fare.

Pollen analysis has established that Easter Island was once covered with forest. Indeed, for at least 30,000 years before humans arrived, the island was a subtropical forest covered with trees, shrubs, herbs, and grasses; that is, a fairly complex shrub layer existed below the trees. All necessary ingredients for making ropes, canoes, and wooden slides for statues could be obtained from forest products. One of the Easter Island palms, the Chilean wine palm, can grow to over 80 feet high and 6 feet in diameter—more than enough tree for a seafaring canoe. The mainstay of the Polynesians' diet was, of course, fish. With large canoes, offshore fishing was not a problem. The inhabitants could easily have traveled hundreds of miles to rich fishing areas in the region. According to Steadman (personal communication), most of the ancient garbage dumps consisted of fish bones. From 900 A.D. to 1300 A.D., porpoise made up part of the protein in the typical diet; however, porpoise in the Polynesian diet is rare elsewhere. Porpoises were found far offshore and therefore must have been hunted in sturdy canoes.

Also in the diet were seabirds. Easter Island must have been an ideal site for nesting seabirds. Without terrestrial mammals, the ground-nesting birds could raise their young with higher success rates. Diamond (1995) suggested Easter Island was one of the richest seabird breeding islands in the Pacific, with at least 25 nesting species. The surrounding waters must have provided much fish for the birds. The islanders ate both birds and fish, based on findings in the garbage dumps.

The historical picture now is beginning to become clearer. Sometime around 400 A.D., the seafaring Polynesians landed on Easter Island, a veritable subtropical paradise in a very remote part of the Pacific. The island was forested, the soil fertile, and the sea rich with fish. Some of the visitors decided to stay. For hundreds of years, they survived and prospered. The human population slowly expanded. Trees were used for canoes and fuel. By 800 A.D., pollen cores show that the destruction of the island's forest was becoming serious and that woody shrubs and grasses were being used for fuel. After 1400 A.D., the palm trees were gone and what once was a forest was now a grassland. Rats had prevented any trees from germinating by consuming seeds. All the native land birds such as rails were caught and eaten. Shellfish were overexploited and wiped out.

Around 1500 A.D., porpoise bones disappear from the dumps. We can conclude that the seafaring canoes were no longer available. Chicken became a mainstay of the diet, and chickens eat seeds. About this time, human bones show up in the garbage dumps. Archeologists confirmed that these bones are not from people dying of old age. Instead, humans began eating humans for food. Cannibalism became a common practice. By the 1600s, warriors with stone spears raided villages and took captives for food. The decline and fall of life in paradise had bottomed out. With the natural resources gone, people turned to hunting people. Since there were no canoes, there was no escape.

Mesopotamia

Most of us have heard of the Cradle of Civilization, the valley of the Tigris and Euphrates rivers, and the Sumerian culture. These rivers flowed highest in the spring due to snowmelt at their sources. This was not ideal for crops that needed more water in the late summer; however, rains in the higher valley acted as a buffer. Lower in the valley, there were fewer rains and higher summer temperatures, thus making irrigation essential to sustain agriculture. Because the land was flat, especially lower in the valley, and the water table was higher, waterlogging and surface salt accumulation were problems. As long as agriculture was restricted to the higher valleys, it was sustainable and the impact on the entire ecosystem was reduced.

The limited amount of easily developed land and an increasing population meant that lower parts of the valley had to be brought under agricultural production. No thought was given to long-term sustainability. Human life spans argued against planning for a distant future. It was in this valley that the first literate society developed, a great achievement for our species.

With literacy came historical records, detailed accounts of a society's rise to prominence and its eventual, and inevitable, fall. So successful were farmers that a military class was created to defend against other rising city-states. Excess food produced by farmers was used to defend, protect, and establish the domination of Sumerian society. While production increases came easily at first, the lower in the valley agriculture extended, the more problems arose. Eventually, environmental degradation through centuries of irrigation and excess production caught up with society.

By 2500 B.C., wheat cultivation was being replaced with barley as a means of keeping production consistent. Barley, it seems, did better in the saline soils that were now common in the lower valley. Slowly over the centuries, wheat production declined up the valley and was replaced by barley. By 1700 B.C., no wheat was grown at all. Throughout the entire region, crop yields decreased.

The human population continued to grow, armies fought other armies for control of the land, and new land was desperately needed. Continued advances in agricultural technology were not enough to sustain the society. Burdened by an army, bureaucracy, and clergy who only consumed, the farmers could not support the society. As early as 2300 B.C., conquests coincided with crop failures. With the Babylonian conquest in 1800 B.C., Mesopotamian society left the Cradle of Civilization for good. Crop yields throughout the valley were less than one-third of those obtained nearly 500 years previously. The ground was white with mineral salts. The great society was no more.

Mesoamerica

The Mayan civilization is also well known. It rose and fell in the lowland tropical forests of Mexico, Guatemala, Honduras, and Belize. The time period coincides with the rise of Sumerian society. The earliest records date back to 2500 B.C. The population grew, and a complex society developed, with temples, stone pyramids, plazas, and other elaborate architectural and scientific wonders. Astronomical observations led to the development of a calendar and the capability to predict positions and phases of the moon. To support a class of builders, astronomers, and other nonproducers, surplus agriculture was necessary.

By 600 A.D., the Mayan empire flourished. In many population centers, pyramids and inscribed stone pillars used for commemorative purposes were erected. The current view of Mayan civilization differs radically from past beliefs. Today, the stone pillars are recognized to be monuments to the rulers of the various cities scattered throughout the empire. They also contain the written history of one city's conquest over another and thus confirm the existence of armies. The deceptive belief of a peaceful religious society, wholly wrapped up in its astronomy and calendar, was flawed. Archeological work has confirmed that an elite class supported by armies and surplus food conducted almost continuous warfare against neighboring cities.

Around the central city and its great temples were masses of laborers who supported the elite. Elaborate agricultural works have been unearthed which show intensive cultivation of the surrounding lowlands. Extensive hillside terraces were used to contain soil erosion. Raised fields in swampy areas also existed. Complex drainage systems were used to control surface water, with material from the ditches used to heighten fields. This is similar to many agricultural areas of south Florida.

Crops of maize and beans sustained the population, while cotton and cacao were also cultivated. "The agricultural system was the foundation for all the achievements of the Maya" (Ponting 1992). Increased warfare, a swelling human population, and ever-more elaborate construction of monuments led to demands on the agricultural system that could not be sustained. Tropical soils are notoriously poor and easily eroded. Cities were clustered around sites of fertile soil, but once the forests were removed, the soils were easily eroded in the tropical rains.

Forests were cleared for the usual reasons: fuel, building material, and to make room for agricultural fields. The Mayans also had no domestic stock to turn weeds into manure for the fields. As the population expanded, more marginal areas were forced into production. Deforestation followed by soil erosion, siltation of the river systems, and general environmental degradation was the predictable outcome.

Human skeletons unearthed from grave sites show increasing nutritional deficiencies. Within decades, the civilization collapsed. The environment of the tropical forest was unable to support a massive human population. Today, the cities are engulfed by tropical rain forest.

Other ancient societies in China and the Mediterranean also collapsed due to long-term persistent environmental degradation. Are human societies now suffering from a similar environmental decline? In times long ago, transportation systems were poorly developed, and most material goods and supplies were made, created, or grown locally. In today's global economy, goods and services can be grown or extracted in one place, assembled or processed in another, and sold in yet another. This has allowed the human population to expand; however, global transportation systems have made possible global exploitation. Our reach has extended around the globe, and exploitation is usually efficient. The local problems faced by ancient societies are similar to the problems modern society faces today. Now, however, we are able to import necessary commodities and thus allow others to sort out the local difficulties. If the producers become too expensive or too inefficient, consumers simply switch to another producer. Does the consumer know or even care that a producer has gone out of business because the local environment is degraded?

Whereas Mesoamericans and Mesopotamians depended on agriculture, modern societies have shifted their dependence to fossil fuels to sustain their economies. Is dependence on a nonrenewable resource such as oil a strategy for a sustainable future?

WILDLIFE ISSUES IN A CHANGING WORLD

Estimates indicate that humans consume nearly 50% of all primary production of the planet. Naturally, while humans are getting their half, all the other creatures of the world are splitting the rest. As the human population increases, the percentage of primary production consumed by humans will increase, leaving less for all other creatures. Advanced technology will enable people to extract more resources and increase primary production; however, it is likely that the human population will increase and consume any excess. An increasing global human population seems a certainty. Wildlife issues are becoming ever-more common across a rapidly shrinking resource base. Rich nations will be able to cope with their problems by purchasing natural resources such as oil from other nations. Third World nations, whose populations are growing most rapidly, will eventually dismiss their wildlife issues as irrelevant. One answer to these problems is global education. What we learn must be translated and retaught to others as efficiently as possible. The Electronic Age offers us an unprecedented opportunity to reach billions of people without using fossil fuels.

EXERCISES

3.1 Identify wildlife issues from all 50 states by reading various local newspapers. Is there a common thread that links the issues regionally?

3.2 Use your favorite search engine to locate wildlife issues on the World Wide Web. Identify issues of concern from other countries.

3.3 Across much of Africa, wildlife is equated with food. Bush meat is routinely eaten. Monkeys are a favorite bush meat. Is there a wildlife issue here? If so, identify the vested interests.

3.4 Are there any wildlife dealers advertising on the World Wide Web? What are the products for sale?

3.5 Visit your local ethnic grocery store and look for interesting foods, medicines, and treatments that are composed of wildlife.

3.6 Do a more thorough investigation of the bear trade. What is the status of the Asian bear today?

3.7 What is the status of the panda in China today?

3.8 Perhaps the most powerful weapon used to solve wildlife crimes is the U.S. Fish and Wildlife Service Forensics Laboratory in Ashland, Oregon. From poisoned bald eagles to dried seal penises, from women's shoulder bags made from cane toads to piles of illegally obtained skins, the lab receives packages from all 50 states and 125 countries that are signatories to CITES. Find out more about the laboratory using the World Wide Web, the library, and by writing for more information.

3.9 Obtain more information about TRAFFIC–USA from the World Wildlife Fund in Washington, D.C. Summarize its activities. Who provides funding for the work carried out by TRAFFIC–USA?

3.10 Trace the history of early Mediterranean societies. What environmental problems caused the collapse of their social systems?

3.11 The northern spotted owl is a famous wildlife issue of the northwest old-growth forests. Summarize what happened. Discuss the so-called "God Squad's" decisions regarding old-growth timber, logging, and the future of the spotted owl.

3.12 Track down some statistics in the international trade of snakes. What is the demand for snakes, and where does this demand originate? How is it satisfied?

3.13 Vicunas are South American mammals prized for their fine, warm hair which makes wonderful sweaters. What is the outlook for this species today?

3.14 The international cat trade, including tigers, is threatening many species of cat. What is happening to snow leopard populations in Asia and ocelot and margay populations in Central and South America? Compare the trade in spotted cats versus cats without spots.

LITERATURE CITED

Brower, L.P. 1995. Understanding and misunderstanding the migration of the monarch butterfly (Nymphalidae) in North America: 1857–1995. *Journal of the Lepidopterists' Society* **49**(4):304–385.

Caughley, G., N. Shepard, and J. Short. 1987. *Kangaroos: Their Ecology and Management in Sheep Rangelands of Australia.* Cambridge University Press, Sydney, Australia.

Colclough, C. 1996. Guatemala's macaws on verge of extinction. The Associated Press, April 30.

Culbert, T.P. 1973. *The Classic Maya Collapse.* University of New Mexico Press, Albuquerque.

Diamond, J.M. 1995. Easter's end. *Discover* August:63–69.

Dold, C. 1996. Shark therapy. *Discover* **17**(4):51–57.

Fitzgerald, S. 1989. *International Wildlife Trade: Whose Business Is It?* World Wildlife Fund, Washington, D.C.

Hughes, J.D. 1973. *Ecology of Ancient Civilizations.* University of New Mexico Press, Albuquerque.

Littell, R. 1992. *Endangered and Other Protected Species: Federal Law and Regulation.* The Bureau of National Affairs, Washington, D.C.

Mills, J. 1992. Milking the bear trade. *International Wildlife* May–June:38–45.

Owens, M. and D. Owens. 1984. *Cry of the Kalahari.* Houghton Mifflin, Boston.

Ponting, C. 1992. *A Green History of the World. The Environment and the Collapse of Great Civilizations.* St. Martin's Press, New York.

Rzoska, J. 1980. *Euphrates and Tigris: Mesopotamian Ecology and Destiny.* W. Junk, The Hague, Netherlands.

Sachs, A. 1991. A grisly and illicit trade. *Time* April 18:67–68.

Safina, C. 1995. The world's imperiled fish. *Scientific American* November:46–53.

TRAFFIC-USA 1995. **4**(2):1–2.

TRAFFIC-USA 1996. **15**(2):1–20.

Williams, T. 1996. The great butterfly bust. *Audubon* **98**(2):30–37.

WHAT IS WILDLIFE?

4

For the purposes of this book, we define *wildlife* to mean any living organism. Although wildlife issues are not limited to any particular taxonomic group, we will emphasize members of the animal kingdom. Our reasons for this bias stem partly from history (the term "wildlife" has traditionally been limited to certain types of animals) and partly from our own expertise and experience. One could further argue that the vast majority of humans are more interested in the fates of animals than in, say, the fate of an endangered bryophyte. This is not to suggest that bryophytes are unworthy of our attention. There was a time historically when the term "wildlife" was applied only to so-called *game* species. Game species were those species (almost exclusively birds, mammals, and fish) that people hunted (we consider fishing to be a modified form of hunting). Of course, if one is willing to classify a handful of species as being "game" species, then the remaining species must all be *nongame* species. In any event, if the term "nongame" refers to any species that is not a game species, then we must define wildlife as any species of living organism. That is to say, we must include all the lower life forms such as unicellular species, as well as the evolutionarily primitive species such as the bacteria.

The brand "wildlife" is no longer limited to birds, mammals, and fish; it now also includes so-called protists, bacteria, fungi, and plants. There may be a bias toward only classifying vertebrate (see below) species as wildlife, but this is a prejudice to which we do not subscribe. Perhaps the main reason for our willingness to relax the boundaries of our definition is the number of issues that arise involving nonvertebrate species. Many of these issues are detailed in this chapter.

CLASSIFYING WILDLIFE

We have already seen that the term wildlife encompasses a vast number of species. Clearly, a classification scheme of some sort is required. A main reason for this lies in developing management plans. If one can group species in a logical fashion, it simplifies, or at least has the potential to simplify, the implementation of management plans or policies. Thus, we might set size limits for harvesting finfish (vertebrates) but not shellfish (invertebrates).

No matter how one chooses to categorize species, the system is based on shared characteristics. Secondarily, the characters should be mutually exclusive. Recall that in our discussion of the scientific method, we stated that hypotheses should be formulated so as to be mutually exclusive. The use of mutually exclusive characteristics here is no accident, as it mirrors the scientific method. Thus, edible species share obviously at least one characteristic, as do inedible species. Inedible species are simply "not edible"; thus, our characteristic indeed has two mutually exclusive states. Note also that we could go further by imposing the standard "tastes good" versus "does not taste good." But this would be futile, because some people like some foods that others simply refuse to eat. Therefore, it is immaterial how the food tastes because human preferences vary. The characters involved here may be shared, but they are rather superficial.

Biologists have long classified species on the basis of observable traits. Such a scheme is referred to as a phenetic scheme. A phenetic scheme can be a powerful system if properly applied but can lead to some very funny conclusions if misapplied. Consider the set of a mosquito, hummingbird, snake, earthworm, and bat. Clearly, we could group species by virtue of their having wings (mosquito, hummingbird, and bat) or not (snake and earthworm). The grouping here ignores evolutionary relationships that, for the sake of argument, we know would place the hummingbird and bat together, and then these two with the snake. This group then would be near the earthworm, and at the other extreme would be the mosquito. Why does the phenetic classification scheme fail? Clearly, it fails because the characters were not weighted. This means that the characters are all assumed to be of equal importance. From an evolutionary perspective, this is weak because some characters are likely more important than others in classifying species. Thus, biologists would consider it more important that the snake, bat, and hummingbird are all vertebrates than that the mosquito, hummingbird, and bat can all fly. In other words, the characteristics associated with being a vertebrate are "weighted" more than the character of mode of locomotion.

In the course of developing our understanding of what species comprise wildlife, we will follow the five-kingdom classification. We will see that there are wildlife issues at nearly all the levels or taxa (singular is taxon). This system is based on shared characteristics, and the characters are mutually exclusive.

The categories used in the scheme are presented below in the form of an example of how to classify an American crow:

Kingdom	Broadest grouping that identifies species that share fundamental similarities in cell structure (e.g., Animalia)
Phylum	Chordata (animals with backbones)
Class	Aves (birds)
Order	Passeriformes (songbirds)
Family	Corvidae (crows, jays, and magpies)
Genus	*Corvus*
Species	*brachyrhynchos*

SPECIES

The genus and species make up the so-called Latin or scientific name. We follow the system of binomial (two names: the genus and the specific name) nomenclature established by Linnaeus. Many species also have a common name; for *Corvus brachyrhynchos,* it is the American crow. A point of caution involving common names: We must be careful today when dealing with some phylogenetic groups of species because many of them have more than one common name; this makes it difficult in some cases to identify a species (i.e., figure out its scientific name) just by the common name.

Here, when we use the term species, it will imply a number of individuals that are reproductively isolated from all other individuals in other populations. Reproductive isolation means the individuals are not able to interbreed with individuals from other populations and produce viable offspring (i.e., their offspring cannot produce offspring of their own).

It is important to note that because it is often unclear whether or not a population is a true species or a subspecies, certain provisions of the Endangered Species Act may apply to just one of several subspecies of a species. The term species is not easy to define either biologically or politically. Because of the difficulty in defining the term, the Endangered Species Act is extended to include subspecies. We simply cannot in every case use the condition of reproductive isolation to identify species versus subspecies (subspecies are geographically distinct subpopulations of a species).

Several wildlife issues are based on the possible confusion over deciding if populations are species or subspecies. The following are examples of some fuzzy cases where this is important:

1. *Red wolf* versus gray wolf (the red wolf is indigenous to the southeastern United States, whereas the gray wolf lives elsewhere)
2. *Florida panther* versus Texas cougar
3. *Concho* water snake versus Harter's water snake

The italicized names may refer to subspecies rather than species, since there is no reproductive isolation except by geography and no general agreement among scientists let alone politicians!

In each of these cases, there are people who claim that these populations are actually different species, not just subspecies. In other words, the red wolf and gray wolf may be different species and not just different subspecies.

THE FIVE KINGDOMS

- Kingdom Monera
- Kingdom Protista
- Kingdom Fungi
- Kingdom Plantae
- Kingdom Animalia

The following are shared characteristics among all these groups:

1. All are made up of cells
2. All have deoxyribonucleic acid (DNA) with the same genetic code

Differences among kingdoms are as follows:

1. **Kingdom Monera**—Comprised of prokaryotic cells, do not have either an organized nucleus or membrane-bound organelles (all other kingdoms have eukaryotic cells, which means they do have an organized nucleus and membrane-bound organelles)
2. **Kingdom Fungi**—Cell wall (chitinous), no chloroplasts, multicellular, no true alternation of generations (see below), heterotrophic
3. **Kingdom Plantae**—Cellulose, cell wall, have chloroplasts, multicellular, true alternation of generations, autotrophic

4. **Kingdom Animalia**—No cell wall, multicellular, no true alternation of generations
5. **Kingdom Protista**—Unicellular, eukaryotes

As stated at the beginning of this chapter, we take the position that any living organism may be considered wildlife. With this in mind, we now consider characteristics of each of the five kingdoms, with special attention devoted to the animals.

KINGDOM MONERA: BACTERIA AND BLUE-GREEN ALGAE

The importance of bacteria to wildlife populations is typically indirect. Humans may go to the field to observe birds, mammals, reptiles, or fish, but typically not bacteria. Nevertheless, bacteria play an important role in wildlife biology in at least three important ways.

First, different bacteria are responsible for numerous wildlife diseases (Forrester 1992), such as Lyme disease, which is transmitted by ticks. The bacterium that causes Lyme disease is found in various species of vertebrates such as rodents and larger mammals, as well as birds. Another example of a bacterium that threatens humans is *Vibrio vulcanicus,* which is found in shellfish (e.g., oysters) and may be lethal to humans.

The second effect of bacteria on wildlife populations is through their role as decomposers. After a recent red tide event in Florida, a large fish kill was caused by bacteria. Decomposing fish can also be a source of disease. Indeed, the relationship of bacteria to red tides may be even more complex, as some authors have suggested that the toxins produced by red tide algae (see Kingdom Protista) may themselves be produced by symbiotic (see below) bacteria that live in close association with the algae (Anderson 1994).

The ability of various types of bacteria to decompose organic polymers and other complex man-made molecules also aids in indirect wildlife concerns, such as cleaning up toxic chemical and petroleum product spills (bacteria are involved in eating petroleum products).

The third effect involves the transfer of nutrients to plants. In particular, certain types of blue-green algae (or, as they are often called today, blue-green bacteria) play an important role in fixing gaseous nitrogen. Plants need nitrogen, just as animals do, for building proteins. Unfortunately, elemental nitrogen exists (albeit abundantly) in the atmosphere as a gas. Certain blue-green algae and fungi are able to "fix" this gaseous nitrogen into a more usable form for plants to take up. Of course, once plants take up the nitrogen, animals can harvest it from the plants (see Chapter 8).

KINGDOM PROTISTA: UNICELLULAR ALGAE AND PROTOZOANS

Red Tides

Our discussion of red tides is based on the work of Anderson (1994). Red tides have long captured the imagination of humans. Recently, red tides and the resultant toxins have been associated with deaths of marine mammals (humpback whales) as well as finfish. Red tides are the result of algal blooms (an algal bloom is basically a population explosion of a type of algae which is a single-celled eukaryote). Red tides can result in massive fish kills due to toxins and are often (but not always!) characterized by a change in water color. Red tides are caused by toxins produced by dinoflagellates and a few other groups of algae. The term red tide is a misnomer since the water may not turn red; it may turn brown or not change color at all. Moreover, some algal blooms cause a change in water color but are not associated with production of any toxin.

There are three types of red tides:

A. Indirect toxic
   1. Dinoflagellates (or associated bacteria) produce a toxin.
   2. The toxin is consumed by shellfish.
   3. Humans eat the shellfish and suffer poisoning (paralysis, diarrhea, neurotoxicity, amnesia).
B. Direct toxic
   1. Dinoflagellate bloom (explosive increase in the number of algal cells in a local area) occurs.
   2. Fish swim by and rupture the dinoflagellate cells.
   3. The toxin released from the cells attacks gills and kills the fish.
C. Ciguatera
   1. Dinoflagellates live in seaweed.
   2. Fish eat the dinoflagellates.
   3. Humans eat fish and suffer ciguatera fish poisoning. Here, the toxins are accumulated in fatty tissues of the fish. The bigger the fish, the more intense the poisoning.

Notice the interesting situation where a unicellular organism is able to cause ecosystem-level changes.

The following factors may favor red tides:

1. **Low resources**—Certain dinoflagellate species revert to sexual reproduction when resources are scarce. As a result of sexual reproduction,
these organisms produce hard-coated cysts which can be translocated
around the world by ship ballast or hurricanes.
2. **Pollution**—Some evidence suggests that red tides are positively correlated with nutrient pollution. More nutrient pollution leads to more red
tides.

Protozoan Parasites

A number of protozoan parasites play an important role in wildlife ecology. For
example, avian malaria is caused by a protozoan in the genus *Plasmodium*. In
Hawaii, bird-watchers can see native forest birds (that are not yet extinct) only
on islands that have high elevations (Kauai, Molokai, Lanai, Hawaii, Oahu,
Maui). The reason for this may be related to the distribution of mosquitoes that
transmit the *Plasmodium* organism to the birds. At lower elevations, temperatures are high enough for mosquitoes to thrive; however, at higher elevations,
mosquitoes apparently cannot survive the chilling rain-soaked nights. Warner
(1968) argued that the distribution of native forest birds was the opposite of
mosquitoes. He suggested that avian malaria was killing the birds that invaded
lower elevation habitats. To test his idea, he conducted the following experiment; note the use of the scientific method.

- **Observation**—Native forest birds largely do not occur at lowland
elevations.
- **Null hypothesis**—Native forest birds cannot live at lowland elevations
(presumably because of exposure to malaria-transmitting mosquitoes).
- **Test**—Place native birds in cages with food and water at lowland elevations and monitor them. If mosquito exposure (malaria) is responsible,
then the birds should die from malaria.
- **Result**—The birds died from malaria.

What was Warner's control? What other factors could have been responsible?

KINGDOM FUNGI:
MUSHROOMS, BLIGHTS, RUSTS, AND MOLDS

This kingdom includes some 70,000 species. Major characteristics are as
follows:

1. Heterotrophs ("hetero" = other and "troph" = eats; therefore, heterotrophs eat other food, as opposed to auto [= self] trophs, which are able to produce their own food via photosynthesis. Ecologists call plants "producers" and animals "consumers.")
2. Cell wall made of chitin
3. Many are symbiotic

Symbiosis: The Art of Living Together

Symbiosis refers to the situation where two or more species live together in close association. There are so many examples of symbiotic relationships in nature that it is difficult to know where to start in describing them. Perhaps the best approach lies in describing the three main forms of symbiosis: competition, where both species suffer; predation/parasitism, where one species suffers and the other benefits; and mutualism, where both species benefit from the interaction. Note that there are costs and benefits here, which means that the decision as to which species suffers and which one benefits is determined by the net effect of the interaction on population size or growth rate. When we say a population suffers, we mean that its population size or growth rate is reduced as a result of the interaction with its symbiont.

The following are examples of symbiotic relationships:

1. **Lichens**—A mutualistic relationship between a fungus and an alga
2. **Mycorrhizae**—Fungus associated with trees roots; the fungus helps with ion transfer, while the tree supplies the fungus with carbohydrates

Fungi play an important role in ecosystems, mostly as decomposers. Decomposers are species that break down tissues into simpler organic molecules that can be used by other organisms. However, certain symbiotic forms such as mycorrhizae play an important role in fixing gaseous nitrogen for plants. Fungi often attack plants and human feet (athlete's foot) and are essential for making important human foods, such as bread and beer. In some countries (e.g., France), various fungi are national delicacies. Finally, as described below, fungi may play an important role in detecting environmental dangers, much the same way that miners once relied on canaries to warn them of reduced oxygen levels.

The Fall of European Fungi and Atmospheric Pollution

In the fall of 1990, mycologist Eef Arnolds of the Netherlands gave a presentation at the Fourth International Mycological Congress in Germany in which he showed evidence of a catastrophic decline in abundance and diversity of ectomycorrhizal fungi—mushrooms (Jaenike 1991). The basic observation reported by Arnolds was that ectomycorrhizal fungi (mushrooms) had suffered major declines in northern Europe between 1970 and 1985. These losses included (1) a loss of species (60% decline in number of species collected per year) and (2) a decline in the abundance of remaining species.

The fungi involved in these declines are associated with trees in a mutualistic (symbiotic, where both species benefit) relationship. The fungi facilitate ion transport (chiefly phosphates and immobile ions) for the trees, and the trees provide the fungi with carbohydrates. Both the fungi and the plants benefit. Scientists now think that with increased nitrogen in the form of deposits from pollution, trees divert carbohydrates to growth of aboveground biomass rather than to roots (for nutrient uptake). Thus, the fungi that are associated with the roots get less and therefore decline.

Other explanations include overharvesting by humans and habitat loss. If overharvesting by humans were the cause, we would predict that only the more desirable species would decline. However, we can reject this hypothesis because of comparable declines in inedible species. Arnolds also rejected the habitat loss hypothesis as being, at best, only a partial explanation.

Other Fungi Important to Wildlife Issues

Chestnut blight reduced hard mast crop bears, and other species that depend on chestnuts were reduced. Ganoderma affects transport tissue. This fungus has attacked palms in Gainesville, Florida. Convulsive ergotism is a condition caused by consuming rye flower that is infested with the fungus *Claviceps purpurea*.

The Salem witchcraft affair is the story of a very localized outbreak in a small area of Massachusetts and one county in Connecticut (Matassian 1982). The symptoms of "bewitchment" were described in Essex County, Massachusetts in 1692. A high percentage of cases (24 of 30) showed convulsions. Many individuals had the sensation of being pinched or bitten. Other symptoms included temporary blindness, deafness, loss of speech, burning sensations, visions of a "ball of fire," the sensation of flying through the air, and spells of laughing and crying.

Most victims were children or teenagers. Original records suggested that the affair was really just an outbreak of convulsive ergotism caused by a fungus that grows on rye in particular. We now know that ergot (*C. purpurea*) is a source of LSD. This fungus is especially common in plants grown in wet areas that have recently been converted to cultivation. Other records showed that due to environmental conditions, specifically wet weather, the people had to rely on rye when other crops produced inadequate yields.

Many mushrooms produce narcotics or toxins. Psilocybin is produced by the fungus *Psilocybe mexicana*. *Amanita phalloides* produces the deadly toxin amanitin, which selectively inhibits mammalian RNA polymerase. Fungi often attack plants. In Florida, there has been much controversy surrounding the use of Benlate, a fungicide manufactured by DuPont that protects certain crops. Unfortunately, it may break down to form compounds that kill plants. The main roles fungi play in ecosystems are as mutualists, as in mycorrhizae, and as decomposers.

In the three kingdoms we have covered so far (Monera, Protista, and Fungi), the categories used to establish relationships among species are based on highly technical, nonintuitive characters. However, in plants and animals, these categories (below the kingdom level) are more familiar to the average person and are also useful in talking about different issues.

KINGDOM PLANTAE

Evolutionary History of Plants

The evolutionary history of plants is fascinating and no doubt played a critical role in the evolution of animals. We must recall that it was only after plants invaded the land and began to produce molecular oxygen that air-breathing animals could survive. The discussion below generally follows Raven et al. (1986).

Kingdom Plantae, which contains 275,000 species, is distinguished by two main characteristics:

1. Cellulose cell wall
2. True alternation of generations:
   - Sporophyte generation (diploid—2N)
   - Gametophyte generation (haploid—N)

The relevance and importance of plants are as follows:

1. As autotrophs, plants fix gaseous carbon from CO_2 into simple sugars via photosynthesis and thus ultimately produce food for themselves, animals, and fungi. For this reason, plants are called primary producers.
2. Plants produce all the oxygen we need, as a by-product of photosynthesis
3. Habitat, at least for terrestrial species, invariably depends on plants.

The nucleus of typical eukaryotic cells contains, among other things, the chromosomes. We say typical because some eukaryotic cells, such as the red blood cells of mammals, have no nucleus. Chromosomes are comprised of DNA and various proteins. Chromosomes are important because they are the bodies that harbor the genetic information that (1) is needed for cells to operate on a day-to-day basis and (2) enables an individual to be different from all other individuals. Chromosomes are the means by which genetic information is passed between generations.

Every cell needs enzymes and other proteins to function properly. A different and highly specific portion of DNA positioned along the chromosomes includes the instructions for an elaborate cell machinery to produce each of the different enzymes and proteins. These portions of DNA are called genes. Every organism has many genes to code for the different proteins. As a simple example, consider the genes that code for the human ABO blood group. The gene has three forms or alleles: one for Type A (IA), one for Type B (IB), and one for Type O (i). The ABO blood group gene occupies a position on a specific chromosome. Since each individual inherits chromosomes in pairs (one from each parent), each of us has two alleles for the ABO blood group gene.

Mitosis and Meiosis

There are two ways in which the nuclei of cells may divide: mitosis and meiosis. In mitosis, the chromosomes duplicate and form sister chromatids. The chromatids condense and line up on the equator of the cell. An elaborate apparatus of microtubules, called the spindle, forms and attaches to the chromosomes and draws them apart toward the ends or poles of the cell. As the chromatids converge at the two poles of the cell, the cytoplasm divides (called cytokinesis), and two daughter cells are formed, each identical to the parent cell (before the chromosomes duplicated to form the chromatids).

Let's say that the parent cell had 20 chromosomes (= 10 pairs). When these duplicate, they form 40 chromatids (= 20 pairs of chromatids). Remember, each chromatid is an exact copy of the original parent cell chromosome. In each daughter cell, there are 20 chromatids (one from each of the original 20 pairs of chromatids). Therefore, the parent cell had 20 chromosomes and the daughter cells have 20 chromosomes each. (Chromatids is a term that refers to the duplicated chromosomes.)

Now we would say that the parent cell had a diploid number of 20 and a haploid number of 10. (The diploid number refers to the total number of chromosomes in a cell, and the haploid number refers to the number of pairs of chromosomes in the cell.) Notice that we began with a diploid cell and ended up with two diploid cells. Mitosis refers to the basic form of nuclear division that nearly all cells use to make new cells.

Meiosis is a very special form of nuclear division that is only involved in one process: sexual reproduction. Consider a cell with the same diploid number as the parent cell above (2N = 20). Not every cell can undergo meiosis, because meiosis is a type of nuclear division reserved for special circumstances.

In meiosis, the chromosomes duplicate as before to form sister chromatids. However, these chromatids will undergo two divisions after this duplication, instead of one as in mitosis.

Before we continue, let's assume one thing about chromosomes: they are all different in size. Now we can identify the chromosomes by numbering them from largest to smallest; thus, the largest chromosome is number 1 and the smallest is number 10. Each individual has chromosomes in pairs and thus has two number 1 chromosomes, two number 2 chromosomes, and so on. The reason for the pairs is that each individual inherits one chromosome of each chromosome pair from each parent. In mitosis, all the pairs of chromatids for all 20 chromosomes line up on the equator. In meiosis, the pairs of chromosomes (each with its own pair of chromatids) line up on the equator. Thus, we see the ten pairs of chromosomes, each with two chromatids, lined up. These are called homologous pairs, because the pair of number 1 chromosomes is together, as is the pair of number 2 chromosomes, and so on. Each homologous pair is comprised of four chromatids. Sometimes these homologous pairs are called bivalents.

In the first division in meiosis, the homologues separate. Thus, two initial daughter cells form, each with both chromatids of one chromosome of each chromosomal pair. Therefore, each cell would get, for example, a chromosome number 10 with both its chromatids. A daughter cell might get the chromosome number 10 that the parent cell inherited from its father and the chromosome number 2 from its mother. There are many ways of dividing up the homologues: There are 2K ways of dividing up K pairs of homologous chromosomes. Thus, if you had 10 homologous pairs of chromosomes, there would be 210 = 1024 ways of dividing up the homologues.

In the second division, the homologues in each daughter cell line up on the equator of the cell and the chromatids separate as in mitosis.

In the end following meiosis, a cell with 20 chromosomes (10 pairs) produces 4 cells each with 10 chromosomes. These chromosomes are not paired, but rather there is a representative of each chromosome. Thus, meiosis begins with a diploid cell and ends with four haploid cells.

Alternation of generations basically consists of an alternation of meiosis and fertilization (which involves fusion of two cells to produce one cell with twice as many chromosomes).

Sporophytes and Gametophytes

In plants, the two stages of the life cycle are the sporophyte (meaning "spore plant") and the gametophyte (meaning "gamete plant"). The sporophyte makes spores (via meiosis), whereas the gametophyte makes gametes (via gametogenesis). Each of these is a distinct free-living entity.

All cells in a typical sporophyte are said to be diploid. This means that all cells have two sets of chromosomes, or at least their chromosomes occur in pairs or multiples of pairs. The sporophtye produces haploid spores (through meiosis). Haploid spores disperse and grow into gametophytes, and gametophytes produce gametes via mitotic cell division. The gametes are the so-called egg and sperm cells. The gametes fuse (fertilization) to produce a zygote, which develops again through mitotic cell division to form the sporophyte.

Sporophyte generation dominates in more evolutionarily advanced species. Gametophyte generation dominates in more primitive species. In flowering plants (the most evolutionarily advanced plants), the male gametophyte is just the pollen grain.

Classification of Plants

Plants can be distinguished as nonvascular and vascular:

1. **Nonvascular**—No xylem or phloem
2. **Vascular**—Xylem and phloem (specialized tissues, cell types, for transporting water and nutrients) are needed for true roots, stems, and leaves

Vascular plants are more advanced in an evolutionary sense than nonvascular plants.

Nonvascular Plants

Bryophytes—This is the single group of nonvascular plants excluding the algae, which in the present classification scheme are considered to be protistans. Mosses (14,500 species), liverworts (9000 species), and hornworts (100 species) are the three subgroups of bryophytes. Bryophytes are characterized by having a free-living gametophyte and no vascular tissue.

Vascular Plants

Seedless Vascular Plants—This group includes the lycophytes, horsetails, and ferns. Although these species have vascular tissue, they are primitive plants. Vascular tissue is needed for a plant to develop true stems, leaves, and roots which allow a plant to become tall. Nevertheless, the lycophytes (about 1000 species) are all small, as are the horsetails (15 species). Although present-day horsetails are mostly small herbaceous plants, in the Paleozoic era they reached their maximum abundance and diversity and were represented by enormous (15 m in height) ancestors.

The ferns, represented by nearly 12,000 species, are by far the most successful of the seedless vascular plants. Ferns are mostly tropical, and some species are truly tree-like in size. Spectacular tree fern forests occur on islands such as the Hawaiian Islands.

Seed Plants—The seed plants are clearly the most evolutionarily advanced group of plants. The least advanced seed plants are the so-called gymnosperms (= naked seed). Among the gymnosperms are the conifers, cycads, gingko, and gnetophytes. Conifers are familiar to most people in regions of the temperate Northern Hemisphere, whereas cycads or sago palms are chiefly tropical or subtropical. The gingko is endemic to China, whereas the gnetophytes occur in deserts and the tropics. There are 550 species of conifers, 100 species of cycads, 1 gingko, and about 70 gnetophytes. As a characteristic, gymnosperms grow quite slowly.

Angiosperms—The angiosperms (= vessel seed), or flowering plants, are the most advanced of all plants. The flowering plants are also highly diverse in structure and have invaded a number of habitats, both aquatic and terrestrial. The angiosperms are subdivided into two groups: monocots and dicots. Monocots are characterized by having flower parts in threes, a single cotyledon, usually parallel leaf venation, scattered vascular bundles, and no vascular cambium to allow for secondary growth. Dicots are characterized by having flower parts in fours or fives, two cotyledons, net-like leaf venation, vascular bundles in a ring, and a vascular cambium.

Major Plant Evolutionary Events

Although we will discuss the history of life on earth in Chapter 7, a brief history of plants is provided here:

1. Invasion of land during the Silurian period of the Paleozoic era.
2. Evolution of vascular tissue (specialized cells for transport) first appears in Upper Silurian (upper refers to not as deep in the sediments and therefore means more recent).
3. Evolution of "naked" seeds, or gymnosperms ("gymno" means naked and "sperm" means seed), during the Permian period of the Paleozoic era. Seeds are an adaptation for a cooling and drying environment.

4. Gymnosperms dominate throughout the Mesozoic era.
5. Angiosperms (covered seeds) evolve in the Cretaceous and dominate the Cenozoic era. These are the most highly evolved plants and are called flowering plants.

Plant Conservation

There are many endangered species of plants in Florida (e.g., Florida scrub species). Many plant species are pests, such as the melaleuca, which was introduced from Australia. Plants can produce some interesting compounds, including drugs and toxins. Castor beans produce ricin, a deadly toxin. Johnsongrass produces glucocyanoside when there is an early freeze. Bracken ferns produce an anticoagulant.

KINGDOM ANIMALIA

The two main characteristics of animals are as follows:

1. Cells lack a cell wall
2. No true alternation of generations

Animals, like fungi, are heterotrophs (i.e., consumers). The diets of primary consumers are as follows:

- Herbivores—eat herbaceous food
- Granivores—eat seeds
- Frugivores—eat fruit
- Foliovores—eat leaves

The diets of secondary consumers are as follows:

- Carnivores—eat primary consumers
- Piscivores—eat fish

The animals can be divided into two main groups: vertebrates and invertebrates. Our goal in the following discussion is to provide a brief description of some of the major groups in terms of wildlife ecology and to use these groups as benchmarks for other taxa mentioned elsewhere in the text.

Invertebrates

The invertebrates comprise numerous phyla, of which we will consider only a handful. The invertebrates are quite diverse. They range from taxa that are little more than aggregations of cells, such as the metazoans and sponges, to such advanced forms as the arthropods and chordates.

Phylum Proifera

These are the sponges. Sponges are very primitive filter feeders that principally occur in marine environments. Sponges are little more than collections of cells. The body is not symmetrical and there are no organs. There are some specialized cells in the bodies of sponges, along with intercellular structures called spicules. Spicules are hard (in some groups they are silicon based, whereas in other taxa they are calcareous) structures that reinforce the body. Water is drawn through openings in the body wall by specialized cells called choanocytes. Food particles are swept into the central canal, and amoebocyte cells engulf and then digest them.

Despite the fact that most sponges are filter feeders, there is an apparent exception: carnivorous sponges (Vacelet and Boury-Esnault 1995). These sponges occur in deep water and live in an environment that is poor in resources. The central adaptations seen in these sponges include loss of choanocytes and the presence of filaments that are efficient at capturing small crustaceans (see below). The captured crustaceans struggle for hours until the filaments that ensnared them shorten and thicken while new slender filaments grow over them. Digestion is completed in a few days.

Phylum Cnidaria

The phylum Cnidaria comprises species with a defined two-cell-layer body and a gut that consists of a blind sac. Among the species in this group are the jellyfish, corals, sea anemones, and their relatives. The specialized cells seen in this group are the nematocysts. These cells are also known as stinging cells. Anyone who has run into a flotilla of sea lice or other such "beach blobs" (also known as moon jellyfish) is probably familiar with the extreme discomfort that nematocysts can inflict.

In the fall of 1994, an invasion of large moon jellyfish (*Aurelia aurita*) hit the west coast of Florida in the vicinity of St. Petersburg. Moon jellyfish are typically pelagic forms, which means they occur in the open ocean far from the coastal or littoral zone. The invasion was apparently a product of heavy storms and accompanying winds that simply blew the jellyfish toward the coast.

Other cnidarians of major importance to wildlife are the corals. Coral reefs are essentially mountains built from calcium carbonate deposited by the reef-building corals. Coral reefs only form when strict environmental conditions of water clarity (for penetration of sunlight), salinity, and temperature are met. Thus, coral reefs are restricted to the zone between 30 degrees north and south latitude (Hickman et al. 1990). Coral reefs provide habitat for numerous species of marine invertebrates, such as sponges, echinoderms, and vertebrates, including numerous bony and cartilaginous fishes.

Phylum Mollusca

The mollusks include several important wildlife species. Among these are the bivalves, which include the scallops, oysters, mussels, and clams; the gastropods, which are comprised of snails and slugs; and the cephalopods, which include squids and octopus.

Many species, including humans, are known to feed on bivalves. Bivalves are filter feeders that typically live in the littoral zone and play an important role in ecosystems as detritus feeders.

The majority of gastropods are herbivores that rasp plant material from surfaces. However, some are predatory and some are scavengers. Snails have long been a food source for humans. In France, native snails have recently been depleted, and imports from Turkey have replaced them in escargot. The important point here is that this may represent an example of human overexploitation of a wildlife resource.

The cephalopods include the octopus and squid, which are active predators. Their prey species include small fish, crustaceans, other mollusks, and worms.

Phylum Echinodermata

The echinoderms include several groups among which are the sea urchins and the sea stars (also known as starfish). Sea stars is a preferred name, as these animals are certainly not fish (which are vertebrates). Sea stars are important predators of other invertebrates on coral reefs. Keep in mind that many invertebrates are either sessile or quite slow (such as bivalves) and thus cannot move away when a sea star approaches. Paine (1966) showed that removal of sea stars from reef plots could result in the loss of total species. His argument was that the sea stars fed heavily on species that were superior competitors to other species. Once the sea stars were removed, the control on the populations of the superior competitors was released, and these species quickly outcompeted (for space) several of the other species, forcing them off the reef.

As a group, the echinoderms are along the evolutionary pathway that led to the vertebrates. Other groups along this line are minor and are not covered here.

Phylum Arthropoda

The arthropods are arguably the most advanced invertebrates. There are numerous taxonomic groups in the phylum, but they can be placed into one of three subphyla: subphylum Chelicerata, subphylum Crustacea, and subphylum Uniramia.

The chelicerates include the spiders, scorpions, horseshoe crabs, ticks, and mites. Spiders are important predators that feed on insects and other small animals, as do the scorpions. Visitors to eastern shores of the United States are undoubtedly familiar with horseshoe crabs, the bodies of which litter many beaches by the thousands.

Many crustaceans are important wildlife species. This group includes the shrimps (several species), crabs, crayfishes, and lobsters. All these species are harvested commercially and recreationally.

The uniramians (unbranched appendages) include the insects, centipedes, and millipedes. The centipedes are predators and may be quite large (several centimeters). Often, they may be found under rocks or rotting logs. They feed on earthworms, insect larvae, and other small animals. The millipedes are herbivorous and, like centipedes, prefer dark places under rocks or logs.

The insects are the most diverse (in number of species) group of animals. Insect species have diverged in a number of interesting ways biologically. Many insects are serious agricultural pests and require the use of massive quantities of insecticides for control. Indeed, one of the worst environmental disasters of modern times involved the use of DDT (dichlorodiphenyltrichloroethane), an insecticide. DDT has been linked to egg shell thinning and the collapse of numerous wildlife populations. Another chemical used as an insecticide is methyl bromide, used by the ton in agricultural enterprises around the world. If nothing else, insects have led humans to impact wildlife populations in indirect but nevertheless severe ways.

Phylum Chordata

Phylum Chordata includes both invertebrates and vertebrates. The invertebrates are important in evolutionary studies, but are nowhere near as important as the vertebrates.

Vertebrates

Vertebrates are not nearly as numerous as invertebrates (of the 1.5 million species of animals, only 50,000 are vertebrates), but they include several important taxa. The best way to view the vertebrates is to look at them in an evolutionary context. In this view, there are two main groups: the jawless forms (agnathans, which includes lampreys and hagfishes) and the jawed forms, which includes all other vertebrates.

Class Agnatha includes the hagfishes and lampreys. Hagfishes are bottom feeders in marine environments. They are scavengers and are only rarely encountered by humans other than marine biologists. Their impact on wildlife populations is not thought to be great at this time.

Lampreys are somewhat more important to wildlife ecology. Several species of lampreys are parasitic. Each is equipped with an oral disk armed with sharp and hard denticles. The lamprey attaches itself to a fish and rasps away at the body wall, ingesting the precious bodily fluids of the host fish. Once sated, the lamprey drops off the hapless fish, which may later die. The sea lamprey (*Petromyzon marinus*) invaded the Great Lakes of the United States and Canada when the Welland Canal around Niagara Falls was deepened in 1918. Invading lampreys, along with overfishing, led to the collapse of the lake trout fishery in Lakes Huron, Erie, Michigan, and Superior in the 1950s.

The classes of vertebrates with jaws are briefly introduced here. More in-depth discussion is provided elsewhere in the text where relevant.

1. **Chondrichthyes**—These are the cartilaginous fishes, sharks, skates, and rays. As far as wildlife issues are concerned, recreational fishers have long pursued sharks, and now commercial fishers are after them too.
2. **Osteichthyes**—These bony fishes comprise the largest group of vertebrates in terms of number of species (>24,000 species). Bony fishes of several species are heavily exploited for food by humans.
3. **Amphibia**—This class includes salamanders, frogs, and toads (4000 species). They are the most primitive of the so-called tetrapods (= four feet). They form the basal group for all the remaining groups (reptiles, mammals, and birds). Amphibians are found on all continents except Antarctica.
4. **Reptilia**—These are the snakes, lizards, turtles, and crocodilians (7000 species). They have epidermal scales and an amniote egg (self-contained egg, no longer dependent on water for reproduction). Reptiles form the stem group for birds and mammals. Both birds and mammals evolved from reptiles in the early part of the Mesozoic era. Both groups began to diversify in the Cretaceous era and continued to diversify in the Cenozoic era, as did flowering plants (angiosperms).
5. **Aves**—This class includes only birds. Members of the class Aves have feathers. Birds are homeothermic and have diverse diets. Some species feed chiefly on fruit, some on seeds, some on other animals, and one (one of Darwin's finches) even takes blood from the bodies of other

birds as they sit on their nests. There are approximately 9000 species of birds, and they occur worldwide in all surface habitats (they do not occur, for example, on the sea floor, but several pelagic species spend much of their lives miles from land).

6. **Mammalia**—The mammals include about 4200 species and are extremely diverse in both morphology and ecology. Like birds, mammals evolved from reptiles and are homeotherms. In place of feathers, most mammals have hair (an exception is the naked mole rat). Mammals are comprised of several important wildlife species, including ourselves. As humans, we have hair, are homeothermic, nurse our young, and possess a number of other characters found only among the mammals.

Mammals are more diverse in size than birds. Consider the shrew *Crocidura* (the smallest mammal, which weighs just a few grams) and the blue whale (which weighs several tons) as opposed to the hummingbird (the smallest bird) and the ostrich (the largest bird). Even though mammals are more diverse in this sense, there still are more than twice as many species of birds as there are mammals. The birds have a much longer evolutionary history.

EXERCISES

4.1 Birds have a much longer evolutionary history than mammals. When did the first flighted birds appear? When did the first flightless birds appear?

4.2 Bats are flighted mammals. When did bats arrive on the evolutionary scene?

4.3 There are many examples of convergent evolution, where similar forms evolved completely independently of each other. For instance, birds and bats are flighted yet have a separate evolutionary history. What other mammals are convergent with kangaroo rats?

4.4 Make a list of the extant flightless birds. Where are they located?

4.5 Why are there so many insects? Should we include insects in a textbook on wildlife issues?

4.6 How many different trees are there? Where do trees reach their highest diversity?

4.7 Explain the relationship between wasps and fig trees. How did this relationship evolve?

4.8 What is a euphorbia and what has it converged with?

4.9 Hornbills are found in the Old World (Asia, Africa, Europe). What have they converged with in the New World (North and South America)?

4.10 Are feral hogs, cats, dogs, and other escaped pets wildlife? Are they of any special concern?

4.11 Are zoo animals wildlife?

4.12 Should we establish reserves to protect rare fungi?

4.13 How many different beetle species are there? How many have been identified with Latin names?

4.14 Why should we care if the panda becomes extinct? If a species is the unit of conservation biology, isn't a mite the equivalent of a panda? Should we be just as concerned for the mite as the panda?

4.15 Only 2% of the people in Florida purchase a hunting license. Couldn't voters outlaw hunting if they wanted to? Would outlawing hunting be a good idea?

LITERATURE CITED

Anderson, D.M. 1994. Red tides. *Scientific American* August:62–68.

Forrester, D.J. 1992. *Parasites and Diseases of Wild Mammals in Florida.* University Press of Florida, Gainesville.

Hickman, C.P., Jr., L.S. Roberts, and F.M. Hickman. 1990. *Biology of Animals,* 5th edition. Mosby, St. Louis.

Jaenike, J. 1991. Mass extinction of European fungi. *Trends in Ecology and Evolution* **6**(6):174–175.

Matossian, M.K. 1982. Ergot and the Salem witchcraft affair. *American Scientist* **70**: 355–357.

Paine, R.T. 1966. Food web complexity and species diversity. *The American Naturalist* **100**:65–75.

Raven, P.H., R.F. Evert, and H. Curtis. 1986. *Biology of Plants,* 4th edition. Worth Publishers, New York.

Vacelet, J. and N. Boury-Esnault. 1995. Carnivorous sponges. *Nature* **373**:333–335.

Warner, R.E. 1968. The role of introduced diseases in the extinction of the endemic Hawaiian avifauna. *Condor* **70**:101–120.

GENETIC DIVERSITY 5

I s a panther from British Columbia, Canada the same as a panther from Venezuela or a panther from Tierra del Fuego, at the tip of South America? If you were a zoo manager in charge of carnivore conservation and wanted to have a panther exhibit, what would you do? Would you choose a panther from Canada and one from the tip of South America to breed, or would you choose two from the same region? If you had to maintain these animals in a zoo for possible reintroduction later, what would your strategy be? Indeed, many Siberian tigers in zoos today are actually the result of crosses with Bengal tigers. Few are pure-bred Siberian tigers, and this raises serious questions regarding the very survival of this beautiful species. For many reasons, knowing the lineage of the animal is critical to maintaining the offspring's pure genetic makeup. It's little wonder genetics is playing a more important role in conservation today.

INHERITANCE AT THE INDIVIDUAL LEVEL

To better appreciate conservation and wildlife issues, we must understand the difference between genetic diversity and species diversity. Gregor J. Mendel (1822–1884) is credited as the father of modern genetics. Sadly, Charles Darwin did not know of Mendel's work, although the two were contemporaries. During Darwin's time, *blending inheritance* was the accepted principle by which inheritance occurred. Darwin doubted blending inheritance but had no other mechanism to explain how traits were passed from parents to offspring. Blending inheritance can be likened to the mixing of traits, as if some averaging was occurring. For instance, if a single species of rose has white flowers on some plants and red flowers on other plants, then breeding or crossing the two plants would lead to a rose with pink flowers—a sort of intermediate form. Mendel knew that this was not the case in nature, however.

Mendel performed hybrid experiments with garden peas and discovered the basis of what is now called *Mendelian inheritance*. Although Mendel had no idea of the mechanism of genetic inheritance, his experiments showed that inheritance was particulate. That is, Mendel demonstrated that traits from the red-flowered plants could be combined with white-flowered plants to produce red-flowered and white-flowered plants, but not pink-flowered plants. Furthermore, red-flowered plants could be crossed to produce both white- and red-flowered plants.

Mendel's concept of *unit characters* was deduced from solid experimental evidence gained from pea plants. The physical traits of his plants were, he reasoned, controlled by what we now call *genes,* which are present in all living organisms. Each gene has two or more *alleles,* which are different forms of a gene that determine alternate characteristics such as color, height, or shape. Thus, if a gene has two alleles, one for red color and one for white color, either color, but not both, can be passed on to offspring in the form of a *gamete.* The separation of the pair of alleles is referred to as *segregation,* which occurs during the maturation of the reproductive cells, called gametes. Since both parents each contribute one gamete, only one allele from each parent can be passed to their offspring. Another way of looking at this is that each new plant has one gamete and hence one allele from each parent. Note that this allele might control the color of the flowers, which could be white or red. Also, gametes carry many alleles for different traits. We say that the *genotype* determines the *phenotype*. This means that the gene, the genotype, determines what you see, the phenotype. Let's look at a simple example.

First, let's assume that the plant is true breeding. By that we mean that if a red-flowered plant breeds with a red-flowered plant, then red-flowered plants always result. Similarly, white-flowered plants breeding with white-flowered plants produce only white-flowered plants. Furthermore, we will assume that the red color is *dominant* over the white color. That is, if a gene with the red allele from one parent is combined with a gene with the white allele for white flowers, the red color will result. The allele for the red color of the flower, labeled **R**, is dominant over the allele coding for the white color, labeled **r**. The allele coding for the white-colored flower is *recessive*. The parents, labeled P, will each be *homozygous*. That is, each will contain two identical alleles, as opposed to being *heterozygous,* which means having two different alleles. The first-generation plants in our experiment are usually labeled the F1 plants, and the offspring of those are labeled F2 plants, for second-generation offspring.

Now let's cross or mate a red-flowered plant with a white-flowered plant, just as Mendel did, and then cross the resulting offspring, again as Mendel did. What happens?

P	**RR** (red, homozygous)	**rr** (white, homozygous)
gametes	R	r
F1		**Rr** (heterozygous)
F1 × F1	**Rr**	× **Rr**
gametes	R r	R r
F2	**R**	**r**
R	**RR** (red, homozygous)	**Rr** (red, heterozygous)
r	**Rr** (red, heterozygous)	**rr** (white, homozygous)

Thus, there will be three red-flowering plants for each white-flowering plant produced in the second generation. The red allele **R** was dominant, as you recall. Furthermore, there will be two homozygous plants and two heterozygous plants. We say that the probability of being heterozygous is thus one-half. The probability of being red is three-fourths and white is one minus three-fourths, or one-fourth. Each parent contributed a single gamete to the *zygote* that forms in the offspring. We know from genetic theory that the contribution from each parent is a random and independent event. The probability of two independent events is equal to the product of the independent probabilities.

Taking the F1 × F1 step above, we know that the probability of an offspring receiving a dominant allele **R** was one-half from each parent. Thus, the probability of being **RR** is $(1/2) \times (1/2) = 1/4$. The probability of receiving an **r** and being recessive or white-flowered is also one-fourth. Thus, the probability of being homozygous is the sum of the two probabilities, or one-half, as shown above. Hence, the probability of being heterozygous is one minus one-half, or one-half.

What is the probability of being red-flowered? Apparently, this is also the probability of receiving at least one **R**, since only one **R** allele is required to express a red flower. But this is simply one minus the probability of receiving no **R**. If the plant receives no **R**s, then it must receive two **r**s. Thus, the probability of a plant having a red flower is just one minus the probability of being white-flowered, or one-fourth, and hence is three-fourths.

This is a simplified example of a very complex problem. We could have used animals instead of plants with no loss of generality. Generally, gametes carry many, many traits. Some traits even skip a generation and are known to be sex linked. Long ago, people noticed traits in a father but not in any of his children, male or female. When these children had families, the trait would surface again in the male offspring. This distinctive pattern suggests that the particular trait is sex linked. Sex-linked traits, such as the inability to recognize the color green, are well studied. It is known that females must receive two recessive alleles to have deficient vision, while males need receive only one. This is because the male sex chromosome carries no color vision *locus,* whereas the female chromosome does. Thus, defective green color vision is a heritable trait. Exactly what traits are heritable?

Many morphological, behavioral, physiological, and life history traits are heritable (Ridley 1993). Indeed, in studies of common houseflies (*Drosophila*), Roff and Mousseau (1987) showed that longevity, fecundity, development time, locomotion, mating activity, and the number of abdominal bristles were all heritable traits. Morphological traits were more heritable than behavioral traits, and life history traits were less heritable. However, chances are if your grandparents and your parents live long and healthy lives, then you might as well plan on living a long and healthy life yourself. That is, you have the right genes.

Genetic diversity within a species is immense; among living creatures, it is incalculable. Nearly every creature is unique in its genetic makeup. Obviously, this raises serious questions with respect to zoos and the species they contain. With so much genetic uniqueness, can we really hope to save any of it in zoos? If a species is experiencing an extinction spasm, such as the whooping cranes of North America, genetic diversity decreases. Alleles are more likely to be bred out of a population simply by chance alone. Keeping a few in zoos is little more than a last-gasp effort, since genetic diversity will almost certainly have been lost forever through the loss of some alleles. Unless we can save the species *in situ*, that is, in its place, and protect its habitat from destruction, then perhaps it is better to limit human involvement altogether. This is most certainly a wildlife issue!

INHERITANCE AT THE POPULATION LEVEL

Animals respond to their environment but do not adapt to it. The English house sparrow (*Passer domesticus*) provides an excellent example. Johnston and Selander (1971) and Gould and Johnston (1972) studied male house sparrow body weights across North America. They discovered that the smallest sparrows were found near San Francisco and Central America, while the heaviest sparrows were found in Minnesota and central Canada. Animals tend to be larger in colder regions because a larger body mass helps to maintain body heat. To be sure, the sparrows were not adapting to their environment. As we will see later, there must have been differential survival among the sparrows. In cold regions, more heavier sparrows survived than lighter ones. Since life history traits are heritable, the heavier sparrows were more likely to survive and thus produced more offspring than the lighter sparrows in these regions. This led to the average sparrow being heavier in the colder regions. We can presume the opposite effect occurred in the southern and western portions of the sparrow's range. Of course, this assumes that no other complicating forces were at work, such as predation. However, there are many similar examples of population diversity.

Geographic variation across a gradient, such as winter temperature, in a species like the house sparrow produces a *cline*, or gradient of continuous variation in a genetic or phenotypic character. Indeed, the two North American meadowlark species are ubiquitous, being found from the east coast to the west coast. During the ice age 22,000 years ago, a great sheet of ice protruded into the northern United States, splitting the population of meadowlarks in half. At that time, meadowlarks were probably one species. Now we recognize two species of meadowlarks, the western meadowlark (*Sturnella neglecta*) and the eastern meadowlark (*S. magna*), although they appear nearly identical. The ice sheet apparently lasted long enough for the single species of meadowlark to separate into two populations that followed divergent evolutionary paths and *speciated*, that is, became separate and distinct species unable to interbreed in nature (Lanyon 1957). Although similar in appearance, the two species are reproductively isolated due to differing behavior and different songs. As the keeper of an aviary for a zoo, you would naturally want both species of meadowlark represented; 22,000 years ago, you would only have required a single pair. Hence, genetic diversity as it changes in time is certainly a consideration in deciding some wildlife issues. Once again, we are using a scientific basis to decide how many and what kind of birds we need for the aviary.

Whereas individuals have genes, populations have gene frequencies. Similarly, individual genotypes are expressed phenotypically, but populations have genotype and phenotype frequencies. One way of analyzing populations of a single species is to assume that the genotype frequency is in equilibrium and then look more closely at deviations from that equilibrium. We say that a population is in Hardy-Weinberg Equilibrium (H-WE) when mating in the population is purely random and there is no selective pressure on any phenotype in the population (Starr and Taggart 1992). What does H-WE mean in terms of genotype frequencies?

We will again consider only one gene with two alleles, **R** and **r**, that have a frequency of p and q, respectively, where p + q = 1. Note that p and q summed must be unity because **R** and **r** are the only two alleles we are considering. Under the assumptions of random mating, and a very large population existing without immigration or emigration, p^2 is the frequency of **RR**, 2pq is the frequency of **Rr**, and q^2 is the frequency of **rr**, just as we saw above in the example using flowers. Note also that $p^2 + 2pq + q^2 = (p + q)^2 = 1$. Now, the claim is that if the population is H-WE, the next generation genotypic frequencies will be stable over succeeding generations, although the genotypic frequencies may have changed initially.

To see this fact, pick out two random individuals from the population and consider the offspring produced. The chance that the offspring will have an **R** is just p, and the chance of having an **r** is then q. Producing an offspring that is an **RR** genotype has probability p^2. Similarly, the chance that the offspring will have an **r** genotype has probability q^2, and finally, the probability of an offspring being **Rr** or **rR** is pq + qp = 2pq. Thus, the allele frequencies did not change in the offspring when compared to the parents. The population is H-WE. When are populations not H-WE?

EVOLUTIONARY FORCES

Populations undergoing evolutionary pressures have changing genotype frequencies, not because the members of the population are adapting to their environments, but because there is differential survival among the offspring due to natural selection acting on the population. Other evolutionary forces such as mutation, inbreeding, and genetic drift may also be acting. The fundamental property of natural selection is described eloquently by the scientist who first used the term. Darwin (1859) described evolution as follows:

> As many more individuals of each species are born that can possibly survive; and as, consequently, there is a frequently recurring struggle for existence, it follows that any being, if it vary however slightly in any manner profitable to itself, under the complex and varying conditions of life, will have a better chance of surviving, and thus be *naturally selected*. From the principle of inheritance, any selected variety will tend to propagate its new and modified form.

Darwin goes on to tell us:

> Natural selection acts solely through the preservation of variations in some ways advantageous, which consequently endure.

Later, he adds:

> Natural selection, it should never be forgotten, can act solely through and for the advantage of each being.

First, Darwin tells us that organisms produce more offspring than can survive. Second, any offspring that is ever so slightly better prepared for its environment will have a better chance of living and reproducing. The organism is naturally selected to reproduce more successfully. The other organisms that do not reproduce as successfully are selected against. Note that, as Darwin tells us, natural selection acts on the individual, that is, on the phenotype and not the genotype. Third, by the rules of inheritance that were discussed previously, the organism will tend to pass on its traits to its offspring, and presumably some of them, but not necessarily all of them, will be differentially naturally selected. The results of natural selection surround us in our everyday lives. Every living organism, from the house sparrow to the elephant, is the product of natural or human-induced selection. Entire orders of organisms have survived for 100 million years and then disappeared from the fossil record forever, never to be seen on earth again. As Darwin said:

Natural selection will not produce absolute perfection...

All living organisms are the product of natural selection. But what is natural selection acting on? A population can change due to natural selection acting on mutation, inbreeding, migration, and genetic drift—natural evolutionary forces changing allele frequencies within a population. Gene mutation can be beneficial, neutral, or harmful depending upon whether or not the organism's *fitness* increases. Fitness is a measure of reproductive success. An organism that reproduces more viable offspring is considered relatively more fit than another organism of the same species. Thus, if one bull elephant sires 20 young in his lifetime and another bull only 10 young, then the first elephant has greater fitness.

Any mutation that increases reproductive success is considered beneficial. In the worst case, if a mutation causes the organism to die at birth, then the mutation can be safely presumed to have been harmful. Most mutations are either neutral or harmful, with the result that the organism is either unaffected or dies before it reproduces. Mutations that increase fitness can be spread through a population because of the differential success of organisms with the mutation. Eventually, the mutated gene will be found more and more often in successive generations.

Thus, gene mutation does not necessarily connote a negative gene transformation. Indeed, natural selection acts on the phenotype produced by the mutant gene and determines the result. If the gene produced a malformed heart in a zebra calf, the chance of the calf surviving to mate would be small. On the other hand, if the calf's chance of survival increased because the mutant gene increased the size of its heart ever so slightly, natural selection would favor this individual. However, the rigors of everyday life are stacked against the zebra calf. Even with a possibly important mutation, the young zebra would have to survive day after day on the African plain, a perfect prey item for hungry lions and hyenas. Natural selection has acted on the predators as well.

Genetic migration acts to decrease differences between populations by *gene transfer*. When an individual or group of individuals migrate from one population to another that is geographically separated and reproduction occurs, the transfer of genes acts to make the two populations more similar. Geographically separate populations of organisms must respond to different environmental variables and thus develop their own gene frequencies that are representative of their ancestral populations. When these populations interbreed, the genetic differences between them eventually disappear, assuming that preferential mating does not take place. Returning to the opening paragraph of this chapter, populations of panthers in British Columbia, Venezuela, and Tierra del Fuego are genetically quite different. If populations from these three very different regions were to interbreed, the resulting panthers would be genetically unique as well. Also, if we were to sample body sizes of panthers along the geographic cline from north to south, we would find variations, with the large body size in the highest latitudes and the smallest in the lower latitudes. These differences in body size could be correlated with certain allele frequencies, although body size is probably accounted for by multiple alleles interacting.

Random genetic drift also occurs in populations, and the smaller the population, the more likely it is that random genetic drift will have a significant impact. Allele frequencies in a population can change simply by chance alone. Furthermore, genetic drift always acts to reduce variability in a population. This means that there is an increase in homozygous individuals in the population at the expense of heterozygous individuals. Recall that homozygous individuals carry two copies of the same allele. In smaller populations, genetic drift reduces heterozygosity and hence variability. Indeed, theoretical studies show that if there are only four individuals in a population, after some 70 generations almost all heterozygosity will have been lost, whereas a population of 1024 individuals will have lost only 8% of its heterozygosity. Obviously, genetic drift can have a powerful impact on small populations. All too often these days, we hear the expression "the vortex of extinction." What this means is that the population of an organism has decreased so that genetic drift is causing the increasing loss of genetic diversity (i.e., genetic variability). Alleles can disappear from a population. When genetic diversity is lost, a population's ability to adapt is reduced simply because the number of alleles expressing phenotypic variation for natural sel   upon has decreased. With increasing loss in genetic variability, e   bability nears unity.

Inbreeding is similar to genetic drift and results when a departure from random mating occurs. That is, if individuals with a certain gene tend to mate with other individuals with the same gene, then nonrandom mating occurs. Inbreeding becomes increasingly more likely with a smaller population. Also, inbreeding is associated with *deleterious* or harmful genes being perpetuated in a population. For instance, there are about 50 Florida panthers living in south Florida in the Big Cypress State Preserve. Many of the panthers are purported to show the effects of inbreeding. That is, many of the panthers have a crooked tail, and breeding males sometimes have but one descended testicle (having none makes them infertile). One breeding female only weighed 40 pounds, about half the size of a normal female at reproductive age. These phenotypic characters are blamed on inbreeding and are believed to be deleterious. A multimillion-dollar introduction of Texas panthers into the Florida population has been undertaken to increase genetic variability. Certainly, over the short term, genetic variability will increase in the Florida panthers. The long-term effects of the introduction program cannot be known with any certainty. A project manager was quoted as saying, "Any panther born in Florida is a Florida panther." Is this a wildlife issue?

QUANTITATIVE GENETICS

Complex traits such as height and weight that vary continuously in a population are known as *quantitative* traits (Strickberger 1990, Futuyma 1986). Most quantitative traits involve the contribution of different alleles from many genes. Furthermore, phenotypic variation can be caused by environmental factors above and beyond that caused by genotypic differences. For instance, suppose there are four different alleles controlling height, A, a, B, and b. Individuals in the population must have two of these alleles. There would be individuals that are AA, Aa, aa, AB, aB, Ab, ab, BB, Bb, and bb. The effects of multiple alleles are usually additive. Hence, the phenotype of the individual is determined as the entire contribution from all the alleles. If each one codes for a different increment in height, for example, then total height would be some base height plus the additive effect of each allele. Imagine the possibilities if a trait were controlled by ten different alleles.

Frequency graphs are most often used to understand quantitative traits. The *x* axis, or *abscissa,* usually represents the trait, such as height, weight, or other characters that can be measured. The *y* axis, or *ordinate,* records the frequency of the trait in the population. The effects of natural selection acting on a trait such as height can be understood by inspecting a frequency graph.

When different rates of survival and reproductive success exist because of some inherited characteristic, natural selection can operate on that character. Natural selection will differentially favor the individuals that exhibit the trait that permits greater reproductive success, and hence greater fitness. On average and over the long term, those individuals with the favorable trait will survive and reproduce more often. Note also that not necessarily all such individuals with the favorable trait will survive. Indeed, the challenges of life demand more than favorable genetic makeup. Generally, natural selection can be stabilizing, directional, or disruptive, and these effects show up in the frequency graphs of the trait that is acted upon.

Stabilizing selection acts to reduce variability of a trait or character. Here, the average individuals in a population have higher fitness than individuals at the extremes. Natural selection is acting against any change from the average. Human birth weight is a classic example of stabilizing selection. Over the course of human evolution, birth weights have stabilized at about 8 pounds. Babies born under- or overweight by 2 pounds have a less than 95% chance of survival, while babies born near the mid range of the birth weight frequency curve have a better than 98% chance of living to age 4 weeks.

Directional selection acts to push a phenotypic character in one direction or another over time. The most famous example of directional selection comes from the experiments of H.B.D. Kettlewell with peppered moths (*Biston betularia*) in England. The most common form of the moth in pre-industrial England was the black and white peppered form or *morph*. The moths rest by day on trees covered with lichens of the same peppered color, camouflaged against visual predators such as birds. With industrialization, the lichens on trees were killed, and hence the peppered morph of the moth was subjected to intense selective pressure by birds. About this time, a black or melanistic morph of the moth appeared more frequently. Camouflaged against the dark tree bark, the melanistic morph was safe from predatory attack. Meanwhile, the peppered morph became rare. Birds were the agents of natural selection. When industrialization was reduced, the lichens responded and once again covered trees. Now the melanistic morph of the moth was subjected to predation, and the peppered morph once again increased in numbers. Here, natural selection was directional, first against the peppered morph and then against the melanistic morph. In both instances, both morphs existed at the same time but in different proportions within the population. Neither was completely removed. Kettlewell's (1973) use of experimentation to test hypotheses remains an excellent example of the scientific method to test evolutionary theories.

Disruptive selection acts to increase variation in a character or trait and is the opposite of stabilizing selection. The phenotypic character at either end of the range is naturally selected for, while the intermediate form is selected against. For instance, disruptive selection can occur when mating is nonrandom. Body size is an inherited characteristic and usually varies smoothly in populations. Suppose that small individuals tended to mate with small individuals and large individuals tended to mate with similar sized individuals. Individuals at the extreme ends of the character frequency curve would have a selective advantage over the intermediate forms in the middle of the curve. Over time, the population might segregate into two groups with different body sizes. Indeed, over a very long time, the groups might become reproductively isolated and speciate.

Why is maintaining variability in a population important? Why haven't all populations stabilized by now? Simply put, maintaining biodiversity means maintaining genetic variability within and between populations of organisms. From plate tectonics to climate change, to variability in the weather, to the competitive advantage of a similar species, organic adaptation is essential to the long-term viability of a species. Recall that individuals do not evolve; populations evolve. Although natural selection acts on the individual, an individual cannot evolve or adapt. The offspring produced will, however, be ever so slightly better adapted to local conditions or, as Darwin put it:

> ...if some of these many species become modified and improved, others will have to be improved in a corresponding degree or they will be exterminated.

If conditions change, there will most likely be differential survival. Indeed, the environment might change, requiring some special feature that most organisms in the population do not possess. Selection can act on these special features, leading to more offspring being produced by the favored organism. Genetic variability will have increased, leading to a population of organisms being better suited to their environment. Genetic variability is the key to the long-term survival of a species, but even species with high genetic variability have no guarantee of surviving forever. We can say that the loss of genetic variation is one step on the road to extinction.

THE VALUE OF GENETIC THEORY

In 1982, the International Whaling Commission (IWC) voted to impose a moratorium on commercial whaling. However, some members of the IWC have continued to take whales for scientific or subsistence purposes, both permitted activities under the ban. A spot check of Japanese retail markets (Baker and

Palumbi 1994) showed that whale products available were not all from species hunted and traded in accordance with the IWC international treaty. The hard evidence came from the genetic analysis of mitochondrial DNA (mtDNA) and demonstrates the ability of genetic techniques to identify not only particular species but also the geographic locations where the species were taken.

Meat products ranging from dried and salted strips of meat, marinated in sesame oil and soy sauce, to unfrozen meat sold as sashimi were purchased from open markets in Japan and analyzed using a portable laboratory. Whale tissue samples from many known species and populations had also been analyzed to construct a library; 17 Japanese samples matched the library specimens closely. Of these, 14 samples were from minke whales, found close to Australia. One sample of marinated meat showed both minke whale and humpback whale sequences. Two samples matched the family Delphinidae, which includes killer whales, dolphins, and pilot whales. One humpback whale sequence was an identical match with known humpback wintering grounds in Mexican, Hawaiian, and Japanese waters. One fin whale sequence was identical to fin whales sampled near Iceland.

Arguments about sustainable whaling are based on the assumption that only abundant species will be hunted and that depleted populations and species will be left to recover. These findings show that such assumptions are ill advised and suggest that active enforcement of IWC rules will be essential if continued whaling is practiced. "Without an adequate system for monitoring and verifying catches, however, history has shown that no species of whale can be considered safe" (Baker and Palumbi 1994).

EXERCISES

5.1 At what level does conservation start? Do we begin conservation at the individual level for birds and mammals and at the species level for insects, for instance?

5.2 Give some examples of the uses of modern genetic techniques in conservation.

5.3 Investigate how zoos ensure against inbreeding of captive populations.

5.4 Is it true that small, highly inbred populations have a necessarily dim long-term survival outlook? Consider the American bison and musk ox populations in the far north.

5.5 Use a search engine on the World Wide Web to identify the range of problems genetics can address.

5.6 Browse the Web for information on zoos. What functions do zoos serve in international conservation?

LITERATURE CITED

Baker, C.S. and S.R. Palumbi. 1994. Which whales are hunted? A molecular genetic approach to monitoring whaling. *Science* **265**:1538–1539.

Darwin, C.R. 1859. *On the Origin of Species.* John Murray, London.

Futuyma, D.J. 1986. *Evolutionary Biology.* Sinauer Associates, Sunderland, Massachusetts.

Gould, S.J. and R.F. Johnston. 1972. Geographic variation. *Annual Review of Ecology and Systematics* **3**:457–498.

Johnston, R.F. and R.K. Selander. 1971. Evolution in the house sparrow. II. Adaptive differentiation in North American populations. *Evolution* **25**:1–18.

Kettlewell, H.B.D. 1973. *The Evolution of Melanism.* Oxford University Press, Oxford, U.K.

Lanyon, W.E. 1957. *The Comparative Biology of the Meadowlarks (Sturnella) in Wisconsin.* Publication of the Nuttal Ornithology Club No. 1. Cambridge, Massachusetts.

Ridley, M. 1993. *Evolution.* Blackwell Scientific, Boston.

Roff, D.A. and T.A. Mousseau. 1987. Quantitative genetics and fitness: lessons from *Drosophila. Heredity* **58**:103–118.

Starr, C. and R. Taggart. 1992. *Biology.* Wadsworth, Belmont, California.

Strickberger, M.W. 1990. *Evolution.* Jones and Bartlett, Boston.

PHYSICAL PROCESSES GOVERNING LIFE ON EARTH

6

Wildlife issues do not exist apart from our everyday life experiences. Indeed, a wildlife issue cannot be fully understood and appreciated unless we understand how the issue arose in the first place and why it came to be an issue. In other words, we must always consider how the issue came into being. Fair questions are: How did this become an issue? What is the history of this issue? Why is the history important? Perhaps no other single factor is more important than history in helping us to reach a fair and equitable solution to a wildlife issue. Both the short- and long-term history of events are important elements in our scientific quest to understand wildlife issues. Consider the following example.

One of the American bison's strongholds is Yellowstone National Park in the northwest corner of Wyoming. Within the park, all wildlife, including bison, are protected. The Yellowstone fires of 1986 showed that park managers are managing Yellowstone as naturally as possible, letting fires started by nature burn nearly uncontrolled. Wildlife is also managed as naturally as possible. In principle, such a policy is easy to execute—or is it?

One winter, a bison attempted to cross Yellowstone Lake, which was, as it turned out, not thickly covered with ice. The bison broke through the ice and was unable to secure its footing to lift itself from an icy death. Three snowmobilers witnessed the incident and reported it. Park rangers had to decide what to do. Without human intervention, the bison would be unable to free itself, but human intervention in a naturally occurring phenomenon was strictly prohibited. Park rangers decided to do nothing, and during the frigid night the bison succumbed. The issue was whether to attempt a rescue of the bison or to do nothing. If you were a park ranger, what would you have done?

First, you might have determined the sequence of events. Unknown to the park rangers, the bison was walking down the snowmobile trail that ran along the lake. Yellowstone was under deep snow, and bison often use snowmobile paths in winter because the snow is compacted and hence less deep. As the bison slowly walked down the path, the snowmobilers approached quickly from around the bend. When the snowmobilers blocked the bison's path, the bison abandoned its course and headed down an embankment that was the bank of Yellowstone Lake. Bison rarely walk across a frozen lake because their hoofs are not well adapted to crossing ice. However, this particular bison was left with little choice. Within five minutes, the bison had crashed through the ice as the snowmobilers watched. Given these new facts, would your course of action change?

The immediate wildlife issue was whether to rescue the bison or to let nature take its most certain course. However, no wildlife issue is ever immediate, and few rarely surprise us from behind. Most often, there is a sequence of events that precipitates what we refer to as a wildlife issue (i.e., an issue that arises because two or more people disagree on a course of action involving wildlife). No decision can be made until the sequence of events is understood as best as possible under the time constraints involved. In our example of the bison, no questions were asked of the snowmobilers. The recreationists reported the incident immediately and were dismissed. Policy was followed and nature did the rest. There was no "discovery" process, no history, no sequence of events. There was simply a bison struggling to free itself, its front legs slipping, pitifully equipped to secure footing on wet ice.

The above events took place in a relatively short period of time. Other events take longer to materialize. For instance, there are two species of African rhinoceros, and both are endangered because of poaching by humans. Rhinos have few natural predators except for lions and hyenas. Ngorongoro Crater in northern Tanzania, East Africa is a wonderful park to enjoy viewing African white rhino. There are about 20 rhino living in the crater, and most are seen each day by the many tourists driving throughout the park. At night, park rangers protect road access to the crater, so the rhino are relatively safe, at least from humans.

Rhinos are notoriously nearsighted, and rhino calves rarely wander more than a short distance from their mother's side. If they do, they are likely to become lost in spite of the fact that they may be only 5 m away. One afternoon in the crater, as the sun set and the tourist trucks drove the steep walls to exit, a rhino calf became "separated" from its mother. Hyenas are opportunistic predators and always seem to be in the right place at the right time. Not surprisingly, one approached the confused calf. A few meters away, the rhino mother grunted and snorted and jerked her head up and down. Leaning backward, with its hindquarters low to the ground, the hyena approached the calf. Slowly the hyena crept forward, and then suddenly, quickly, its jaws secured the rhino calf by the nose. The jaws of the hyena are among the most powerful of any predator, able to crush bone for the marrow contained within it. The calf resisted and broke free but did not flee. These events were witnessed by a professional wildlife photographer who had spent a lifetime in Africa. Had you been a park ranger on the scene, what would you have done? Would a factor in your decision be that white rhinos are endangered because humans have poached them to the brink of extinction? Or would you follow the stated wildlife policy, which is to let the animals work out their own struggles? The photographer filmed the gruesome sequence of events.

Unrelenting human poaching has led to the mass extirpation of the white rhino across Africa. Unless humans intervene on behalf of the rhino, extinction will be the result. The history of both species of African rhino is well documented. Intervention by humans on behalf of the species must take place inside as well as outside of parks and preserves if the rhino is to survive. Very few African parks are even remotely "wild" today, and most are extensively managed. Deciding on a form of "natural" management policy is certainly one of the most complex wildlife issues of our day. Each conservation biologist must decide when to intervene and when to be an observer—well before the situation arises.

In both examples, the importance of history and understanding the sequence of events should have carried some weight in helping us reach a decision. That is, the importance of history cannot be ignored, and an understanding of the historical events that preceded the wildlife issue frequently leads to a more comprehensive understanding and deeper appreciation of the issue at hand. Indeed, history, even ancient history, is of profound importance in resolving many wildlife issues. Without a historical perspective, many issues are impossible to resolve. Thus, a historical understanding of life on earth is essential, and understanding how we got to where we are today is crucial.

Biogeography is the scientific study of the distributions of extinct and living organisms. With more than 1.6 million named plants and animals living today and from 5 to 30 million organisms thought to exist today, this is not an easy task. Indeed, when we include all extinct organisms, which account for more than 90% of all known life, the task seems insurmountable. Nevertheless, more progress in understanding the distributions of organisms, alive and dead, has been made in the last 150 years than had been made in the entire history of mankind. The questions biogeographers must answer are simple to appreciate: What are the causes of the variation of life from place to place? How does this variety of life differ from place to place? Appreciating the history of life is an important first step in deciding most wildlife issues. Importantly, the rise of the scientific method in the 1500s led to challenges in ancient and incorrect beliefs and made possible the replacement of dogma with hypotheses that could be rigorously tested and replaced with new ones if necessary.

THE DOWNFALL OF PTOLEMY'S UNIVERSE

That the earth was the center of the known universe was once an accepted truth. The Ptolemaic System, the astronomical view that the earth was the center of the universe, was set forth in 150 A.D. by Ptolemy of Alexandria in his classic work *Almagest*. It was based on previous works, notably by Apollonius of Perga (220 B.C.) and Hipparchus of Rhodes (about 150 B.C.). Ptolemy had advanced such a theory, and long after his death most people still accepted that the sun, moon, and planets revolved about the earth. This belief had become a scientific paradigm.

Polish astronomer Nicolaus Copernicus (1473–1543) is credited with founding modern astronomy. As a product of the European Renaissance, he, like many of his contemporaries, studied astronomy, law, mathematics, and medicine. Copernicus became fascinated with what he perceived as a serious flaw in the Ptolemaic version of the known universe he had studied as a student. Knowing the importance of the work done before him, he reviewed previous manuscripts on the study of the universe and discovered that a few thinkers had placed the sun instead of the earth at the center of the universe. Copernicus set about to demonstrate that a belief held by a majority of people for more than 1400 years was not necessarily correct.

So profound was his revelation that it shaped forever the way science is used to create theories supported by observed facts. Indeed, it is clear to nearly every human that the sun rises in the east and sets in the west and, furthermore, that the moon also rises and sets. Indeed, all heavenly bodies *appear* to revolve around the earth. What nearly everyone who had ever lived failed to realize was that they too shared in the earth's constant motion. By carefully charting the motion of the planets, Copernicus put forth a theory supported by facts—that the sun, and not the earth, was the center of the known universe. It was not until 150 years later that Sir Isaac Newton (1642–1727) grasped the true significance of these facts.

Certainly one of the most recognized scientists ever, Newton is regarded as the most original and influential theorist in the history of science. Even today, most schoolchildren recognize his name. As the keystone of the scientific revolution in the 17th century, Newton's work combined the contributions of his predecessors into a new and powerful synthesis. The magnificence of Newton's achievements and his very presence in England enabled a golden age of science to flourish. However, it was not until the late 1700s and early 1800s that the evolution of the earth was even remotely accurately described.

As late as the middle of the 1800s, most people believed that the earth was little more than 6000 years old and that life was created shortly after the earth was born. Religious beliefs of the time held that all life was created at the same time and that humans were placed on earth by the Creator about 4000 B.C. Once again, the scientific method was put to the test, not as an instrument against the church, but as a way of creating a theory based upon facts that could be tested.

ACTUALISM

The principle of actualism is attributed to James Hutton (1726–1797) and Charles Lyell (1797–1875); however, Jean-Baptiste Lamarck (1744–1829) was an outspoken proponent. Lamarck suggested that geological discontinuities were the result of gradual changes working slowly over long periods of time. He proposed that environmental changes led to the creation of new species from then extant species that have since disappeared. As geologists, both Hutton and Lyell realized that the earth was much older than believed. The term actualism refers to the theory which holds that all geological phenomena (as well as the processes of speciation and extinction) can be explained as the result of existing forces operating uniformly as a consequence of physical laws at least since the origin of the earth. Of course, this is also a belief that cannot be tested. However, most scientists accept that the physical laws of the universe have remained unchanged at least since the origin of the earth and so accept these theories.

CATASTROPHISM

French anatomist Georges Cuvier (1769–1832) was a formidable advocate of catastrophism. The theory of catastrophism held that new species of life were created by great natural events, such as the Great Flood, glaciations, or other supernatural cataclysms. To some, such as Louis Agassiz (1807–1873), there had been many divine interventions in the past. Evidence abounded to support this theory as well. Large boulders in the middle of cultivated fields across Europe were testimonials of the flood. Indeed, how else could fossil fish and shells be found on mountain slopes if there had been no flood? The theory of catastrophism was supported by facts and gave rise to hypotheses that could be tested. Many philosophers argue that the only way science advances is by disproving hypotheses. If most hypotheses were accepted as true, there could be no new theories to advance. Thus, science advances by disproving old theories and advancing new theories, oftentimes in the complete absence of new facts.

Catastrophism was accepted by many because it explained fossils as extinct species that had been replaced by new extant species and also agreed well with the biblical flood and left open the possibility of future divine events.

There is no single day, year, or even decade when one theory dies and another is accepted. Thus, science advances in a sort of biased random walk, first going to the left, then right, back left, but always forward, ever so slightly. Where concepts such as the evolution of life and the origin of species were hotly debated, work by geologists continued. Catastrophic discontinuities were not found in geographically distributed areas, suggesting they were local events. Past changes had obviously occurred as a result of natural forces, such as erosion, volcanism, mountain building, and local flooding. Thus, no supernatural causes had to be investigated. Finally, the earth had to be much older because natural forces generally work slowly. Catastrophic events did occur and were recorded in the geologic history, to be sure, but for most known areas around the Victorian world, events that shaped the past left an identifiable signature.

Certainly one of the most famous scientists of any time was Charles Darwin (1809–1882), a biologist by trade. Darwin carried Lyell's book *Principles of Geology* with him on his historic five-year voyage of H.M.S. Beagle in 1831. The publication of Darwin's *On the Origin of Species* in 1859 commanded the attention of the scientific world. However, we must continue here with our geological discoveries. Evolution of species will be considered later, and by looking back from our more modern vantage point, we can better put Darwin's work into perspective.

PLATE TECTONICS AND CONTINENTAL DRIFT

Over a century ago, geographers noticed how the coastlines of some of the continents fit together like a jigsaw puzzle. In 1858, Antonio Snider-Pelliginin proposed that the continents had actually split apart and drifted away from each other. Odd occurrences of coal in Antarctica and glacier-scoured rocks in the Sahara Desert gave rise to bizarre scientific speculations. Alfred Wegener (1880–1930), a German meteorologist, became one of the speculators in 1912 (Gould 1993).

The scientific paradigm of Wegener's time was that the continents were fixed from the time the earth had coalesced billions of years in the past. Wegener suggested that long ago the continents had indeed been joined and, furthermore, they had drifted apart. Wegener's theory rocked the very foundations of all physical sciences and opened the door for the full expression of theories that speculated on the origin and distribution of extinct and living organisms. Today, we accept the theory of continental drift, but it was not until after World War II that scientists around the world began to amass powerful evidence to support plate tectonics. Without this knowledge, the origin and distribution of living organisms would be a complete mystery, and we would be unable to explain why marsupials are common in Australia but only one is found in North America. We could only speculate why similar fossil leaves have been found in Antarctica, other southern continents, and India! Knowing the history of life on earth is crucial to understanding wildlife issues of the present.

All life on earth lives within a 20-km band that stretches around the earth. Living organisms have been found from the bottom of the ocean floor to about 9 km altitude. Yet 95% of all life lives within a 5-km band. If the earth was a basketball, life would exist in a band on its surface no wider than a human hair. Thus, it is not hard to see that if the basketball were to end up resting on a patch of snow, life on the cold side of the sphere would be forced to endure or perish. By far the most significant factor causing long-term changes in the distribution and abundance of life is the slow movement of the land masses as they journey across the surface of the earth. This movement in turn causes climatic shifts, alters ocean currents, and creates new challenges for organisms.

Although on a human time scale the positions of the continents are static, clear evidence abounds to support the theory that the earth's surface is truly in a dynamic state. The San Andreas fault in California is a striking feature of the landscape running roughly north–south. Land west of the fault is slowly, inexorably moving northward while land to the east of the fault is moving westward. Earthquakes are common around the globe and are located along certain fault lines that correspond to the nine major plates, as shown in Figure 6.1. The continents are riding on these plates. Sea floor spreading is the mechanism for the moving continents. What's more, we can calculate just how fast the continents are spreading.

Even the most casual observer can scarcely mistake the features of eastern South America, western Africa, eastern North America, and western Europe.

FIGURE 6.1   Tectonic plates (solid lines), major trenches (dashed lines), and direction of movement.

These regions appear as though they were once joined together. The fossil evidence shared by the regions that once abutted suggests that Brazil in South America and the western equator of Africa were joined 65 million years ago (MYA), as were North America and Europe. They are now about 2000 miles or 3000 km apart. We can therefore calculate that the rate of spreading is about 6 mm per year. The mid-Atlantic ridge that runs between the continents is spreading them apart by forcing new land outward from beneath the ocean floor. As new sea floor appears, so must existing land disappear. Indeed, as the subcontinent of India crashes into the Eurasian continent, the Himalayan mountain chain is growing, while part of India is disappearing beneath the plate on which part of Asia rides.

But why is plate tectonics important? Why is biogeography relevant? Isn't it enough to know that elephants are found in Africa and Asia and not in North America? Let's suppose that you were alive a mere 10,000 years ago and that you were employed as a park ranger. North America was in the grip of an ice age that was aging rapidly. The peninsula of Florida was about three times as wide as it is today because sea level was about 100 m lower than at present. You have been given the task of establishing a large national park to be called Pleistocene National Park in peninsular Florida. The park is to hold in perpetuity a representative sample of the great megafauna of North America that existed at that time. The park will include 3-m-tall giant beavers, mastodons and mammoths easily as big as present-day elephants, giant ground sloths 5 m tall and tipping the scales at 3000 kg, and short-nosed bears bigger than Florida black bears of today and much faster runners. Your park will include much of the past coastal plain and border the Gulf of Mexico on the west coast of Florida. What would be your advice to your supervisors regarding the establishment of the park? How would you use the scientific method to support your arguments? Is biogeographic history of any use in your arguments?

A BRIEF HISTORY OF THE PHYSICAL EARTH

The approximate accepted age of the earth is about 4.5 billion years, based on analysis of the rate of radioactive decay of uranium and thorium. The oldest known basalt outcrops are about 4 billion years. The oldest known fossils are about 3.4 billion years. Various other techniques are used to date rocks and fossils. For instance, the direction of minute iron particles within igneous rocks as they formed can be measured quite accurately. These particles tended to align along the earth's magnetic field when the rocks cooled. Since these rocks have been moving throughout time, the direction they now point to does not align with the earth's magnetic field. Depending on the strata where a fossil is located, specific types of radioactive decay products can be assessed.

No history of the earth can be given without the aid of the geologic time scale, and none can be appreciated without showing the relationships of the continents. As scientists venture into the deep past, the reconstruction of the positions of the continents becomes less clear. Nevertheless, much work has been done around the world to reconstruct the geologic history of the earth. Plate tectonics have been operating for at least 2 billion years. By 375 MYA, during the Devonian, the Age of Fishes, life was well developed in the continental seas and on land. There were no flowering plants at that time, but vegetation covered the land. The continents were closer together than today and they were moving even closer. The continents we know as Africa and South America had been joined together since deep time and remained joined. About 325 MYA, in the Carboniferous, the continent we now call North America

abutted Africa. India was located east of Madagascar. In the late Carboniferous, a Southern Hemisphere glaciation occurred that is evident in the fossil
record of *Glossopteris* flora of the southern land masses. The Carboniferous
period is important to us today because our coal and oil deposits date back to
this time.

About 275 MYA, during the Permian period, the continents came together
once again to form the supercontinent of Pangaea, consisting of Gondwana in
the south and Laurasia in the north. As the supercontinent moved slowly northward, the ice cap melted. Although there are many puzzles yet to be worked
out, and new theories may suggest otherwise, Pangaea existed throughout the
Triassic and began breaking up about 200 MYA, in the late Jurassic. To be
sure, life thrived and was well developed. The continental shelf was full of life
and large lizards roamed the earth during this Age of Dinosaurs (Gould 1993).

Africa and South America had been joined for at least 400 million years,
and now they were slowly torn apart. During the Cretaceous period, about 100
MYA, flowering plants appeared, insect diversity exploded, and the continents
that we know and recognize today assumed their forms. India separated from
Madagascar and began its long journey northward. Humans appeared only
about 4 MYA, when all the continents were in place just as they are today.

PLEISTOCENE CLIMATES AND THE
MILANKOVIC CYCLES: WHERE WE ARE TODAY

In 1837, Louis Agassiz, president of the Swiss Society of Natural Sciences,
presented a paper at the annual meeting on the possible origin of erratics (ir-
regular large boulders strewn across landscape). Agassiz, a creationist, believed
that erratics were actually transported by glaciers. When the ice retreated, the
erratics were left behind. The popular idea developed by Lyell was that ice-
bergs had transported the erratics during the Great Flood. Needless to say,
Agassiz failed miserably to convince his colleagues and after several years
returned to his work on fossil fish.

Late in 1846, Agassiz sailed to Boston and in 1847 was offered a profes-
sorship at Harvard University. He found that his glacial theory had preceded
him. Indeed, shortly after his 1837 address, several American geologists delivered talks in America offering supporting evidence of ice age glaciers. Agassiz
never left Harvard, and by the mid-1860s the glacial theory was accepted in
both Europe and America. Now the most difficult task remained—figuring out
what had caused the glaciers, why they retreated, how many times in the past
they had occurred, and whether they would appear again.

Physical evidence continued to accumulate in Europe and North America. Agassiz himself found evidence of glaciations in South America. James Croll (1821–1890), a Scotsman, proposed in 1864 what became know as the Astronomical Theory of glaciation. More than a century earlier, the famous French mathematician Jean le Rond d'Alembert showed that the earth's axis rotated in a circular path that required 26,000 years to complete. He also showed that independently the tilt of the earth's axis varied about 1.5 degrees on either side of its average angle of 23.5 degrees. This cycle was 22,000 years. Croll knew these facts, and French astronomer Urbain Leverrier (1811–1877) had recently shown that the elongation of the earth's orbit, the orbital eccentricity, slowly changed from nearly circular to elliptical. It took Leverrier ten years to complete his calculations and he used information on the seven known planets. So meticulous were his calculations that they led to the discovery of Neptune. Note that none of the calculations could have been made were it not for the work of Newton.

Croll reasoned that one hemisphere or the other would experience an ice age whenever the earth's orbit was highly elliptical and the winter solstice occurred far from the sun. Croll predicted that ice ages would last 10,000 years and occur first in one hemisphere and then another in response to the 22,000-year processional cycle. According to Croll, the glacial epoch began about 250,000 years ago and ended 80,000 years ago. Since then, there would have been no ice age because of the highly circular orbit. Later he included the tilt of the earth's axis in his theory and refined his predictions and timetable for ice ages. He published *Climate and Time* in 1875.

Finally scientists had a theory from which to make predictions that could be tested. During the last quarter of the 19th century, the glacial theory of Croll was hotly debated and tested. By 1894, American geologists had accumulated enough evidence to disregard Croll's glacial theory. The bulk of substantive evidence suggested that the last ice age ended not 80,000 years in the past but between 10,000 and 15,000 years ago. Meanwhile, the Europeans favored Croll's explanation, but as time went on and the century ended, Europeans too accepted that the last glaciation had ended relatively recently. The bulk of scientific evidence was against Croll, who fortunately did not live long enough to see his theory relegated to the dustbin—almost.

The stage was set for Milutin Milankovitch (1879–1958), a Serbian mathematician and professor of applied mathematics at the University of Belgrade. Milankovitch resolved to calculate the solar radiation impinging on the surface of Earth, Mars, and Venus. He also realized that Adhemar and Croll, both pioneers of astronomical theories of climate variation, did not possess the mathematical skills necessary to calculate solar effects accurately. Had

Milankovitch realized that such a task would require his entire professional lifetime, he might have decided otherwise (Imbrie and Imbrie 1979).

Fortunately, Ludwig Pilgrim, a German mathematician, had worked out the three principal properties of the earth (eccentricity, precession, and tilt) he required to begin his investigations. The amount of solar radiation falling on the earth's surface is a function of the earth's distance from the sun and the angle the sun's rays strike the surface. Thus, Milankovitch realized that it would be simple, in principle, to complete his tasks. In 1914, Milankovitch published a report entitled "On the Problem of the Astronomical Theory of the Ice Ages" in which he showed that solar radiation was more important than Croll had appreciated.

A few years later, he was a prisoner of war but was placed in the custody of a fellow mathematician in Budapest. There he continued to work on his theory of earth's climate and also that of Mars and Venus. He published his results in 1920 and showed mathematically that variations in the three fundamental properties of the earth's orbital parameters were sufficient to produce ice ages. Moreover, he had developed formulas to calculate the amount of solar radiation impinging on any part of the earth at any time, past, present, or future. Later he collaborated with Alfred Wegener and Wegener's father-in-law, the widely respected German climatologist Vladimir Köppen (1846–1940).

Basically, a decrease in the tilt of the earth's axis causes a decrease in the amount of solar insolation (incoming radiation). A decrease in the distance between the earth and the sun obviously causes an increase in solar insolation. The tilt cycle was now well known to be 41,000 years, and precession was acting on a 22,000-year cycle. Furthermore, the influences of these two parameters vary in latitude, due to a strong influence in the high latitudes by the tilt cycle. Finally, Milankovitch was able to predict mathematically the altitude of the snowline based upon the solar insolation.

Once again the scientific method could be used to make predictions from Milankovitch's theory. Naturally, by the mid-1950s the theory was in jeopardy of rejection by the scientific community. The most damning evidence came from a new method of dating fossils called radiocarbon dating. Geologists used radiocarbon dating in America and Europe to discredit the theory because evidence for several glacial advances over the past 80,000 years had been shown, whereas the Milankovitch theory explained only one. However, radiocarbon dating is accurate only to 40,000 years ago. By 1969, however, the Milankovitch theory was not taken seriously.

With improvements in dating techniques, geologists again were able to explore the deeper past. Indeed, important sea level rises occurred 125,000,

105,000, and 82,000 years ago. Modifications in the effect of the earth's precession were made in Milankovitch's mathematical formulas to match the geologic facts. Cores from the ocean depths supported the Milankovitch theory. An article published in *Science* in 1976 declared that variations in the earth's orbit were indeed the cause of the ice ages, and Milankovitch's theory is accepted today.

We now know that the average temperature is rising. This rise has been linked to human use of fossil fuels. Whether this rise in temperature will be enough to prevent the next ice age is not clear. What is clear is that a few decades after the discovery of the Milankovitch cycles, a new and more powerful force can influence the global climate.

The long journey of the land masses across the face of the earth continues today, and the effects are no less fundamental. Just as islands are born and invaded by life, so too can life be wiped clean when an island volcano explodes, as Krakatau did off the coast of Java. The major fault zones around the world threaten human creations; we are in the middle of a glacial period, and rising sea levels will consume coastal cities unless the northern polar ice cap begins expanding. CO_2 levels are increasing and the global average temperature is rising. Variability of local climates is increasing. Volcanoes in Indonesia, mud slides in South America, and tidal waves occur yearly. Humans call these events disasters, yet they are fundamental disturbances that have shaped and tested life throughout the earth's history. Now humans are creating disturbances that are influencing the global climate and, without doubt, these influences must be factored into our investigation of issues affecting wildlife.

EXERCISES

6.1 Using the World Wide Web, do a search on "climate change" and prepare a summary of the issues climate change raises.

6.2 Run a search on "volcanoes" on the World Wide Web and summarize the results. How can volcanoes play an important role in climate change? Are low-latitude, high-aerosol volcanoes important?

6.3 Run a search using "biogeography" and "zoogeography" as separate keywords. Summarize the results.

6.4 Use the keywords "Miocene," "Eocene," "Pleistocene," and "Holocene" to run searches. What comes up?

6.5 Run a search on "El Nino" and summarize what you learn.

6.6 Is plate tectonics a theory or a fact? How can we prove that the laws of physics were applicable 2 billion years ago?

6.7 Is there a journal dedicated to studying plate tectonics? What are some of the recent research topics?

LITERATURE CITED

Gould, S.J. (Ed.). 1993. *The Book of Life*. W.W. Norton, New York.

Imbrie, J. and K.P. Imbrie. 1979. *Ice Ages*. Harvard University Press, Cambridge, Massachusetts.

ORIGIN AND
DISTRIBUTION OF
BIODIVERSITY

7

E.O. Wilson (1988) wrote about the amount of biological diversity. There are about 750,000 insects, 43,000 vertebrates, and 250,000 plants that have been classified. Of the vertebrates, 4200 are mammals, 9000 are birds, 6300 are reptiles, 4200 are amphibians, 18,000 are bony fishes, and 900 are jawless fishes and cartilaginous fishes. Add to this number sponges, nematodes, algae, fungi, bacteria, mollusks, and arthropods and the total comes to about 1.5 million known species. We have already seen that within-species diversity is enormous as well. What is even more astounding is that Wilson estimates there may be from 5 million to 30 million species worldwide. In short, humans have only begun to appreciate the number of species that coexist on planet earth.

These numbers seem bewildering, especially to people living in temperate North America. Whereas some forests in North America have perhaps a dozen or so species of tree, on the island of Borneo there may be 500 species of tree *per hectare*. And since each different tree has its own peculiar community of insects, the number of animals inhabiting these highly diverse forests is as yet unknown. How do we measure such biodiversity? How do we begin to organize our understanding? The patterns of distribution and abundance we see in nature now are the result of the past history of life on earth.

Raven (1994) suggests that biodiversity is the sum total of genetic variation and the interactions of all living organisms on earth, or in a particular area. The term biodiversity is a way of encompassing, in a single word, all of life's history and complexity on earth. Raven estimates that between two-thirds and

135

three-fourths of all species on earth occur somewhere in the tropics, and more than half live in tropical rain forests. Yet rain forests occupy only 7% of the earth's terrestrial surface, and this amount is decreasing.

Many oddities confound the modern observer of wildlife distributions. For instance, fossilized leaves of the so-called *Glossopteris* flora (Schopf 1970, Brown and Gibson 1983) have been found in Permian deposits in Antarctica, South America, Africa, India, Australia, and Papua New Guinea. Hence the evidence suggests that either this ancient conifer-like form somehow rafted to many southern continents and India or that these land masses were once much closer together. Indeed, we now know that these land masses were at one time a single continent called Gondwana. To understand more clearly the present distribution of life on earth, we must understand the distribution and abundance of life throughout the history of the earth (McKinney 1993). From life's earliest beginnings, the dynamic nature of the earth has carried life along, and life has modified the land, sea, and atmosphere so as to sustain and promote life. In short, we cannot fully understand and appreciate the present distribution and abundance of living organisms without knowing how things got to where they are today.

THE ORIGIN OF BIODIVERSITY

Paleozoic: Old Life

The famous paleontologist G.G. Simpson (1969) wrote: "The existence of a natural community, or ecosystem, is the result of evolution." Evolution is responsible for biodiversity. Certainly evolution is driven, in part, by the dynamic geological phenomenon of plate tectonics. After all, *Glossopteris* flora rode into the Northern Hemisphere on India. Here, we are interested in understanding the evolution of life and how past changes in the distribution of organisms have determined present distributions. Indeed, today even the most casual observer notices that the distribution of most living organisms is limited. No species, save humans and their parasites, are cosmopolitan.

Life is hypothesized to have started about 3.5 billion years ago (BYA), when the atmosphere of the earth consisted of methane, carbon dioxide, and gaseous nitrogen compounds—an atmosphere that would poison life today. Bacterial communities consisting of cyanobacteria that could photosynthesize are known today as fossilized stromatolites. Limestone stromatolites are found on nearly every continent. Those in Australia are found along the seacoast and look like large stone toadstools. These cyanobacteria expelled poisonous oxygen as a waste product. About 2 BYA, iron began to rust as the oxygen content of the primitive atmosphere began to rise. Bacteria were oxidizing the earth, beginning with the ocean. Once the iron supply of earth was reduced, the atmospheric oxygen content rose further. By the time earth was 2.5 billion years old, life had transformed the atmosphere and the stage was set for an explosion of biological activity. From simple bacteria, more complex life forms developed.

About 800 million years ago (MYA), the supercontinent of Pangaea, which had merged from separate land masses, began to break up. The earth's surface has never stopped moving. The earliest animals are 580- to 560-million-year-old Cambrian rocks that hold fossils of arthropods, brachiopods, mollusks, and others known as metazoans. From these beginnings arose the first life forms that can be easily recognized with the unaided eye. An explosion in shells and skeletons of calcium carbonate and silica occurred as life continued to evolve. Some 500 MYA, the Cambrian ended with marine organisms having diversified into gastropods that today include snails, cephalopods with their single shell (whose only example today is the nautilus), and echinoderms, such as sea lilies, on stalks attached to the sea bottom in the inner tidal zones.

The Ordovician land mass locations were nothing like the land mass locations today. Laurentia was an isolated continent. Gondwana included Australia, Antarctica, India, Africa, and South America. Other massive islands existed where none are found today. Marine life expanded its ecological range and continued to diversify. Hinged shells evolved during this time. Starfish evolved as well, preying on shelled mollusks attached to rocks. Sponges, corals, snails, bryozoans, and many other creatures populated nearshore coasts. However, the end of the Ordovician was marked in the fossil record when some 70% of marine species disappeared. For sea creatures, this was a mass extinction, perhaps the second most all-encompassing setback. Entire reef-constructing communities disappeared from the fossil record. The emerged land masses were on the move into less favorable positions on the globe. The megacontinent of Gondwana had now drifted over the South Pole. With so much of the earth's land mass crowded around the South Pole, a great ice sheet formed, the seas cooled, and polar faunas grew within 10 degrees of the equator. The expansive ice cap sequestered water and global sea levels fell, exposing Laurentia's surrounding coral reefs. Toward the end of the Ordovician, the polar ice caps melted as land masses drifted away from the South Pole. Sea levels again rose and drowned coastal flora and fauna.

The Silurian began about 438 MYA and lasted only 30 million years. The first plants moved onto land during this time. They were simple forms, such as *Cooksonia,* that had vascular conducting strands to carry water and nutrients through the stem. Fish began to diversify, and toward the end of the Silurian, the fossil record contains jawless armored fishes less than 20 cm in length. Sea life was beginning to explore greater depths.

The Devonian began about 408 MYA with the reappearance of reef communities of corals, sponges, brachiopods, bryozoans, and echinoderms. According to Cox and Moore (1994), separate floras and fish faunas can be distinguished in different parts of the world as it was then. Amphibians, the first land vertebrates, emerged during the late Devonian, and the first reptiles evolved from amphibians. The key to success on land was the evolution of the hard-shelled egg that freed the land-dwelling reptiles from the necessity of having to return to water to lay their eggs. Fossils suggest that these land creatures first evolved on the continent of Laurentia, which had been located on the equator. The Devonian also saw an explosive radiation of land plants, no doubt affecting the global climate by reducing *albedo*, or reflectance, of the earth's surface and also reducing the CO_2 content of the atmosphere further still. The Devonian closed with another mass extinction.

The next period in the history of life began about 360 MYA with the Carboniferous period and lasted until 286 MYA. During this time, terrestrial life forms diversified and multiplied. Trees, ferns, insects, dragonflies, and amphibians were common. However, life had not been freed from its aquatic past. All amphibians must return to the water to lay their eggs. The land masses of the Carboniferous were coming together again. Africa and South America were connected, and North America abutted Africa. India, Antarctica, Australia, and Europe were all close to Africa and each other. Africa was traveling northward to its present position on the globe. The Carboniferous forests were lush and green in the lowland swamps and estuarine areas that were routinely inundated by the sea.

Cockroaches, spiders, scorpions, and centipedes were thriving in the green regions of earth. The southern part of the Gondwana was glaciated extensively. Central and Southern Africa, most of South America, and all of Australia were covered with ice at one time during the Carboniferous. Our vast coal deposits of today date back to the Carboniferous period. Major coal deposits today are found in what is called Laurasia—the eastern United States, Europe, Siberia, China, and part of Australia—which is presumed to have been more tropical. These tropical forests provided suitable habitat for the amphibians and reptiles.

Laurasia lay on the equator, and the seas were rich with life. Sharks hunted the waters; starfish, gastropods, crinoids, corals, and sea urchins would be familiar to us. The bony fishes were evolving as well and competing for space. Indeed, these bony fishes make up 90% of all fish today. Most of the fish at this time were bony fishes, but a second group, the lobe-finned fishes, were also present. Although unimportant during the Carboniferous, the lobe-finned fishes had great evolutionary significance. They were the vanguard for the invasion of land. Those lobed fins were supported structurally with bone and were the forerunner to legs. Several reptile groups are known from the Carboniferous as well.

The Paleozoic era closed with the Permian period, which began 286 MYA and ended 245 MYA. During this time, the continents were moving closer together than in the Carboniferous period. Laurasia and Gondwana merged to become Pangaea. The vast ice cap that had formed during the Carboniferous began to shrink. The northern parts of Pangaea became hotter and drier, and the great wet forests of Laurentia began to dry out. The mosses, horsetails, and other wet-adapted flora were replaced by conifers, cycads, ginkgoes, and seed ferns—gymnosperms. The Gondwana ice cap completely disappeared during the Permian and *Glossopteris* spread throughout the southern land mass. Rich beds of fossil amphibians and reptiles are found in the Permian basin of Texas.

The end of the Permian period and the Paleozoic era was also the end of ancient life on earth. The Paleozoic ended with the most devastating mass extinction ever. Nearly 75% of all amphibians and reptiles were erased from the annals of life. Trilobites, perhaps the most familiar fossils, were never to occur again. Some 50% of all marine families were wiped out. Many of the forms that survived have never fully recovered their former glory. The assembly of the land masses of earth into the supercontinent Pangaea is believed to have precipitated the mass extinctions. Volcanoes, falling sea levels, global climate change, and the creation of a single land mass giving rise to a single global ocean all have been suggested as possible causes of the mass extinctions. Using the number of extant families as a measure, life was set back to mid Ordovician times—a setback of some 300 million years.

Mesozoic: Middle Life

The Triassic period lasted from 245 MYA to 208 MYA. The supercontinent Pangaea was at its maximum contiguous size at about the middle of the Triassic. With the exception of ferns, most of the forests from which coal would eventually form were gone. The extant reptiles of the Triassic are the thecodonts, the precursors of the dinosaurs. The earliest recognizable frogs (order Anura) from the early Triassic are found in Madagascar and became more common in the fossil record throughout time. The Karroo, an arid region in South Africa, is known for the number of Triassic fossils discovered there. Among the fossils are the therapsids, mammal-like reptiles of both carnivorous and herbivorous forms.

Since the continents abutted, there existed a single global ocean. A large finger of ocean, the Tethys Seaway, penetrated the land. On the vast shoreline and in the warm seas, sea life slowly recovered. Large reptiles, such as ichthyosaurs, efficient swimming reptiles, caught fish, and placondonts, with their specialized jaws and teeth, grazed on mollusks by first stripping the creatures from the rocks and then crushing them with powerful jaws and plate-like teeth. The fish so common in today's waters were but an unimportant group in the Triassic. Significantly, it was during the Triassic that the archosaurs were undergoing a transformation from what Gould (1993) refers to as "a sprawling gait," such as that of a modern crocodile, to "an erect gait," like that of the much later Tyrannosaurs. Changes in the skeletal structure allowed some groups to walk upright.

The reptiles we refer to as dinosaurs appeared in the latter half of the Triassic, along with several other important groups. The first turtles appeared, as well as the first crocodilians, pterosaurs, and mammals. The Paleozoic reptiles were gone, and many of the forms we see today have their origin in the late Triassic. Birds, however, had to wait another 40 million years to appear.

From 208 MYA to 114 MYA, during the Jurassic and all through the Cretaceous, ending 65 MYA, the dinosaurs flourished. Cycads, ferns, and ginkgoes diversified while seed ferns disappeared. Conifers also diversified, and the angiosperms (the flowering plants) radiated gloriously about 150 MYA during the Jurassic, replacing the gymnosperms as the earth's dominant vegetation. Crocodiles of the Jurassic would be familiar to us, but other inhabitants would not. The theropods (*Tyrannosaurus rex*), sauropods (*Brontosaurus*), ornithopods (duck-billed dinosaurs such as Tsintaosaurus), ceratopsians (*Triceratops*), stegosaurs (*Stegasaurus*), and ankylosaurs (heavy club tails) were true dinosaurs that spread across the earth.

During the Jurassic, Pangaea started breaking up, and by the mid-Cretaceous (100 MYA), the land masses were separate and their trajectories were carrying them into their present positions. South America had just separated from Africa and was on a westward trajectory. Africa was moving slowly northward and rotating slightly into its place on the present globe. India was accelerating northward but was still just north of Antarctica. Europe had barely separated from North America. Pangaea had broken up—again. There is little doubt the continents will once again come together and give rise to another Pangaea in the distant future.

The flying reptiles, pterosaurs, are known from early and middle Jurassic fossils. These were the first vertebrates to be freed from terrestrial life. The oldest known reptilian flyer was *Eudimorphodon*, a fish-eating form with a 1-m wingspan. The pterosaurs consisted of two highly differentiated groups. The rhamphoryncoids had a tail and a toothed beak, while the pterodactyloids lacked these features. Some of these flying reptiles were adapted to catching insects on the wing.

Perhaps the best-known bird fossil ever found is of Archaeopteryx, discovered in 150-million-year-old limestone in Bavaria, Germany. Archaeopteryx had more dinosaur affinities than modern bird attributes. For instance, it had teeth, a heavy skull, a long slender tail, and long fingers which modern birds lack. Modern birds also have large wishbones; Archaeoptryx had a reptilian wishbone. Indeed, it was classified as a meat-eating reptile for many years before it was re-examined and found to have feathers.

The explosive radiation of the angiosperms about 100 MYA during the Cretaceous gave rise to an increase in insect diversification. With the large variety of plants and flowers, and differing climatic conditions, the insects speciated. Bees are known to have originated during the Cretaceous, for instance, with the radiation of flowering plants.

Mammals were an unimportant group during the Jurassic and Cretaceous. They arose from therapsid reptiles, mammal-like reptiles in the Triassic. The earliest true mammals were the morganucodontids. These diminutive creatures were as small as present-day shrews, probably nocturnal, and insectivorous. They are presumed to have laid eggs. Before the end of the Cretaceous, mammals evolved into three groups that still exist today: monotremes, marsupials, and placentals. Some groups such as the multituberculates, for instance, radiated and existed for 160 million years before disappearing. The most primitive group, the monotremes, still lays eggs. However, even by the end of the Cretaceous, many mammals were delivering live young.

The end of the Mesozoic era and the Cretaceous 65 MYA came with yet another mass extinction. No dinosaur fossils are known beyond this time. Other forms such as flying reptiles and large marine animals died out as well. Compared to the Permian extinctions, only 70% of all species died out. All the surviving animals were small, including the mammals. Many floral species passed into extinction.

What caused the so-called K-T (Cretaceous-Tertiary, the next geological period) extinction? Alvarez et al. (1980) suggested that a meteorite 10 km in diameter struck the earth and led directly to the mass extinction. The fossil record shows that within a few years, 70% of all species vanished forever. The evidence was based solely on the discovery of an iridium layer in Cretaceous rock in Italy. Iridium is exceedingly rare on earth but is a common element found in meteorites (that is, meteors that strike the earth). Alvarez and his team suggested that this iridium layer would be found around the world and was caused by an extraterrestrial object impacting the earth.

Since 1980, evidence has continued to accumulate which indeed shows that iridium is found in a layer around the earth. If a meteorite of the size Alvarez and his team suggested did strike the earth, an enormous amount of dust and debris would be thrown into the atmosphere. In a few days, most of the heavier particles would have fallen back to the ground; however, the lighter aerosols would have remained suspended in the upper atmosphere. High-aerosol, low-latitude volcanoes such as Mount Pinetubo reduced temperatures worldwide. The K-T meteor would have had a similar but extensive effect. The dust cloud would have blackened the sky, especially in the tropics. Photosynthesis would have been interrupted, causing the death of plants in a few weeks. Global temperatures would have dropped, more so in the tropics than in the higher latitudes, but most life is in the tropics. There would have been a crash in animal populations as large animals died out first across the globe. Smaller flesh eaters would have survived somewhat longer, feasting on the dead.

Other meteor impacts have been recorded without causing global extinctions. However, these impacts were in Canada and Siberia, both high-latitude locations. Similarly, Mount Saint Helens exploded, throwing smoke and ash into the atmosphere. Obviously, the earth's global inhabitants did not suffer. However, volcanoes like El Chichon did lower global temperatures. El Chichon was a high-aerosol, low-latitude volcano. In contrast, Mount Saint Helens was a high-latitude, low-aerosol volcano. In any case, most scientists agree with the meteorite hypothesis, and the impact crater is believed to be located on the coast of the Yucatan Peninsula in the Gulf of Mexico. The mass extinctions of the K-T boundary once again wiped away a majority of the earth's inhabitants and species. The continents were separated and moving apart. Whatever survived the K-T boundary would be the precursors of life on the separate continents for 65 million years.

Cenozoic: New Life

The Cretaceous period lasted nearly 80 million years and ended abruptly with an extinction spasm. The Tertiary period of the Cenozoic era began 65 MYA with the Paleocene epoch and lasted a mere 8 million years. Evidence of possible mammals as far back as the Triassic period (about 220 MYA) shows that these proto-mammals were small creatures—much smaller than the dinosaurs with which they co-existed. Certainly, true mammals existed by 210 MYA in the Triassic. True birds evolved about 60 million years after mammals, around 150 MYA. However, with the K-T extinctions, the playing field was wide open. The multituberculate mammals had made it thus far.

Mammals that made it through the K-T boundary now radiated to fill new niches left by their extinct competitors. Marsupials, placentals, multituberculates, and monotremes all were extant forms. The continents were moving into their present positions; however, India and Australia were noticeably out of place. The global climate was warmer and damper than today. Most mammals, although strange, would be recognizable herbivores, carnivores, or insectivores. Regional differences began to show in the fossil record. Since the continents were moving apart, it is not surprising that different forms were evolving according to differing climates and other ecological opportunities. The Eocene epoch began 57 MYA and lasted until 34 MYA. India was midway on its journey to Asia, and Australia and New Guinea were approaching their present positions. Many living orders and even families of mammals trace their ancestors to the Eocene. Indeed, Gould (1993) points out that three living orders of today arose in the Eocene. The Chiroptera (bats) arose in the early Eocene, while Cetacea (whales) and Sirenia (sea cows and manatees) arose in the late Eocene. Early primates also appeared in the Eocene. The important point to realize is the continents had split apart and were moving into place. Mammals were radiating from archaic stocks *in situ*. Whereas Australia had many marsupials, primates occurred in North America.

Climate change in the late Eocene forced tropical vegetation to the lower latitudes, and conifer forests spread in the high latitudes in response to colder temperatures. The late Eocene saw the loss of many ancient forms of mammals. The multituberculates died out, ending a 160-million-year existence—by far the most successful mammalian group ever to have existed. Not all groups retreated, however. Rodents, for instance, radiated and in sheer numbers of species comprise one-fifth of all present-day mammals. In the Oligocene epoch, 34 MYA to 23 MYA, the earth was cooler than previously and the temperate forests ruled the high latitudes in both hemispheres. Strange camel-like mammals roamed North America but later went extinct. The earliest seal comes from the Oligocene. Around 23 MYA, the Miocene began during a period of mountain building. India was crashing into Asia, creating the Himalayas, which are still growing today.

A warming trend expanded the tropical forests, and mammals thrived in the rich coastal waters. Whales radiated during this time. Africa made contact with Europe, and mammals crossed between the two continents. The Proboscideans existed in three groups: deinotheres, mastodonts, and gomphotheres. Ancient horses radiated spectacularly and spread across the Northern Hemisphere during the Miocene. Cats such as the saber-toothed machairodontids were present, and fossils have been found in North America. The Miocene epoch lasted until only 5 MYA. About 11 MYA, North America was much like the Serengeti of Africa is today, with an array of different herbivores and carnivores.

The Pliocene epoch lasted from 5 MYA to 1.8 MYA. During this time, the earth grew cooler and drier. Grasslands grew more extensive and more treeless plains came into existence. Mammal diversity decreased due to a less diverse environment. North America lost most of its Miocene fauna and during the Pleistocene epoch lost some 54 large mammals over 45 kg. The megafauna of North America were gone before modern humans could enjoy them. The Florida peninsula was about three times as wide during the glacial period as it is today. It was also an area of high vertebrate biodiversity. An alternating sequence of glaciers now grips the earth, and we are currently enjoying an interglacial period. Both the Indian subcontinent and Africa support a large complement of megafauna similar to what North America contained only 12,000 years ago. Now that the polar ice cap has retreated, two-thirds of what was Florida is underwater.

The disappearance of the North American megafauna from across the continent is perplexing. Some have suggested that climate change is responsible. Others note that around this time, humans spread across the continent and into South America. For whatever reason, the megafauna—the mastodon and mammoth, the tapir and camel, the cheetah and lion, the giant ground sloth, the giant beaver, the four-horned pronghorn antelope, the short-faced bear, two species of bison, the saber-toothed cat, and the teratorn (a giant bird)—all are gone from North America. Some lament their passing.

MODERN DISTRIBUTION AND ABUNDANCE

Looking outside your window, you may see trees and squirrels or perhaps cactus and birds. They did not just happen by one day. Their distribution is the result of the entire past history of life, at least 600 million years of life, before they arrived as ancestors of the riders on the continents before them. The distribution and abundance of living things is controlled by many factors. For instance, Birch (1957) suggests that "weather is a component of the environment of animals which effectively determines the limits to distribution and the abundance of some species." There is no doubt that weather plays a vital role in affecting the geographical limits of species from plants to animals. Competition between species also plays a role, as do predation, food resources, a place to live and reproduce, and a host of other biological and physical factors. Huston (1994) summarized landscape patterns of species distributions and biological diversity. The fastest rates of change result from mortality-causing disturbances, such as fires or volcanic eruptions. Moderate rates of change result from vegetation changes. Slow change occurs as a result of gradual processes, such as natural climate change, or soil development processes. Finally, the slowest changes are caused by geologic processes of plate tectonics and the movement of land masses. Currently, the earth's biota is undergoing a rapid change.

Today, wildlife across the globe is under immense pressure, principally from direct and indirect human causes. For many species, extinction is a real possibility as their populations become ever more fragmented and isolated. Ecological processes such as the monarch butterfly migration are also threatened. As we have just seen, there have been many extinctions in the fossil record. Indeed, many periods and eras in the earth's history are divided by these so-called mass extinctions, yet life has always recovered and continued to diversify, always reaching higher levels of previous diversity. In one instance, 300 million years was required to attain the former diversity, but life, if nothing else, is tenacious. After all, it led to the evolution of humans in spite of mass extinctions and catastrophic losses of biodiversity. Indeed, it is because of these mass extinctions that we even have humans on earth! Extinction is, without doubt, the ultimate fate of all species, including humans.

Today, we read about this or that species going extinct. We do not even have a verb form of the adjective "extinct." It must be that humans have little interest in the final event of the last member of a species. We will never see the passenger pigeon again, yet as little as 80 years ago flocks turned the sky black. We will never hear the high notes of the Carolina parakeet, yet just 100 years ago it was a common winter migrant to Florida. The ivory-billed woodpecker must have been a spectacular bird to see, its bright ivory-white bill gleaming in the sun. The dusky seaside sparrow is another bird gone in our lifetime. These are just a few of the creatures we will never enjoy. But extinction is normal. Indeed, 99.9% of all species ever to have lived are extinct! What, then, is the big deal? It is the rate of extinction around the world that has attracted attention.

Pimm et. al. (1995) suggest that recent extinction rates are 100 to 1000 times their pre-human levels in well-understood diverse groups of organisms from many different environments. The ultimate fate of every species is to evolve into a new form and hence become extinct, but Wilson (1988) warns that:

> The current reduction of diversity seems destined to approach that of the great natural catastrophes at the end of the Paleozoic and Mesozoic eras—in other words, the most extreme in the past 65 million years. In at least one important respect the modern episode exceeds anything in the geological past. In the earlier mass extinctions, which some scientists believe were caused by large meteorite strikes, most of the plants survived even though animal diversity

was severely reduced. Now, for the first time, plant diversity is declining sharply.

Some argue that since extinctions have been part of life's history, we should not be concerned about modern extinctions. Some insects, such as mosquitoes and malaria-causing flies, and some viruses, like the HIV and Ebola viruses, they say, should be driven to extinction. Certainly both camps can agree that extinction is a wildlife issue.

Humans depend on biodiversity to sustain them. Indeed, humans arose in a diverse world, not in a depaurate one. The fruit and grains we consume are but a tiny fraction of all that we might one day utilize. Babbitt (1995) suggests that we do not need more laws to protect biodiversity. "Eco-showdowns" must be avoided because they polarize people, making a compromise difficult to achieve. In the same article, Babbitt, as secretary of the interior, announced the formation of the National Biological Service (NBS). In late 1995, the U.S. Congress demoted the service to a department under the U.S. Geological Survey. The new mission for the NBS was to "examine the status and trends for all U.S. wildlife habitats." Its budget was cut by 25% to $146 million, a fraction of what it takes to run a single government weapons laboratory.

There are about 270 million people living in the United States. Before Europeans arrived, there were about 12 million Native Americans. Since European arrival, more than 90% of the tallgrass prairies, 55% of wetlands, 26% of all forests, 50% of tropical forests, and 75% of all old-growth forests have been destroyed. Since 1620, over 500 species and subspecies of native plants and animals have been erased forever. According to Raven (1988), the earth may be losing 100 species per day. One way to preserve biodiversity and mitigate wildlife issues is through private sector initiatives (Edwards 1995). We will discuss this further in Chapter 17.

EXERCISES

7.1 Do a search on the World Wide Web using the keywords "biodiversity" and "biological diversity" to look for interesting wildlife issues. Summarize your results.

7.2 Look for the Econet site on the World Wide Web. Identify countries that seem to have an interest in wildlife issues. Which countries are represented on the World Wide Web?

7.3 Run a search on "Pangaea" and "Gondwana" using your favorite search engine. What comes up?

7.4 Go to the science library on campus and browse through the journal section. Are there any journals devoted to studying biogeography or plate tectonics? If so, select an interesting article to report on.

7.5 Run a search on "tectonics" or "plate tectonics" on the World Wide Web. Report on your findings.

LITERATURE CITED

Alvarez, L.W., W. Alvarez, F. Asaro, and H.V. Michel. 1980. Extraterrestrial cause for the Cretaceous-Tertiary extinctions: experiment and theory. *Science* **208**:1095–1108.

Babbitt, B. 1995. Protecting biodiversity. *Nature Conservancy* Jan./Feb.:17–21.

Birch, L.C. 1957. The role of weather in determining the distribution and abundance of animals. *in Population Studies: Animal Ecology and Demography, Cold Spring Harbor Symposia on Quantitative Biology,* Vol. XXII. The Biological Laboratory, Cold Spring Harbor, New York.

Brown, J.H. and A.C. Gibson. 1983. *Biogeography.* C.V. Mosby, St. Louis.

Cox, C.B. and P.D. Moore. 1994. *Biogeography.* Blackwell Scientific, Boston.

Edwards, V. 1995. *Dealing in Diversity.* Cambridge University Press, New York.

Gould, S.J. 1993. *The Book of Life.* W.W. Norton, New York.

Huston, M.A. 1994. *Biological Diversity.* Cambridge University Press, Cambridge, U.K.

McKinney, M.L. 1993. *Evolution of Life.* Prentice-Hall, Englewood Cliffs, New Jersey.

Pimm, S.L., G.J. Russell, J.L. Gittleman, and T.M. Brooks. 1995. The future of biodiversity. *Science* **269**:347–350.

Raven, P.H. 1988. Our diminishing tropical forests. *in* Wilson, E.O. (Ed.). *Biodiversity.* National Academy Press, Washington, D.C.

Raven, P.H. 1994. Defining biodiversity. *Nature Conservancy* Jan./Feb.:11–15.

Schopf, T.J.M. 1970. Relation of flora of the Southern Hemisphere to continental drift. *Taxon* **19**:657–674.

Simpson. G.G. 1969. The first three billion years of community evolution. *in Diversity and Stability in Ecological Systems.* Brookhaven National Laboratory, Upton, New York.

Wilson, E.O. 1988. The current state of biological diversity. *in* Wilson, E.O. (Ed.). *Biodiversity.* National Academy Press, Washington, D.C.

ECOSYSTEMS OF THE WORLD

8

S chultz (1995) introduced the term _ecozones_ as divisions of the earth's surface that share climatic factors, soil-forming processes, and living conditions for flora and fauna. Ecozones are characterized by the average conditions within them. The boundaries between ecozones are not important. Thus, ecozones are a way of organizing, at the highest level, biotic and abiotic factors and processes that control the ecosystems of earth. Our discussion follows Schultz (1995).

According to Schultz, the earth has nine ecozones, with some ecozones having at most two subregions within them. Table 8.1 list the ecozones, their areas, and percent landmass. Figure 8.1 shows the ecozones of the world.

As an example, consider the island of New Guinea, located just below the equator and north of Australia. According to Figure 8.1, New Guinea contains two ecozones: humid tropics and semi-tropical grasslands. However, there are snow-capped peaks along the central spine of New Guinea and rocky mountain slopes bare of vegetation. These ecozones could hardly be considered tropical. Indeed, using the ecozone classification, parts of New Guinea would be considered polar. Nevertheless, the usefulness of the ecozone classification scheme lies not in the details but in its ability to allow comparison of geographically distant regions of the earth.

For instance, the Mediterranean subtropical ecozone has components along California's west coast; Perth, Australia; and Capetown, South Africa; as well as Spain. On visiting these areas, one could expect to see many of the same kinds of plants—but not necessarily the same species—sharing the same ecological adaptations.

Net primary production (NPP) is an important term associated with plant growth. NPP refers to the gain in tissue and energy of plants and is typically

149

TABLE 8.1   Ecozones of the Earth According to Schultz (1995)

Ecozone	Size (million km²)	% landmass
1. Polar/subpolar	22.1	14.8
1.1 Tundras and frost debris	5.8	3.9
1.2 Ice deserts	16.3	10.9
2. Boreal	19.5	13.0
3. Humid mid-latitudes	14.5	9.7
4. Arid mid-latitudes	16.4	11.0
4.1 Grass steppes	11.9	8.0
4.2 Deserts and semi-deserts	4.5	3.0
5. Tropical/subtropical arid lands	31.2	20.9
5.1 Thornbush, thornscrub savanna	13.6	9.2
5.2 Deserts and semi-deserts	17.6	11.7
6. Mediterranean subtropics	2.7	1.8
7. Seasonal tropics	24.4	16.3
8. Humid subtropics	6.1	4.1
9. Humid tropics	12.5	8.3

measured in metric tons per hectare per year. In short, NPP is the amount of mass plants gain in a year.

POLAR/SUBPOLAR ECOZONE

The northernmost portions of Alaska, Canada, Greenland, Siberia, and Antarctica make up the polar/subpolar zone. The topography is ancient and hence very flat. Plants, birds, and mammals have circumpolar distributions in this ecozone. The polar bear, musk ox, and reindeer (caribou) have wide distributions, and their total numbers are comparatively low because the environment cannot support great numbers. Many animals and birds migrate toward the equator in winter. In the northern tundra, the growing season begins in June and ends in September. Lichens, mosses, and dwarf shrubs dominate the plant community. Trees are hardy dwarfs such as birches and willows. Permafrost hinders infiltration and percolation of water. Soil formation is limited to that part near the soil surface that thaws. Litter decomposition is very slow. Compared with tropical forests, NPP is 10 times as low, and litter decomposition is 100 to 1000 years or longer. NPP is about 2 in this ecozone. Precipitation rarely exceeds 300 mm annually.

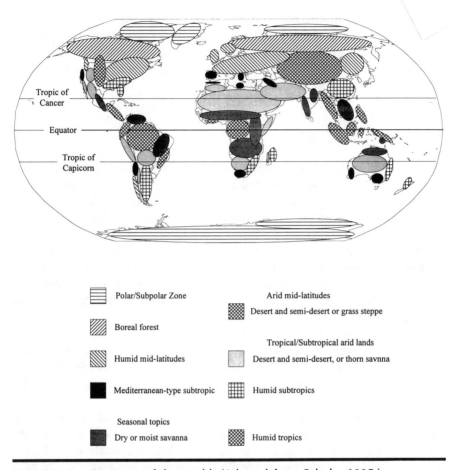

FIGURE 8.1 Ecozones of the world. (Adapted from Schultz 1995.)

The polar/subpolar zone is the least populated of all the ecozones, with a population of only two million people, all in the Northern Hemisphere in the subarctic tundra. Indeed, there are more reindeer (about 3.25 million) than people. Some 40 to 80 ha or more is required for grazing each reindeer. Some people believe that because the tundra is so vast, this ecozone could become an important food-producing region through good reindeer management. Musk ox wool is an important but expensive commodity.

The Arctic is important strategically because 15% of the world's recoverable oil lies beneath its surface, as does 50% of the earth's natural gas. Much coal and ore are also found, especially in Russia. However, the tundra is a sensitive ecosystem, and man's activities can easily damage it. The Alaska pipeline, for instance, stands mostly above the tundra on platforms. Oil drilling and transportation at the Alaskan oil fields are usually done in winter, when the tundra is frozen, so as to avoid damaging it and allowing roads to become quagmires.

BOREAL ECOZONE

This is the only zone that is found exclusively in the Northern Hemisphere. The boreal ecozone covers most of Alaska, Canada, Scandinavia, northern Russia, and Siberia and thus is one of the largest ecozones. It is the largest forested zone on earth, covered by quite uniform coniferous forests. Traveling through the boreal ecozone northward, the boreal coniferous forest becomes more stunted and sparse, until no trees are found in the polar ecozone. Most of us are familiar with the extensive spruce/birch forests of Canada that are typical of the boreal zone. Topographically, the boreal zone is a very ancient land and hence has been weathered flat, except for a few mountain ranges formed during the late Cretaceous/Tertiary.

While the winters are extremely cold, summers are relatively warm, so that the annual temperature range is the largest of all ecozones. Along the coasts of the boreal zone, temperature is moderated by the sea. The growing season is 3 to 6 months. Precipitation is 250 to 500 mm a year. Lakes and swamps are common in the boreal zone.

The pine forests of the boreal zone are species poor. Forest fires and insect damage contribute to a changing mosaic pattern that creates and maintains the forest. Although local changes occur, the forest has been stable since the last ice age. Organic litter accumulates and is slow to decay because of winter cold, acidic soils, and the high resinous content of pine needles. For three forests in Alaska, Cole and Rapp (1981) estimated that 353 years is required for litter to decompose. NPP is about 4 to 8, or 2 to 4 times that of the polar zone.

The boreal zone is sparsely populated because the climate is hostile to agriculture. Hunting and fur trapping support human activities. Bear and moose are found in low densities. The lynx and hare populations of the boreal forests have been studied by many wildlife biologists.

Siberia

On September 4, 1995, the cover of *Time* magazine read, "The Rape of Siberia." The article commented that "The natural wonders of the majestic Bikin

Valley capture the imagination but also tempt poachers and lumbermen." Note that poachers and lumbermen received equal billing as plunderers of the earth. Siberia, as Linden (1995) wrote, reminds one of a wasteland where subversives of the former Soviet Union were sent to work until they died. This image would be correct. More than 20 million people died in Siberia's gulag. Now, however, portions of Siberia are dying.

Parts of Siberia resemble Alaska in many ways. Glaciers, brown bears, and volcanoes remind one of the Kenai Peninsula of Alaska, although equally rugged Siberia is far more remote and less densely populated. Yet even remote parts of Siberia have been under attack by humans. Plutonium wastes from nuclear reactors have contaminated rivers. Linden suggests that the world's single largest source of air pollution comes from a complex of smelters in central Siberia. The haze, he claims, troubles people as far away as Canada and contributes to global warming. "Perhaps never has so vast an area been so despoiled so rapidly" at the hand of man. Of course, not all of Siberia has been ruined, but then Siberia is about 5 million square miles, about eight times as big as Alaska. The Sakha Republic is seven times the size of California and is but one of Siberia's 12 political regions.

Siberia is mostly taiga (boreal forest), a vast area of timber. Being a newly independent state, Siberia's economy needs hard cash. These timberlands are already attracting extraction companies. But Siberia has more than forests to offer foreign companies. Oil and gas deposits are believed to rival Saudi Arabia's enormous wealth. Diamonds and rich mineral deposits have been found. Linden claims that much of the gold comes from riverbeds, a clear indication that humans have not explored here before. Already a plethora of companies are exploring for mineral deposits.

With a population of 30 million, a vast area, few environmental laws, and even fewer resources to enforce the laws, poachers have hunted freely. The Siberian tiger once roamed a vast area; now the tiger is endangered and only 180 remain. The Amur leopard is one of the most elusive creatures on earth; fewer than 50 are believed to exist. Logging concessions are routinely given to friends by the very officials appointed to protect the forests. Oil spills have occurred in Siberia, and the permafrost allows the oil to flood large areas. Even our local news programs have shown oil spills in otherwise pristine wetlands in Siberia.

Once again, the United States is leading the environmental charge, in spite of its history of protecting species of plants and animals. Siberia has 25% of its forests intact, fully five times as much as the United States. While the U.S. Congress debates opening the Arctic National Wildlife Refuge to oil drilling, the United States is urging Siberia to set aside vast areas of protected lands that probably contain rich deposits of oil and gas. However, the former Soviet republics had access to an excellent educational system. Fortunately, many highly trained ecologists appreciate the problems Siberia faces. Hopefully, their concerns will be addressed before the rush for resources plunders Siberia.

HUMID MID-LATITUDES ECOZONE

The humid mid-latitudes spread discontinuously from the Pacific Northwest to the northeastern United States and cover most of Europe and western Russia. Parts of Turkey, Japan, and China are considered part of the humid mid-latitude ecozone. The coast of Chile south of Santiago, the south island of New Zealand, Tasmania, and the southernmost part of Australia are also in the humid mid-latitudes. Again, most of the humid mid-latitudes lies in the Northern Hemisphere. This is the so-called deciduous forest ecosystem that once covered Europe.

The humid mid-latitudes are located at about 40 degrees north and south latitude, and seasonal temperature changes are therefore important. Generally, temperatures are not as low in winter as in the boreal zone. As is typical, those regions near the coast have a moderate climate. Much of the humid mid-latitudes was covered with glaciers 20,000 years ago, and many mountains show the U-shaped valleys created by ice. The soils are much higher in nutrient content than soils of the boreal zone, and soil fauna are more diverse.

Plant distributions of the humid mid-latitudes were contiguous when the land masses abutted during the Miocene, 20 million years ago, but as the land masses broke up, the distribution separated. During the glacial period of the Pleistocene, the plants retreated southward. Mountain ranges that ran latitudinally acted as barriers to southward plant migration, and many plants became extinct as a result. Thus, as Schultz points out, Europe has fewer plant species than does North America. The species richness is, as would be expected, higher than in the previous two zones discussed. Temperate rain forests of Tasmania, Chile, and the south island of New Zealand contain not pine but broadleaf hardwoods. NPP is about 10, or twice that of the boreal zone. Litter requires about 4 years to return to the soil, which is 90 times faster than in the boreal forests. Precipitation averages between 50 and 100 mm a year. Naturally, humans have taken advantage of the generally fertile soils, decomposition rates, and precipitation by farming and ranching much of the humid mid-latitudes.

The humid mid-latitudes are one of the most heavily populated zones on earth. Europe is densely populated, as is the American northeast. These are also the most heavily industrialized regions, and as a result, environmental alteration and degradation have already occurred. Indeed, mean population densities are the highest on earth.

ARID MID-LATITUDES ECOZONE

About one-third of terrestrial earth is considered arid. Due to climatic factors, global wind patterns, and the confluence of planetary-scale wind currents descending, the arid zone is between 15 and 35 degrees north and south latitude, although some arid regions such as the Gobi Desert of China are continental deserts. The annual amount of precipitation, 0 to 500 mm, is misleading. Precipitation is lower than potential evapotranspiration. Also, rainfall evaporates quickly, and often within an hour it is not readily apparent that it has rained at all. Soils develop differently in humid and arid regions. Alkaline soils generally found in the arid mid-latitudes are due to the rainshadow effect of longitudinal mountain chains, the leeward side of the mountains being drier. Such is the case with the Rocky Mountains of North America.

Within the ecozone there are forests, tall- and short-grass prairies, deserts, and semi-deserts. Wheat is grown in this region, as in the Great Plains of the United States. Wind plays an important role in the arid mid-latitudes by transporting soils. Soil erosion by wind is a common problem, especially when soil is left exposed by lack of vegetation or other process. Wind strips the soil down to pebbles and transports the dust to cover other areas. Thus, when stripped of vegetation, a thorn scrub or grass steppe can be transformed into a desert.

During the Pleistocene, large ungulate herds roamed the steppes of Eurasia and North America. The American buffalo and the saiga antelope of Asia are examples. Voles, lemmings, and numerous rodents still find the arid mid-latitudes hospitable. Litter decomposition requires about one year (Schultz 1995). NPP is 4 to 10.

Aral Sea

Without doubt, the drying of the Aral Sea is one of the most rapidly occurring environmental disasters ever recorded. The creation of a huge agricultural scheme based on cotton and the opening of the Kara Kum Canal in 1956 precipitated the current problem. The Aral Sea of central Asia, once the world's fourth largest inland body of water, has turned into a mere puddle compared to its former size. This is one of only a few examples where an entire ecosystem has been destroyed so quickly and whose impact is so broad. The sea has contracted by some two-thirds of its surface area. Being an inland sea, as sea level declined, salinity increased. By 1977, the large fishing industry was in ruins. Fish catch had declined by over 75%. Within seven years, the commercial fishery had been eliminated. An industry that employed 60,000 is gone, and once prosperous seaports are now 50 km from the water. Where fruits and vegetables were once grown by local people and fish provided necessary protein, there is now only a wasteland and no fish.

Because the need for hard currency was so great, a large cotton project was begun around the Aral Sea. The hope was that water from feeder rivers could be used to irrigate the cotton crop which could be sold on the world market. The diversion scheme was successful—at first. In 1991, cotton made up 33.6% of Uzbekistan's exports. Cotton continues to be the country's leading hard-currency commodity. Some 17% of the work force was employed in agriculture. In neighboring Kazakhstan, the figures are similar. A substantial proportion of the economies of both nations depends on the canal diversion and the climate moderation provided by the Aral Sea. However, the Aral Sea is the same latitude as North Dakota, and its climate is less than ideal for cotton. Unfortunately, water was not all that the Aral Sea provided for the entire region. Like Easter Island, Mesa Verde, Mesopotamia, and so many places before it, the region has been laid to waste, a victim of ecological arrogance and misuse of man's technology.

The two major freshwater rivers, the Amu Darya (which flows into the Aral Sea from the south) and the Syr Darya (which empties into the sea in the north), were harnessed to irrigate the vast cotton crops. Irrigation canals were built of soil without even plastic liners. As a result, only a small fraction of the water reached its destination. The bulk of the water was sequestered in the walls of the irrigation canals. Indeed, so much water was lost that land nearby the canals began turning to swamp (Ellis 1990).

The Kara Kum Canal diverted large amounts of water from the Amu Darya into the Turkmenistan desert, irrigating millions of hectares of land. As more fresh water was diverted, the sea began to lose surface area and shrink. The sea had received about 50 km^3 water per year in 1965. By the early 1980s, this had been reduced to zero. Everything seemed fine for a while, and it was thought that as the sea dried, bottomlands could be put into production. However, the ecosystem services performed by the sea were never considered important. The Aral Sea, as it turned out, was the great moderator of the local climate. The sea's existence provided a mass of water-vapor-laden air that protected the region from the fierce dry winds from the north. The seasonal dry winds would blow, but the sea's presence would eventually assert itself, providing a buffer that prevented the surface soil from drying.

As the sea surface area was reduced through feeder river diversion, the regional climate began to change. Summers became hotter and drier. Winters, once moderate, became longer and much colder. The climate was hard on people, but it was much harder on cotton. Drier soils fell prey to wind erosion, and windblown salt precipitated from the shrinking sea added to human misery and also blew across the fields, coating the soil and sucking up what little moisture was left. As Mathews (1994) put it, "Thousands of square miles of farmland cannot now grow anything, and on thousands more productivity is dropping, propped up by fertilizer and pesticides and more and more water to rinse the fields of salts after each harvest." Nearly 30,000 km^2 of lake bed, poisoned with salts and chemicals, is toxic to plants. The dry lake bed sediments became windblown, poisoned dust clouds which damaged crops, and were hazardous to humans.

Naturally, more fertilizer makes for more salts, which further exacerbates the fundamental problem. As the sea dried and became saltier, the local fish died. Now, toxic water combined with an inadequate healthcare system threaten people's lives. According to Mathews, infant mortality may be among the highest in the world. Groundwater supplies were contaminated. And now the Aral Sea is shared not by one country but by two independent countries. Any solution must be mutually agreed upon before there is any hope of rescuing an already desperate situation.

TROPICAL/SUBTROPICAL ARID LANDS ECOZONE

Schultz's (1995) approach is to include semi-arid transitional zones with the traditional arid lands in the tropical/subtropical arid lands ecozone. This brings the total terrestrial surface occupied to almost 21%. The previous ecozone, the arid mid-latitudes, occupies 16.4% of the land surface. Together, some 37% of the earth is thus arid land! These lands include the great deserts of the earth: the Sahara Desert of North Africa (larger in extent than the continental United States); the Sahel on the southern border of the Sahara; the southwestern deserts of the United States and Mexico; the Great Basin of the American West; the Atacama and Monte of Peru; the East African arid lands; the Kalahari and Namib of South Africa; the southwest portion of Madagascar; the great Arabian desert; the Negev desert of the Middle East; the deserts of Iraq, Iran, and India; and the extensive deserts of Australia.

These deserts are due to the circulation patterns of the planetary winds, caused by the rotation of the earth and the resulting Coriolis force. In other words, most lands around 30 degrees north and south of the equator will be deserts unless other forces are able to overcome these planetary winds. Soils are poorly developed and wind movement of surface soil is important. Desert-adapted plants are some of the most unusual plants on earth. Cactus in the New World and euphorbias in Africa have many of the same adaptations to mitigate moisture loss. Trees in the Namib are some of the most unusual plants on earth. Some plants can leaf out repeatedly, leafing when rain occurs and dropping their leaves until the next rain. Fire in this ecozone is not generally important, although desert plants do catch fire. Usually, the occurrence of a fire is hardly noticed after a few weeks, as only dead grass and sticks burn. Fires do not spread easily over sparsely covered ground.

Precipitation can vary enormously. In some areas of the Atacama Desert of Peru, rain has not fallen for ten consecutive years. When rain falls, locally heavy accumulation is possible, while nearby areas receive almost no rain. Frequently, rain falls but never reaches the ground due to evaporation. Rainfall is highly variable and completely undependable, and hence humans have not been able to penetrate this ecozone effectively. Peoples who do live in the deserts are often nomadic and do not maintain land holdings.

Litter decomposition requires many years. Saguaro cactus of the Sonoran Desert that died and toppled in 1900 still lay decomposing today. When compared with recent identical photographs, photographs of desert scenes taken before the turn of the century show the same small shrubs occupying the same ground. Even leaf litter requires years to return to the soil.

MEDITERRANEAN SUBTROPICS ECOZONE

Located between 30 and 40 degrees north and south latitude, the Mediterranean-type subtropics covers but 1.8% of the earth's land surface, some 2.7 million km², and is the smallest ecozone. It is found on five continents and is highly fragmented.

The west coast of California, a small portion of the west coast of Chile, the southwest coast of Africa around Capetown, the southwest coast of Australia around Perth, and the border lands surrounding the Mediterranean and Caspian seas make up this ecozone. All lands are within 100 km of the coast except in Spain, where the ecozone penetrates inland. A distinguishing feature of the climate is the wet winter (cool season) and dry summer. These are also areas of high floral endemism and hence uniqueness. Thus, similar but unrelated forms of plants appear in all these disjointed regions. Along the ocean coasts, these are areas where cold water upwells from the ocean depths, causing cooler summer temperatures and fog.

Many plants have special adaptations that prevent summer loss of moisture. Leathery leaves are common; some have wavy coatings, hairy surfaces, or oils that slow water loss. Other environmentally induced plant adaptations occurred in these widely separated areas. Fires are not as prevalent in this ecozone. Litter decomposition requires around three years. Because the growing season lacks water, NPP is about 5 tons per hectare per year.

Humans have altered this ecozone as well, despite the unfavorable growing season. Irrigation schemes are common, vegetation changes have occurred because of human-induced fires, and in times past, cattle grazing was a common practice aided by the use of different summer and winter ranges. The damaging effects of human activity in this ecozone are well known. Massive soil erosion caused by overgrazing the land has caused local economic collapse.

SEASONAL TROPICS ECOZONE

The seasonal tropics ecozone is found on five continents and covers much of Mexico including the Yucatan Peninsula, Cuba, the western edge of Central America, parts of Venezuela, much of Brazil, Africa around the Congo Basin, western Madagascar, India, Indochina, the southern lowland portion of New Guinea, and northern Australia. The term savanna, or savanna zone, has become synonymous with this ecozone. The region is seasonal because there is usually a summer rainy season and a dry winter. The Florida Everglades lies in this region, for instance.

Near the equator, precipitation peaks occur in spring and fall. The llanos (grasslands) of Venezuela are parched dry part of the year and have standing water on them during the wet season. As the distance from the equator increases, the peaks of rain come closer together, eventually forming a single peak. The rainy season can last 9 months, and 1000 to 1500 mm of rain falls. In other areas, rain falls for only 4 months, and only 500 mm a year is typical.

Chemical weathering of the soils occurs in the ecozone, and clay-rich soils have developed and the underlying rock is decomposed. Nevertheless, water infiltration is good, but runoff occurs during the wet season. This ecozone has semi-evergreen forests, dry forests, savanna woodlands, shrubs, and grass savannas.

Grasshoppers and locusts are the most important herbivores in this ecozone. During the rainy season, caterpillars are also important. Appearing in a rich variety, spiders and ants are secondary consumers. The mammals of the seasonal tropics are recognizable to most everyone, and nowhere are the large mammals more varied than in Africa. The unforgettable congregations of wildebeests, elephants, zebras, antelopes, African buffalo, hippos, and lions immediately come to mind when Africa is mentioned. The seasonal tropics of India also support large mammals such as gaur, sambar, chital, tigers, blackbuck, and nilgai. South America had many large mammals as well, but they are now extinct. In Australia, marsupials such as kangaroos are found in the ecozone.

Fire is an important process in maintaining the vegetation community of the seasonal tropics. Lightning strikes and humans cause fires. With the onset of the rainy season, lightning is a common phenomenon. Fires burn away excess biomass and provide a flush of nutrients in time for the rains. Indeed, fire maintains the diversity of the vegetation community.

Litter decomposition takes place in several ways but is achieved in about a year. Termites are important decomposers that live on dead plant material. In some highly productive areas, termite densities can reach 100 million per hectare. NPP varies depending on the type of ecosystem. In a West African savanna, the NPP is 27 tons per hectare per year.

This ecozone is the most heavily populated and agriculturally altered region of the tropics for a variety of reasons. The soils are fertile and receive seasonal rainfall, grasslands are utilized by cattle, plant growth is high, and atmospheric conditions permit more sunlight to reach the plants. In numerous areas, seasonal rainfall is sufficient to raise crops. Given these favorable conditions, it is not surprising that the human population has doubled in the seasonal tropics in the last quarter century and agricultural expansion has occurred. Overgrazing is now occurring and degrading vast areas. Furthermore, the feedback mechanisms as a result of stripping the vegetation acts to prevent plants from growing. For instance, where overgrazing has occurred, the soils degrade and are blown or washed away, leaving only bare pebbles.

HUMID SUBTROPICS ECOZONE

The humid subtropics cover the southeastern United States, the southern part of Argentina, China, southeastern Australia, the southeastern part of Africa, part of Japan, and the north island of New Zealand in the latitude range between 25 to 35 degrees north and south. The number of humid months varies from 5 to 12, depending on the location. There is no true dry season, however, and many drought-resistant plants are able to grow year round.

The humid subtropics is a transition ecozone between the humid tropics and the humid mid-latitudes. The forests are less developed than the typical luxuriant lowland tropical rain forest. Soils are typically acidic, a result of weathering and leaching.

The vegetation of this ecozone is dense rain forest where there is adequate rainfall. As rainfall decreases geographically, the moist forests are replaced by dry forest or even grasslands. Litter decomposes in about two years. NPP varies from forests to grasslands at 14.4 tons per hectare per year, with one-third of the net being produced underground.

The human influence in this ecozone has been considerable, and often the vegetation has been completely altered. Forests have been felled and replaced by production agriculture. Since most regions have mild winters and only light frosts, citrus and tea are occasionally grown. The poor soils can be improved to support rice, soybeans, groundnuts, cotton, and tobacco. In southern Florida, around Lake Okeechobee, large orange groves have replaced the mixed savanna and forest mosaic. Once, much of the southeastern United States was covered with longleaf pine forests. These forests were logged out many years ago, and areas were replanted with faster growing slash pine. Many even-aged stands have thus replaced the native vegetation, reducing biodiversity and causing the extinction of many native birds.

HUMID TROPICS ECOZONE

The humid tropics are equatorial, occurring within 10 degrees north and south of the equator. Most of New Guinea, Java, Sumatra, Borneo, the Philippines, Malaysia, Equatorial Africa (but not East Africa), the Amazon of South America, and Central America make up the humid tropics. The climate is uniform all year. The sun rises at about 6:30 A.M. and sets about 6:30 P.M. The nearer the equator, the less the climate varies seasonally. Plant growth continues all year. Precipitation is 2000 to 3000 mm annually.

Chemical breakdown of the soil takes place because of high soil moisture content and year-round temperatures. However, physical types of weathering do not occur. Hence, bare rock does not break down. Streams and rivers are ubiquitous in the humid tropics, channeling the precipitation to the sea.

On the steeper slopes of the humid tropics, landslides are common and are the result of thick, saturated soil accumulation that slides off the rock surface. Probably all steeper hillsides are eventually affected. The bare soil surfaces are quickly colonized by opportunistic plants.

Evergreen tropical lowland rain forests are the world's "tropical forests." They occupy less than half their original extent. Some 20 million ha are now felled annually. However, "there are still larger percentages of primeval forest than in any other ecozone" (Schultz 1995). Aboveground plant biomass is the highest of any ecozone. Under the forest emergents, the canopy is uneven but dense. Trees can make up 70% of the vegetation. In some areas, the diversity of woody plants is so high that it is difficult to find two trees of the same species nearby.

Walking through a lowland tropical forest is an experience. While the wind can be gusting above the canopy, the air is typically still, hot, and humid at ground level. The forest floor has a thin layer of vegetation, and the forest is open. One is able to see many meters in all directions. The soil is clay-like, hard, and slippery. Pockets of hot and humid air exist, and one moves in and out of them. Small streams dissect the ground. The air smells like decaying plant material. Clothes become moisture-laden. At the edges of open areas, a breeze cools the visitor.

Many of the trees have strange root systems called buttress roots. Buttress roots are fan-like structures that act as stabilizers to anchor the tree to the ground and also help the tree respire, since the soil is wet. Annual growth rings of trees are almost nonexistent since the growing season lasts throughout the year. Also, flowering, fruiting, and leaf loss can occur anytime. This, in part, accounts for the high diversity of life that is supported by a tropical forest.

The wildlife of the humid tropics is typically heard before it is observed, if it is observed at all. Most species are sparse, but diversity is high, as it is for the plants. The multilayered structure of the forest supports a multitude of forest insects, amphibians, birds, and mammals. Thus, we say that there is high species diversity, but low species density.

The NPP of the humid tropics is the highest of any ecozone and is estimated at 20 to 30 tons per hectare annually. Leaf litter decay occurs quickly, usually within a few months. Despite the potential amount of leaves, the forest floor is only sparsely covered with litter because of the high decay rate.

The humid tropics are sparsely populated by today's standards. Slash-and-burn agriculture takes place on a shifting basis. A landowner might cut and burn 2 hectares of forest. Burning releases a flush of nutrients that supply food crops. After about two years, the landowner burns another area and allows the former area to return to forest. Much worse for the forest are ranching operations that burn the forest and plant grass for cattle. After a few years, heavy rains wash away the topsoil, aided by the trampling of heavy cattle, and another tract of forest must be felled. With the soil removed, the former tract may require hundreds or thousands of years to recover. The anti-beef/tropical forest campaigns of the early 1980s focused on eliminating such grazing practices. Examples of sustainable multicrop plots that rely on native trees to hold the soil and provide shade can be found.

EXERCISES

8.1 What other classification schemes are used to categorize ecological regions of the earth? How do these compare with the classification scheme used here?

8.2 Compare life history strategies of mammals in the different ecozones. For instance, compare different species of deer in the different ecozones. Which have the largest antlers? When are the antlers lost? Offer an explanation of your results.

8.3 Everglades National Park once had millions of wading birds. Even as late as the 1930s, a million or more birds existed in the greater Everglades region. Why are there so few now?

8.4 Not too long ago, there were many species similar to elephants. What were their distributions and how do they compare to distributions of *Loxodonta* and *Elephas* today?

8.5 Do a World Wide Web search for "Aral Sea." Summarize the present situation. Compare maps of the sea before and after the irrigation canal was built.

8.6 Find other regional examples of environmental disasters. What ecozone factors were ignored that made the disaster worse?

8.7 The ecozones we see today did not always exist in their present positions. Using the ecozone system explained here, make an ecozone map of the Carboniferous period 350 million years ago.

8.8 Make an ecozone map of the world during the height of the last glaciation, 22,000 years ago. Where was the boreal forest of North America?

8.9 Tropical forests of the humid tropics are being lost at an alarming rate. How will these losses affect precipitation in that ecozone?

8.10 How does the body size of animals of the same taxa differ across ecozones? Compare the body size of different bears across ecozones. How does body size of panthers differ across ecozones?

8.11 China has proposed building dams along the Yangtze River. Speculate on the long-term environmental ramifications of this action using ecozone information.

LITERATURE CITED

Cole, D.W. and M. Rapp. 1981. Elemental cycling in forest ecosystems. *in* Rieichle, D.E. (Ed.). *Dynamic Properties of Forest Ecosystems.* International Biological Program 23. Cambridge University Press, Cambridge, U.K.

Ellis, W.S. 1990. A Soviet sea lies dying. *National Geographic* **177**:72–93.

Linden, E. 1995. The rape of Siberia. *Time* September 4:45–49, 51–53.

Mathews, J. 1994. Hard lessons from the death of the Aral Sea. *St. Petersburg Times.* October 19.

Schultz, J. 1995. *The Ecozones of the World.* Springer-Verlag, New York.

EXTINCTION

The history of life on earth is punctuated with extinctions. Yet each time, life rebounded, diversified, and took new forms. The most successful mammalian radiation occurred with the multituberculates and lasted 160 million years. Today there are none. Based simply on the number of species extant today, biodiversity has never been higher in spite of the stunning fact that 98 to 99% of all species that ever lived are now extinct. Biological organisms are a force to be dealt with. The fact of the matter is that all species evolve or become extinct. Another way of putting it is that all species disappear one way or another. Why are some people concerned about extinction when it is as natural as life itself?

THE WAY THINGS WERE

A few vignettes will set the stage for our examination of the present dilemma. George Cavendish Taylor visited Florida to collect birds in the spring of 1861 and wrote about his trip (Taylor 1862). Most of the wildlife he observed remains common today. He suggested that Florida be called the "Mockingbird State" because mockingbirds (*Mimus polyglottus*) were common. They remain so today. Other birds Taylor saw are not as common. His list included the ivory-billed woodpecker (*Campephilus principalis*) and the Carolina parakeet (*Conurus carolinensis*). Today, the Carolina parakeet is extinct and the ivory-billed woodpecker is believed to be extinct (Lammertink and Estrada 1995). Perhaps Taylor's sightings were just luck.

Taylor's trip aboard the steamship *Darlington* took him up the St. Johns River. South of Lake George, the captain of the ship took several rifles to his post on the top deck and proceeded to shoot alligators sunning on the banks of the river. The captain suggested that alligators had greatly decreased in number in that part of the river in recent years. However, above Lakes Jessup and Harney, higher up the St. Johns, alligators were more common and "cannot do harm in a country where the population is so scanty as in Florida." The captain shot at some turkeys. Both turkeys and deer were noticeably diminishing in numbers by this time.

The steamship reached its destination, Lake Monroe, in a day. The captain shot another alligator. Taylor observed ivory-billed woodpeckers from his room. The next day, Taylor traveled by horse-drawn cart to New Smyrna, near the Atlantic coast. Along the way, he happened by country settlers referred to as "crackers." "One of them told me that there were a 'smart' of Bears, Wolves, and Turkeys about. The Wolves had been 'bad' on his hogs, and he had killed a good many of them with strychnine."

Near some lagoons, Taylor again sighted a flock of parakeets (Parroquets in his text). He raised his gun to bag them, but the sun prevented him from getting a clear shot and the parakeets made their escape. The next morning, he bagged a few Florida shrub jays (*Cyanocitta floridana*). That afternoon, he again saw parakeets and shot two. He observed another ivory-billed woodpecker. His companion bagged an opossum but left it behind. Taylor stated that the barred owls were so tame he could approach within a few feet of them before shooting them.

Quail were abundant around Smyrna, but Taylor was without a dog to hunt them. Taylor met two Englishmen visiting on a sporting outing. The two had just returned from killing a female bear, but the cub they shot at had escaped. That morning, the two had killed four deer, a "good many alligators," and enjoyed harpooning sawfish with 3-foot saw-like snouts. They also saw parakeets and "large" woodpeckers but did not shoot any.

Taylor wrote about a Sir Francis Sykes who spent three winters hunting in Florida. "One winter they killed as many as thirty-five bears, principally on Merritt's Island near Cape Canaveral, where they were camping out. A few years ago Roseate Spoonbills were plentiful down by the Indian River, but of late their numbers have greatly diminished, owing to their being shot for the sake of the wings, which are greatly in demand for the purpose of making fans." Later, Taylor saw the ground full of holes, "like large rabbit-burrows, made by the Land-tortoises, here called Gophers (*Testudo carolina*). These tortoises are extracted from their burrows by hooks with long handles, and are, I believe, used for food."

Later, Taylor shot "a fine Pileated woodpecker" and shot at "a pair of Swallow-tailed kites" but could not see the result. The parakeets were nesting at this time of the year and "generally breed in the cypress-swamps. They roost in company, making use of a hollow tree as their nesting-place. I am told that some live-oak-cutters, up the Halifax River, saw a flock go one evening into a hole in a tree to roost; next day, while the birds were absent, they cut the trunk of the tree nearly through, only leaving just enough uncut to keep it standing. After the Parroquets had gone in to roost, they felled it with a few blows of the axe, and secured them all."

In a letter to Taylor, one Dr. Bryant, who wrote "Notes on the Birds of Florida," which was published as Volume VII of the Proceedings of the Boston Society of Natural History, expressed regret that although the eggs of the ivory-billed woodpecker would be an important contribution to science, he was never able to collect any. "There are some birds, common enough, the eggs of which I have never succeeded in getting, such as the Ivory-billed Woodpecker, which would be a most important acquisition to science, and a most ornamental and curious egg, *never likely to be common*, and growing rarer every year as the bird does."

Later, on the same steamship with the same trigger-happy captain, Taylor described with disgust the shooters aboard. "Soon after the steamer has left Lake Monroe and has arrived in the narrow river, we see a flock of Turkeys on the right bank, consisting of a 'gobbler' and a few hens. Captain Brock and several others have their rifles ready, and blaze away at them, unfortunately wounding the 'gobbler.' This I consider shameful destruction, and unsportsmanlike in the extreme." More alligators were killed. "One of the gunners shoots an unfortunate Fish-Hawk [osprey] while bearing a fish to its nest. It drops the fish, falls in the woods, and perishes uselessly."

One day on Deep Creek, a tributary of the St. Johns, Taylor spent time in dense swamp with many large cypress trees and apparently many ivory-billed and pileated woodpeckers. "I saw the Swallow-tailed Kites coming nearer, and gliding just clear of the tops of the trees, where, no doubt, they find a good supply of lizards, tree-frogs, and insects. At last one came within shot, and I killed it....I obtained a specimen of Bonaparte's Gull, which I shot while it was running along the shore of the river."

"Red-bellied and Red-cockaded Woodpeckers were common around Orange-Mills, and easily obtained....I saw a single flock of ten Parroquets, and next day went again to the same locality in search of them, but without success." Apparently, killing in the name of science was an acceptable alternative to the wanton destruction of the gunners. Nevertheless, the result was the same.

Just 130 years ago, millions of wading birds inhabited the Everglades and Big Cypress. One roost area contained an estimated one million birds. First, the plume hunters decimated roosting sites. Later, water management policies destroyed what the hunters could not. Today, estimates are that fewer than 50,000 wading birds live in the Everglades. What have we lost in Florida? Perhaps we should ask what there is left to lose in Florida.

One problem is that most people do not know what used to be in Florida or in any other place. We have all read about, heard about, or seen on television the great wildlife of Africa. By comparison, North America appears almost devoid of wildlife. However, the situation has not always been so. Imagine a Florida inhabited by more wolves, panthers, bears, and deer than humans. Try to imagine wading bird flocks in the hundreds of thousands coming in to roost. Imagine 60 million American bison roaming the interior of the United States. A roadside information sign in Kansas tells us that a person could stand at the site and watch for *five days* as a great bison herd moved by. Few people know that American elk were plains animals and retreated into the high-elevation forests as humans increased their hunting pressure on them. A mere 800,000 American pronghorn antelope survive today in the western plains. Imagine how many roamed the West just 200 years ago. What have we lost? Many people suggest we have lost far too much.

The majority of Americans do not appreciate what has been lost and do not understand that life has not always been the way it was just yesterday. Humans are an infinitely adaptable species with almost no memory of the past. Indeed, most people do not know that Lake Powell in Utah is the result of a hydroelectric power plant concrete and steel dam placed in a narrowing of the canyon walls between the Grand Canyon and what used to be Glen Canyon. Were it not for the full-page advertisements placed in major metropolitan newspapers across the United States, a series of dams would exist in what is now Grand Canyon National Park. How many people born since 1970 would suggest that the Glen Canyon dam be removed? Not many. Why? The answer is that *the dam has always been there.*

DOCUMENTED EXTINCTIONS

Islands have been the scene of many extinctions, particularly bird extinctions, since most remote islands did not have native mammals. Human-caused extinctions began thousands of years ago on islands in the tropical Pacific. Steadman (1995) estimates that perhaps as many as 2000 species of land and sea birds were exterminated by prehistoric human activities. Such a figure represents nearly 20% of all bird species. Native birds across a vast area vanished as human invaders cleared forests and introduced mammals. Most of these birds evolved in the absence of mammalian predators and probably had not learned to fear humans before they were driven to extinction. Many extinctions have been well documented. One such story is told by Bailey (1956).

The Hawaiian Island chain extends northwestward from the big island of Hawaii to Kauai, and on to Laysan, Pearl, Midway, and Kure islands. Midway, as the name implies, is centrally located in the mid-Pacific between China and San Francisco and is about the same distance from Australia. Laysan is between Midway and Kauai.

Bailey reported that "Laysan was considered one of the most remarkable bird islands of the world because of the five species of indigenous birds which had evolved there, and because of the thousands of sea birds assembling during the nesting season." Captain John Paty annexed Laysan Island to the Hawaiian Kingdom on May 1, 1857. Despite being only 25 to 30 feet high, about 3 miles long, and 1.5 miles wide, with a lagoon about 1 mile long and a half mile wide, Paty reported that Laysan was quite literally covered with birds whose numbers he estimated at 800,000. He also recorded that seals and turtles were tame and too numerous to avoid stepping on.

In 1859, Captain N.C. Brooks visited Laysan and harvested 1500 Hawaiian monk seals (a federally endangered species today). The piles of bird guano, however, doomed the island fauna and flora. On March 29, 1890, Laysan was leased to the North Pacific Phosphate and Fertilizer Company for a 20-year period. Guano digging commenced in 1894 and ended in 1904. Despite these mining activities, the five endemic species survived, but it was only a matter of time.

Around 1903, the manager of the mining operation, Max Schlemmer, introduced rabbits and guinea pigs to Laysan to act as his food supply and as a profitable business venture. The animals thrived in the absence of predators and "literally every green leaf on the island was devoured except for a tobacco patch." With no vegetation left, the island quickly became an almost "uninhabitable desert," and three species of endemics became extinct. Drifting sands buried tens of thousands of birds alive. In 1909, more than 200,000 albatrosses and other birds were killed by Japanese feather hunters. However, it was the rabbit and guinea pig invasion that finally did in Laysan's avifauna.

As for Midway Island, Captain N.C. Brooks first discovered the island on July 8, 1859. In 1902, Midway was visited by the naturalist W.A. Bryan. He reported on the activities of the Japanese feather hunters who killed hundreds of thousands of birds for the fashion industry. Bryan found the island covered with bones. On other nearby islands, the same destruction occurred from the Japanese feather trade. On the island of Lisianski, an estimated 300,000 albatrosses and other sea birds were killed before the feather hunters were interrupted in their work. As a result of these grizzly activities,

President Theodore Roosevelt set aside all the islands as bird sanctuaries in 1909.

A tiny grayish-brown warbler, the so-called miller bird (*Acrocephalus familiaris*), was unique to Laysan and became extinct when rabbits destroyed the vegetation on Laysan. In 1902, Fisher (1903) reported that "The miller bird is one of the most abundant of the strictly land birds peculiar to Laysan." Bailey (1956) reported that the birds were abundant on Laysan in 1913 and the warblers were common visitors to the buildings on the island. They were so tame that "they would land upon our heads" in search of millers (a variety of moth) and caterpillars. By 1923, they were extinct.

The Laysan honey-eaters (*Himatione sabguinea fraithii*) were beautiful scarlet-vermillion birds "with slender down-turned beaks and eyes of reddish-yellow." Fisher (1903) wrote that "This brilliant little bird is found all over the island, but is most abundant in the interior among the tall grass and low bushes, bordering the open stretches near the lagoon, where all the land birds seem fond of congregating." Bailey (1956) cites Palmer's diary wherein he described securing one. "A most touching thing occurred: I caught a little red Honey-eater in the net, and when I took it out the little thing began to sing in my hand. I answered it with a whistle, which it returned and continued to do so for some minutes, not being the least frightened."

Dill (1913) visited Laysan in 1911, shortly after the rabbits began the destruction of the vegetation there. He estimated 300 honey-eaters remained. "The honey-eater is not common on Laysan." Bailey and Willett arrived in 1912, and the brightly colored birds greeted them. Because of the rapidly disappearing vegetation, "the birds we noted about the island were few, and were confined to patches of wild tobacco, and the few remaining clumps of *Scaevola* and bunch grass." The sad end of the Laysan honey-eater came in 1923, when the rabbits had completely denuded the entire island.

Bailey writes, "The last naturalists to see these birds alive were the members of the Tananger Expedition, and the late Donal Dickey was probably the last to take photographs when he secured his dramatic motion picture of a male in full song on a coral rock twig—one of three survivors of the race which was doomed to extinction in swirling dust a few days later." Wetmore (1924) pulled the curtain on three of the native birds on Laysan when he wrote:

> In spite of the rabbits, a few dozen Laysan finches still end their sprightly songs above the buildings or hopped among the rocks near the lagoon. Three individuals alone of the little Honey-eater remained on our arrival: these perished during a three-day gale that enveloped everything in the cloud of swirling sand. The Miller-bird had disappeared entirely, and of the Laysan Rail but two remained.

The Laysan rail (*Porzanula palmeri*) was unique to Laysan. Munro (1946) reported that the rails were "plentiful all over the island" in 1981. Fisher (1903) wrote, "The rails were everywhere on Laysan in great numbers" and photographed them. Dill (1913) reported them to be abundant during his visit to Laysan. Wetmore (1925) was probably the last to see the living bird. None were seen during a visit to Laysan in 1936. Although the rails survived on Midway until 1942, their destruction was rapid. Rats succeeded in getting ashore on Midway during World War II.

The Laysan finch (*Psittirostra cantrans cantrans*) was the hardiest of the three endemic perching birds of Laysan, and it was able to find food even after the destruction of the vegetation. It even outlasted the rabbits and was there when new growth returned. On Midway, however, it was no match for the rats and eventually succumbed.

Who cares about a few birds on remote islands where few people live? And if we don't care about a few birds, why, for instance, should we care about whether or not a wasp becomes extinct? The answer is, of course, that we do not know all the possible ramifications species have in the natural world. Indeed, we cannot know. After all, mammals were given their chance with the extinction of the dinosaurs brought about by a chance meteorite impact. An example from Borneo illustrates what can happen when this balance is upset.

Harrison (1968) tried to illustrate the interrelationships with an example given to him by a biologist who had spent five years in Borneo. The island of Borneo was suffering an outbreak of mosquitos. To control the pests, the World Health Organization decided to spray heavily with the pesticide DDT. This was before the long-lasting detrimental effects of DDT were understood. Much DDT was used to deal the mosquitos a severe blow. For the local people, however, their problems were not solved—they were only beginning. Unfortunately, the DDT killed a large fraction of the wasp population as well. As a result, the caterpillars, whose main threat was the wasps, were devouring the thatched roofs of the local houses, causing them to collapse.

The houses were now open to flies, and further DDT spraying was done to reduce their population. The gecko lizards, which were a common feature in every home, also controlled the flies indoors. Now the bodies of the flies were laced with DDT. The geckos consumed the flies and accumulated the toxins in their bodies. When the fatal toxic level was reached, the geckos died, and their corpses were, in turn, consumed by the other common pet, a house cat. Soon the house cats also died as they too consumed the poisons.

With the death of the cats, another outbreak was visited upon Borneo. Freed from the terror of house cats, rat populations exploded; they invaded the houses and consumed food. Now the circle was complete, and the attacker became the attacked. The rats were "potential plague carriers." In the end, house cats were airlifted by the World Health Organization to remote villages to control the rats. The ecological web is a complex one, and no one can say for certain what will happen when this or that species is lost. All we can be sure of is that nature is complex, and humans must find a way to live with and not without nature. As C.S. Holling points out (*Natural History* 1968), "We do know that, despite the arguments for the delicate balance of nature, natural systems are profoundly resistant to change." Humans evolved in a natural system. Can we now live without them?

Mammalian extinctions have also occurred. The vast herds of elephants across Africa are no more. Rhino are extremely rare. The Bengal tiger is once again under intense human pressure. Of the Siberian tigers, only 200 remain in the wild. The last Tasmanian wolf died in captivity in 1938. In the last 100,000 years or less, some 70% of North American, South American, and Australian large mammals and 40% of the genera of large mammals in Africa have become extinct (Martin and Klein 1984). In the next 50 years, we could well witness the extinction of the African Cape hunting dog (*Lycaon pictus*), the panda (*Ailuropoda melanoleuca*), and a host of others. The consequences of these extinctions are unimaginable.

The mechanisms most responsible for modern extinctions were discussed by Diamond (1989). He listed them as (1) habitat destruction and fragmentation, (2) introduced species, (3) chains of extinctions, and (4) overkill and labeled them "the evil quartet." In Florida, habitat destruction is a main cause of the extinction of wolves and ivory-billed woodpeckers, as well as the near elimination of panthers. Diamond (1989) suggested that overhunting by humans may have caused the Pleistocene extinctions of as many as 45 species of large mammals in the New World, although this is still debated today.

The islands of Hawaii are world famous for the extraordinary number of successfully introduced exotic species and for the resulting chains of extinctions that eliminated native plants and birds. As Hafernik (1992) points out, 870 nonnative plants have been successfully transplanted to Hawaii, and that approximates the number of native plants that once existed on Hawaii. Some 2000 invertebrates and 81 vertebrates have also been introduced in Hawaii. Cattle, pigs, rats, mongooses, goats, and birds of all sorts have been established on Hawaii, and their effects on the native flora and fauna have been nothing short of devastating. Indeed, a number of brown tree snakes have been recovered at the airport. These are the same snakes that devastated the island of Guam.

EXTINCTION RATES

Ehrlich (1995) claims that extinction rates are so high that "a major extinction episode is clearly underway." We already know that five major extinctions occurred in the past: the Ordovician 440 million years ago, the Devonian 365 million years ago, the Permian 250 million years ago, the Triassic 210 million years ago, and the Cretaceous 65 million years ago—all of which were catastrophes for life (see Figure 9.1). How does the modern "extinction" compare with these past setbacks?

Four of the previous mass extinctions eliminated 65 to 85% of all animal life in the ocean. The Permian extinction was far more devastating, erasing 95% or more of all marine species. These facts led Jablonski (1995) to suggest that "extensive as today's species losses probably are, they have yet to equal any of the 'Big Five' mass extinctions." Moreover, he points out that over 90% of all past extinctions occurred at times other than during the "Big Five" mass

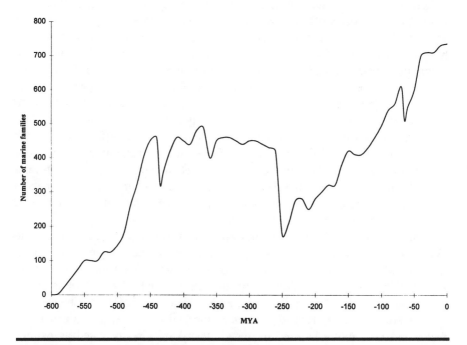

FIGURE 9.1 Approximate number of families of marine body fossils. (Adapted from Droser and Fortey 1996.)

extinctions. Rebounds from mass extinctions, Jablonski points out, are "geologically rapid and ecologically slow," and biodiversity recovery might happen in only 5 to 10 million years. What is there to worry about? Since 1600, we have only lost 1% of the known bird species, and most of these losses occurred on islands. Whales are making a comeback. Whooping cranes introduced in Florida are surviving. Are we coming back from the brink?

Recall Diamond's evil quartet. The most important factor in extinction is habitat destruction. Habitat loss is a pervasive long-term problem. Complete habitat loss is usually preceded by habitat fragmentation. That is, large, contiguous habitat is broken up, or fragmented, into smaller portions. As fragmentation occurs, certain species, such as ivory-billed woodpeckers, are especially susceptible to population declines. Nest parasitizers such as cowbirds do well in fragmented habitats and accelerate the loss of certain species. As the world becomes more populated, less land is available to all other plants and animals.

Is the human population the problem? Not directly. There are about 5.5 billion humans. The state of Alaska is 586,400 square miles (375,296,000 acres). If the average household worldwide is four people, then every household on earth could have more than one-quarter acre and live in Alaska. However, humans have to eat. Humans require about 40% of all primary production to maintain themselves. Crops and livestock require huge amounts of land. When land is converted to food crops, habitat loss for most other species occurs. There is little doubt that habitat fragmentation continues to be a threat to biodiversity. Many species can survive in fragmented habitat; however, their long-term viability is questionable. Indeed, human impacts affect species well beyond human population centers and where habitat fragmentation is a major factor (Nott et al. 1995). Furthermore, Nott et al. point out that freshwater mussels and freshwater fish in North America, mammals in Australia, plants in South Africa, and amphibians worldwide are suffering rates of extinction 1000 times higher than extinction rates of the past.

The rate of the modern extinction event is cause for concern. According to Wilson (1992), one-fifth of all bird species worldwide have been eliminated in the past 2000 years, a rate far higher following human expansion. Another 1000 are globally threatened. Additionally, migratory songbird populations in the eastern United States have fallen 50%. Fully 20% of the world's freshwater fish species are extinct or close to it. Even in the United States, plants and freshwater and land mollusks are threatened. Many are already listed as extinct. Others are declining. In many instances, we know what the problem is, but we lack the will to carry out the solution. For some, enough has been lost and another loss is intolerable. For others, species losses are part of progress. This begs the question, "What do we mean by progress?"

Sadly, it seems inevitable that we will look back in 50 years and ask why nothing was done to save this or that creature from extinction. Why wasn't the manatee fully protected? Why does the Alaska Fish and Game Department shoot wolves? Why wasn't something done to save habitat for ivory-billed woodpeckers? Some resent not being able to see this giant woodpecker. How can we sit by and watch rhinos become extinct in the wild without doing something to help? Extinction is more than a wildlife issue. It is the single most important issue of our time. The legacy of extinction will be found in museum drawers across the world for all future generations to see.

The road to extinction for a species is usually, but not always, a long one. Clearly, rarity is a prelude to extinction. However, species do not have to be rare for very long before they become extinct. The passenger pigeon was so ubiquitous that harvesters were convinced the species could be harvested forever. Populations of American buffalo are estimated to have been as many as 60 million during the early 1800s. Within half a century, the population was reduced to less than 10,000. Modern-day extinctions are no less dramatic. On the continent of Africa, the large ungulate population has been reduced by an estimated 95%. Populations of both species of rhinos and the African elephant have been reduced to a tiny fraction of their former glory, although rhino populations in Africa are now increasing.

Many instances exist, however, that indicate our true ignorance of present situations. No one knows how many African okapi exist. We have no clue how many snow leopards haunt the high Himalayas. What is true is that these animals are habitat specialists and they are rare. Perhaps they have been rare throughout the history of their species. Certainly we would expect top predators to be rare. After all, if they were common, their prey would be even less common and hence could not support them. But how rare is rare, and when does a rare animal demand special attention?

THE SEVEN FORMS OF RARITY

In a classic analysis, Rabinowitz et al. (1986) discussed the seven forms of rarity. Although their original analysis was for plants, the forms of rarity apply to wildlife as well.

In our discussion, we will use the same terms these authors used in their paper. First, the geographic distribution of a species is of utmost importance.

The distribution can be broad or narrow. By broad we mean that the range of the species is large. For instance, the polar bear has a wide geographic range extending across the far north. The panther's geographic distribution extends from Canada to Tierra del Fuego at the tip of South America. In contrast, golden lion tammarins are found in small remnants of the Atlantic Forest in Brazil. Within each of these two categories, species can have a broad or restricted habitat specificity. That is, within the geographic distribution, is the habitat of the species broad or small? Panthers are generalists able to live in forests, the Sonoran Desert of Arizona, and the rain forests of Central America. The polar bear requires seals to eat, and seals are found in the sea. Thus, the polar bear's habitat specificity is fairly restricted. The Herrero chat, a small bird, is found only in a very restricted region of northern Namibia. The chat's geographic distribution is narrow, and its habitat specificity is restricted.

Lastly, the local population size of the species can be small everywhere or large somewhere within the geographic range and habitat specificity. Thus, a species can have many small populations and a central large population, or perhaps just small isolated populations. The chat has a single small population, making it one of the rarest birds on earth. The panther is, as a top carnivore, never locally abundant, but where it is found there are usually healthy populations. This way of looking at rarity yields a matrix of the following form:

Geographic distribution	Wide		Narrow	
Habitat specificity	Broad	Restricted	Broad	Restricted
Local population size				
Somewhere large	Wildebeest	Red crossbill	Polynesian triller	Cape Sable seaside sparrow
Everywhere small	Snow leopard	Red-cockaded woodpecker	Kodkod	Black-footed ferret

The analysis does not take into account the trophic level of the species, which is equally important in determining abundance. Predators are never found in greater abundance than their prey. Species lower on the trophic ladder are usually more abundant locally than species higher on the trophic ladder. Nevertheless, thinking about where species belong in the rarity matrix forces us to understand species requirements and conservation implications of the actions we take.

RED DATA BOOK

The threatened species categories used today have been in place for about 30 years. Words like "extinct," "endangered," and "vulnerable" and such terms as "extinct in the wild" and "critically endangered" are used by everyone across the world concerned with conservation. Even governments and organizations use and apply them. As we saw earlier, the terms "threatened" and "endangered" are defined in the Endangered Species Act. The remaining terms in popular usage are contained in the so-called Red Data Book, whose categories provide "an easily and widely understood method for highlighting those species under higher extinction risk, so as to focus attention on conservation measures designed to protect them" (IUCN 1994).

In 1988, the Species Survival Commission of the IUCN invited G. Mace to propose a population-based risk assessment system for species. Version 1.0 is based on the Mace-Lande criteria (Mace and Lande 1991) and has been applied and found to be most appropriate for higher vertebrates (Mace et al. 1992). Subsequent meetings resulted in creation of Version 2.0 in 1992, Version 2.1 in 1993, Version 2.2 in 1994, and the version described here in December 1994.

The categorization process applies to wild populations inside their natural ranges and to populations resulting from benign introductions, that is, from attempts to establish a species, for the purpose of conservation, outside its recorded distribution but within an appropriate habitat and ecogeographic area. The categories typically apply to species but can apply to subspecies and races as well.

The categories and definitions according to the Red Data List (IUCN 1994) are as follows.

Extinct—A taxon is extinct when there is no reasonable doubt that the last individual has died.

Extinct in the Wild—A taxon is extinct in the wild when it is known only to survive in cultivation, in captivity, or as a naturalized population (or populations) well outside the past range.

Critically Endangered—A taxon is critically endangered when it is facing an extremely high risk of extinction in the wild in the immediate future, as defined by any of the following criteria:

    A. Population reduction in the form of either of the following:
          1. An observed, estimated, inferred, or suspected reduction of at least 80% over the last ten years or three generations, whichever is longer

    2. A reduction of at least 80%, projected or suspected to be met within the next ten years or three generations, whichever is longer

B. Extent of occurrence estimated to be less than 100 km² or area of occupancy estimated to be less than 10 km², and estimates indicating any two of the following:

    1. Severely fragmented or known to exist at only a single location

    2. Continuing decline observed, inferred, or projected in any of the following:

        a. Extent of occurrence

        b. Area of occupancy

        c. Area, extent, and/or quality of habitat

        d. Number of locations or subpopulations

        e. Number of mature individuals

    3. Extreme fluctuations in any of the following:

        a. Extent of occurrence

        b. Area of occupancy

        c. Number of locations or subpopulations

        d. Number of mature individuals

C. Population estimated to number less than 250 mature individuals and either:

    1. An estimated continuing decline of at least 25% within three years or one generation, whichever is longer

    2. A continuing decline observed, projected, or inferred in numbers of mature individuals and population structure in the form of either:

        a. Severely fragmented (i.e., no subpopulation estimated to contain more than 50 mature individuals)

        b. All individuals are in a single subpopulation

D. Population estimated to number less than 50 mature individuals

E. Quantitative analysis showing the probability of extinction in the wild is at least 50% within ten years or three generations, whichever is longer

Endangered—A taxon is endangered when it is not critically endangered but is facing a very high risk of extinction in the wild in the near future, as defined by any of the following criteria:

A. Population reduction in the form of either of the following:

    1. An observed, estimated, inferred, or suspected reduction of at least 50% over the last ten years or three generations, whichever is longer, based on (and specifying) any of the following:

    a. Direct observation

    b. An index of abundance appropriate for the taxon

    c. A decline in area of occupancy, extent of occurrence, and/or quality of habitat

    d. Actual or potential levels of exploitation

    e. The effects of introduced taxa, hybridization, pathogens, pollutants, competitors, or parasites

2. A reduction of at least 50% projected or suspected to be met within the next ten years or three generations, whichever is longer, based on (and specifying) any of (b), (c), (d), or (e) above

B. Extent of occurrence estimated to be less than 5000 km^2 or area of occupancy estimated to be less than 500 km^2, and estimates indicating any two of the following:

    1. Severely fragmented or known to exist at no more than five locations

    2. Continuing decline inferred, observed, or projected in any of the following:

        a. Extent of occurrence

        b. Area of occupancy

        c. Area, extent, and/or quality of habitat

        d. Number of locations or subpopulations

        e. Number of mature individuals

    3. Extreme fluctuation in any of the following:

        a. Extent of occurrence

        b. Area of occupancy

        c. Number of locations or subpopulations

        d. Number of mature individuals

C. Population estimated to number less than 2500 mature individuals and either:

    1. An estimated continuing decline of at least 20% within five years or two generations, whichever is longer

    2. A continuing decline observed, projected, or inferred in number of mature individuals and population structure in the form of either:

        a. Severely fragmented (i.e., no subpopulation estimated to contain more than 250 mature individuals)

        b. All individuals are in a single subpopulation

D. Population estimated to number less than 250 mature individuals

E. Quantitative analysis showing the probability of extinction in the wild is at least 20% within 20 years or 5 generations, whichever is longer

Vulnerable—A taxon is vulnerable when it is not critically endangered or endangered but is facing a high risk of extinction in the wild in the medium-term future, as defined by any of the following criteria:

A. Population reduction in the form of either of the following:
   1. An observed, estimated, inferred, or suspected reduction of at least 20% over the last ten years or three generations, whichever is longer, based on (and specifying) any of the following:
      a. Direct observation
      b. An index of abundance appropriate for the taxon
      c. A decline in area of occupancy, extent of occurrence, and/or quality of habitat
      d. Actual or potential levels of exploitation
      e. The effects of introduced taxa, hybridization, pathogens, pollutants, competitors, or parasites
   2. A reduction of at least 20% projected or suspected to be met within the next ten years or three generations, whichever is longer, based on (and specifying) any of (b), (c), (d), or (e) above
B. Extent of occurrence estimated to be less than 20,000 km^2 or area of occupancy estimated to be less than 2000 km^2, and estimates indicating any two of the following:
   1. Severely fragmented or known to exist at no more than ten locations
   2. Continuing decline inferred, observed, or projected in any of the following:
      a. Extent of occurrence
      b. Area of occupancy
      c. Area, extent, and/or quality of habitat
      d. Number of locations or subpopulations
      e. Number of mature individuals
   3. Extreme fluctuation in any of the following:
      a. Extent of occurrence
      b. Area of occupancy
      c. Number of locations or subpopulations
      d. Number of mature individuals
C. Population estimated to number less than 10,000 mature individuals and either:
   1. An estimated continuing decline of at least 10% within ten years or three generations, whichever is longer
   2. A continuing decline observed, projected, or inferred in number of mature individuals and population structure in the form of either:

     a. Severely fragmented (i.e., no subpopulation estimated to contain more than 1000 mature individuals)

     b. All individuals are in a single subpopulation

D. Population very small or restricted in the form of either of the following:

    1. Population estimated to number less than 1000 mature individuals

    2. Population is characterized by an acute restriction in its area of occupancy (typically less than 100 km^2) or in the number of locations (typically less than five). Such a taxon would thus be prone to the effects of human activities (or stochastic events whose impact is increased by human activities) within a very short period of time in an unforeseeable future, thus capable of becoming critically endangered or even extinct in a very short period.

E. Quantitative analysis showing the probability of extinction in the wild is at least 10% within 100 years

Lower Risk—A taxon is lower risk when it has been evaluated and does not satisfy the criteria for any of the categories critically endangered, endangered, or vulnerable. Taxa included in the lower risk category can be separated into three subcategories:

1. *Conservation Dependent (cd)*—Taxa that are the focus of a continuing taxon-specific or habitat-specific conservation program targeted toward the taxon in question, the cessation of which would result in the taxon qualifying for one of the threatened categories above within a period of five years

2. *Near Threatened (nt)*—Taxa which do not qualify for conservation dependent, but which are close to qualifying for vulnerable

3. *Least Concern (lc)*—Taxa which do not qualify for conservation dependent or near threatened

Data Deficient—A taxon is data deficient when there is inadequate information to make a direct or indirect assessment of its risk of extinction based on its distribution and/or population status. A taxon in this category may be well studied and its biology well known, but appropriate data on abundance and/or distribution are lacking. Data deficient is therefore not a category of endangered or lower risk. Listing of a taxon in this category indicates that more information is required and acknowledges the possibility that future research will show that threatened classification is appropriate. It is important to make positive use of whatever data are available. In many cases, great care should be exercised in choosing between data deficient and threatened status. If the range of a taxon is suspected to be relatively circumscribed and a considerable period of time has elapsed since the last record of the taxon, threatened status may well be justified.

Not Evaluated—A taxon is not evaluated when it has not yet been assessed against the criteria.

Scientifically, we know what most of the problems are and how to stop or even reverse declines of species. However, scientists have not been able to convince politicians that very real threats exist. A New Mexico state game and wildlife officer said it best: "The scientists give us the facts, but the public tells us what to do."

EXERCISES

9.1 Do a search on "extinction" and "extinct" on the World Wide Web. Summarize the results.

9.2 Look for "manatee" on the World Wide Web. Is there an organization dedicated to ensuring the survival of manatees?

9.3 Look for "rhino," "elephant," and "penguin" on the World Wide Web. How many species and subspecies of these animals are recognized? What is the status of each?

9.4 The extinction of the dusky seaside sparrow was a sad day in modern wildlife history. Many subspecies of sparrows existed in Florida as a result of the Pleistocene glacial retreat. Look for an article on Florida's sparrows in the journal *Ecology*. Use the library and the Web to construct a history of these subspecies. Predict the future of these subspecies, given global climate change.

9.5 How many pandas are left in the wild and how many exist in zoos around the world? What is it about the breeding biology of the panda that lessens the species' chances of surviving the next century? How many pandas have been bred in zoos? If the panda is lost to extinction in the wild, will zoos be able to reintroduce pandas?

9.6 How do the Red Data Book listings compare to CITES Appendices I, II, and III listings?

9.7 Run a keyword search on the World Wide Web for "threatened" and "endangered." Summarize the results.

9.8 Do a search for "CITES," "IUCN," and "WCMC." Are there databases containing information on ranges of endangered species?

9.9 Using the criteria in the Red Data Book, determine if pandas should be threatened or endangered. How about elephants and rhinos? What about whooping cranes? What biological parameters are important to an endangered species?

LITERATURE CITED

Bailey, A.M. 1956. *Birds of Midway and Laysan Islands.* Denver Museum of Natural History, Denver.

Diamond, J.E. 1989. Overview of recent extinctions. pp. 37–41 *in* Western, D. and M. Pearl (Eds.). *Conservation for the Twenty-First Century.* Oxford University Press, Oxford, U.K.

Dill, H.R. 1913. The albatross of Laysan. *American Museum Journal* **13**:185–192.

Droser, M.L. and X.Li. Fortey. 1996. The Ordovician radiation. *American Scientist* March–April:122–131.

Ehrlich, P.R. 1995. The scale of the human enterprise and biodiversity loss. pp. 214–226 *in* Lawton, J.H. and R.M. May (Eds.). *Extinction Rates.* Oxford University Press, Oxford, U.K.

Fisher, W.K. 1903. Notes on the birds peculiar to Laysan Island, Hawaiian group. *Auk* **20**:384–397.

Hafernik, J.E. 1992. Threats to invertebrate biodiversity: implications for conservation strategies. pp. 171–195 *in* Fiedler, P.L. and S.K. Jain (Eds.). *Conservation Biology.* Chapman & Hall, New York.

IUCN. 1994. *IUCN Red List Categories.* Gland, Switzerland.

Jablonski, D. 1995. Extinctions in the fossil record. pp. 25–44 *in* Lawton, J.H. and R.M. May (Eds.). *Extinction Rates.* Oxford University Press, Oxford, U.K.

Lammertink, M. and A.R. Estrada. 1995. Status of the ivory-billed woodpecker *Campephilus principalis* in Cuba: almost certainly extinct. *Bird Conservation International* **5**:53–59.

Mace, G.M. and R. Lande. 1991. Assessing extinction threats: toward a reevaluation of IUCN threatened species categories. *Conservation Biology* **5**(2):148–157.

Mace, G.M., N. Collar, J. Cooke, K. Gaston, J. Ginsberg, N. Leader Williams, M. Maunder, and E.J. Milner-Gulland. 1992. The development of new criteria for listing species on the IUCN Red List. *Species* **19**:16–22.

Martin, P.S. and R.G. Klein. 1984. *Quaternary Extinctions: A Prehistoric Evolution.* University of Arizona Press, Tucson.

Munro, G.C. 1946. Laysan Island in 1891. *Elepaio* **8**:24–25.

Natural History. 1968. Ecology: the new great chain of being. **77**(10):8–16, 60–69.

Nott, M.P., E. Rodgers, and S. Pimm. 1995. Modern extinctions in the kilo-death range. *Current Biology* **5**(1):14–17.

Rabinowitz, D., S. Cairns, and T. Dillon. 1986. Seven forms of rarity and their frequency in the flora of the British Isles. pp. 182–204 *in* Soule, M. (Ed.). *Conservation Biology: The Science of Scarcity and Diversity.* Sinauer, Sunderland, Massachusetts.

Steadman, D.W. 1995. Prehistoric extinctions of Pacific Island birds: biodiversity meets zooarchaeology. *Science* **267**:1123–1131.

Taylor, G.C. 1862. Five weeks in the peninsula of Florida during the spring of 1861, with notes on the birds observed there. Part I. *The Ibis* **IV**:127–142, 197–207.

Wetmore, A. 1925. Bird life among lava rocks and coral sand. *National Geographic* **48**:77–108.

Wilson, E.O. 1992. *The Diversity of Life.* W.W. Norton, New York.

CURRENT WILDLIFE ISSUES IN FLORIDA

10

The geographic location of Florida, its favorable climate (the Sunshine State), and its geologic history have set the stage for some very interesting wildlife. Add to this unique stage 13.7 million people, with a projected 19 million by 2020 (892 new people per day—1692 entering, 800 leaving), and very little public land and wildlife issues will arise. There are 23 nonindigenous birds, and 27% of the state's plants are nonindigenous. During the ice age 18,000 years ago, the peninsula of Florida was twice as wide as it is today. Northern North America was covered by the massive Laurentide Ice Sheet, and the Cordilleran Ice Sheet extended up the northern Pacific coast. By about 7000 years ago, the ice sheets had retreated (Pielou 1991). With all that fresh water locked up in great ice sheets, the sea level 18,000 years ago was at least 85 m lower than today and perhaps as much as 130 m lower. Huge tracts of land along the continental shelf were exposed. Instead of being a long and narrow finger, Florida was a broad but still very flat platform of land (Hoffmeister 1974). As the ice retreated, the sea level rose, and sea water encroached and inundated the land. Peninsular Florida, lacking topographic relief, lost half of its peninsular land to the sea.

At the full extent of the glaciation, Florida had a complex array of large mammals that are no longer found there or anywhere else for that matter. Between 12,000 and 10,000 years ago, mammoths and mastodonts disappeared from the earth. Fossil mastodonts have been found in Florida. Florida lost 20 mammals whose body weights were over 45 kg.

The rise in sea level and the loss of so much biodiversity raise an interesting issue. Suppose you were alive 18,000 years ago. Your tribe was comparatively well off because you were living in Florida along what was then its west coast.

185

At the annual gathering of tribes, it was decided that in order to protect the rich hunting grounds, a large reserve should be established so that the animals could breed and roam freely within the reserve. Excess animals leaving the reserve could be hunted without doing harm to the breeding population within the sanctuary. With these goals in mind, a large sanctuary was established and its boundary agreed upon. You were put in charge of the sanctuary. Your assigned task was to do nothing and to make certain no one else did anything either.

For generations, the sanctuary functioned properly. The hunting grounds beyond the protected area remained rich, and people colonized these areas, although they remained somewhat nomadic. People began to depend on the sanctuary for excess animals. You were proud of the fact that people, for the most part, respected the boundary of the sanctuary and your authority. You became a legend, and you passed your position and your duties to your offspring.

Slowly the climate began to change. Whereas the western park was once a dry savanna, it was now holding more water. The plant community began to change. Wetland plants began moving in, and dry savanna-adapted plants no longer were common. The animal community also responded to these changes. Stories of the sanctuary, a verbal history of the area handed down from you to your offspring and in turn to their offspring, told of the western boundary being a dry savanna. Now the area was more like a wetland. The eastern boundary of the sanctuary had not changed, but because of the changes on the western boundary, animals within the park were utilizing the eastern part of the pro- tected area more frequently. When the animals ventured beyond the agreed upon boundary that was now clearly marked by human settlements, they were quickly dispatched and eaten. Indeed, so many people had moved in on the eastern border that poaching along the full extent was becoming a problem.

Year after year, decade after decade, the western wetland invaded eastward. What was once the far western part of the sanctuary became a beach where sea turtles nested. The sanctuary was becoming one dimensional, extending north and south. The east to west extent was shrinking. From human generation to human generation, the sea advanced westward and the sanctuary began losing its wildlife. Mastodonts were the first to disappear. The large ground sloths were next. Other animals were only rarely seen. The plant community extended well beyond the eastern boundary of the sanctuary but had been altered by humans. The animals within the sanctuary were trapped between the advancing sea and humans. They were doomed. Your offspring concluded that no sanc- tuary would be big enough given that the climate was changing and the human population was growing.

Although the above scenario is completely fictitious, the conclusions your offspring reached are valid. Boundaries that keep humans out and keep wildlife in won't work over the long run. The national parks and preserves in place today are cages that must be artificially maintained to survive. The laws that established and maintained these parks are not going to change this human generation. Your task will be to undo these laws and establish new laws that allow people and parks to co-exist across the landscape—all across North America.

SANDHILL CRANES

On April 1, 1996, the front page of the *Tampa Tribune* reported that Florida sandhill cranes (*Grus canadensis pratensis*) were showing up in people's back-yards. It was no April Fools' joke. The Florida Game and Freshwater Fish Commission estimates that there are between 4000 and 6000 Florida sandhill cranes remaining. The Florida sandhill crane is a recognized subspecies of sandhill crane; unlike other sandhill cranes, it does not migrate out of Florida to breed. The fact that cranes are showing up in residents' backyards might be a joy for local people, but it sounded an alarm for some ornithologists. More and more sandhill cranes are showing up in urban settings such as golf courses, highway medians, and backyards. There could be several reasons for their appearance.

One reason cranes are more commonly seen is that their population is increasing. Sandhill cranes typically lay two eggs and raise two chicks each year. Another reason might be native habitat destruction. In Pasco County near Tampa, one ornithologist estimated that up to 100 crane nesting sites remain today: 100 ago there were thousands of nesting sites. Sandhill cranes require natural wetlands with short grass to nest and feed. The South Florida Water Management District reported that overpumping of groundwater sources has led to a decrease in the number of local wetlands in Hillsborough, Pasco, and Pinellas (near Tampa) counties. The wellfield drawdown is the number one concern of the Tampa Audubon Society. Entire wetland communities, of which the cranes are a visible part, are disappearing. Wellfield drawdown, however, is a symptom of a more widespread problem.

The reason the sandhill cranes are showing up along highway medians is that water runoff from the highways collects in the medians, forming ephemeral wetlands. The cranes then feed in these temporary wetlands. Fortunately, the cranes also nest in other parts of Florida, but this is just one more setback for cranes. Slowly, the crane's habitat is being lost to overdevelopment. Subdivisions, shopping malls, ranchettes, and fast-food restaurants are springing up all over Florida. Most of the land in Florida is privately held. Once development occurs nearby, cashing out becomes the hope of many large tract holders. Taxes increase near developments, making it impossible to make a living from ranching or farming. Habitat destruction due to overdevelopment is the most important problem for the sandhill cranes and for most species living in Florida.

MANATEES

The Florida manatee (*Trichechus manatus latirostris*) is a subspecies of the West Indian manatee (*T. manatus)* and is one of the largest inshore mammals of the North American continent. Adults typically weigh 1000 pounds and are about 10 feet long. They are completely aquatic and herbivorous. Manatees are found in shallow, slow-moving rivers, estuaries, canals, and coastal waterways. They are without natural predators and can live 60 years. Annual migrations of some individual manatees are 1700 km (O'Shea et al. 1995). The manatees are protected under the Florida Manatee Sanctuary Act of 1978 (which designated the entire state as a refuge and sanctuary for the manatees), the Endangered Species Act of 1973, and the Marine Mammal Protection Act of 1972 and their amendments. Manatees were federally listed as endangered in 1967.

Federal management activities are directed to improve the population status of the Florida manatee so that the subspecies can be removed from the endangered species list. To achieve this goal, healthy marine ecosystems where the manatee resides must be sustained. Twenty-five years ago, manatees were studied by a single scientist; today, millions of dollars are spent annually on the research and management of the species. Much of what is known about the Florida manatee is presented in detail by O'Shea et al. (1995). After perusing this publication, one would think that everything humans need to know to save manatees is already known. In addition, in October 1989, Florida's governor and cabinet directed the Florida Department of Environmental Protection to work with 13 key manatee counties in Florida where over 80% of manatee deaths occurred to reduce injuries and deaths. Furthermore, anyone can call the Florida Marine Patrol manatee hotline (1-800-DIAL-FMP) anytime to report injured, dead, harassed, tagged, or orphaned manatees. How could anything go wrong? Apparently, everyone is behind saving manatees and there is no wildlife issue here.

On March 28, 1996, the front page of the *Tampa Tribune* read, "Concern mounts as more manatees die." Dead manatees were being found in "alarming" numbers in nearshore waters off southwest Florida. The second paragraph of the article summed up the crisis: "If the current death rates continue, the population of manatees in this region could be wiped out by fall." The most recent counts pegged Florida's manatee population at 1822 and the population of the four-county area including Sarasota County at 726 manatees. The article went on to say that there were 163 manatee deaths statewide in the first 87 days of the year. "At the current rate, nearly four deaths per day [sic], the population could theoretically be wiped out by the first week of September." Things always have a way of being worse than they appear, especially when calculations are off by a factor of two.

As a result of the manatee deaths, Florida assigned 35 more professionals to investigate, doubling the number of researchers working on manatees. On April 4, 1996, the *Tampa Tribune* reported on previous manatee research. For all of 1995, 201 manatees died. This total was less than the 206 manatees that died in 1990, when cold weather stressed the manatees. In 1994, 193 manatees died. Table 10.1 summarizes the causes of deaths for 1994 and 1995.

On April 15, 1996, the *Tampa Tribune* ran another article: "Influx of dead manatees crowds marine research lab." Manatees were dying in record numbers. The lab had run out of cold storage space for carcasses awaiting examination. Bodies were lining up side by side. The article hinted that scientists suspected a virus. Statewide, 200 manatees had been found dead, and this was one shy of all of 1995. So far, the dead manatees are all from southwest Florida. The deaths appeared "unrelated to a rise in the deaths of green turtles and cormorants on the Gulf of Mexico coast," one researcher reported. The endangered turtles are reported to have a cancer-like ailment that causes tumors. Cormorants are diving sea birds, and their ailment seems to be the result of eating fish killed by red tide, a natural marine toxin that blooms in the Gulf

TABLE 10.1   Causes of Manatee Deaths

Cause of death	1994	1995
Watercraft related	49	42
Floodgate/canal lock	18	8
Other human related	5	5
Perinatal (newborn)	46	56
Cold stress	4	0
Other natural	33	35
Undetermined	37	53
Verified, not recovered	3	2
Total	195	201

of Mexico. As for manatees, "The only permanent populations in the United States are in Florida, where a count this year put them at 2639." Between the beginning of 1996 and April 5, 1996, the population of manatees statewide somehow grew by nearly 800. Despite more than 200 deaths so far in 1996, population counts showed an all-time high. Moreover, aerial surveys have shown that since the 1985 census, when there were an estimated 1200 manatees, the population of manatees has grown steadily. The figure 2639 is the result of better counting procedures and therefore is the actual minimum number of manatees in Florida on April 5, 1996.

On May 2, Beeman (1996) reported that manatee deaths had tapered off. Red tide (a dinoflagellate) was blamed for the deaths. A finger of 68-degree water laden with so-called red tide, a highly toxic algae, was located 40 miles off the coast of Florida, due southwest of Tampa. A cold front in March may have been enough to stress manatees already weakened by the toxic algae. As the algae is washed near shore, it breaks up in the waves and emits a neurotoxin in the form of an aerosol. Since manatees come up for air, they inhale the neurotoxin. Their lungs also become irritated. Since January 1, 1996, a record 258 manatees have died, 52 more than the previous record of 252 in 1990. About two-thirds of the deaths are blamed on red tide. However, there are also a record number of manatees living in Florida coastal waters. What is the wildlife issue here?

From 1974 to 1992, Ackerman et al. (1995) analyzed mortality patterns and trends in manatees. As shown in Table 10.1, human-caused deaths of manatees outnumber all other causes of death after manatees are a few months old. Furthermore, destruction of prime manatee coastal and estuarine habitat continues. Humans and their activities are the greatest threat to manatee populations. Humans and manatees interact along Florida's waterways, and rarely does the manatee come out on top. Wright et al. (1995) reported that 1376 sets of fatal or healed propeller wounds were found on 628 dead manatees from 1979 to 1991. Collisions with watercraft caused 406 deaths. Nearly two-thirds of the manatees were killed by humans! Watercraft impacts caused more deaths than propeller cuts. The total number of registered boats in Florida has steadily increased with the human population. Many manatees are identified by their healed scars from boats. Perhaps as many as 40% of the manatees have scars. Private boaters report seeing groups of manatees all scarred by propellers.

Manatees are migratory mammals; hence, establishing a sanctuary where propeller-driven boats are prohibited will work only part of the time. As soon as the manatees leave the sanctuary, they become nothing more than speed bumps for boaters. Many boaters feel that their right to own a boat and drive it as fast as they desire is just that—a right. Apparently the grass roots campaign that stopped net fishing off the Florida coast cannot be repeated for the gentle manatee. Even a law requiring boaters to install something as simple as a flexible plastic propeller protector is too difficult to impose. We already know that habitat destruction cannot be outlawed.

Continued research on manatees will refine what we already know, and no surprises are anticipated. Destruction of wetland habitat will continue throughout Florida. Many of the fresh and marine grass beds where manatees graze have been reduced or entirely destroyed by water pollution, herbicides, and dredging projects. The human population of Florida will continue to increase at about 2.7% per year, and the number of boats on the water will increase at a rate of about 3.4% per year. The number of manatees dying from collisions with boats will probably increase by about 9.3% per year in the future. With less available habitat for manatees, the chances of an infectious disease spreading increases. Natural population constraints will take hold when the density of manatees in an area increases beyond its holding capacity. Long-distance migration will occur more frequently as the manatees become relatively more crowded.

As The Associated Press reported on May 21, 1996, "Manatee protection hurts tourism, some say." Seven manatee sanctuaries have been named by the federal government as off limits to people and boats from November 15 to March 31. This is peak tourist season in Florida, of course. Several other sites such as the Crystal River might also be added to the sanctuary list. Dive shop owners, developers, and others dependent on tourism are not likely to support the sanctuary idea. In Crystal River, some 30 to 40 manatees gather and attract 70 or more tourists at a time. A wildlife biologist accused the Save the Manatee Club of being extremist for backing the sanctuary idea. What will future generations think if no sanctuary is created?

Reintroducing Manatees

Wildlife introductions have occurred, and indeed continue to occur, worldwide. There is a worldwide homogenization of plants and animals taking place before our eyes. Prickly pear cactus, rabbits, foxes, and dingoes were all introduced in Australia. The results have been catastrophic. Twenty-one parrot species live and breed in and around Miami. The English house sparrow is found nearly everywhere in North America. Coyotes are now invading Florida. Native Hawaiian birds have been displaced by introduced species. Yet some introductions fail. In 1995, 19 manatees were returned to their native habitat. During 1994, ten were reintroduced to the wild. Injured manatees found in the wild are treated and released. Orphaned newborns are cared for and then released. Care for captive animals is expensive, time consuming, and at times heartbreaking. In the wild, a young animal learns much from its mother. Learning in a natural setting sometimes makes the difference between life and death. Because of the number of manatees in southwest Florida, the *Tampa Tribune* published an article on manatee introductions on April 6, 1996. Individual manatees were named by the researchers. Several of the released manatees were outfitted with radio transmitters.

A young female manatee named MD came to the Lowry Park Zoo in Tampa in 1992 after being hit by a boat. She was treated in captivity and then released in June 1993. In August, she gave birth. Later she was hit by a boat that crushed her satellite transmitter, disabling it. MD was lucky she survived. Baby J. Coral was brought in after being entangled in ropes and dragged around a concrete block. She was treated and released. Eight months later, she was found starved to death after being stuck in a culvert.

Naples was in captivity for seven years before being released in July 1994 with her captive-born two-year-old calf Andrea. Also released with her was four-year-old Timehri, an orphaned wild calf she adopted as a newborn. Naples is reportedly doing fine and gave birth to a new calf in August 1995. Timehri's transmitter quit in November 1994 but she is believed to still be alive. After setting off on her own, Andrea attempted to return to the place where humans had cared for her. When cold weather came, she showed no signs of leaving. Manatees are cold water intolerant, and she was moved by humans to a nearby power plant with artificially warmed waters. Researchers noted that she had survived the winter and was on her way to becoming the first introduced manatee to make the transition to a free-ranging lifestyle. Sadly, Andrea was found crushed to death in the summer of 1995 in the Caloosahatchee River's Ortona lock. Apparently she had not learned on her own about the dangers and hazards all free-roaming manatees face.

A young male manatee named Palmer was outfitted with a transmitter before his release. Unfortunately, Palmer was too used to humans and took advantage of boaters wanting to pet him. He was caught in the act of begging junk food from the back of a boat. Palmer was addicted to attention from humans.

Round-the-clock rescue efforts at Lowry Park Zoo failed to save three of four cold-stressed manatees. A fourth was released after less than two weeks in captivity. Lucky Frank was injured and later released. New Bob was brought in for treatment in 1992 as an orphaned newborn. He was released at a special "halfway house" for manatees at the Merritt Island National Wildlife Refuge but was soon back in captivity. In 1995, four manatees between three and four years old "showed promise" in their unsuccessful return to the wild. Marjorie and Valentine (her captive-born calf) and an orphan calf named Graham visited

Lowry Park Zoo for three weeks on their way to freedom. They were flown to the Everglades and released in September 1995. Marjorie lost her transmitter and is believed to still be alive. Valentine and Graham are now free-ranging manatees in the company of others of their kind near Ten Thousand Islands. Successes do happen.

Soon after his release, Moose, an orphaned manatee rehabilitated at Sea World in Miami, was killed by a boat. Three other captive-born manatees also failed to survive their releases. Harvey failed to find warm water during a cold spell and died. Foster was captured for failing to learn the same lesson and was sent back to captivity. Indie set off on a journey of 200 miles before he was hit and killed by a boat. Many dedicated people, specially designed facilities, rehabilitation centers, halfway refuges, expensive satellite transmitters, and flights to monitor the manatees every week are part of the program to save the manatee. Millions of dollars, ten of thousands of hours donated by concerned people, and the best research top scientists can produce are up against habitat destruction and mobile boaters. Then again, nuclear power plants have provided artificial warm water sanctuaries that have acted to increase the population and create habitat. We can only wonder how the next generation will judge our efforts to save the gentle manatee from extinction.

FRESHWATER FISH

On September 26, 1995, a Florida Game and Fresh Water Fish Commission news release reported that an investigation into the sale of illegal game fish resulted in 27 arrests. Two days earlier, wildlife officers had fanned out across four Florida counties and issued citations to individuals selling bluegill, crappie, channel catfish, largemouth bass, redear sunfish, striped bass, and sunshine bass. They had exceeded the state-established bag limits, most often deliberately. The individuals arrested had buyers lined up before they ever caught fish, and some even made repeated trips while stashing fish at home or other locations. Officers purchased more than 1100 pounds of fish.

Citizen complaints tipped the officers off. Most complaints of illegal commercialization of freshwater fish are investigated, and steps are usually taken to halt the practice immediately. The charges range from second-degree misdemeanors to infractions. The penalty for a misdemeanor or conviction is a fine of $500 and/or 60 days in jail. An infraction carries a preset fine and court costs. Most people who enjoy recreational fishing do it fully within the law. However, if a few wildlife officers can make 27 arrests in two days, the problem of illegal commercial fishing could be seriously impacting Florida's freshwater fish.

FLORIDA PANTHERS

No other animal in Florida symbolizes wildlife issues more than the Florida panther. Coyotes are now invading Florida, and ranchers are shooting them on sight. So-called coy-dogs (a cross between domestic dogs and wild coyotes) are rumored to be domestic dogs by day and evil coyotes by night, striking fear into anyone caught outside after dark! Yet it is the Florida panther that is most hated by some who fear big government and most beloved by others as a symbol of wild places, of what once was in Florida and what could be.

U.S. Fish and Wildlife Service authorities introduced 19 Texas panthers into the wilds of northern Florida to test whether panthers could survive there. Most succeeded but all were eventually removed. The male panthers were all neutered by professionals—well, almost all were neutered. At the time of his capture, Waldo was a free-ranging panther in north Florida near the small town of Waldo. Waldo's genetic makeup indicated that he was of Texas panther descent. His capture was disappointing to many residents, and "Free Waldo" T-shirts announced their ire. Many called for Waldo's release, including U.S. Senator Connie Mack (R-Fla.), who questioned the legality of removing an endangered species from Florida. The State Division of Wildlife director announced that "its existence near Waldo did not occur naturally, and would have been potentially harmful to Florida wildlife if we had not removed it from the wild."

There is no doubt that panthers are carnivores, and hence some wildlife are harmed by panthers. Let's just admit that panthers eat other wildlife for food. A U.S. Fish and Wildlife Service manager working on the project had earlier been quoted as declaring that "all panthers born in Florida are Florida panthers"—except for Waldo apparently. The contradictions are transparent in so volatile an issue as the Florida panther. And this is just the tip of the iceberg. Six pure-bred, authentic "born in Florida" Florida panthers are caged at a private state-of-the-art captive breeding facility in north Florida. Males are separated from females, and they are prevented from breeding. Many people are asking why. The facility has been prevented from breeding them and is now asking the federal government to find another home for its most controversial occupants.

Some 50 panthers roam freely in Florida, mostly on private land. Habitat destruction is the principal cause of the panther's decline. One hundred years ago, panthers were found from one end of Florida to the other and from coast to coast. So was the eastern timber wolf. Bears were ubiquitous. Bobcats are still everywhere. And there were no coyotes. Some suggest the Florida panther suffers from inbreeding. Some panthers have crooked tails and cowlicks. Some males have only one descended testicle. Without at least one they would be sterile. Panthers fight for territories, and males kill other males in their territory. The few that remain are found east of Tampa. Florida has not been kind to panthers.

Cramer (1995) surveyed north Florida residents as part of the Northeast Florida Panther Education Program sponsored by the Florida Advisory Council on Environmental Education. From February 1993 to July 1995, a small population of radio-collared Texas panthers was released in the Pinhook Swamp area near the Georgia–Florida border. Cramer found that fully 73% of the residents favored panther reintroductions into their own county or surrounding counties. Fully 49% felt there should be land development restrictions to preserve natural panther habitat, while 86.7% of the respondents felt that saving wildlife habitat was a good idea. Tax breaks and cooperation from regulatory agencies (state and federal) were favored incentives by 81% of the residents.

Despite the overwhelming apparent support for the panther reintroduction program, Cramer also revealed many interesting problems. Landowners with more than 10 acres (31%) were less supportive of panther reintroduction. Education level played a major role in people's decisions. People with less education showed the least support for the program (55%), the highest level of ignorance of the program (30%), and the highest outright opposition (15%) to the reintroduction program. Those with a high-school degree or more favored the program (85%). More men (62.6%) felt that panthers were probably not a threat to deer populations, while only 42.5% of women felt the same way. More women (53%) than men (41.5%) felt that panthers were a threat to children.

A closer look at the question of preserving habitat for wildlife revealed an interesting trend. When asked whether the responsibility for habitat preservation was the landowner's, 100% of respondents with 10 acres or more used for residential purposes agreed that saving habitat was their responsibility, whereas 94.1% who used their land for forestry agreed, 86.7% who used their land for ranching agreed, and 72.0% who used their land for farming agreed. Clearly, the more land was used, the less responsibility for habitat preservation people were willing to accept. Nevertheless, seven out of ten agreed it was an important responsibility of the landowner.

Demographically, respondents 18 to 49 years old supported the panther reintroduction program in higher percentages than did those over 49 years of age. Those 60 and over saw the panther as a threat. All landowners with 10 or more acres were asked if they would allow certain species to live on their land. Again the trend was clear. Fully 86.5% would permit gopher tortoises, 92.2% red-cockaded woodpeckers, 93.8% fox squirrels, 84.4% otters, 64.6% bobcats,

57.8% panthers, and 53.1% black bears. Only 11% of respondents said they presently did not take any actions to benefit wildlife.

Specialty license plates in Florida are carried on 12% of registered vehicles, and at $27 each, total revenues were nearly $4 million for the state coffers in 1995. Since its introduction in 1990, 217,737 Florida panther specialty license plates have been sold, raising $13.2 million. The Challenger license plate, introduced in 1987, has sold 597,685 plates and has raised $28.7 million. The manatee plate is second at 323,288 plates and $14.4 million raised. Fees vary from plate to plate, but the popularity of specialty plates is so broad that there are 36 for the public to choose from. Although each new introduction dilutes the effectiveness of each individual plate, the manatee and the panther both continue to be leading license plates, which indicates that these two popular species will continue to be of concern to Florida residents.

The Florida panther issue is extremely complex, and books have been written describing efforts to save the species (Alvarez 1993, Maehr 1996). Maehr was chief of the state game commission for eight years. He suggested that the commission's strategy to interbreed Texas panthers with Florida panthers was poorly conceived (Maehr personal communication). Data show that the native Florida panthers are reproducing just fine. Who cares if a panther has a crooked tail or a cowlick, as long as the females continue to have an average of 2.3 cubs per year. Maehr claims that habitat destruction, in part caused by poor water management, is the panther's principal enemy. Furthermore, more panthers are located on private rather than state or federal lands, and hence more money should be spent to create beneficial relationships with local landowners. Logan, director of research for the Florida Game and Fresh Water Fish Commission, agrees that spending any additional funds on a population of panthers that is expected to remain at about 50 for the foreseeable future is irresponsible. Yet in 1995 alone, Florida specialty license plates generated about $1.7 million to save the panther. That kind of money is worth fighting over even if the panther cannot be saved. Thus, political problems are bound to occur.

In 1993, a woman jogger in New Mexico was threatened by a panther. Panthers are found throughout New Mexico. Several residents tried to get a glimpse of the cat but failed. Indeed, seeing a panther in the wild is a unique experience, and most people who enjoy the outdoors would welcome the opportunity to see a panther. However, most backpackers in New Mexico will never see a panther, although the chances are excellent that a panther has seen them. As one professor at the University of Florida bluntly put it, if we are worried about people being killed, we should do away with all cars. In fact, you probably have a better chance of finding a winning lottery ticket on the street than of being killed by a panther in Florida. Panthers simply avoid people.

The Arizona State Game and Fish Department estimates that 3000 panthers live in Arizona. Until 1970, the state paid a bounty of $200 for each panther killed. A few people in Arizona consider panthers to be a nuisance. Ranchers routinely hire private hunters to kill panthers.

FROG GIGGING

On April 29, 1996, an article on frog gigging appeared in the *Miami Herald.* Two days later, another article reported that frog gigging in Big Cypress National Preserve would be outlawed the following day. The disclosure that poachers (a word not used in the April 29 article) had been hauling tons of frogs a month out of the national preserve had caused a public outcry. Commercial giggers had plundered too much, too often. Also, two endangered birds that used the marshes were a consideration.

Sportsmen and conservationists were outraged by the previous report and demanded the preserve be closed to such activities. The preserve is 2400 square miles and supports hunting, fishing, and off-road vehicles. It took but two days of public pressure for the chief ranger to close the preserve to gigging. Intense, relentless public pressure did what scientists could not do. The South Florida Sportsmen's Association was among the groups calling for an end to the pillaging of resources. The Everglades Coordinating Council, a coalition of 14 sportsmen's groups, had already called for statewide regulation of frogging.

The chief ranger suggested that the ban will eventually be lifted when limits are placed on the number of frogs giggers can take. Other areas of the state have already established limits. For instance, no more than 50 frogs a night can be taken from the Miccosukee Indian Reservation.

As is the case in many instances, scientists understand the intricate food web of aquatic systems and the role each animal and insect plays, but it is the public that tells the park service what to do. When the public gets behind a wildlife issue, one way or another, the issue will be resolved. What the public demands, the public gets.

RABIES AND SMALL MAMMALS

With the loss of Florida's wolves and panthers, small mammals have been able to thrive. Raccoons, opossums, armadillos, bobcats, feral hogs, and foxes are often seen. They have no top predator to control their populations, and some of them are able to profit from a landscape dominated by humans. Raccoons are ubiquitous in Florida. Many people feed raccoons in the mistaken belief that they are helping to save wildlife, when in reality the opposite is true. With the rise of so-called meso-mammals, eggs of ground-nesting birds are more likely to be eaten. Even the eggs of some birds of prey are eaten by raccoons.

Alligators are top predators in Florida wetlands. Although female alligators guard their nests, raccoons often prey on the eggs. There has been a role reversal in Florida. The alligator eggs are eaten by raccoons, but because there are fewer alligators, fewer raccoons fall prey to them. Raccoons in the drier parts of Florida find gopher tortoise eggs a delicacy. Some raccoons have learned that the tortoises carry the eggs around inside them before they are laid. The raccoons attack the tortoises for their eggs and in doing so kill the tortoises. Gopher tortoises are threatened in Florida.

On January 6, 1994, the *Gainesville Sun* reported that cases of rabies were on the rise in 1995. Thirteen cases of rabies were reported in Alachua County in the first seven months of 1995. Aside from two cases in a neighboring county, there were no cases of rabies in Alachua County in the 18 previous months before the first reported case. In 1995, there were 251 cases of rabies and 258 cases in 1994. Of the 1995 cases, 184 were from raccoons, 18 from foxes, and 27 from domestic cats. The domestic cats may have contracted rabies from encounters with raccoons.

With the increasing numbers of raccoons and other meso-mammals, disease outbreaks such as rabies are more common. When populations increase beyond historical limits, aided in part by humans, the density becomes too high. Viral epidemics such as rabies pass through a population quickly, knocking the numbers, and hence the density, back.

RED-COCKADED WOODPECKERS

Old-growth longleaf pine forests are the home of the red-cockaded woodpecker (RCW), a federally endangered species. Of course, longleaf pine forests are themselves rare. Once, longleaf pine forests covered extensive areas of the southeastern United States and much of Florida. Trees more than a meter thick were common. Today, the longleaf pine forests are disappearing. RCWs are primary cavity nesters; that is, over a period of months, they excavate their own nest sites in dying or dead trees. RCWs favor longleaf pine trees but will nest in other dead or dying pine trees. They create holes in trees to nest, which other birds can occupy after the RCWs leave.

RCWs have declined throughout their range because of extensive loss of nest trees. They usually nest in trees more than 80 years old. Traditional forestry practices require harvesting trees between 40 and 50 years old. Thus, the trees favored by the birds have disappeared. Furthermore, other less favorable tree species such as slash pine have been planted. Harvesting trees and replanting with other species more favorable to harvesting has led to a steady decline in RCW numbers. There are an estimated 700 nesting pairs of RCWs in the entire state of Florida and 2000 in the southeastern United States, their traditional range.

RCWs are cooperative breeding birds. That is, young birds from the previous brood help to raise the young of their parents. In the morning, the RCWs all fly off together to feed. They return to their cavity nests just before the sun sets. The sight of them returning to the nest site is an experience enjoyed by a decreasing number of people. The squawking birds all fly into the nest stand together, land on the sides of their respective trees, and immediately hop into their cavities, which are about 20 feet off the ground. One of North America's most beautiful birds, the RCW is a symbol of a healthy forest with many old-growth trees and snags. The U.S. Forest Service plans to regulate timber cutting on more than 3000 square miles of land around nesting sites in an attempt to increase RCW numbers. Also, the U.S. Fish and Wildlife Service plans to replace harvested areas with slower growing longleaf pines. The Florida Forestry Association has suggested that such a policy is unfavorably restrictive.

EXERCISES

10.1 Whooping cranes are being released in Florida by the U.S. Fish and Wildlife Service. Investigate the status of whooping cranes using the World Wide Web and a conventional library, and summarize your findings.

10.2 Find more information on the Florida Manatee Sanctuary Act of 1978. What does the act provide for? Are fines assessed for violating the act?

10.3 Do a more thorough study of manatee introductions and reintroductions. Do reintroductions succeed more often than introductions? Offer an explanation.

10.4 Armadillos invaded eastward from Texas and into Florida. How did they cross the Mississippi River? Investigate this fascinating story of the successful armadillo invasion. What was it about the breeding biology of this diminutive creature that helped it succeed?

10.5 Investigate the coyote invasion into Florida. Why is this happening? Can it be prevented? Why didn't it happen 100 years ago?

10.6 Find out where specialty license plate money is spent in your state. How much money really goes to conservation of the species on the license plate?

10.7 Speculate on the complete loss of a primary cavity maker such as the red-cockaded woodpecker. What effect would its demise have on other birds?

10.8 The Clinton administration wants to restore the Florida Everglades to its former glory and bring back the massive colonies of wading birds that once existed. How many species of wading birds use the Everglades, and what were their populations in 1850? Trace the history of the wading birds of south Florida. Why are there so few today?

LITERATURE CITED

Ackerman, B.B., S.D. Wright, R.K. Bonde, D.K. Odell, and D.J. Banowetz. 1995. Trends and patterns in mortality of manatees in Florida, 1974–1992. *in* O'Shea, T.J., B.B. Ackerman, and H.F. Percival (Eds.). *Population Biology of the Florida Manatee.* National Biological Service, Washington, D.C.

Alvarez, K. 1993. *Twilight of the Panther.* Myakka River Publishing, Sarasota, Florida.

Beeman, K. 1996. Manatees dying less frequently. *Tampa Tribune* May 2.

Cramer, P. 1995. The Northeast Florida Panther Education Program. Florida Advisory Council on Environmental Education, Tallahassee.

Hoffmeister, J.E. 1974. *Land from the Sea.* University of Miami Press, Coral Gables, Florida.

Maehr, D. 1996. *The Florida Panther.* University of Chicago Press, Chicago.

O'Shea, T.J., B.B. Ackerman, and H.F. Percival. 1995. *Population Biology of the Florida Manatee.* National Biological Service, Washington, D.C.

Pielou, E.C. 1991. *After the Ice Age.* University of Chicago Press, Chicago.

Wright, D.D., B.B. Ackerman, R.K. Bonde, C.A. Beck, and D.J. Banowetz. 1995. Analysis of watercraft-related mortality of manatees in Florida, 1979–1991. *in* O'Shea, T.J., B.B. Ackerman, and H.F. Percival (Eds.). *Population Biology of the Florida Manatee.* National Biological Service, Washington, D.C.

NATIONAL AND INTERNATIONAL ISSUES

11

Dewar (1996) makes a compelling point—America's wildlife is dwindling. Meanwhile, 300 million people visited America's national parks in 1995. Populations of bees, birds, frogs, and many other species, including native plants, are declining. Populations of raccoons, armadillos, fire ants, and introduced species of plants and animals are increasing in the United States. Clearly, something is terribly wrong. More than half of the neotropical migrant birds are declining in number. The American goldfinch population has declined 25%. Raccoons are becoming nuisance wildlife. Bees are disappearing. In fact, in California and Florida bees are brought in to pollinate crops. And these bees are usually European bees! America's native bees are checking out. As Dewar points out, bobwhite populations are crashing along the east coast, the common honeybee is becoming rare, frogs are disappearing worldwide, butterflies are vanishing, once common eastern meadowlarks are losing ground, and even prairie dogs are disappearing across the short-grass prairie. What is happening?

In the *Albuquerque Journal* on April 21, 1996, Dewar summarized what people are seeing across the United States—strange invasions of coyotes into Florida, mesopredator populations such as red foxes increasing dramatically, the once common summer tanager of New Mexico now rarely seen. The tanager depends on riparian habitat that is shrinking or damaged by river projects. Even snakes such as the eastern indigo snake are now endangered. And when insect populations decline, something is definitely wrong. A recent study by The Nature Conservancy showed that 17% of America's butterflies are experiencing population declines.

Who should care about insects? Fully 60% of U.S. agricultural crops are pollinated by bees. Some 3000 varieties of native bees are in trouble. Nabhan of the Arizona–Sonoran Desert Museum estimates that 25% of all managed beehives have died in the last five years, having fallen victim to a pair of parasites from Asia and Europe.

Habitat loss and introduced species are partly to blame. Human activities are responsible for both, however. Fortunately, we are entering crisis mode, and people often seem to mobilize around crises. Like a sleeping giant, nothing seems to motivate us until a crisis occurs. However, Americans seem to respond to crises like no other society. Their solutions are bold, unprecedented, and cannot be predicted. The status quo is thrown aside completely. Dramatic new laws are passed without regard to the shackles of tradition or grandfather laws. Bold, sweeping, grand proposals become law. Private citizens step forward with new initiatives. The private sector responds just as it did 220 years ago when the nation was established.

Hardly a day passes without one wildlife issue or another appearing in a local newspaper in every city and town across the United States. Every child learns about wildlife and is attracted to wildlife every day. Parents encourage their children to enjoy wildlife. Nature shows appear daily on television across the United States. Presidential candidates and members of Congress want to be seen supporting wildlife. Some 300 million people visit national parks to see what is left of our natural world, which is fast disappearing. People are catching on that if you want to see wildlife, now is the time. Something is happening across the United States. If the history of the dusky seaside sparrow is representative, perhaps it is crisis time.

DUSKY SEASIDE SPARROW

At one time, there were ten recognized species and subspecies of seaside sparrows and three species and subspecies of sharp-tailed sparrows from the Texas Gulf coast to the Gulf of St. Lawrence in Canada. Beecher (1955) pointed out that the Texas seaside sparrow (*Ammodramus maritima sennetti*) and the Acadian sharp-tailed sparrow (*A. caudacuta subvirgata*) of the Gulf of Saint Lawrence are closely related species. The seaside sparrows range from the Texas Gulf coast to the coast of Massachusetts. The sharp-tailed sparrows range from Delaware to the Gulf of Saint Lawrence, and so overlap of the seaside and sharp-tailed sparrows occurs on the Atlantic coast.

As the Pleistocene glaciers melted, the sea level rose some 100 m, and North America's coastal crust also rose due to the loss of an immense weight of ice. Beecher suggested that the loss of land along the Gulf and Atlantic coasts brought about the isolation of a once contiguous population of an ancestral sparrow species. As land was inundated by the rising ocean, the ancestral sparrows became isolated populations and therefore speciated in response to differing environmental conditions. The Delaware River, for instance, separates the common sharp-tailed sparrow (*A. caudacuta caudacuta*) from the southern sharp-tailed sparrow (*A. caudata diversa*). Galveston Bay separates the Texas seaside sparrow from the Louisiana seaside sparrow (*A. maritima fisheri*). The Mississippi River divides the Wakulla seaside sparrow (*A. maritima macgillivrayii*) from the Louisiana seaside sparrow. Traveling eastward along the Gulf coast, the bay at Mobile divides Scott's seaside sparrow (*A. maritima peninsulae*), and the Cape Sable seaside sparrow (*A. maritima mirabilis*) is isolated in the Everglades. The dusky seaside sparrow (*A. maritima nigrescens*) was on the east coast of Florida near Merritt Island, which, according to Beecher, "could have been greatly affected by rise in sea level." Continuing further north up the Atlantic coast, other populations of seaside and sharp-tailed sparrows are similarly isolated.

Complicating Beecher's analysis is the fact that glacial advances have occurred at least 18 times during the Pleistocene and that each advance and recession of the great ice sheets has affected the sparrow populations differently. Any seaside sparrow populations would have been driven southward during glacial growth. Indeed, other populations of seaside and sharp-tailed sparrows probably existed and have become extinct. Environmental processes such as hurricanes act to maintain the isolation between populations. So does extinction.

The extinction of the dusky seaside sparrow is the story of jobs and growth versus those who would set aside even a small piece of ground to save a bird (Walters 1992). Dusky seaside sparrows inhabited the salt-marsh areas of broomgrass and rushes. Before Merritt Island became the site of America's launch pad for the space race, nests were reported to be 10 to 15 m apart. The size of a typical sparrow, duskies lived on insects, caterpillars, and spiders. In the 1960s, NASA bought much of Cape Canaveral and North and South Merritt Island and built Kennedy Space Center. The U.S. Air Force had previously used the area as a launch site. Mosquito spraying eliminated an important food source for the duskies and had reduced their population even before NASA arrived. As early as 1955, Longstreet (1955) warned that mosquito control programs might harm the dusky population. But mosquitos became a public menace and had to be done away with. In 1960, it was realized that the diminutive dusky was already in trouble.

Indeed, the mosquito problem was apparently so bad that NASA decided to construct dikes on the Indian River to inundate mosquito breeding grounds.

Naturally, neither the loss of a food source nor the flooding of critical habitat was good for the dusky, but few cared. The vegetation community also changed. The avian community responded to the vegetation change, and larger birds such as red-winged blackbirds and boat-tailed grackles moved in. Salt water was replaced by fresh water. Fresh water enabled ducks to take residence, and so, at first appearance, it seemed that the number of birds increased and all was well. Of course, the delicate balance of the salt marsh was broken. The Spartina grass where the duskies nested was almost gone. Without appropriate nesting habitat, the bird would disappear.

In 1967, the Endangered Species Act of 1966 (see Chapter 2) passed through Congress and was signed into law by the president. The original endangered species list included more than 50 animals; among the ten from Florida were the West Indian manatee, the Florida panther, the Everglades kite (snail kite), the Cape Sable seaside sparrow, and the dusky seaside sparrow. In 1969, the duskies on Merritt Island were disappearing, but another population was found to the west in the coastal marshes of the St. Johns River. By 1973, only three dusky seaside sparrows remained on Merritt Island, their population a victim of overzealous mosquito control. Unfortunately for the approximately 2000 remaining duskies in the marshes at St. Johns, the state wanted to build a highway through the middle of their habitat. Today, the Beeline Expressway in Brevard County cuts through what was once prime dusky habitat.

With the new highways came real estate developers. Canaveral Groves and Port St. Johns now abut what was prime habitat for duskies. By 1968, the entire population of duskies had been reduced to only a few. Land purchases by the Nature Conservancy and U.S. Fish and Wildlife Service established the St. Johns National Wildlife Refuge around 1970 and provided the dusky a temporary reprieve. With the borders of the 4200-acre refuge established, the countdown to the dusky's extinction had begun.

We will see later (Chapter 16) that even large reserves fail to prevent extinction. Furthermore, a heterogeneous landscape is needed to support many species. If, for instance, the dusky could only nest in areas of vegetation that had been burned three years prior and could only survive in those areas for four years, then a heterogeneous landscape maintained by periodic fires widely spread around the landscape would be essential to the dusky's survival. Such a regime would be impossible to maintain in a small refuge. Six fires, in fact, burned in the refuge from 1970 to 1977, but because the refuge was too small, several fires were damaging. By 1976, only 28 males remained in the refuge. Despite repeated past warnings about the devastating effect fires might have, it was not until 1979 that the U.S. Fish and Wildlife Service cut fire lanes. It was already too late, however. By then, only a few males survived, presumably along with an unknown number of females.

By 1979, reality had set in, and the dusky's slide to extinction caused a bureaucratic panic. By 1980, only four birds remained in the wild, three of which joined others that had been captured earlier. The last wild dusky, a male, eluded capture and presumably died in the wild. All the duskies in captivity were males, but the dusky was not extinct yet. A dusky could presumably be crossed with another of the seaside sparrows; by crossing and then crossing the offspring again, each time with a dusky male, a nearly purebred dusky could be recreated in six generations. Indeed, a female Scott's seaside sparrow from the Florida Gulf coast had been successfully crossed with a dusky in captivity and viable offspring were produced. However, the U.S. Fish and Wildlife Service refused to allow a cross-breeding program. The late Herb Kale, a vice president of the Florida Audubon Society and a central figure in the story of the dusky, was furious. "The decision by USF&W was one of the worst decisions made anywhere at any time" (Kale personal communication).

Having searched for more duskies, the U.S. Fish and Wildlife Service insisted that a female could be found. One has to ask, if a female could be found in the wild, couldn't the males do a better job of it than humans? Kale simply never gave up. He hatched a plan to transfer the three (two died earlier) remaining males to Disney World, where a captive breeding program began. But it was too late, and old age had taken its toll. In July 1987, the last pure dusky died. The aviary at the Disney facility where the hybrids were kept was neglected and in disrepair when rats ate them. Even the hybrids had been lost through the carelessness of humans.

FISHING IN U.S. AND INTERNATIONAL WATERS

Atlantic bluefin tuna can weigh up to three-quarters of a ton and are able to swim 50 miles per hour. On the docks of Halifax, Nova Scotia, bluefin can sell for $20,000 apiece. In Japan, however, a bluefin can sell for $350 a pound. In 1975, the northwest Atlantic population of bluefin tuna was estimated to be 250,000. Twenty years of overfishing has reduced the population to about 22,000. In 1995, the bluefin was proposed for listing as an internationally endangered species. Man's greed is solely responsible for the decline.

The Magnuson Fisheries Conservation and Management Act (the Fish Conservation and Management Act, see Chapter 2) set up regional fishery management councils that are today dominated by fishing interests as regulators (Swardson 1994). As a result, the U.S. fishing industry underwent massive growth, in part subsidized by federal loan guarantees. With improving technology and a complete reluctance to regulate itself, the fishing industry is overcapitalized and far too large. Unfortunately, the seas were found to harbor only finite resources. The situation in the United States is not unique however. Worldwide harvests of fish in 1989 brought in a catch worth about $70 billion. The cost to operate the global fishing fleet was about $90 billion. The difference had to be subsidized. The Japanese government extended $19 billion in credit to its troubled fishing industry, and no one seriously expects the money to be paid back. Even the fiscally conservative Norwegians subsidized their fleet at $150 million. In 1994, the Clinton administration issued a $30 million aid package for the sinking New England fishing industry. Canada must of course support the Newfoundland economy.

Who consumes all this fish? It is estimated that 6.6% of the animal protein consumption of North Americans comes from fish. Fish accounts for 12% of European consumption of protein. In Africa, the figure is 19% and in Asia 29%. It is thus no surprise that Asians lead in aquaculture technology. It is easy to suggest that the people of Third World countries will ultimately pay for depleted fish stocks worldwide. However, their investment in capital equipment such as processing factories and large fleets is much less. As is usually the case, subsidies will spread the cost throughout the economy.

On March 11, 1995, the *St. Petersburg Times* reported that Canada had seized one of 14 Spanish fishing trawlers operating within Canada's international waters. Canadian gunboats fired across the bow and gained control of the ship after a chase on the high seas. Relationships between the European Economic Community and Canada have since deteriorated sharply over the dispute, the article suggested. Canada continues to protect its dwindling fish stocks after the failure of intense high-level political negotiations. As we saw, Canadian fish stocks, especially in the northwest Atlantic, are in trouble.

One day later, on March 12, 1995, the *Miami Herald* reported that United Nations Food and Agricultural Organization (FAO) experts had concluded that oceans around the world are being "ravaged by overfishing that has decimated natural stocks and jeopardizes the future of the seas as a source of food for the Earth's rapidly growing, ever-hungrier population." The experts concluded that the history of fishing is to deplete the resource until there are no fish. The world's fish catch was a stagnant 101 million tons in 1993, about 83 million tons of which were caught in marine and freshwater fisheries. Aquaculture accounted for the remaining 18 million tons, and this figure has been increasing yearly for some time. Approximately 85% of fish farms are in Asia, and aquaculture is now a $30 billion industry annually.

The world take of Atlantic cod and such prized species as haddock, hake, flounder, and shrimp has declined principally because of overfishing. Less valuable fish such as Alaskan pollock, Peruvian anchoveta, and Chilean jack mackerel are now sought-after species. According to the FAO, over 70% of all conventional species are fully exploited, overexploited, depleted, or are in the process of recovering from overexploitation. In West Africa, Bangladesh, and Southeast Asia, fish that were once taken when they were 1 m in length are now taken at 10 cm in length. The world's fishing fleets have swelled over the past quarter century so that fishing effort has increased to bring in the same tonnage each year. Twenty nations account for over 80% of the total harvest of fish. China leads the world with 10 million tons caught offshore. Japan, Peru, Chile, and the United States follow with 5.8 millions tons.

The FAO researchers claim that fishermen discard upwards of 27 million tons of fish yearly, a tremendous loss. Less valuable fish are tossed overboard to make room for more valuable fish. How to manage the world's fisheries is a difficult problem. In developing nations, populations are growing faster than food output, and thus it is nearly impossible to limit the number of fishermen. High unemployment, political upheaval, and pest outbreaks all drive people to fish for themselves. If all fishing were to stop immediately, some fish stocks would require a decade or more to recover. "What we are talking about is a worldwide management crisis of natural resources," said one U.N. official.

The U.S. fisheries also suffer from overharvesting. Fish resources in Puget Sound in the Pacific Northwest have seriously declined, and harvests are at their lowest level in over 55 years. Annual catches of over 26 million pounds were routinely harvested in the past. Now the total harvest is a pitiful 3.6 million pounds. Populations of Pacific cod, hake, and pollock have been severely reduced. One researcher suggested that "essentially the fisheries have pretty much ceased for these three stocks."

Outraged by foreign fishing fleets slightly more than 3 miles off U.S. coastlines, the U.S. Congress expanded the coastal economic zone to 200 miles in the 1970s. Although the foreign fleets backed off, U.S. factory ships quickly filled the void. Driven by greed, these trawlers were said to take everything "their nets could snag." On March 15, 1995, the *Miami Herald* reported that Oregon Indian tribes urged President Clinton to declare a state of emergency in the Pacific Northwest to make good on a 140-year-old treaty that would help bring salmon populations back. The tribes have depended on the salmon fishery for more than 10,000 years. Hydroelectric dams have caused the demise of several species of salmon that have been added to the federal list of threatened and endangered species. The Indian tribes, state fish and wildlife officials, and conservation groups sued the federal government over its failure to protect the salmon.

Dams have been shown to block fish migrations upstream to breed and to slow travel downstream after the fish spawn. The National Marine Fisheries Service proposed barging fish, but conservationists claim that more water needs to be spilled over dams to speed migration to the sea and also lower reservoir levels. Such measures are opposed by irrigation farmers, shippers, and the aluminum industry, all of which depend on water from the rivers. The Indian tribes claim that if nothing is done, the several salmon species will be extinct by the turn of the century. If the salmon become extinct, the very culture and religion of the tribes will be lost as well. Clearly, there is a wildlife issue here.

Northwest Pacific salmon such as coho salmon are born in freshwater streams, migrate to live in the sea, and then return to freshwater streams to spawn and die. Each year, fewer and fewer fish return to their place of birth to spawn. In 1995, the National Marine Fisheries Service reported that West Coast ocean catches of coho fell to only 292,000 fish in 1993 from 5.3 million fish in 1976, a 95% decline. The Chinook salmon catch declined by 80% from 1988 to 1992. Sockeye salmon populations also declined. Steelhead trout are being considered for the endangered species list.

On Oregon's Rogue River, all migrating salmon must pass through a narrow underwater passage to get around Gold Ray Dam. Each passing salmon is recorded by a video camera. Biologists in the region agree that most species of Pacific salmon are in deep trouble as a result of overfishing at sea and destruction of their freshwater habitat by dams, agricultural schemes, and industrial and urban development. Logging near upstream spawning areas caused massive siltation of the gravel beds where the salmon laid their eggs. Insect populations that fed salmon were decimated when the trees were taken. Streams were straightened, obstructions removed, and as a result, the complex environment so necessary to support salmon was destroyed. Man's activities were blamed for the loss of fish. As one logger put it, "I've got to feed my family. It's either us or them fish."

INTRODUCED FISH

Introduced species are one of the principal causes of extirpation of native species. The *Washington Post National Weekly Edition* for October 17–23, 1994 ran a story about Yellowstone Lake in Yellowstone National Park, Wyoming. Yellowstone Lake supports a native cutthroat trout population that federal authorities have spent years protecting. As a result, Yellowstone Lake is one of the favorite sportfishing lakes in the Rocky Mountains. Now, however, lake trout have been discovered in Yellowstone Lake. Lake trout are native to the Great Lakes and not western rivers. Lake trout are larger than cutthroat trout, and one fish biologist referred to the species as "freshwater sharks." Fears are that lake trout will prey upon the smaller cutthroat trout.

Since the 1970s, the U.S. Fish and Wildlife Service has managed the Yellowstone cutthroat fishery actively. Every spring, the lake's cutthroats migrate up more than half of Yellowstone Lake's 124 feeder streams to spawn and thus provide grizzly bears with a source of protein after a winter of hibernation. Lake trout, on the other hand, spawn deep in the lake and thus do not become food for bears. Federal officials have offered a $10,000 reward for information leading to the arrest of those responsible for introducing the large lake trout. However, knowing who perpetrated the crime will not solve the problem.

Because some of its waters come from thermal vents, Yellowstone Lake is unusually productive for an alpine lake. Biologists have found several strains of cutthroat trout within the lake. Protecting the cutthroat trout also protects eagles, ospreys, and otters within the park. Montana has long been a magnet for sportfishing, and rivers like the Madison, Yellowstone, and Big Hole are known for their great fishing. However, the brown trout and rainbow trout for which the rivers are known are introduced species. Brown trout were introduced from Europe and rainbow trout were introduced from the Pacific coast. Native fish throughout North America are facing threats from logging, development, ranching, and introduced species. Until a species is declared threatened or endangered, with few exceptions, there are few laws that protect it.

Throughout the West, aquatic systems are collapsing. Grazing activities have had a devastating effect on many western streams and riparian areas. Among the native species in trouble are the bull trout, the westslope cutthroat trout, the fluvial grayling, and the white sturgeon, which was placed on the endangered species list. Many other species of freshwater fish are in trouble. In Colorado, the squawfish is about to be lost forever. Although many blame introduced fish species, habitat loss and dams contribute to the problem. Water, it seems, is a valuable commodity to humans.

AMPHIBIAN POPULATIONS DECLINE WORLDWIDE

Frogs, toads, and salamanders worldwide are in trouble, and populations are thought to be disappearing (Phillips 1994). Every continent has documented losses, except Antarctica, which has none. In Australia, 26 of 202 species of frogs have declining populations. Some frogs have not been seen in over a decade. In Costa Rica, the golden toad (*Bufo periglenes*) has not been observed in significant numbers since 1987. Scientists working in Brazil reported declining populations of amphibians in the early 1980s. Amphibians are thought to be sensitive environmental indicators.

Since the decline appears to be happening worldwide, factors such as climate change and increased atmospheric pollution have been blamed. Scientists are alarmed because even populations in protected areas have declined; hence the reasons sought are not always associated with habitat loss or other proximal causes.

At a meeting in Irvine, California in 1990, scientists reported on declining ranges and populations (Blaustein and Wake 1990). Although amphibian populations fluctuate, sometimes wildly, it is the accumulation of evidence worldwide that indicates a global phenomenon. For instance, only 2% of the lakes in the Sierra Nevada Mountains of California that contained yellow-legged frogs (*Rana muscosa*) in the mid-1970s had them in 1989. Similarly, Blaustein documented the decline of three species in the American Northwest. Other species have disappeared from undisturbed lakes in the American Southwest.

A unique gastric brooding frog (*Rheobatrachus silus*) from Australia was discovered in 1973. The frog is interesting because its eggs hatch and develop in the mother's stomach. In 1981, it was thought to be extinct. There is little evidence, however, that declines of low-latitude, low-altitude amphibians are also occurring aside from those adversely impacted by habitat loss.

As Blaustein and Wake assert, amphibians are critical components of many ecosystems, often constituting the highest fraction of vertebrate biomass. Amphibians are carnivores that consume insects and are themselves preyed upon by birds, fish, mammals, and also some insects. They occupy the middle trophic level in the web of life. Acid rain, climate change, air pollution, UV radiation, and introduced predators have all been suggested as causes of amphibian declines.

RAPTORS

Swainson's hawks are birds of prey that spend spring and summer in western North American grasslands (Di Silvestro 1996). Before the North American fall, the hawks migrate to South American grasslands where they spend another spring and summer. By migrating, the hawks live a life of springs and summers. Since the 1940s, the number of Swainson's hawks has declined by 90%, yet few dead birds had been found in the United States or Canada. Either migration was killing the birds or something was going on in their southern range. Most of the band recoveries from Swainson's hawks came from Argentina. To discover what was happening, two Swainson's hawks were outfitted with 30-g satellite transmitters in California. (As an aside, Swainson's hawks weigh from 700 to 1000 g. The federal weight limit for transmitters is that they must be less than 3% of the body weight of the bird.) They were tracked to the Argentinian pampas.

Biologists visited Argentina, where the outfitted Swainson's hawks settled. Near La Pampa in north-central Argentina, introduced Australian eucalyptus trees grow in isolated stands called montes. Swainson's hawks and other birds of prey roost in the montes. One flock of hawks numbered 4000. An additional 700 birds were found dead. The deaths were suspected to be due to pesticide spraying. One of the dead Swainson's hawks was banded in Saskatchewan, Canada. In all, some 450,000 Swainson's hawks, nearly all the North American population, winters in Argentina.

La Pampa was mostly cattle country and alfalfa, but ten years ago agricultural crops were replaced with sunflowers. Recent irrigation developments have encouraged the development of cultivation. Large agricultural areas attract hordes of insects, especially grasshoppers. Swainson's hawks are attracted to the large swarms of grasshoppers. Unfortunately, the insecticide monocrotophos and other pesticides were sprayed to control grasshoppers in alfalfa and sunflower fields. A survey found 4100 dead Swainson's hawks. Total deaths were probably much higher.

Canadians also expressed an interest in the study. Two Swainson's hawks that had satellite transmitters attached in Alberta were at the same location as the dead hawks in Argentina. Of 12 leg bands that have been recovered from the dead Swainson's hawks, 9 originated in Alberta and Saskatchewan and 1 each in Colorado, Idaho, and California. Most of the dead hawks were in the white color phase, indicating that they were from Canada and the adjacent Great Plains of the United States, and 90% were adults.

The pesticides were sprayed from planes and air blasters towed by tractors. The hawks were following the tractors to catch disturbed grasshoppers. Not only did the hawks receive a direct spray, but they also received a secondary dosage from the ingested grasshoppers. The life cycle of the grasshoppers required multiple pesticide applications. Hence, hawks were probably subjected to multiple doses of insecticide. Unfortunately, many of the dead hawks were quickly scavenged by carrion-feeding birds such as caracaras and vultures. Efforts are now underway to find a replacement insecticide that kills grasshoppers but does not harm top predators such as Swainson's hawks. Other North American birds such as dickcissels also winter in South and Central America. These too are subjected to agricultural pesticides.

According to the *Albuquerque Journal* on April 23, 1996, the Forest Conservation Council, the National Audubon Society, the Carson Forest Watch, and the Forest Guardians warned the U.S. Department of Agriculture that timber sales in the Carson National Forest of New Mexico threaten wildlife habitat for the endangered Mexican spotted owl and the northern goshawk. According to the Department of Agriculture, 30% of the old-growth trees have been set aside as habitat, while only 18% is required. Both sides will convene in a courtroom to reach a decision.

Mexican spotted owls were added to the endangered species list in 1993. They are found in canyons and forests of Utah, Colorado, New Mexico, Arizona, and on the New Mexico–Texas–Mexico border. About 90% of the owls live within national forests.

NORTHERN WHITE RHINOCEROS

The northern white rhinoceros (*Ceratotherium simum cottoni*) is a rare race of white rhino. Its nearest relative is 1500 miles away in South Africa. Garamba National Park in Zaire was declared a national park in 1938 and is nearly 2000 square miles. Another 3000 square miles bordering three sides of the park is protected as a wildlife reserve with sustainable use of natural resources. In the mid-1970s, there were 400 to 800 rhinos in the park and 15,000 to 30,000 elephants (Karesh 1996).

By 1984, there were 15 rhinos and 4500 scared elephants. Poachers had decimated one of the last great herds in Africa. Shortly after that, conservation efforts led by Institut Zairois pour la Conservation de la Nature were able to increase elephant herds to 11,000 and the rhino population doubled to 30.

Zaire's economy was doing (and continues to do) poorly, and refugees from numerous warring nations east of Zaire have moved into areas surrounding Garamba. Park guards make five dollars a month and routinely risk their lives protecting the wildlife. International organizations are interested in increasing their activities in Garamba.

For the second time in 1996, poachers killed northern white rhino in Zaire's Garamba National Park. Garamba has the world's last 28 wild white rhinos. In mid-February 1996, poachers killed a male rhino and hacked away its horn and meat. It was the first confirmed rhino poaching in 12 years. About one month later, a pregnant female was found dead and hornless. Rhino horn can sell for $15,000 to $50,000 a kilogram in Yemen, where the horns are used to make dagger handles. In China, rhino horn is used to lower a child's temperature and hence is purchased for medicinal uses. There are some 7500 white rhinos left, most of which are in South Africa; however, these rhinos are in captivity.

Conservationists have urged the Zaire government to stop the poachers. However, Garamba is in northeastern Zaire, far from the capital. Unless conservationists are willing to provide funding to support an antipoaching patrol

FIGURE 11.1 A mother rhino and her calf in Ngorongoro National Park, Tanzania. She is guarded 24 hours a day by an armed guard.

staff and increase security for the rhinos, nothing will stop the poachers save the supply of rhinos. Dehorning the rhinos might also be a solution. However, poachers who follow rhino tracks around for several days don't appreciate finding a dehorned rhino. So as not to waste time tracking them repeatedly, poachers kill the rhino in any case.

The penis of a rhino can sell for $600 and is used as an aphrodisiac. In India, one zoo sells rhino urine for 44 cents a liter. The urine is presumed to cure asthma and sore throats. At least the urine is a sustainable product and requires that the rhino be living! The World Wildlife Fund claims there are fewer than 11,000 rhino of all five species in the wild. Sadly, the two rhinos in Figure 11.1 may be the last of an ancient lineage.

RATTLESNAKE ROUNDUP

Fifteen species of rattlesnakes are found in the United States. The western diamondback rattler (*Crotalus atrox*) is perhaps the most recognized, although it is found only in New Mexico, Texas, and Oklahoma. Snakes are economically valuable species because of the services they perform for humans. Many snakes eat rodents and thus perform valuable ecosystem functions for farmers. The U.S. trade in rattlesnakes is unregulated, and TRAFFIC–USA estimates that up to 125,000 rattlesnakes have been traded annually since 1990. A three-foot diamondback is worth about $21. What is so curious are the so-called "rattlesnake roundups" that are economically important events in some towns.

The Sweetwater, Texas Rattlesnake Roundup is the largest and most publicized event of its kind (Weir 1992). Upwards of 35,000 spectators and 18,000 snakes could be seen over a weekend in 1989. The roundup is now in its 39th year. Gross income for 1989 was $55,000 and net income was about $30,000.

Rattlesnake roundups are held in New Mexico, Pennsylvania, and Texas, as well as other states. Prizes are offered to participants and large crowds are attracted to the spectacle. The chance to behead a snake is not uncommon. When a snake is decapitated, the head and body continue to writhe because of the snake's slow metabolism. Some people find it interesting to bet on when the head and body will actually stop wiggling. Any number of snake curios and oddities can be had, such as snakehead earrings, snakehead belt buckles, and snakeskin boots. If none of these interest you, you might want to bungie jump with a snake or perhaps stand in a pit of snakes. All this fun can be had at a rattlesnake roundup for about five dollars.

Cash prizes are often awarded for the largest snake, the smallest snake, most pounds collected, and to the collector who brings in the most snakes. Knowing this, some snake collectors precollect, or bring in the largest home-raised snake they can find. Rounding up rattlesnakes does require a bit of skill. Techniques for collecting are highly sophisticated. A common method in Texas is to carry around a tank of gasoline that can be pumped up with air and used as a sprayer. The tank is pressurized and the gasoline is sprayed into the snake's den, usually in some boulder field. Care must be taken not to spray in front of the den because the snake only backs into its den. If too much gasoline is sprayed, the snake simply dies in its den and cannot be recovered. If the spray is directed deep in the den, the snake will flee. With patience and experience, this technique works every time! When the blinded and confused snake emerges, a collecting pole is used to snare it around the neck. The snake is then placed into a sack. Even a pillowcase can hold a dozen snakes. Dazed, starved, dehydrated, and near death, the snakes are delivered to holding pens for public viewing.

Some rattlesnake hunts raise money for charity, others are motivated by the profit from admission fees, and some towns just need a reason to exist. No license is required to participate. No research has been done on the effect on snake populations. As for the ethical treatment of snakes that participate in the roundup, standards simply do not exist, and it is unlikely that any will anytime soon.

The impact on all snake species is, as one might expect, not healthy. Many types of snakes are taken during the hunts. For every 100 rattlesnakes taken, 40 harmless snakes are also killed. Regarding the rattlesnake hunt, Shelton (1981) states that the "purpose of the Sweetwater Jaycees Rattlesnake Round-up has never been to exterminate the specie [sic] but to aid nature in controlling overpopulation of rattlers in the area." Later, Shelton implies that deer hunting may actually have increased deer populations. Thus, Shelton's contradiction becomes clear. In 1982, 8166 snakes weighing 17,986 kg, were taken. In 1991, 2031 snakes, weighing 4474 kg, were harvested. No one has studied small mammal populations in these areas to see if they are increasing. Rattlesnakes consume rats, mice, ground squirrels, and gophers that would otherwise damage crops and pastures. Sadly, an outbreak of plague must occur before people realize that snakes are beneficial.

ZEBRA MUSSELS

On October 8, 1995, the *Miami Herald* proclaimed in bold print: "Mussels strain water world." Zebra mussels are tiny striped mollusks that successfully invaded North America in the late 1980s, when they were detected in the Great Lakes. The mussels are freshwater organisms but can tolerate salt water for short periods of time. They are believed to have been introduced from northern Europe after being transported on the hulls and bilges of ships. Within two years of being recorded in Lake Erie, some areas had 35,000 individual zebra mussels per square meter. They have shut down power plants, destroyed native clam beds, and disrupted natural aquatic functions. Like other mollusks, zebra mussels are filter feeders, taking in algae and bacteria and ejecting clarified water. Their feeding activities thus concentrate pollutants. However, they are not native to North America, and thus their long-term impact is not known. Two-thirds of all native freshwater mussels are endangered in the United States and Canada, perhaps because of exposure to contaminants.

What is known is that the zebra mussels are being transported across the United States. Boats and barges transport the mussels and their larvae up and down the Mississippi River. Pleasure boaters inadvertently have transported them to California. Meanwhile, the zebra mussels continue to adapt to their new environments. A mollusk's reproductive capacity is enormous; hence, adapting to a new environment is enhanced. Natural selection can quickly select against offspring that are poorly adapted. Thus, speciation is occurring in the zebra mussels. Boaters are being asked to check their boats for the mussels, but the zebra mussel's larvae are microscopic and hence nearly undetectable. It seems certain that it is just a matter of time before the entire United States is invaded by this adaptable menace. The biology and ecology of the zebra mussel will allow the organism to gain access to most, if not all, of North America's freshwater systems.

The Tennessee Valley Authority is emptying some of the lakes it manages to control the infestation of zebra mussels. The mussel population is so dense that water pipes become clogged by mussels. Screens installed to prevent fish from entering pipes have allowed mussels to completely close off water pipes. So far, the only way to eradicate an infestation is to drain the lake. However, the larvae follow the water out and settle elsewhere. From the zebra mussel in fresh water to introduced fish, birds, mammals, and plants, North America and most every other populated area is becoming homogenized.

GRIZZLY BEARS

Grizzly bears (*Ursos arctos horribilis*) existed across much of the western United States from as far south as the Mexican border up through Canada and into Alaska. The bear on the California State flag is a grizzly bear. Sadly, grizzly bear populations have crashed across their range. They have been extirpated from Oregon south and from Colorado south as well. Occasionally, a grizzly bear report comes from the San Juan Mountains of southern Colorado. The U.S. Fish and Wildlife Service has created a grizzly bear recovery plan to aid one of America's most mythical creatures, a symbol of all that was wild and free and without any predators save primitive human hunters.

Grizzly bear populations in the lower 48 states now exist in five forested areas in the northwest. In Yellowstone National Park, an estimated 250 bears survive. Several hundred occupy Glacier National Park as well as an adjacent national forest in northern Montana and Canadian forests. Little more than a dozen live in the Cabinet Mountains on the Idaho–Montana border. A few dozen are believed to inhabit the Selkirk Mountains of northeastern Washington and Idaho. Perhaps grizzly bears use the Northern Cascade Mountains in north-central Washington. Other mountainous areas nearby, such as the Selway-Bitterroot Mountains in Idaho, are being considered as a reintroduction area.

Seeing a grizzly bear in Denali National Park in Alaska is an exciting experience. Most visitors see them from inside one of the many buses that take people back and forth across the park. However, this experience does not compare to seeing a grizzly bear on foot out in the middle of the park. Picture, for a moment, hiking across one of the braided gravel rivers found in Denali. Far above you and several miles away is the road where the tiny yellow buses move back and forth. You cross a stream on foot when you see a grizzly sow and three cubs making their way toward the stream. The cubs are trailing, turning over rocks and poking their noses into everything. Suddenly the wind shifts and the mother bear has picked up your scent more than a mile away. For a moment, fear washes over you like a warm wave. You freeze and your legs feel weak. The bear could make up the distance between you in less than two minutes. You turn and calmly walk directly away from the bear as she goes about her routine. Bear attacks on humans in Denali are extremely rare and almost always caused by humans bumbling onto bears. It's a good feeling to know that grizzlies are still around and we can experience them on their terms.

Once again all the laws on the books won't save the grizzly bear unless something is done to save suitable habitat. Grizzly bears are top carnivores. Their requirements are enormous and, as in many, many other cases, their habitat is shrinking. Grizzly bears are known to have large home ranges and thus need large areas to exist. Unfortunately, roads in one form or another run through most areas. Large roadless areas are few and far between. The approach of modern forest management is to designate land as limited access or no access and then attempt to connect these large tracts of forest with smaller unoccupied corridors through which wildlife, including bears, can move. The Kootenai National Forest, which includes the Cabinet Mountains, is a good example of what is wrong with the present management scheme. Since the grizzly was "promoted" to the federal threatened list in 1975, nearly 7000 miles of roads for loggers have been built in the forest and some 5 billion board feet have been removed. To be an effective bear sanctuary, the roads would have to be blocked off, logging would have to cease, and hunting would have to be discontinued.

Some people favor multiple use of public land. If the grizzly bears disappears from the lower 48 states, they can just as easily go to Alaska or Canada to see them. Others suggest that all logging on public land, including national forests, must stop for the foreseeable future. Millions of miles of roads in these forests must be removed and revegetated. Hunting would be restricted to certain areas known to have no bears. These people are not radical environmentalists—they are you and me.

SOUTHWESTERN WILLOW FLYCATCHERS

The *Arizona Republic* reported that Phoenix and five other area cities agreed to share the $440 million cost of raising Roosevelt Dam by 77 feet in the belief that the cities would receive more water. However, the habitat of 40 southwestern willow flycatchers (*Empidonax traillii extrimus*), an endangered species listed on February 20, 1995, would be significantly altered so as to be useless to the small birds. The birds migrate between Central America and the Southwest riparian habitats. About 160 willow flycatchers live along Arizona's rivers, and additional birds are found in New Mexico and southern California. No environmental assessment was undertaken by the Salt River Project (which manages the dam) and the city partners have already invested millions of dollars in the project. Willow flycatchers have "high site fidelity," that is, they return to the same sites to nest and raise their young.

The Endangered Species Act not only may prevent the loss of the partners' initial investment but will probably force cancellation of the entire project. Creation of new habitat is very expensive and probably will fail in the long term.

Raising the level of the dam to impound more water is not a viable long-term solution. The dam "improvement" project would have allowed 1 million more people to move into the Phoenix area. This would have taken a decade. Then what would be done? Is more growth the answer? Is more water the answer? How much is enough? The long-term survival of the willow flycatcher seems inconsequential when addressing the heart of the issue. Are we really treating the disease or just its symptoms?

LOCUSTS

In April 1996, an enormous swarm of locusts moved across agricultural lands of the former Soviet Republic of Tajikistan and posed a serious threat to the economy of the nation. At least 250,000 acres of cotton and fruit crops were the insects' target. The locusts invaded from the southern plains of the Pamir Mountains to the east. The swarm was so huge that no attempts were made to stop it.

MEXICAN WOLVES

On May 2, 1996, The Associated Press reported that ranchers who see a reintroduced Mexican wolf attack and kill their livestock on private land can kill the wolf. The rule was proposed by the U.S. Fish and Wildlife Service because it wants to reintroduce wolves in New Mexico and Arizona. Al Schneberger, director of the New Mexico Cattle Growers Association, was quoted as saying that such proposals "aren't worth the paper they are printed on." The cattlemen distrust the federal government and believe federal authorities would renounce the agreement once wolves are reintroduced.

The Endangered Species Act has a special section that allows designation of the Mexican wolves as "non-essential and experimental," thus allowing more flexibility in their management. One problem cattlemen have is that if a Mexican wolf is attacking stock on public land, the wolf cannot be harmed. In the West, it is common for a rancher to own and live on one acre and pay less than two dollars per head per month grazing fees to use public land. Of course, grazing rights are a privilege and not a right. Thus, a simple solution would be to not grant any grazing rights to the public land occupied by the wolves.

The Arizona State Congress threatened to pass a law offering a bounty on any Mexican wolves shot in the state.

CALIFORNIA GNATCATCHER

The California gnatcatcher (*Polioptila california californica*) lives in coastal sage scrub in southern California, south of Los Angeles. Developable land in this part of the United States can be extremely expensive. On March 30, 1993, the gnatcatcher was listed as threatened under the Endangered Species Act. However, many other species living in the coastal scrub are just as unique as the gnatcatcher, and all need protection in one of the world's most rapidly developing regions.

Mann and Plummer (1995) described an encounter between developers who purchased land, environmentalists who want the land left alone, and the U.S. Fish and Wildlife Service, which is responsible for protecting species. In the high-stakes world of modern development, tens of millions of dollars ride on housing layouts and access roads. Environmentalists argue that setting aside a connected sequence of reserves is essential to protecting species. An isolated sequence of reserves dissected by roads and billboards won't work, they say.

The gnatcatcher has already temporarily halted development on prime developable land. A southern California developer purchased a large tract of coastal scrub for $180 million in northern San Diego County. The developer planned to build 3000 upper-middle-class homes on the property. Oddly, the property was purchased by the development company *before* professional biologists surveyed it. Had the company paid biologists to survey first, the developers would have saved their money. Instead, the profit motive drove them to purchase the property first and ask questions later. This was a serious mistake as it turned out. Habitat conservation plans, amendments to the Endangered

Species Act in 1982, and the formation of the Natural Communities Conservation Planning (NCCP) program in California in 1991 resulted. The NCCP was supposed to "inaugurate a new era of consensus" between all interested parties, developers and endangered species alike.

The very beauty of the California coastal sage scrub, which drew some people to live near it, is driving developers to destroy it. It is prime developable land. Meanwhile, more controversies over development across the United States are occurring. Are more shopping centers needed? How much habitat is going to be lost? There will be more and more issues similar to the California gnatcatchers, spotted owls, and manatees.

KILLER BEES

Four swarms of Africanized "killer bees" were reported in Nicaragua, the *Albuquerque Tribune* reported in April 1996. One swarm killed two elderly people. Eleven people were hospitalized after being stung during a Holy Week procession. In Costa Rica, one person died after being stung.

EXOTICS

During the 1960s, the New Mexico State Game Commission began a program to introduce nonnative, big game wildlife into New Mexico to garner sportsmen's dollars (see Chapter 16). Barbary sheep from Africa, Persian ibex from Iran, Siberian ibex from Siberia, and oryx from Africa were introduced, and all succeeded. By the mid-1980s, the introduced species' populations exploded and overpopulation became a problem. The introductions outcompeted native wildlife and ate native plants, some of which were endangered. Ibex in some areas of the state can be hunted all year. Population control programs for the oryx were started.

PETS

More than ten million animals are euthanized (killed) every year in the United States. There simply are too many pets that are making even more pets. Pet overpopulation is an immense problem. Even pet owners turn in their pets to be killed. Our disposable society throws away even a family pet. People allow their pets to roam at large, without neutering them. Wild cats and dogs breed freely. Cats are wild birds' second worst enemy.

POACHING

Undercover agents working for U.S. Fish and Wildlife Service's Division of Law Enforcement see some gruesome activities. In a *Time* magazine article, Van Biema (1994) wrote about rampant poaching in U.S. parks. He suggested that 300 bears are poached every year for their body parts, including gallbladders. Not even bear cubs are immune from the illegal hunters. From spiders to elk and from butterflies to bighorn sheep, the slaughter in all 366 parks continues. Figure 11.2 shows the efforts of one poacher in a Rwandan national park.

Van Biema estimated that poaching of animals is a $200 million cash business. Species such as the hawksbill sea turtle, brown pelican, peregrine falcon,

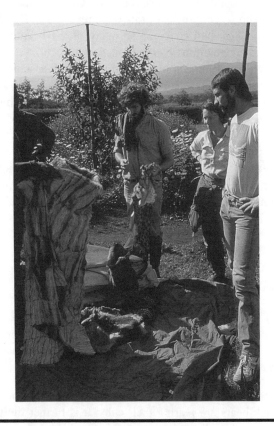

FIGURE 11.2 A poacher's bounty is confiscated in Rwanda. The skin of a cerval, an African cat, is held by the ranger in the center. On the left is a blanket of more than a dozen antelope skins.

and Schaus' swallowtail are endangered but are shot or taken anyway. Of course, with budget cuts poaching is a lucrative business. In 1994, there were 60 full-time rangers to patrol Yellowstone National Park, which is the size of Delaware and Rhode Island.

What drives poaching? The answer is money. Poaching is defined by federal law as hunting protected wildlife for $350 or more. A mounted bighorn sheep can be worth as much as $10,000. A grizzly bear can go for $25,000. A bear gallbladder can be worth $64,000 in Asia. Some poachers are notorious and are preoccupied with fame. One poacher was videotaped attacking a herd of elk in Yellowstone National Park. He was fined a mere $15,000 and served only 30 days of an 18-month prison term. The courts, it seems, do not take wildlife crimes seriously.

Van Biema also reported on a snake poaching ring. Snakes are caught for skins and for pet shops. Outbreaks of rats were reported in Big Bend National Park in Texas. Poachers had collected so many of the beautiful gray-banded king snakes that rat populations had exploded.

In Bandelier National Park in New Mexico, mule deer and elk poaching is a problem. Several years ago, a ranger disguised himself as a hunter. Four poachers entered the park from the western boundary in the Jemez Mountains. One of the hunters shot a large mule deer. The ranger heard the shots and located the hunters. The ranger turned on a hidden microphone and also took out his camera. Suspecting nothing, the hunters each posed with the trophy deer. The ranger took their addresses so he could "send them pictures." Within a week, all four hunters were arrested for poaching. Sound, photos, and the ranger's testimony led to pleas of no contest by the four men. They were fined $100 each and their guns were confiscated for the remainder of the hunting season.

VOTING ISSUES AND HUMAN VALUES

Both Idaho and Michigan have referenda prohibiting the use of dogs when hunting bears. It is no small task to get a proposed initiative on a state ballot. In Idaho, at least 41,335 (10% of registered voters) signatures were required in 1996. The Idaho initiative reads:

> It is the intent of this act to prohibit the taking of black bears when female black bears are rearing their cubs. It is further the intent of this act to promote the concept of fair chase by eliminating the taking of black bears through the use of bait and dogs.

Voters will decide the issue. In 1995, 96% of all bear hunts in Michigan used dogs, and 30% of 5600 permittees were successful. We do not know whether male and female bears were taken. Oregon voters passed similar legislation in 1994. Only about half as many bears were killed in 1995 as the previous year. Perhaps as a result, nuisance bear complaints were up 39% and 205 bears had to be destroyed. Are we certain that the reduced number of bears killed led to the increase in the number of nuisance bears? What did the bear population as a whole do? What did the human population do? Is it possible that there are fewer bears and many more humans, for instance?

Across the United States, voters are demanding that action be taken on a variety of issues ranging from gambling, term limits, child care, school choice, taxes, and even the legality of smoking marijuana. Wildlife issues are appearing on state ballots as well. In most cases, the long-term ramifications of successful initiatives will not be known.

Recall what the New Mexico state wildlife official said: "Scientists tell us what is going on, but the public tells us what to do." Typically, scientists gather facts, organize them, and make these facts available. Generally, scientists do not make policy decisions, although their recommendations are heard. In the coming months and years, voters will decide many wildlife issues.

According to Eisler and Buckley, the National Rifle Association claims that the public is not educated enough on issues regarding hunting, wildlife management, and science to make informed wildlife management decisions. Animal rights groups suggest that the public is on their side when it comes to hunting and that it is their elected officials who will not carry out the will of the public.

Scientists can help educate the public and bureaucrats alike but cannot answer the moral questions that always arise. Now that humans have altered forever the delicate predator–prey relationships, humans must decide what to do. Of course, the best management strategy would be to manage ourselves into a position where no management decisions have to be made. This is the way things existed for hundreds of millions of years—before human impacts became the dominant force they are today.

Unfortunately, there are no easy answers. Albuquerque, New Mexico seems an unlikely place to have too many beavers—but it does. Beavers live in bank dens along the Rio Grande. They routinely attack orchards and New Mexico's beloved cottonwood trees. Beavers have been blamed for the lack of regeneration of the cottonwoods, but, in fact, cottonwoods require spring flooding to germinate. Flood control programs have effectively prevented floods. Irrigation channels act as invasion corridors for beavers to penetrate to city limits, bringing beavers and pets into conflict. Beavers have become a wildlife issue in Albuquerque. Should hunters be allowed to take beavers?

Florida residents' fear of panthers is not shared by California voters who rejected a plan to allow hunting of the animals, even though a woman jogger was killed by a panther.

No doubt, more wildlife issues will find their way onto more state ballots. One result of a successful initiative will be that the number of nuisance animals will increase. There will then be a need to better define nuisance animals. When is a bear a nuisance bear or an alligator a nuisance alligator?

In Florida, a nuisance alligator is in the eyes of the beholder. If an alligator is sunning itself near a boat, it can be considered a nuisance. One call to the local state wildlife office is all that is required. A professional state-certified hunter will "harvest" the alligator at no charge to the state or the caller. In return, the hunter can sell the meat and hide and pocket the profit. The hunters are always successful.

In 1967, the American alligator was one of the original entries on the endangered species list. Today, there is a hunting season on alligators in Florida. Some 5500 nuisance alligators were killed in 1995, and the number of nuisance alligators continues to increase. Indeed, the number of legally hunted alligators is less than the number culled as nuisances!

If a female bear cannot find enough food for herself, she will often abandon her cub. The cub usually starves to death for lack of food. Is a bear cub a nuisance if it turns over a garbage can looking for food? Should it be destroyed? Should the female bear be destroyed if she raids a dumpster?

Normally, bears do not raid dumpsters unless they are driven to do so. Humans have, in many cases, destroyed the natural habitat of the bears. We have logged the forests and probably overgrazed them as well. Humans have altered the fire regime and damaged the streams so they no longer support fish. Housing developments abut wilderness areas, and the prime lots are those on the perimeter of wildlife areas. In every way, humans have reduced the quantity and quality of wildlife habitat. Is it any wonder there are nuisance animals?

Much money is at stake in these initiatives. The National Rifle Association spent $100,000 trying to advance a panther hunt in California. The Humane Society spent $60,000 urging voters to prevent the hunting of panthers. These issues are seen in the larger framework by organizations on both sides. One side might see the issue as follows: "If panther hunting is prevented in California, all hunting will eventually be stopped in the state. Then 'they' will ask us to turn in our guns. The end is near." The other side might see things differently: "If we don't stop the panther hunt, 'they' will want to hunt everything. Soon the hunting season will be 12 months long and everything will be killed by any and all means." Fortunately, public beliefs are somewhere in the middle. A study by the U.S. Fish and Wildlife Service found that 75% of Americans approve of hunting, but a majority of those people also believe that a lot of hunters break laws. Hunters, its seems, are their own worst enemy.

ANIMAL DAMAGE CONTROL

In a throwback to the 1800s, the U.S. Department of Agriculture continues to support an Animal Damage Control (ADC) agency. The agency apparently hates coyotes for some reason and believes they should be poisoned. ADC's method of choice is to use a spring-loaded, meat-baited device known in the trade as an M-44. It sprays poison sodium cyanide pellets into the coyote's mouth and nose. The coyote dies an excruciating death. ADC has been trying to exterminate coyotes for as long as it has been in existence and has not succeeded. In the tradition of all good bounty hunters, ADC has learned that if it were to kill all its prey, it would go out of business. The only thing worse than coyotes, it seems, is no coyotes!

In all 1995 in New Mexico, coyotes killed 7 adult cows and 105 calves valued at about $38,200, according to the Agriculture Department. The report did not say whether the cattle were killed on public or private land. However, 3 to 5 coyotes were killed on public land and 19 on private land. One full-time ADC officer would cost the taxpayers about three times that amount. It would be just as ludicrous to compensate ranchers for their losses. A better solution is simply not to permit grazing on public lands where coyotes are present.

Several questions come to mind. Why is the government killing coyotes on private land? Ranchers are supposed to object to the federal government telling them what to do, particularly when it comes to canines such as wolves and coyotes. Why should ADC still exist? It has not been able to eradicate coyotes and never will. Killing those coyotes responsible for killing cattle would not serve as an example to all other coyotes. Other species that eat the poisoned coyotes also die. Why is there still grazing on public lands? Cattle grazing has destroyed immense tracts of land in the West. Furthermore, grazing on public lands amounts to a subsidy that private ranchers, especially those east of the Rockies, do not receive. Is grazing on public lands a wildlife issue? You bet it is.

In February 1993, an ADC hunter was charged with "wanton destruction of wildlife." U.S. Fish and Wildlife Service officers discovered "mutilated bear carcasses" at the hunter's home near Moab, Utah. The ADC hunter apparently killed two bear cubs after killing the mother, who was trying to feed her cubs. Earlier, another ADC agent was found taking gallbladders and paws from the bears he killed. It was not known whether the agent was killing the bears for their parts alone. Several years earlier, ADC agents captured an endangered bald eagle in a leg-hold trap. The eagle had to be destroyed. In 1991, a Utah television station reported that ADC killed over 4000 coyotes, 16 black bears, 11 bobcats, and 37 cougars in Utah alone. ADC claims it takes no pleasure in killing wildlife and that only when wildlife comes in conflict with people's interests does it "address the problem in a professional manner."

MANAGEMENT PRACTICES

Cattle grazing in unique riparian habitat along the Rio Grande in New Mexico, the so-called Rio Grande Bosque, is a big problem for outdoor recreationists. Cattle roam freely and are "destroying the wildlife habitat," one fisherman told the *Albuquerque Journal.* Some of the local residents claim they have grand-father laws that allow them to let their cattle roam at large. In New Mexico, fences are built to keep cattle out, not in. One duck hunter suggested that the Bosque looked like a corral. Locked gates were installed to keep people from driving in and dumping trash, cutting wood, and shooting guns and to keep cattle out as well.

The *Albuquerque Journal* reported that on May 20, 1996, Santa Fe-based Forest Guardians sued to force the U.S. Bureau of Land Management to con-duct studies to determine how grazing on public lands was affecting several endangered birds and fish. Forest Guardians questions whether any level of grazing along streams and rivers is appropriate. Forest Guardians and other environmental groups have an ongoing injunction against logging in New Mexico and Arizona. It remains in effect until studies are completed to determine how the Forest Service's timber plans affect the Mexican spotted owl.

Both lawsuits demand studies on how listed species are affected by wide-ranging land management practices. The idea here is to look not only at the "content" of an area but also its "context." That is, grazing may not affect southwestern willow flycatchers in the immediate area, but a cattle-damaged mountain stream may silt up and foul water where there are willow flycatchers. In New Mexico, the Bureau of Land Management manages 500 miles of stream-side land and 13 million acres.

COMMUNITY GROWTH

If growth is good for communities, more growth must be better. Most people are, in fact, pro-growth. But is growth really good? Who benefits from growth?

How many development projects are taking place within town limits across the United States? Such development projects are merely filling in areas and are not expansive. But who really benefits from such projects? Certainly the developer benefits. Local construction company workers benefit, temporarily at least. Do residents surrounding such projects benefit? The next time you are sitting in your car at a traffic light, ask yourself, "Am I benefiting from the growth of my community?" Chances are you are not. Your taxes have probably increased to pay for widening the streets to accommodate the increased traffic. Perhaps the police force had to be increased. New residents must pay taxes. How much comes back into the community? How have you personally benefited from this growth? Has this growth enhanced the quality of your personal life?

EXERCISES

11.1 Make a list of the freshwater fish in several states in different parts of the United States. Where are many native freshwater fish in trouble?

11.2 Make a list of fish species introduced in the United States. Investigate some of these introductions in detail. What has been their role with respect to native species?

11.3 Freshwater fish have unique evolutionary histories. Compare freshwater fish in New Guinea to Australian freshwater fish.

11.4 Use the Web to search for information on migratory birds. What kind of information comes up?

11.5 Do a Web search using "salmon" as a keyword. Summarize some interesting findings.

11.6 Search the Web for information on sashimi and sushi bars. What meat do they serve?

11.7 Do a library and a Web search for "pupfish." How many species of pupfish are there? How did they get to be where they are today?

11.8 Investigate the introduction of Nile perch into Lake Victoria in Africa, where millions of people depend on the lake fishery for food.

11.9 Suggest how to test theoretical causes of declining amphibian populations using the scientific methodology discussed in Chapter 1. How can low-latitude effects be isolated?

11.10 Can the effect of UV radiation be tested directly on amphibians to determine their susceptibility? Suggest an experiment.

11.11 Formulate testable hypotheses regarding the issue of bears and humans. How would you gather data to test your hypotheses?

LITERATURE CITED

Beecher, W.J. 1955. Late-Pleistocene isolation in salt-marsh sparrows. *Ecology* **36**(1): 23–28.

Blaustein, A.R. and D.B. Wake. 1990. Declining amphibian populations: a global perspective. *Trends in Ecology and Evolution* **5**(7):203–204.

Dewar, H. 1996. Not in your backyard. *Albuquerque Journal* April 21.

Di Silvestro, R. 1996. What's killing the Swainson's hawk? *International Wildlife* May/June:38–43.

Karesh, W.B. 1996. Rhino relations. *Wildlife Conservation* **99**(2):38–43.

Longstreet, R.J. 1955. Dusky seaside colony endangered. *The Florida Naturalist* **26**:78.

Mann, C.C. and M.L. Plummer. 1995. California vs. gnatcatcher. *Audubon Magazine* **97**(1):38–48, 100–104.

Shelton, H. 1981. A history of the Sweetwater Jaycees Rattlesnake Round-up. pp. 95–234 *in* Kilmon, J. and H. Shelton (Eds.). *Rattlesnakes in America*. Shelton Press, Sweetwater, Texas.

Swardson, A. 1994. A loss that's deeper than the ocean. *Washington Post National Weekly Edition* October:124–130.

Van Biema, D. 1994. The killing fields. *Time* August 22:36–37.

Walters, M.J. 1992. *A Shadow and a Song*. Chelsea Green Publishing, Post Mills, Vermont.

Weir, J. 1992. The Sweetwater Rattlesnake Round-up: a case study in environmental ethics. *Conservation Biology* **6**(1):116–127.

THE NORTHWEST ATLANTIC OCEAN

12

I n summarizing a recent conference, Baker (1995) concluded that "tensions between commercial and recreational fishermen, between U.S. and foreign fleets, and among fishing interests, environmentalists, and resource managers create a climate of finger-pointing rather than common purpose." Few trust the government or regulators. "If there is uncertainty, we need to err on the side of protection of the resource," said D. Hall, deputy administrator for the National Oceanic and Atmospheric Administration. It seems that politicians do not want to err on this side. In truth, we are witnessing the end of a cycle of human mismanagement of a world resource. With each harp seal death, biodiversity decreases and more predatory fish that feed on young cod survive. The cod are being hit with a "double whammy." They have been overfished by humans, and now their underwater protectors are being decimated by humans. Without cod to eat, predatory fish will switch to another resource, such as hake, and decimate their populations. A downward spiral will ensue, and the richness and abundance of species that have co-existed for millions of years will have collapsed directly by the hand of humans.

HARP SEALS AND ATLANTIC COD

As noted earlier, the Canadian government blamed the harp seal (*Phoca groenlandica*) for the decimation of one of the richest and most productive fisheries on earth, although harp seals have been harvested commercially since about 1700 (Busch 1985) (see Figures 12.1 and 12.2). As a result, harp seals have been harvested for fun and profit since 1987. In 1996, Fisheries Minister

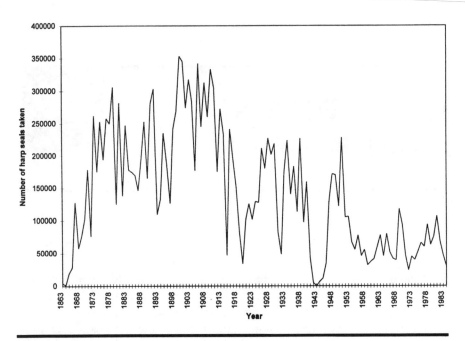

FIGURE 12.1 Annual Newfoundland harp seal harvest.

Brian Tobin announced that the total allowable harp seal harvest for the year would be raised from 186,000 seals to 250,000 seals. Even more importantly, a 15 cents per pound bounty was placed on seals. The government also encouraged the use of large vessels to help hunters reach breeding colonies on offshore ice floes. In this way, large colonies of breeding females could be harvested, or massacred, depending on your viewpoint. Canada was not alone; Iceland, the Faroe Islands, Norway, and Russia also announced harvests of seals. An environmental group, Animal People, reported that Canada was close to signing an agreement with an Asian country that called for delivering 250,000 seal carcasses a year.

Environmentalists reacted strongly against the raised quota and the bounty. The International Wildlife Coalition and the International Fund for Animal Welfare, for instance, condemned the action. Clubbing the helpless seals seems like a senseless act of violence. Who among us has not seen the tiny, white ball of fur with coal-black nose and eyes staring so innocently? Is the hunt humane? Environmentalists say no. The hunt is inherently uncontrollable, because there are only a few inspectors and the range of the seals is enormous across the frozen North Atlantic. Monitoring the hunt is impossible.

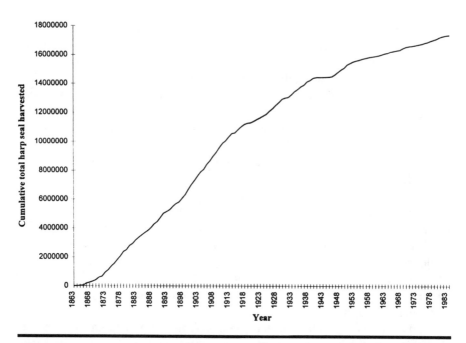

FIGURE 12.2 Cumulative number of Newfoundland harp seals harvested.

The Canadian government and the environmentalists have faced off against each other in a public battle. Indeed, by focusing attention on the harp seal harvest, public attention is being deflected from the real wildlife issue. Is the real wildlife issue the clubbing of baby seals or the loss of the entire North Atlantic fishery? Is the real problem the Canadian government policymakers or the harp seals? How can we, as scientists, address this issue? Do politicians have the will to turn scientific information into policy?

The Canadian government closed the largest Atlantic cod (*Gadus morhua*) fishery on July 2, 1992 for a two-year period. The Newfoundland fishing industry was the backbone of the province's economy, and for fishing communities scattered along the harsh coast, the closing was a disaster. For 350 years, the fishery meant life to these communities. Survey data from fishing ships showed a dramatic decline in fish size taken from 1989 to 1992 however.

Historically, northern cod catches peaked in about 1968 at about 800,000 metric tons. The historical average preceding that spectacular catch was 200,000 metric tons. Foreign trawlers—fish factory ships—were largely responsible for the additional catch. The catch of 1968 caused catch forecasts for other years to be raised. In 1977, the offshore fishery belonged to Canada when Canada declared a 200-mile fishery zone from its shores. During the 1980s, the fishing in Newfoundland strengthened. Cod population assessments by scientists led to lowered quotas. Many untestable statements were made, such as "the fish are hiding" and "unusually cold weather did them in." Another statement was testable: "the seals ate them." A 1992 survey indicated that the cod fishery was on the verge of commercial collapse and the fishery was closed. The usual quotations from sea captains appeared in the media: "I've been fishing cod out of these waters for 20 years and there are more cod now than there were when I got started." Despite such statements, the cod population has not rebounded.

Many theories have been offered to explain why the fishery collapsed. Some suggest overfishing by humans caused the population to collapse beyond its ability to sustain itself. The so-called *tragedy of the commons* is typically invoked to explain people's behavior toward a shared resource, where the attitude might be something like, "I better get mine before someone else does." Foreign floating fish factories were blamed for taking too many fish before the 200-mile limit was established. However, cod stocks located beyond the limit were then fished out.

Cod are omnivorous feeders and attain weights of up to 35 kg (Serchuck et al. 1994). These fish can live in excess of 20 years, although young fish make up most catches. Cod can breed as early as 2 years old and certainly by the age of 4 (Trippel 1995). The Georges Bank of Newfoundland and the Gulf of Maine cod fisheries have been heavily exploited until recently. The 1991 fishing season yielded 48,000 metric tons. In 1992, 39,500 metric tons of cod was harvested from these two fisheries. The total cod fishery take in 1993 was 31,400 metric tons. Both Canadian and U.S. harvests declined.

Survey data show a consistent trend toward catching, on average, younger and younger fish each year. Other results show that individual cod born in 1987 have been fished out almost entirely. Commercial landings in 1993 were dominated by the 1990 year class, which accounted for 55% of the catch by number and 41% by weight. Older fish were almost nonexistent in the catches and middle-age fish were marginally represented. Examination of on-board catches in 1994 showed that the year classes of 1991, 1992, and 1993 were the lowest on record. Recruitment into the population was extremely poor. Worse still, spawning stocks were expected to decline to unprecedented low levels. The Georges Bank cod stock "is at a very low biomass level, and is overexploited. Without substantial reductions in mortality, there is a possibility of stock collapse" (Serchuck et al. 1994).

Scientists were responsible for gathering data to make surveys and projections, but we now know that their research methods and assessments were flawed. For instance, separate cod populations were treated as a single unit. Natural mortality, recruitment, and other variables were treated as constants in models that then gave overly optimistic results. Scientists also collected data aboard ships. However, it was common practice to omit undersized fish whose numbers seemed to increase as harvested stocks decreased. Such blunders led to underestimates of mortality and overestimates of cod populations. The harvests continued until fishermen were shut down completely. In 1992, a way of life for hundreds of years was tossed into the dustbin of history. The Canadian government blames the harp seals for this demise.

"There's only one major player still fishing that stock. Its first name is harp; its second name is seal," said Canadian Fisheries Minister Brian Tobin. But are harp seals responsible for the collapse of the fishery? Can it be that unless harp and hooded seal populations are regulated by man, they could decimate the fishery?

The pinnipeds (fur seals, harbor seals, and walruses) are mammals that returned to the sea approximately 23 million years ago. Their former mammalian limbs became flippers. Enaliarctos (sea bear) is the earliest known seal and comes from the late Oligocene or early Miocene of the Pacific Ocean near what is now California (Janis 1993). Enaliarctos was otter sized and might have looked like an otter with flippers. Unlike modern seals, Enaliarctos lacked the specialized features of the inner ear that enable modern seals to deep dive. From the North Pacific, they dispersed and speciated into the pinnipeds we know today. Today, pinnipeds generally occupy polar and subpolar regions; however, exceptions to this rule are the Hawaiian monk seal (*Monachus schauinslandi*), the Caribbean monk seal (*M. tropicalis*) (now presumed extinct), the Mediterranean monk seal (*M. monachus*), and the Galapagos fur seal (*Arctocephalus galapagoensis*) (Lavigne and Kovacs 1988). The Caspian Sea, the largest inland body of water, is occupied by seals—evidence that this sea was once connected to the Black Sea and the Mediterranean Sea.

Adult harp seals are about 1.7 m (5.5 feet) long and weigh about 120 kg (285 pounds). Harp seal distribution and range limit are determined by pack ice throughout the North Atlantic (Lavigne and Kovacs 1988). Their distribution spreads across the North Atlantic from northern Newfoundland and Labrador, part way into Hudson Bay, along most of the coast of Greenland, and across the North Atlantic to Iceland, the Scandinavian countries, and the coast of Russia. In late autumn, the harp seals move in front of the advancing ice sheet. After a winter spent feeding in the frigid waters, adult females assemble by the thousands on their traditional whelping (pupping) grounds. Most give birth to a single pup.

The northwest harp seals give birth in late February and mid March. There are three principal breeding grounds, and morphological studies show that there is little mixing of the populations. After pups are weaned, the adult females join the males for the annual mating season. Shortly thereafter, the harp seals molt. During the annual molt, the coat and surface layers of skin are replaced. The seals then migrate north to traditional feeding grounds. Since pups are born on the ice floes and molt on their whelping grounds, no one understands how the inexperienced pups migrate to the feeding grounds. During the summer months, seals disperse to feed.

Perhaps the most photographed animal in the world is the harp seal pup or whitecoat. Since a female will feed only her own young, an abandoned whitecoat faces certain starvation. A female harp seal defends the territory around her pup. The pup grows quickly from the female's milk, which is about nine times as rich as cow's milk. Within a week, the pup is a fat whitecoat. Within two weeks, the pup can reach 30 kg (66 pounds), at which time the female abandons it. The pup's call for food is unanswered and eventually it becomes quiet. The pup then molts its long, fluffy white fur and replaces it with a so-called ragged jacket. When the pup finally enters the water, it typically feeds on crustaceans, not cod. The pup is known as a beater, perhaps because of its poor swimming skills. Harp seals reach sexual maturity at 4 years, and their normal life span is 35 to 40 years.

During the nursing period, the female does not feed. Thus, all the weight that the pup gains comes from the female's body. In addition, there is always a net loss of weight through body maintenance and thermoregulation. A female can lose up to 3 kg per day. Thus, the entire process of birth, whelping, and weaning must take place rapidly.

Cod and harp seals have shared the same seas for millions of years. If harp seals decimated the fisheries, there would be no harp seals. Indeed, because they have co-existed for so long, we must conclude that neither could exist without the other. If the seals had decimated the cod, then the seals would have switched to more abundant prey and allowed the cod to recover. Most likely, the seals feed on a variety of prey. The aquatic food web is complex, and we must appreciate that predatory fish also feed on other fish, including cod. Top predators such as the harp seal undoubtedly permit a higher biodiversity to exist by regulating the populations of predatory fish.

For hundreds of years, humans have hunted harp seals, and this is by far the greatest cause of death (Lavigne and Kovacs 1988). Certainly natural causes of death occur. Polar bears hunt seals, as do Greenland sharks and orcas. Archaic Indians living on the coast of Newfoundland hunted seals. The diaries of early visitors to the east coast of Canada, such as John Cabot (1497) and others, recorded that aboriginal people hunted seals for a variety of products. Subsistence living probably depended on abundant seal populations. It was not until Europeans arrived that serious slaughter began.

HISTORICAL SEAL HUNTING

The gray seal (*Halichoeruss grypus*) was also slaughtered by the tens of thousands from New England to Newfoundland. Hunting gray seals year round was a way to make a living. By 1860, the population had been nearly wiped out. By 1950, the gray seal was thought to be extinct in eastern Canada. As with the walrus, commercial uses led to its demise. The harbor seal (*Phoca vitulina*) was not commercially exploited but was nevertheless hunted by local people for food, fuel, and leather products. It too was easily massacred because of its habit of congregating. The Lake Ontario population of harbor seals was obliterated in 1824. That harbor seals survive at all today in sparse scattered populations is but luck.

The ice-breeding seals, the harp and hood (*Cystophora cristata*) seals, were also discovered further north and hunted relentlessly. Because of their habit of remaining mostly in the water, these seals were the last to be exploited. However, because of their huge populations, they too have been commercially exploited since the 1600s. The local Innuit people used nets made of sealskin to catch seals, and this technique was adopted by Europeans. By the 1850s, a lucrative so-called "fishing" industry was built on harp seal exploitation.

As more was learned about harp seal behavior, seal hunts were expanded. By 1723, the harp seal hunt was making a contribution to the economy of Newfoundland, mainly from the export of seal oil. Between 1723 and 1795, hunts yielded between 7000 and 128,000 seals annually. When whelping ice occasionally carried pups close to shore, the young whitecoats were heavily exploited. In 1773, for instance, 128,000 seals were harvested, some 50,000 of which were whitecoats. At the beginning of the 1800s, seal hunting became a serious business. Sealers took to the sea in search of their quarry. The cod fishery was harvested in summer and fall, while the seals were harvested in winter and spring. Exploiting the bounty of the sea became a full-time occupation. Between 1803 and 1816, harvests averaged 117,000 seals per year. Between 1818 and the turn of the century, annual seal harvests totaled more than 200,000 seals for all but three years. In many years, the annual harvest exceeded half a million seals! By the middle of the 1800s, seal harvests were the second largest contributor to the Newfoundland economy. Cod fishing was first.

An indication of the immense number of seals comes from the years 1831, 1832, and 1844, when 680,000, 740,000, and 686,000 seals were harvested, respectively (Lavigne and Kovacs 1988). In 1857, more than half a million seals were taken. At the height of the Golden Age of Sealing, when 370 large sailing vessels and 13,600 sailors participated in the seasonal hunts, the number of seals hunted began to fall. From 1850 to 1862, the harvest went from 329,185 to 268,624. Despite technological improvements and capital investments, seal harvests had seen their limits. A century of relentless hunting had taken its toll, and the years of overkill finally did in the seemingly inexhaustible resource. From 1890 to 1895, seal harvests averaged 307,000. The total harvest for all seals during the 1800s on the North American seacoast was a staggering 33,000,000 seals. It did not cease, however.

During the early 1900s, annual hunts claimed 266,000 seals. In 1914, 234,000 seals were killed. Between 1915 and 1919, the average annual hunts yielded 143,000 seals. From 1920 to 1929, average annual hunts brought in 154,000 seals. From 1940 to 1945, the number of seals killed plummeted to a mere 20,000 annually. During the remainder of the 1940s, however, catches averaged 200,000 seals annually. Between 1950 and 1959, 312,000 seals were harvested. In 1951, for instance, 430,000 seals were taken. During the 1960s, total annual catches of seals averaged 284,000. In 1971, the hunt brought in 230,966 harp seals.

Around the world, large numbers of seals are being killed to supply penises to the Far East for aphrodisiacs and to protect fisheries. A seal marketing strategy report paid for by the Canadian government confirmed that over half of the income from seals was derived from the sale of penises. The average price paid to sealers for a seal penis was about $23. In Namibia, Cape fur seals (*Arctocephalus pusillus pusillus*) are hunted for trophies and penises. In 1994, 120,000 seals died for inexplicable reasons and 55,000 were taken by hunters. Norway accounts for up to 20,000 seal deaths per year. In Russia, 30,000 harp seals have been taken every year for several years. The Mediterranean monk seal is one of the 12 most endangered animals in the world. The International Fund for Animal Welfare claims that 70% of Canadians are opposed to killing seals as there is virtually no market for their fur. Indeed, the marketing report also found no viable markets for seal meat or oil. Lack of a market was the reason used to explain why only 67,000 harp seals were taken in 1995 when the quota was 186,000, but that was before the bounty was established.

Scientific studies have shown that, on average, less than 1% of a seal's diet is cod. In fact, large predatory fish are probably the young cod's most formidable enemy. Removing harp seals that eat large fish will have an immediate and severe negative impact on Atlantic cod. Apparently, the logic of this statement has escaped the Canadian government. Harp seals are a keystone predator, acting to maintain a high biodiversity through their predatory activities. Because harp seals consume fish that prey on young cod, we suggest that there are more young cod when harp seals are present.

THE BOUNTY OF THE SEA

Harp seal hunting is directed mainly at whitecoats because the mothers are usually in the water near their young. Hooded seal mothers, in contrast, stay with their young and thus both are easily killed. In 1974, only 9995 hooded seals were taken, and the quota of 15,000 seals was not reached. Since 1976, annual quotas have not been exceeded. In 1987, for instance, a quota of 2340 was established, but 2008 were taken. As for the seal's voracious appetite for fish, scientists now suggest that Atlantic harp seal fish consumption has been overestimated by anywhere from five- to tenfold. The potential impact of harp seals on fish populations is far less than was previously claimed (Lavigne and Kovacs 1988).

A growing human population and advances in technology have led to increased pressure on fish stocks worldwide. In the Gulf of Mexico, habitat deterioration was blamed for decreasing harvests. Dams and logging in the Pacific Northwest have led to declines in salmon populations. Salmon populations in the Columbia River are 5% of their historic levels because of dams and habitat destruction from upstream logging and agricultural activities.

Many of the world's fisheries will continue to decline unless better management decisions are made and put into practice (Baker 1995). While scientists often understand the situation and know what needs to be done, policymakers are unwilling or unable to end overfishing until a crisis occurs. In the United States, 40% of fish stocks are overexploited (Baker 1995), and overfishing is destroying many fisheries worldwide. New England's Georges Bank fishery has been overexploited by people. The fishery was one of the richest in the world and was considered inexhaustible. J. Cato, director of the Florida Sea Grant, blamed the media, industry leaders, and policymakers for "cowardice" in the face of an obvious need to act (Baker 1995). In Alaska, on the other hand, when biologists say a fishery must be closed, there is no appeal. Hence, Alaska's salmon populations are at record levels. However, Alaskan rivers have not suffered the intrusion of dams and pollution from industry and agriculture. Habitat loss, however, should not be considered the scapegoat for overfishing.

WALRUS

Walruses (*Odobenus rosmarus*) were once abundant on the northeast coast of North America from Cape Cod, through the St. Lawrence River, and up the coast to the Magdalen Islands. Magnificent congregations bred and proliferated. Today, there are none. Their loss is a tragic story of merciless exploitation beginning in the 1600s. Lavigne and Kovacs (1988) summarize their complete and total demise. The last walrus in Massachusetts was killed in 1754. By 1680, the St. Lawrence population was wiped out. A lone walrus was sighted off the Magdalen Islands in 1800. The St. Lawrence walrus population was officially declared extirpated 187 years later by a Canadian committee on endangered wildlife. The walrus was not alone, however.

Looking back hundreds of years, it is clear that the bounty of the sea was a treasure of nature. Walruses by the ten of thousands sunned themselves from Cape Cod to the Magdalen Islands. Harp and hooded seals with populations in the millions occupied the sea waters and raised their young on ice floes. Tens of millions of cod, hake, shrimp, crab, and capelin were but a few of the undersea biotic riches. Native peoples with little or no technology plied the seas for a living and harvested seals as needed. Commercial interests simply did not exist. Something that took nature millions of years to create has been nearly wiped out in 300 years. Today, we are witnessing the death of a truly unique resource. Perhaps it will come back when the walrus returns to the North Atlantic.

EXERCISES

12.1 Do a search on the World Wide Web for "harp seal" and "seals." Pursue your leads into their biology and management. Summarize your results.

12.2 What other fisheries have been decimated since 1900? Find information on the Peruvian anchovy fishery.

12.3 Search in the library and on the World Wide Web for information on the world's fisheries. Write a brief summary of your findings.

12.4 Have any freshwater fisheries been decimated?

12.5 Investigate aquaculture more thoroughly using the library and the World Wide Web. What aquatic species lend themselves to aquaculture technology?

LITERATURE CITED

Baker, B. 1995. Is overfishing or habitat destruction the key culprit in fishery depletion? *Bioscience* **45**(11):751.

Busch, B.C. 1985. *The War Against the Seals*. McGill-Queen's University Press, Montreal.

Janis, C. 1993. Victors by default. in Gould, S.J. (Ed.). *The Book of Life*. W.W. Norton, New York.

Lavigne, D.M. and K.M. Kovacs. 1988. *Harps & Hoods*. University of Waterloo Press, Ontario, Canada.

Phillips, K. 1994. *Tracking the Vanishing Frogs*. Penguin Books, New York.

Serchuck, F.M., M.D. Grosslein, R.G. Lough, D.G. Mountain, and L. O'Brien. 1994. Fishery and environmental factors affecting trends and fluctuations in the Georges Bank and Gulf of Maine cod stocks: an overview. *International Council for the Exploration of the Sea (ICES) Marine Science Symposium* **198**:77–109.

Trippel, E.A. 1995. Age at maturity as a stress indicator in fisheries. *Bioscience* **45**(11):759–770.

AN IN-DEPTH CASE STUDY OF GORILLAS

13

A visit to a habituated group of gorillas is certainly one of the most exciting adventures any wildlife enthusiast can experience. One of the authors (JGS) visited the mountain gorillas in Rwanda in November 1985, shortly before the murder of Dian Fossey. At the time, a trip to see the gorillas cost $100 and most openings were filled six months in advance. The registration center was located in the small village of Kinigi on the volcanic slopes of Mt. Sabinyo. Four groups of gorillas had been habituated to the presence of humans. Each day 24 people in groups of six visited these gorillas for one hour only, six people and their guide per group of gorillas.

The trek to the edge of the forest was two hours at an altitude of 8000 feet. Before entering the Parc des Volcans, the guide and his assistant recited the rules governing all tourist visits to the gorillas: no pointing at the gorillas, no smoking near the gorillas, no staring at the gorillas, no eating near the gorillas, no flash photographs, no running away if the gorillas approach, no breathing on a gorilla if it approaches, and so forth. Everyone was anxious to get started. Soon the darkness of the forest enveloped the tourists. The trail was muddy and slippery and the vegetation foreign, with stinging nettles and strange mushrooms. Some people walked for several hours before encountering a group of gorillas. Others encountered them in ten minutes. Most people remember the moments just before contact because their excitement level was especially high as the guide came back and ushered them forward. The guide also made low rumbling sounds to comfort the gorillas and make them aware that their daily routine was about to be interrupted.

By the time the first contact is made, the tourist's heart is pounding with excitement and anticipation. An hour with the gorillas is certainly one of the fastest hours anyone can experience. At all times the visitors are kneeling and watching, listening, and taking photographs. A few juvenile gorillas are playing, a silver-back male is eating in front of you, several females are feeding together, and a young might be nursing. It is surely as if you have invaded the privacy of an intimate family in their own home; while they go about their daily routine, you are crawling around taking pictures of them. When the hour is almost up, most people are ready to return and feel grief or guilt that they have interrupted the lives of these peaceful creatures. Many people liken the visit to a surrealistic voyage to a distant time and place far away from the middle of poverty-stricken Africa, to a place primeval where animals have not yet learned to fear humans, the way it once must have been. Most who visit cannot experience the gorillas only once. Some cannot get enough.

CONSERVATION, SCIENCE, AND WILDLIFE ISSUES

Today, scientists recognize three subspecies of gorillas in Africa. The western lowland gorilla (*Gorilla gorilla gorilla*), the eastern lowland gorilla (*G. gorilla graueri*), and the rarest of the three, the mountain gorilla (*G. gorilla beringei*), all live in forested regions of central Africa. As shown in Figure 13.1, the western lowland gorilla is located in Cameroon, Nigeria, Congo, Gabon, and the Central African Republic. The eastern lowland gorilla is located in eastern Zaire and is at least 2000 km from the western lowland populations. The mountain gorilla lives on isolated and remote mountains in eastern Zaire, Rwanda, and Uganda. Yet 150 years ago, the existence of gorillas was only a vague rumor and a frightening one at that. Their dense, remote habitat and their rumored strength and fearlessness made human contact without a gun impossible. Today, tourists enjoy visiting gentle gorillas. Some enjoy gorilla heads, hands, and feet as trophies, and others find gorilla flesh good eating. Certainly, these different interest groups cannot all be satisfied for long. What are the current wildlife issues concerning wild gorillas, and how can science be used to meet the conservation needs of these unique creatures? Again we must take a historical perspective.

Since the discovery in 1847 of what is now known as the western lowland gorilla, gorilla taxonomy has been controversial. The mountain gorilla was not even discovered until 1903, when Captain Oskar von Beringe shot two "large black monkeys." Coolidge (1929) and Schouteden in 1947 both accepted a single species. In 1961, Vogel proposed that the western lowland gorillas and eastern lowland gorillas were separate species. He further divided the eastern

FIGURE 13.1 The distribution of gorillas in Africa. Habitat destruction in western Africa and political instability in eastern Africa threaten the existence of gorillas.

lowland and mountain gorillas into distinct subspecies. Schaller (1959) accepted Coolidge's classification when he ventured into central Africa to perform ecological studies of gorillas. Fortunately for all later generations, Akeley (1923) was able to convince the ruling Belgians to set aside a sanctuary for the gorillas in 1922. In 1929, the boundary of the Parc des Volcans was enlarged to include much of the known mountain gorilla habitat. Groves (1970) analyzed 747 gorilla skulls and concluded that there are three gorilla subspecies.

Kahuzi-Biega National Park in eastern Zaire presumably protects the eastern lowland gorillas, and several parks in Cameroon, Central African Republic, and Gabon protect western lowland gorillas. In principle, all gorillas are protected under international treaties. In addition, since the present populations of gorillas are recognized and differentiated only to the level of subspecies, we could, without loss of biodiversity, lose one or two subspecies completely without adverse impacts. For instance, if the remaining mountain gorillas vanished, under present taxonomic status there would be no loss of biodiversity since biodiversity is typically measured at the species level. Harcourt (1996) estimates there are 125,000 gorillas in Africa, double the previous estimate. Some of the areas may contain more than a thousand individuals. With the present parks, it would appear to the casual observer that the gorillas are in fine shape. Nothing could be further from the truth.

MOUNTAIN GORILLAS

When civil war exploded in Rwanda in early 1991, conservation organizations feared the worst for the mountain gorillas of the Parc des Volcans. Harboring the last 300 mountain gorillas on earth, Parc des Volcans straddles three of the poorest countries on earth—Rwanda, Uganda, and Zaire. Refugees began leaving Rwanda by the tens of thousands. Fighting took place within the Parc des Volcans. Land mines were planted within the park by both factions and no maps were kept. People leaving Rwanda moved into the forested part of the Parc des Volcans in eastern Zaire. In Uganda, the rebel invaders camped in the Parc. Conservationists quietly pleaded with both sides to leave the gorillas alone. Akegera National Park in Rwanda was completely sacked and overrun. Most of the wild animals were eaten for food by Rwandan rebels. Those that were not consumed during the war were consumed afterward. The park was destroyed. Mercifully, the Parc des Volcans was spared, although at least one gorilla was killed when it surprised rebel forces.

In the spring of 1995, four mountain gorillas were killed in the Bwindi Forest in Uganda, site of the Bwindi National Park and home to some 300 eastern lowland gorillas. These gorillas were speared by poachers to reach a nursing infant, such as the one shown in Figure 13.2. Suspected poachers were detained, but no arrests were made. Four months later, three more mountain gorillas were killed in Zaire in Virunga National Park (the Zaire part of the Parc des Volcans) just hours after tourists had visited them. In 1995, seven mountain gorillas were known to have been killed by poachers. The actual number of slain gorillas is unknown.

On February 1, 1996, news reports out of Zaire indicated that 750,000 Rwandan refugees were creating an "environmental hell" in Africa's oldest World Heritage National Park, the Parc des Volcans. Rwandan Hutu tribe refugees were destroying the Virunga National Park and carrying away an estimated 1000 tons of trees per day to be used for fuel and charcoal. Twenty thousand acres of prime bamboo forest, a staple gorilla food, had been completely destroyed to make mats and furniture.

FIGURE 13.2   Mountain gorilla mother and infant find sanctuary in the Parc des Volcans, Rwanda. The infant is sucking its thumb.

The environmental coordinator for the United Nations High Commissioner for Refugees was reported to have said, "Some things disappear and never come back—only in 200, 300 years." Hutu militants are now suspected to be training in the Parc des Volcans to begin a cross-border rebellion inside Rwanda. New attempts to smuggle infant gorillas outside Rwanda to buyers in Asia and the new Soviet republics might be made under the guise of being surprised by gorillas in the forest and accidentally killing them. Six Italian tourists were killed in Zaire in August 1995 by an unidentified gunman. Near the refugee camps, previously planted mines explode daily. Antelope, buffalo, and other bush meat is sold regularly for food.

Meanwhile, tourist visits to the gorillas increased. Driven by greed, visits to habituated gorillas in Zaire doubled by allowing two groups of tourists to visit daily. A single human with a sniffle can wipe out a gorilla group because gorillas have no built-in immunity to human colds. A tourist with the measles could wipe out the entire population of gorillas. This is why a distance of 5 m is kept at all times between humans and gorillas. In the past, this minimum distance was honored. Now, for a small tip, tourists can have a closer encounter with a rare and endangered species.

Part of the Virunga National Park in Zaire is a grassland, and the Rutshuru

River was once known for its huge population of hippos. In March 1996, reports from the former park headquarters described a slaughter of horrific proportion. The banks of the river are "littered with hippo bones," evidence that the traditional snares and hand-pounded metal spears have been replaced by modern automatic weapons. Is it any wonder park rangers look the other way?

On the Ugandan side of the Parc des Volcans, Klaus-Jürgen Sucker was responsible for preventing incursions into the forest and maintaining gorilla patrols. Klaus made certain people and agriculture were kept out of the forest. He lived in a makeshift tented camp in the foothills of Mt. Gahinga before he relocated to the small town of Kisoro after two years. When the Rwandan civil war began, Klaus stepped up patrols in the forest. Rwandan rebels intent on the overthrow of the government established camps around Mt. Gahinga. Klaus met with them and asked them to safeguard the gorillas and not to shoot if by chance they surprised a gorilla in the forest. On June 20, 1994, Klaus was found dead in his home. There was a noose around his neck and his feet were on the floor. No arrests were ever made.

Klaus's death is shrouded in mystery. A few days before his death, he was ordered by the Uganda government to vacate his position as director of the Mgahinga Mountain Gorilla Project. He was told to report to work in Kidepo Valley National Park in northeastern Uganda, about as far from Kisoro as a person can get and still be in Uganda. Powerful forces and big money were at work undermining years of Klaus's work. Certainly Uganda National Parks, a government agency, was aware of his achievements.

Klaus was no stranger to life on the edge. Naturally, he was not popular among the poachers and wood cutters in the region. His patrols put many of his enemies out of work. During the first year of his project, his tented camp was attacked by a small unit of unknown people armed with Russian Kalashnikov machine guns. Two were aimed directly at Klaus in an attempt to scare him off. "You go ahead and shoot," he said. Later, a small park headquarters was built. Mgahinga was declared a national park. Klaus stepped up patrols on dedication day; he knew the park's enemies only too well.

After the Rio de Janeiro Earth Summit, several multiple-use projects were planned for Mgahinga National Park by several U.S. organizations. Klaus opposed these projects because they allowed harvesting of honey, herbs, and bamboo, an important gorilla food. No controls or limits on so-called subsistence gathering were ever discussed. After all, he reasoned, Mgahinga was only 35 km^2, of which 10 km^2 was severely degraded and just recovering and therefore highly susceptible to disturbance. Together with Uganda National Parks and international scientists, Klaus argued effectively against subsistence use. Except for a small number of highly controlled tourists, no one was to enter the forest except to patrol. When the survival of the gorillas was at stake, Klaus believed, people would just have to take second place.

A month before his departure, Klaus discovered his mail was routinely being opened. The chief park warden of Mgahinga had a key to the post office in Kabale where the mail was received. Klaus never received a confidential letter mailed only to himself and one other person. Yet at least one employee of a widely known donor organization had a copy—marked confidential. His departure from Mgahinga was a guarded secret. However, it seems others knew about it. In the end, it cost Klaus his life. His death was not the first and will not be the last. Gorilla protection is a serious business. The gorillas in Uganda, Rwanda, and Zaire are listed as endangered. Harcourt (1996) discusses this classification.

EASTERN LOWLAND GORILLAS

The Hollywood movie *Gorillas in the Mist* was filmed in Rwanda and Zaire in the 1980s. The film portrayed the life and death of Dian Fossey (see Figure 13.3), who is widely credited with saving the mountain gorillas of the Parc des

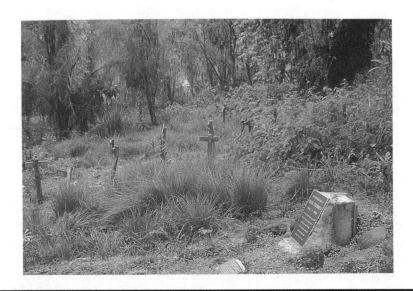

FIGURE 13.3 The grave of Dian Fossey in Rwanda among the gorillas fallen to poachers.

FIGURE 13.4   Maheshe, an eastern lowland gorilla in Zaire, appeared in the movie *Gorillas in the Mist*. In 1993, he was killed so his head, hands, and feet could be sold as souvenirs.

Volcans in Rwanda (Fossey 1983). One of the stars of the movie was a gorilla named Maheshe (see Figure 13.4), a silver-back male eastern lowland gorilla living with his group in Zaire's Kahuzi-Biega National Park. Maheshe was a gentle gorilla who took command of his group in 1975 when he was 15 years old. His group was eventually habituated to the visits of humans before he became a movie star.

Maheshe means *the chief* in the local tribal language. In 1987, when Maheshe was in his prime, his group consisted of 28 gorillas. In 1990, the group had 24 individuals; in 1993, 16 members were protected by Maheshe. In November 1993, Maheshe disappeared suddenly. He had not shown any signs of deteriorating health, and poachers were suspected. In August 1995, his corpse was located and unearthed after a tip-off from a local person. Maheshe's head and hands were missing, indicating that he had been killed for the so-called "trophies." Today, his hands are probably used as an ashtray or perhaps a soap dish. His moth-eaten head may grace a wall or perhaps his skull is used to hold a candle. From wastebaskets made from elephant feet to brooms made from monkey tails to ashtrays made from gorilla hands—native African wildlife is used in many interesting ways.

Eastern lowland gorillas (*Gorilla gorilla graueri*) are found in isolated forests in eastern Zaire and Uganda along the border with Burundi and in Rwanda. No wild gorilla populations exist in Kenya or Tanzania, although similar habitats are found. The Bwindi–Impenetrable Forest National Park in Uganda has about 300 eastern lowland gorillas. Kahuzi-Biega National Park on the shores of Lake Kivu contains about 1000 eastern lowland gorillas. Mt. Tshiaberimu on the northwest shore of Lake Edward in Zaire supports an estimated 16 eastern lowland gorillas (see Figure 13.5). Other populations of unknown numbers of gorillas exist on isolated mountains in Zaire.

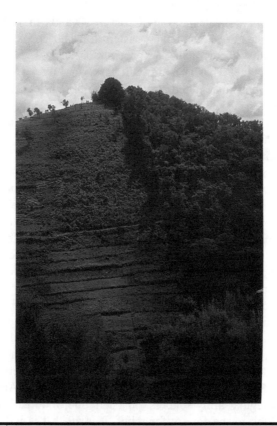

FIGURE 13.5 All across Africa, parks are surrounded by agricultural fields. On one side is the Bwindi–Impenetrable Forest National Park in Uganda, home to some 300 eastern lowland gorillas.

The greatest threat to the eastern lowland gorilla populations is habitat destruction. These isolated mountaintops are surrounded by agricultural fields, and the gorillas have been pushed ever higher up the slopes of the mountains. Logging for fuelwood is extensive in and around these mountaintops. Bush meat hunting is a way of life for many rural people in eastern Zaire. Even where protected areas exist, constant vigilance is necessary to keep loggers and poachers out. Often the brother of an anti-poaching patrol officer is one of the most efficient poachers.

Wages for guards can be five dollars a month, and bush meat hunting is thus essential to feed their families. Who can blame them? Life in modern Zaire is difficult for rural people. Often the reason parks and reserves are created is because the soils are too poor to support crops. Nevertheless, trees can still be harvested for building material and fuel.

Rwandan refugees fleeing the civil war in Rwanda in 1994 relocated to many of the forested areas containing eastern lowland gorillas. Organizations such as the Institut Zairois pour la Conservation de la Nature have tried to minimize the damage. This is a difficult task. In July 1994, over 700,000 refugees fled Rwanda and entered North Lake Kivu District, Zaire (Lanjouw et al. 1995). In spite of a United Nations decree against locating refugee camps near national parks and protected areas, the United Nations High Commission on Refugees established refugee camps on the edge of Africa's oldest national park, Parc National des Virunga, a World Heritage Site.

Mt. Tshiaberimu is also located within Parc National des Virunga. Once famous for its large concentrations of hippos, Cape buffalo, and elephants, the park has since been decimated. Poachers armed with machine guns destroyed the hippos in a few months. Poaching is now rampant and park guards are reluctant to intervene. Why should they? It is already impossible to keep people out of the park. The slopes of Mt. Tshiaberimu are now occupied by small numbers of refugees just trying to stay alive. Various conservation organizations are trying to reduce the impacts of the refugees.

In 1995, poachers killed four lowland gorillas and captured an infant in the Bwindi–Impenetrable Forest National Park in Uganda. The infant was never recovered. More lowland gorillas were killed in Kahuzi-Biega National Park in Zaire. Although gorilla tourism brings so-called hard currency into cash-strapped Zaire and Uganda, the murder of gorillas continues. The international border between Zaire, Rwanda, and Uganda is a high-risk zone. Armed refugees, former Rwanda regular army soldiers, poachers, fuelwood gatherers, and hungry people all look to the forests for relief. It is all that is left.

Anti-poaching patrol guards were issued bullet-proof jackets and other essential field gear. The gorillas in some areas were receiving 24-hour protection.

The situation continues to be precarious at best. Tourism is nonexistent and the flow of foreign hard currency has dried up. People are hungry and hence willing to do whatever it takes to obtain food. Gorilla populations across Africa are under the most intense pressure ever. Unlike the bush meat trade that threatens the western lowland gorillas, the eastern lowland gorilla's greatest present threat continues to be habitat destruction brought about by man's inhumanity toward man. The gorillas are simply caught in the middle.

WESTERN LOWLAND GORILLAS

Until recently, the gorillas of western Africa had been relatively safe. Now there is a connection between a beautiful, new wood table made in Cameroon and a western lowland gorilla. In the western stronghold of the gorillas, bush meat is a delicacy and gorillas and chimps are eaten as food. Gorillas were protected more by remote location than by any laws humans might choose to make. Now, however, their forests have been invaded and destroyed by French and German logging companies. With the new logging roads cut into pristine forests came the bush meat hunters. However, bush meat, when plentiful, is heavy, and transportation is always hard to come by in the forest. Enter once again the loggers and their heavy trucks. European loggers have not only opened huge virgin tracts of timber but have solved the transportation problem that formerly made bush meat hunting a losing proposition.

Drivers of the logging equipment purchase fresh bush meat of gorillas, chimps, and forest antelopes directly from the hunters on the logging roads. In makeshift shanty towns and villages, the loggers act as middlemen and market the fresh meat to waiting buyers. International treaties cannot be enforced in remote logging tracts, and the profit motive is a powerful incentive. Now there is a burgeoning market for fresh gorilla and chimp bush meat. Demand exceeds supply and prices are high. The problem here is that we do not know how many western lowland gorillas exist. Some reports suggest three gorillas and three chimps are now being killed each day to meet the demand for bush meat. This harvesting cannot be sustained.

Pictures of young orphaned gorillas and chimps (see Figure 13.6) are finding their way onto the World Wide Web. These young primates will almost certainly die of starvation without their mothers' milk for nourishment. Some conservation organizations use these pictures as scare tactics to raise funds to support some sort of conservation effort. Nothing seems to be working. Most wildlife conservation organizations are mute. If objections are raised over the issue of bush meat consumption, the conservation organization's operations

FIGURE 13.6 George and Martha, chimpanzee infants stolen from the wild in Zaire and then confiscated. The rest of the family of 40 chimps was killed trying to protect them.

might be curtailed in that country. If no objections surface, all is assumed to be fine. These organizations have learned not to object too strongly lest they lose "part of their portfolio" of wildlife projects—the very projects they use in mailing campaigns to raise money. Typical requests for funds are quite emotional: "Orphaned as a by-product of the logging concessions, their parents shot dead for bush meat, these tiny babies will die a slow, excruciating death by starvation unless we raise $50,000 to create a primate orphan sanctuary..." However, they are correct and factual.

The assault on Africa's elephants, rhinos, lions, hunting dogs (Figure 13.7), gorillas, chimps, and other animals continues. Powered by greed, demand for food is outstripping supply. The plight of the gorillas is a less familiar story. How can science be combined with conservation efforts to offer a solution to the gorilla's plight? That is the question facing a conservation biologist. No less than the survival of all the gorillas is at stake. If killing gorillas and chimps is acceptable, how big a step is it to killing humans?. Thus, our own fate may be inextricably linked to the survival of the gorillas. What can be done? What are some possible solutions?

FIGURE 13.7 Wild dogs in Serengeti National Park, where they no longer roam the savannas.

RECENT TAXONOMIC STATUS

New genetic evidence suggests that the western lowland gorilla (*Gorilla gorilla gorilla*) and the eastern lowland gorilla (*G. gorilla graueri*) appear to be more distinct from one another than are members of two established chimp species. The mitochondrial DNA differences in the two gorilla subspecies lead to the conclusion that gorillas separated from chimps between 8 and 10 million years ago. Humans and chimps separated 6 million years ago. Morell (1995) reported that the eastern and western gorillas separated about 3 million years ago and hence should be considered separate species. Others suggest that humans, chimps, and gorillas diverged at the same time. In any case, genetic information is accumulating and perhaps the questions will be resolved before any of the gorilla populations are destroyed.

Esteban Sarmiento of the American Museum of Natural History has looked at morphological differences between the two mountain gorilla populations in the Parc des Volcans in Rwanda and the Bwindi Forest in Uganda (Sarmiento, personal communication). He reported that Bwindi gorillas live at lower elevations and warmer temperatures, are much more arboreal, have longer day ranges and larger home ranges, and eat much more fruit and pith and less bamboo and leaves than Parc des Volcans gorillas. Bwindi gorillas have smaller bodies; longer limbs, hands, and feet; shorter trunks and thumbs; big toes and tooth row lengths; and narrower trunks and orbital breadths than the other gorillas. Sarmiento suggests that the Bwindi gorillas should be considered a separate taxon from the Parc des Volcans gorillas. But are the Bwindi gorillas related more closely to eastern lowland gorillas or mountain gorillas?

Ecological, morphological, and behavioral differences between the Parc des Volcans gorillas and the Bwindi gorillas show that the gorillas have responded to different selective forces. Perhaps the Parc des Volcans gorillas are indeed only mountain gorillas and their population of 300 is all that remains on earth. Perhaps they are a unique species that requires special attention. Mammalian taxonomists will almost certainly recognize the western lowland gorilla and the eastern lowland gorilla as separate species. The mountain gorillas of Rwanda will most likely be recognized as a subspecies of eastern lowland gorillas.

Thus, at least two and perhaps three species of gorillas will emerge, and each will demand its own conservation strategy. The loss of a gorilla species will not be permitted by anyone, and conservation organizations will unite and stop worrying about being ejected from a country for bringing the international community's attention to wildlife atrocities. A new conservation ethos will emerge from the rubble of previous failed efforts. Conservation biologists will be supported by logging concessions to create parks and reserves within logging tracts to harbor gorillas and other fauna in western Africa. In the tri-border area of Rwanda, Uganda, and Zaire, gorilla tourism offers a hope for conservationists. Gorilla tourism was formerly a lucrative business, bringing in much needed foreign currency. Indeed, visits to the Rwandan mountain gorillas provided the second largest source of so-called hard currency in Rwanda (Vedder and Weber 1990). Cross-border agreements will limit tourism and increase the price of visits. Revenues will be shared among the three nations according to rules set in a treaty governing gorilla visits. Moreover, a broader tourism base will off-load gorilla visitation with birding and hiking trips. Concessions run by local cooperatives will allow more local people to participate in the revenue stream. Local hotels and eateries will be established. A holistic, comprehensive conservation plan will be created. Or is this wishful thinking?

Of course, community-based conservation education programs could create the groundswell of local support that all successful conservation programs require. Scientific research opportunities abound in the remote African forests. For instance, almost nothing is known about the mammals, insects, and plants of the gorilla strongholds. Thus, science can play a vital role in constructing and maintaining strong research programs that ensure a steady stream of researchers. Scientific understanding of local ecological processes is essential to the conservation of the local resources, gorillas included. There is simply no substitute for a strong scientific base. Scientists have demonstrated again and again in widely varying parts of the world that overexploitation of resources has potentially catastrophic consequences. Once the resource is depleted or destroyed, recovery is usually long and slow under the best of circumstances. Too many tourists getting too close to the gorillas will almost certainly lead to their destruction. Sustainable tourism is possible. The price of a visit to the gorilla should be driven by market forces. Just as OPEC controls the price of world oil, so too can these countries control the price of a visit.

In west Africa, the logging companies will be required to support conservation efforts. Laws and enforcement of those laws will make it impossible to transport bush meat. Multinational banks, whose lending practices make possible expensive logging schemes like those in west Africa, will demand change when they see for themselves that their lending policies, while permitting short-term profits, lead to collapsing wildlife populations over the longer term (Wilkie et al. 1992). While selective logging may not harm the forest, the peripheral activities associated with logging have certainly damaged wildlife populations, and especially primates such as gorillas.

CURRENT ISSUES IN GORILLA CONSERVATION

An unprecedented number of gorilla killings was witnessed in 1995 in Bwindi–Impenetrable Forest National Park in Uganda and in the Virunga/Parc des Volcans Zaire–Rwanda–Uganda World Heritage Parks. Accusations and recriminations worldwide fail to frame the relevant questions necessary to address this problem and define solutions that enable better protection for the gorillas. We asked two leading authorities to address several critical questions: H. Dieter Steklis of Rutgers University and director of the Dian Fossey Gorilla Fund and Esteban Sarmiento of the American Museum of Natural History. Both have extensive experience with the gorilla projects.

What is the motive behind the gorilla killings?

Dr. Steklis—The presumed motive in all cases (Uganda and Zaire) is capturing immatures for sale on the black market. But it may be more complex in some cases; that is, politics may also be involved. Political infighting and power struggles have been suggested as motives in Uganda, and in Zaire at least one death may have been caused by angry refugees.

Dr. Sarmiento—The most often quoted motive, that the killings were perpetrated for the capture and sale of gorilla infants, has never been substantiated. There is no evidence in any one of these incidents that infants were actually taken and sold. At Bwindi, group number counts taken before and after the killings account exactly for the four recovered corpses. Furthermore, given the trade restrictions, it is no longer possible to freely move gorillas out of any one country without alerting government authorities and a multitude of watchdog organizations. Notably, none of the supposedly abducted infants has surfaced, further arguing against the likelihood that they were sold or traded. Unfortunately, the autopsy report does not mention the condition of the slain female's uterus to confirm whether she had recently given birth and substantiate the possibility that the infant taken may have escaped census.

Given their abundance, political motives are most likely to be behind the gorilla killings. Disgruntled employees, job availability, uneven distribution of donor funds, and restrictions on local use of forest resources are all viable motives at the local level. Possible motives at the national and international level are as an attention-seeking device to resolve other political issues or to increase funding and public awareness and as a means of sabotaging tourism revenues. The perceived economic worth of Virunga and Bwindi gorillas, created by heavy funding of these areas and the associated media attention, has made them vulnerable to political maneuvering and terrorism and put these populations as well as the tourists who visit them in jeopardy. The one to two million Hutu refugees in Zaire between Goma and Rutshuru and the political problems in Rwanda, therefore, may presently pose the biggest threat to the safety of these gorillas. In part, this threat can be traced to the large sums of external aid Rwanda received during the 1970s and 1980s and the population explosion and social inequality that such funding helped to precipitate. Unfortunately, there aren't any readily clear solutions to the multitude of political problems in the area. Developments over the last 20 years, however, strongly suggest that throwing money at or around the forests in which gorillas live without carefully planned long-term goals is more likely to exacerbate the problem of protecting gorillas than solve it.

Why weren't the killings prevented? Is it a problem with the present policy or with its implementation? What changes in policy or implementation could be undertaken to better protect the animals?

Dr. Steklis—In the Uganda cases, internal politics cannot possibly prevent or protect gorillas from getting caught in the middle of some personal dispute among the very officials charged with their protection. Otherwise, better patrols in the area should be sufficient to prevent killings. This strategy has worked in Rwanda.

In Zaire, the refugee situation has heightened the structural chaos that normally prevails there. Moreover, the presence of the former Rwandan soldiers in the park has made it virtually impossible for Institut Zairois pour la Conservation de la Nature (IZCN) patrols to work safely (that's why IGCP [International Gorilla Conservation Project] outfitted them with bulletproof vests!) or efficiently. Until the refugee problem is solved and they are gone from the park area, little can be done effectively without starting a small war.

Dr. Sarmiento—For all these killings, it is easy to blame the park rangers for either falling short of their responsibility to patrol the forests or promptly reporting to their superiors the suspicious behaviors of trespassers. The warden in charge is also easily criticized for not having the necessary presence, rapport, and/or control over his subordinates to ensure that they do their jobs. Without a strong voice in the media or professional "spin-meisters" working on their behalf, neither wardens nor the rangers when blamed have much to say in their defense. If their voices could be heard, they would complain as to the lack of equipment, working communication systems, and transportation necessary to do their job effectively. Undoubtedly, they would also complain about their salary. If they received a wage sufficient to feed their families and send their children to school, they wouldn't need to sacrifice their working schedule by taking on other jobs.

Such is the economy of Third World countries that they are unable to provide funds for adequately protecting these World Heritage sites. Supposedly, this is why these sites have been designated World Heritage sites in the first place and why so much donor money each year is funneled into them. Both the taxes collected by Western donor nations and donations to NGOs [nongovernment organizations] by an environmentally conscious populace are supposed to ensure that these sites are protected from such incidences. Bwindi–Impenetrable Forest National Park and the Virungas volcanoes both have their fair share of NGOs touting conservation (IGCP, CARE, and World Wildlife Fund at Bwindi; IGCP, CARE, Dian Fossey Gorilla Fund, and Morris Animal Fund at Virunga).

Given that the resources for conserving these areas exist, why weren't the killings prevented? The answer is simple: the NGOs aren't doing what they proposed to do with the donations they are busy collecting. Why? Primarily, because there is no motivation for them to do so. There is no accountability. They would receive future funding whether or not the jobs they proposed to do are done very well or are not done at all. It is logical, therefore, that instead of investing the majority of their resources to see their proposals through, NGOs invest the majority of their resources to come up with new proposals and collect more money. Ironically, the killings have been used as a rallying cry by NGOs to ask for more money, instead of an indication to donors that these organizations are not providing the necessary protection to these areas. Thus, the problem is not one of implementing the existing conservation programs, but of formulating effective policy that will not only help protect the gorillas and their habitat, but will also assure us NGOs will do what they propose to with the funds they receive. At the moment, there simply is no carefully thought out, long-term tested policy for implementing, or the motivation to formulate one.

To protect rhinoceroses, the Kenyan parks department assigns armed guards to each animal 24 hours a day. Couldn't gorillas also benefit from this type of protection?

Dr. Sarmiento—The World Bank endowment to Bwindi can ensure an armed guard for each and every gorilla in the forest 24 hours a day. With limited funds, however, the expense to patrol individual gorillas may not be worth it. In the case of Bwindi and the Virungas, no one could convincingly argue that these past killings, if they don't continue, will have any effect whatsoever on either population. The Virunga population was heavily hunted at the turn of the century, with records for over 50 specimens collected in the 15 years following Captain Beringei's discovery. The actual number hunted was probably much higher. Population numbers, however, were never shown to be adversely affected. It is estimated that approximately the same number of gorillas exist in the Virungas now as existed when Beringei originally discovered them. More importantly, there is no certainty that keeping poachers away from gorillas or locals from using the forest in the long run will ensure their survival. It is conceivable that in some cases limited use may be maintaining the conditions that everyone wants to conserve. Deterioration of their present habitat with population growth, increased intensity of agriculture, and development of surrounding areas poses a much larger long-term threat to the gorillas.

The long-term threats to gorilla survival that these killings alerted us to point to a much more serious shortcoming of conservation policy. Such threats also plead for a more precise definition of conservation, aside from a word that evokes sympathy and justifies the expenditure of vast sums of money. Unfortunately, there is no known magic policy that can ensure the protection of these animals and their habitats. Both Bwindi and the Virungas are relatively small tracts of land, surrounded by relatively dense populations containing relatively large mammals (i.e., elephants, Cape buffalo, and gorillas). Being small tracts of land, they have a proportionally larger perimeter relative to their surface area and hence are much more susceptible to the influx of exotic plants, animals, and/or pests and degradation from adjoining populated areas. Furthermore, because these areas are relatively small, the fauna may be expected to have a more profound impact. Conservation methods used in American national parks that are relatively large tracts of land often buffered by large uninhabited expanses and generally contain smaller sized fauna are unlikely to prove effective without modifications. In this regard, whatever management policies are implemented, they have to be tested for long- and short-term effects.

In the long run, what role will ecotourism have in conserving gorilla populations? What must be done to ensure that tourism and the development that goes along with it will have a positive effect?

Dr. Sarmiento—Although eagerly embraced by donor countries looking for justification to pour in Western funds, Weber and Vedder's proposal [see Vedder and Weber 1990] that revolves around making gorillas an economic asset to the local population has never been adequately tested. It is uncertain whether following a policy of this type would protect the gorillas in the long run. If the recent situation in the Virungas and Bwindi is any indication, this policy is likely to cause more problems for protecting these animals than solving them. The same applies to the oxymoron currently popular with donors: "development through conservation." While debate on the merits of these policies can be argued eternally, careful testing is the only way to gauge their effectiveness. In this regard, the conservation methods presently used at Bwindi and the Virungas are experimental and have to be carefully and painstakingly researched. It is mind-boggling how many NGOs and donor countries flaunt policies of not supporting research with the tacit suggestion that research is a frivolous expenditure when setting out to do conservation.

Prior to undertaking research on the success of implemented conservation programs, research as to systematics and ecological relationships of the flora and fauna that presently exist in these parks has to be undertaken. In this regard, the Virungas area is far ahead of Bwindi, but there is still much work that needs to be done in both. Once systematic and ecological relationships are clear, careful monitoring of the park's flora and fauna can gauge the effects of implemented programs within the forest (i.e., tourism, limited use of forest resources) or in the areas surrounding the forest (crop changes in adjacent fields, more intensive agriculture, new roads, dams, waterways, etc.).

Who is to take responsibility and make the necessary changes to ensure that these killings do not continue?

Dr. Steklis—The international community needs to take a far stronger, more concerted stand on Zaire's tolerance of the Rwandan army on its soil. The present regime in Zaire is basking in aid dollars that have once again poured in because of the refugees, so the government has no immediate motivation to end the crisis, especially as dozens of agencies are making high profits themselves seeking solutions to the environmental degradation caused by the refugees. All are "band-aid" solutions, like cutting wood for the refugees elsewhere (virgin forest) rather than getting rid of the refugees. If all aid to Zaire were stopped today, the refugees would be gone tomorrow! Unfortunately, it is all big business for governments and NGOs alike, because both profit from crises!

Dr. Sarmiento—Ultimately, the donors have to, since they control the assets the conservation NGOs seek to attract and thus are the only ones that hold the rein of accountability. This points a finger at each and every one of us that donates to gorilla conservation groups and also to USAID [U.S. Aid for International Development], which is one of the largest donors in the Bwindi and Virunga areas.

All of us clearly agree conservation of gorillas and their habitat is a good cause, but that is not enough to justify our donation to any group that uses all the "politically correct" but hollow catchphrases. NGOs worthy of funding should have a proven track record of implementing conservation programs successfully. They should have clearly set long- and short-term goals and a feasible carefully outlined conservation program for each and every area they propose to conserve. More importantly, they should not confuse proven versus experimental programs and implement aggressive research policies in cases where program implementation is experimental. As individual donors, to hold NGOs accountable we have to take the time to familiarize ourselves with their accomplishments, ideologies, and conservation policies. As noted, blindly throwing money at both Virunga and Bwindi areas may be causing more harm than good.

To implement a system of accountability, major donors or donor countries must have a working knowledge of what is needed to establish and carry through effective conservation programs in areas they plan to fund. This should include estimates of the cost of carrying out such programs. This would effectively eliminate NGOs from working at cross purposes in any one area. Because they are donating this money in the name of taxpayers who supposedly want to support conservation, donor countries should have a clear and precise policy as to the types of conservation programs they are willing to fund for each area and how effective each program must be. For example, will it fund only tested, proven methods of conservation or will it fund experimental ones? Because USAID is part of the U.S. federal government, if you are an American voter, you have some say through your district representative as to how this organization donates money. If you want to help, write to your congressman and tell them you want the government to implement programs of accountability in international conservation policy. These programs should impartially gauge the effectiveness of NGOs in implementing proposed programs, cease funding NGOs that aren't successful in carrying out their proposals, and hold them accountable for funds if the proposed work was not satisfactory. Add that you do not want untested conservation programs to be implemented unless accompanied by rigorous scientific testing.

Fortunately, if these gorilla killings do not continue, what damage has been done is negligible. Like every ominous grey cloud that mars a perfect blue sky, the killings have a silver lining. In this case, they alerted us to the fact that our efforts to conserve Virunga and Bwindi gorillas are far from satisfactory. Contrary to what the popular press would have one believe, the major reason for this has not been lack of concern or funds, but the lack of holding those who receive these funds accountable.

EXERCISES

13.1 Run a search for "gorilla" on the World Wide Web using your favorite search engine. There are official and unofficial Web pages. Often, other Web sites such as news networks have information on gorillas. Besides habitat destruction, what are the latest threats to gorilla populations?

13.2 What other information on primates is available on the World Wide Web? Is there any information on New World primates such as tamarins and marmosets?

13.3 Look for more information on primates. How many species are recognized today? What genera have converged with other genera on different continents?

13.4 Compare and contrast the plight of gorillas and other primates on a country-by-country basis. Use the Web to check on countries such as Zaire, Nigeria, and Equatorial Guinea. Is there information on chimpanzees?

LITERATURE CITED

Akeley, C. 1923. *In Brightest Africa.* Garden City Publishers, Garden City, New York.

Coolidge, H.J. 1929. A revision of the genus *Gorilla. Memoirs of the Harvard Museum of Comparative Zoology* **50**:293–381.

Fossey, D. 1983. *Gorillas in the Mist.* Houghton Mifflin, Boston.

Groves, C. 1970. Population systematics of gorilla. *Journal of Zoology* **161**:287–300.

Harcourt, A.H. 1996. Is the gorilla a threatened species? How should we judge? *Biological Conservation* **75**:165–176.

Lanjouw, A., G. Cummings, and J. Miller. 1995. Gorilla conservation problems and activities in North Kivu, eastern Zaire. *African Primates* **1**(2):44–46.

Morell, V.W. 1995. Will primate genetics split one gorilla into two? *Science* **265**:1661.

Schaller, G.B. 1959. *The Mountain Gorilla.* University of Chicago Press, Chicago.

Vedder, A. and W. Weber. 1990. The Mountain Gorilla Project (Volcanoes National Park). *in* Kiss, A. (Ed.). *Living with Wildlife: Wildlife Resource Management with Local Participation in Africa.* World Bank, Washington, D.C.

Wilkie, D.S., J.G. Sidle, and G.C. Boundzanga. 1992. Mechanized logging, market hunting, and a bank loan in Congo. *Conservation Biology* **6**(4):570–580.

INTERNATIONAL WILDLIFE ISSUES: IRIAN JAYA

14

Many wildlife issues are of international importance and affect all of us in one way or another. Many birds, for instance, summer in the United States but winter in South America, where they are subjected to agricultural pesticides that have long been banned in the United States. Combined with habitat destruction in the United States, these species face trouble at both ends of their range. Logging in Panama to supply the Japanese with select hardwoods for their bathrooms destroys habitat for U.S. songbirds as well. Gold mining by an Australian company on the Irian Jaya border is destroying immense tracts of pristine forest but is providing nearly 20,000 badly needed jobs. Seared kangaroo is a delicacy at a restaurant in Australia. Dogs are regular table fare in the Philippines, while millions of dogs and cats are euthanized and incinerated in the United States. How can we appreciate the wildlife issues of our time? Many issues are resolved by default before we have a chance to confront the problem. We never even learn about others until it is too late.

According to Sawhill (1995), Indonesia is a "true biodiversity hot spot." However, Indonesia has 210 endangered species, more than any other country in the world. Indonesia's rain forests and marine ecosystems are some of the most diverse areas on earth. Fully 10% of the world's rain forests remain in Indonesia on some of its 17,000 islands. Indonesia contains 10% of the world's plant species, 12% of its birds, 12% of its mammals, and 16% of the world's reptiles and amphibians.

PARADISE AND PARADISE LOST

As discussed earlier, a wildlife issue requires two people and a difference of opinion regarding a wildlife resource. In many cases, human invaders have caused extinctions (Steadman 1995). In other instances, humans have used wildlife resources for thousands of years without damaging them. In Irian Jaya, for instance, bird of paradise feathers are an important part of ceremonial life. Wild pigs are traded for brides. The men of some villages all sleep under one roof away from the women of the village, who sleep in the upper story above the pigs. The world still holds strange and wonderful surprises for those willing to appreciate them. However, there are some issues we never hear or read about because they are thought by those who bring us the news to be unimportant or uninteresting to us. Such is the case with Irian Jaya, a nation state of Indonesia.

During the Cretaceous, New Guinea and Australia were beneath sea level. New Guinea first emerged from the sea in the Eocene, about 40 million years ago, at about 35 degrees south latitude (Axelrod and Raven 1982). Since then, the island has been a changing landscape of emergent islands, and biotic events have been strongly influenced by changing sea levels, particularly during the Pleistocene. Throughout the geologic history of the island, the central mountain range has acted to separate biotic interactions. The flora of Australia and New Guinea is derived from Gondwana stocks. However, the Dipterocarpaceae so common in Indonesia are rare in New Guinea. Cores from the middle Miocene about 15 million years ago show pollen from vegetation that was common to Australia. The chain of islands extending southward from Indonesia contains a transition of predominately Asian flowering plants and placental mammals, while Australia contains marsupial mammals and different flowering forms. Plant geographers view New Guinea as principally Malaysian. Zoologists noted both marsupial and placental forms on New Guinea and also that the avifauna was more like Australian forms. During the glacial periods of the Pleistocene, extensive grasslands and savannas formed on New Guinea, which was joined with Australia. These regions contain dry-adapted, fire-resistant flora. New habitat was created when the central mountain range was uplifted during the Pliocene and early Pleistocene, and as a result, the extant floral and faunal forms further diversified. Wallacea, the region containing New Guinea, Timor, and Sulawesi, actually contains few mammals from either Australian or Asian stocks. Many plant families are shared, but most species are unique to New Guinea. Thus, New Guinea's tectonic history and interesting mixture of Australian and Asian forms make the island unusual.

Indonesia's population of about 200 million has had a direct negative environmental impact (Hardjono 1991). The most common cause of degradation is deforestation, followed naturally by soil erosion. Erosion has caused the sedimentation in some lakes to reduce their holding capacity and hence provide less extensive wetlands used for rice crops. The population growth of the so-called "inner islands" like Java is forcing agricultural lands to be converted to urban housing. Asian demand for wood products is now forcing open timber tracts on the so-called "outer islands" such as Irian Jaya and Kalimantan. After two decades of harvesting on Kalimantan, the forests have been completely logged over, and never again will the size and thickness of the trees approach the scale that once existed. New roads in Papua New Guinea have also destroyed pristine forests (Figure 14.1). The indigenous people such as the Dayaks have been relocated, so extensive is the damage (Potter 1991).

Irian Jaya is the western half of the world's second largest island, New Guinea; the eastern half is Papua New Guinea. Irian Jaya is part of Indonesia, the fifth most populous country after China, India, the United States, and Brazil. Indonesia is, in general, densely populated. Irian Jaya, however, is the least populated island, with only 1.35 million people. From 1848 to 1963, Irian Jaya was Dutch New Guinea and was a protectorate of the Netherlands. After existing under the United Nations flag for several years, West Irian, as the country was called, was integrated, against its own desires, into Indonesia.

FIGURE 14.1 Tropical rain forest destruction for a new road in Papua New Guinea.

FIGURE 14.2   Human cultural diversity is celebrated at the Mt. Hagen Sing-Sing, a gathering of over 100 tribes, in Papua New Guinea.

The indigenous people of Irian Jaya have a long and unchanged history of subsistence fishing, agriculture, and living off the land. Many continue to maintain their culture, as do their neighbors in Papua New Guinea (Figure 14.2). Some live off Sago palm pulp, while others eat the larvae of the Capricorn beetle as a source of protein. Highland crops include sweet potatoes and taro. Pigs are raised for food and traded for brides. Well over 250 languages are thought to be spoken, so isolated are many of the local tribes. Even through the middle of this century, Stone Age people lived as headhunters and practiced cannibalism and ritual warfare. Superstition was a powerful force in their lives. Now, however, these beliefs and practices are becoming a thing of the past. Some lament their passing. Since 1969, many local natives have waged a war of freedom against their more heavily armed Indonesian oppressors (Osborne 1985, Whittaker 1990).

On February 17, 1996, an earthquake of magnitude 7.5 rocked Irian Jaya. Twenty-four people were killed and many more were presumed dead from numerous mud slides. Subsequently there were 19 aftershocks measuring 4 to 5 on the Richter scale. Only six days passed before another quake was felt. Remote villages in the interior of Irian Jaya have virtually no contact with the rest of the world; hence there is no way of knowing who needs help. Dysentery is always a problem after earthquakes and other natural disasters, and therefore, the number of dead undoubtedly rises. The tidal waves that struck the villages of Borarsi, Borobudur, Fanindi, and Wosi also killed many people and damaged houses. On February 27, 1996, news reached the outside world that a pig epidemic in the remote villages of Brome and Ndugwa, near Wamena, Irian Jaya, killed 177 people. Symptoms included breathing distress, vomiting blood, and then death. Medical teams were dispatched on receiving the news but were days too late. Because of a hostage case involving foreign graduate students, mail couriers feared leaving the villages. How much of this news reaches people in the United States?

The Indonesian Army Strategic Reserve Command sent Battalion 432 Airborne, an elite commando unit, to assist in the rescue of 3 British graduate students, 2 Dutch, a German, and 17 Indonesians. The graduate students had been researching local tribesmen, who still carry on subsistence living, in an attempt to learn more about an isolated area of high floral and faunal diversity, when they were taken hostage. In the past, these so-called Stone Age tribesmen used handmade long bows and arrows to defend their territory against Indonesia government helicopter gunships and paratroopers. The local people's knowledge of the region was no match for the more heavily armed government army. Within a few days, not a single paratrooper was alive. One result of the paratroopers' dropping in was that these primitive tribal people received a supply of the latest in automatic weapons, such as M-16s, and regular armed forces standard weapons and ammunition (Osborne 1985).

A team from the International Commission of the Red Cross was attempting to establish contact with a group of freedom fighters, or rebels as the Indonesians refer to them, who still withhold the whereabouts of researchers around Mapunduma Village, Tiom District. As of March 10, 1996, the whereabouts of the hostages was unknown.

No accurate vegetation map of Irian Jaya exists, even on a crude scale (Perocz 1989). Some hill tribes were not even discovered by the outside world until the 1930s (Archbold and Rand 1940). Indeed, before 1824, Europeans believed that birds of paradise were mystical creatures without legs that lived on dew and survived permanently on the wing until death. The discovery of birds of paradise by the European fashion industry led to the demise of over 50,000 birds for the feather trade shortly before 1900. For thousands of years, natives lived essentially in harmony with nature and the birds of paradise. The indigenous people use the birds for their headdresses as ceremonial ornaments. The more colorful sexually mature male birds are only taken after they have reproduced. Most local people over the age of ten know most of the birds in their area and are familiar with the natural history of the birds they value.

The fauna of the island of New Guinea lies at the intersection of the Oriental region and the Australian region, an area referred to as Wallacea, named after the great naturalist–explorer Alfred Russell Wallace. It contains a mixture of Australian and Oriental floral and faunal forms. According to Perocz (1989), Irian Jaya contains the richest concentration of plant life in the country of Indonesia, a "floristic diversity of tremendous proportions." A conservative list contains well over 20,000 species. An astounding 124 genera of flowering plants are endemic, compared with 59 for the island of Borneo, 17 for Sumatra, and only 10 for Java. Species endemism is extraordinarily high—90% of all species are endemic. Leach and Osborne (1985) report that this region contains the highest number of plants useful to humans. However, members of the family of trees Dipterocarpaceae are rare and hence the forests are generally not of interest to timber companies. Many indigenous uses of plants have yet to be described and will undoubtedly one day contribute to the health and welfare of the human race if we can only learn to appreciate the fact that these "primitive Stone Age people" have forgotten more about plants than most of us will ever learn.

Surprisingly, orchids make up nearly one-third of all flowering plants on Irian Jaya. Giant epiphytic anthouse plants can reach 2 m in length and house thousands of ants. Some pitcher plants are carnivorous, living on ants. From glowing fungi that emit an iridescent light from their gills, to the fruit of the *Amorphahallus campanulatus* that stinks like rotting flesh, Irian Jaya holds a fantastically diverse flora waiting to be explored.

As for land mammals, Irian Jaya has 2 monotremes, 57 marsupials, 63 chiroptera, a single carnivore, 2 artiodactyls, and 49 rodentia. These forms place the island of New Guinea at the intersection of two zoogeographic regions, with the first two orders being Australian and the remaining orders more closely related to Oriental forms. Several of the mammals are curious forms, such as the echidnas, the eight species of cuscus, pygmy possums, and four species of tree kangaroos. Large carnivorous predators are absent from New Guinea.

The avifauna of the island of New Guinea is legendary, with approximately 700 species known. Of these, 643 species occur in Irian Jaya, including 269 endemic species. The birds also show affinities to Australian and Oriental forms. "Birds have attracted the attention of visitors and voyagers to New Guinea since its discovery, and they are well known and utilized for many purposes by the indigenous peoples." Of course, the birds of paradise are unique among the world's birds and many consider them the most beautiful birds on earth. For instance, the blue bird of paradise's mating call sounds like an electric guitar. The male hangs upside down from a branch, puffs up its plumage, and emits an almost electronic sound while it bobs up and down, displaying for the drab female. The nocturnal Papuan frogmouth sits with its mouth open, catching insects. Strange bower birds build large nests of sticks called bowers, and some even line the entrance with blue berries and flowers. The cassowary is a deadly flightless bird that has been known to disembowel a human with a single kick. Almost nothing is known about the birds of prey. We don't even know what the nests look like. They still remain unknown to us. No one has found a nest—ever!

The reptiles and amphibians are equally strange and beautiful. Although 250 reptiles are known, it is suspected that 100 snakes and 200 lizards may actually occur. There are legless lizards, arboreal dragon lizards, and the non-venomous green tree python. Approximately 120 tree frogs are known to occur and more can be expected to be discovered. As for fish, there are between 6000 and 7000 species in nearby coastal seas. The surrounding seas have been the principal evolutionary center from which the entire Indo-Pacific region has been populated (Carcasson 1977). This total represents fully one-third of all species of fish. Allen and Cross (1982) note that of about 158 freshwater species, only 11 occur on either side of the central mountain range. Little is known about the insects, but estimates range from 80,000 to 120,000 species. The spectacular birdwing butterflies, the Ornithopterids, occur in Irian Jaya. There are some 800 spiders, including the giant bird-eating spider. Some stick insects are 25 cm in length. Of all groups, insects have been investigated the least, and biologists will undoubtedly be surprised by new discoveries. Colorful coral reef communities like none other on earth are found off the coasts of Irian Jaya. In most areas of Indonesia, mollusks have been depleted, but Irian Jaya has rich and diverse offshore resources. Among the offshore islands are also strange life forms, such as the world's largest terrestrial arthropod, the coconut crab (*Birgus latro*). Of the smaller organisms, scientists have not even ventured a guess as to how many exist. Indeed, the smaller the organism, the more likely it is that it has yet to be described.

Perocz (1989) estimated that over 80% or more of Irian Jaya remains in a pristine state. Traditional tribal practices maintained a low population density and communal land practices prevented anyone from accumulating large land holdings. Now, however, development is proceeding at a rapid pace, and age-old practices are being condemned as standing in the face of progress. In the past, protected areas were never established because there was no need for them. Indeed, the concept of a protected area is a modern one because large-scale development creates a need to protect relatively small areas after the fact. These areas are usually, for one reason or another, not developable at the time. As the tribal value system is torn apart and the local people displaced, conservation areas become a popular subject.

Two species of crocodiles have been harvested in Irian Jaya for many years.

The saltwater crocodile (*Crocodylus parosus*) is listed in the IUCN Red Data Book as an endangered species, while the New Guinea crocodile (*C. novaeguinea*) is considered vulnerable. Most crocodile farms depend on wild crocodiles to stay in business. As of 1989, only one farm had been able to produce crocodiles in captivity. The crocodile industry exists mainly to supply a growing export market. It remains to be seen if crocodile farms can wean themselves from wild-caught crocodiles and wild egg exploitation.

The birds of paradise have also been harvested, perhaps for thousands of years. There are 26 species of birds of paradise and the most beautiful are highly valued. Pigs are often traded for the finest feathers. All the birds of paradise are protected by Indonesian law. There are also 44 species of parrots, 5 of which are protected by law. Frequently, these laws are not enforced, and fine caged birds of almost any kind can be found in the local markets. Before the illegal pet trade was established, traditional uses of the birds, and especially the birds of paradise, were controlled by cultural barriers and social taboos. No birds of paradise are known to have been driven to extinction by the indigenous people. Perocz (1989) suggests that as the bird trade became more commercialized and markets outside Irian Jaya were established, certain species of birds of paradise were driven to extinction in parts of their range. The parrot trade has also thrived in spite of laws designed to prevent it. Once a commercial trade is established, market hunters must harvest birds continuously. As the birds become more rare and their value increases, market hunters are forced to drive them to extinction. The need for a quick profit in a competitive marketplace puts enormous pressure on resources, as we have previously seen. From orchids and butterflies to giant clams—all are under increasing pressure now, principally because of external market forces above and beyond traditional uses.

Marine vertebrates such as sea turtles and dugongs are also exploited for food. Irian Jaya has nesting grounds of leatherback (*Dermochelys coriacea*), green (*Chelonia mydas*), hawksbill (*Eretmochelys imbricata*), and olive ridley (*Lepidochelys olivacea*) sea turtles. All are now endangered. The dugong (*Dugong dugon*), the Irian Jaya form of the Florida manatee, is widely distributed and suffers from uncontrolled hunting pressure throughout its range. The dugong is considered a delicacy and its teeth are used for cigarette holders. Nietschmann and Nietschmann (1981) studied dugongs in the Torres Strait between New Guinea and Australia. Here the dugong is a part of the indigenous people's culture, tradition, economy, and religion. Thus, the dugong is conserved for perpetuity here. Elsewhere across Irian Jaya, netting and spearing these gentle creatures continue unchecked.

According to Perocsz (1989), many species are protected under Indonesian law. "Among these are whales, the three species of cassowary, all birds of paradise, all tree kangaroos and cuscuses, three species of marine turtles, and some fish....According to this law, the hunting, killing, capturing, trading (dead or alive), and even the mere possession of these species are forbidden. The law, furthermore, states that it is also forbidden to export these species from country to country or to possess or trade their skins, feathers, and other parts of the body, or the products made thereof, or to disturb, collect, trade, and possess their eggs and nests." Of course, having laws on the books and enforcing them are two very different things. In Irian Jaya, these Indonesian laws are totally ignored. Yet are we to blame the indigenous people for the commercial exportation of certain species? An International Institute for Environment and Development/Government of Indonesia (1985) report singled out the World Bank and its continued financial support for the transmigration program as the largest contributor toward the destruction of the forests on Kalimantan (Potter 1991). Will the same happen to Irian Jaya?

TRANSMIGRATION

With its low population, Irian Jaya is an attractive destination for the largest human transmigration program on earth. Hundreds of thousands of native Indonesians from the central islands surrounding Java have been relocated to the outer islands of the empire, such as Irian Jaya. As the world's demand for hardwoods increases, logging companies have established claims on 70% of Irian Jaya's virgin and virtually unknown forests (Perocz 1989). Social, political, and technological changes are rapidly wiping aside thousands of years of cultural diversity. Some suggest that "Indonesia's secret war" is nothing less than a genocidal war to remove the native Melanesian people and replace them with true Indonesians from the inner islands.

The massive transmigration program was announced to the world by Indonesia in 1963. Since then, hundreds of thousands of people have been relocated from the heavily populated inner islands of Java, Bali, Madura, and Lombok to the less heavily populated outer islands of Kalimantan, East Timor, Sumatra, and Irian Jaya. Often missionary societies provide the initial foothold by penetrating the remote areas of Irian Jaya under the guise of religious reform. Of course, mission stations and airstrips must be established to secure outside supplies. For this privilege, the local people donate part of their land holdings. Thereafter, a small military outpost is established. With mission services flying into remote areas, military and aid-agency personnel are frequent passengers. According to Indonesia national law, all unimproved land is state property. Thus, the native forests that have supported indigenous people for thousands of years, by definition, are owned by the state. Transmigrants are usually Islamic, and cross-cultural conflicts are common. The Indonesian Minister of Transmigration admitted that an intended result of transmigration was that different ethnic groups would in the long run disappear (Colchester 1986).

Of course, land tenure in Irian Jaya is fundamentally different than in the West. Typically, a tribe holds communal property and people live on tribal lands. Living on the land confers certain rights and privileges but not outright ownership. If an individual "sells" the lands, he is merely conferring certain rights for a specific period of time. Hence, the land can be sold many times, much like renting property, for instance, and growing crops, with the provision that the land will revert back to the community after some time.

Ten percent of the transmigration funding was initially provided by the World Bank in the form of loans. After about 30,000 families were relocated, Indonesian and foreign companies invested money in the scheme in the hope of reaping future profits. According to Monbiot (1989), Indonesian Army operations and transmigrants often make refugees of the indigenous people, forcing them to vacate their tribal lands and, in some cases, relocate to the neighboring independent country of Papua New Guinea. Unfortunately, without knowledge of the local growing conditions, the transmigrants' crops often fail, and without some local assistance, transmigrants go hungry. Both the new lords and the refugees became victims of grand plans and grim reality (Whittaker 1990).

NATURAL RESOURCE EXPLOITATION

Irian Jaya is rich in other natural resources, including timber, minerals (such as copper, zinc, and gold), and petroleum. The United States, Japan, and South Africa have been quick to take advantage of the prospects where almost no environmental laws are enforced. Some of the world's largest oil companies are already pumping oil. In the Cyclops Mountains between Irian Jaya and Papua New Guinea lays one of the largest mines in the world. In 1967, Freeport Indonesia Inc. received its contract to begin operations and produced its first copper in 1972. Oddly, in 1978, the Lorentz Strict Nature Reserve was created by Irian Jaya; it contained the entire mine, all the local housing, the airport, and the port facility far to the south on the coast. As of 1989, 45% of the mine was inside the park but underground. The reserve was designated a World Heritage Site in 1982 as one of the greatest natural areas on earth. Formerly, the area was remote and sparsely occupied. More than 17,000 people work at the mine in an area where good jobs are otherwise nonexistent. But very few jobs go to poorly trained and unskilled native people who are mostly laborers.

Perocsz (1989) reported that "slag and gravel disposal and particularly water contamination of the Otomona River will have an impact on the reserve through tidal transfer at the Arafura Sea. Untreated waters full of metal oxides will affect the well-being of the vast resettlement project downstream near Timka, the largest settlement program of its kind in the province." Just six years later, tons of toxic wastes may be harming fish and other wildlife resources on portions of the river and contaminating tropical forest. One problem is that the wilderness is virtually off limits except for invited guests. The few visitors who have seen this region have remarked on the degradation that has occurred in the relatively small areas they saw, such as along the trails. The cost of implementing sound environmental awareness is incidental to a mining operation that unearths titanic amounts of ore each day. Figure 14.3 shows siltation in the Ok

FIGURE 14.3 River siltation has destroyed the local fishery on the Ok Tedi in Papua New Guinea, near the Irian Jaya border.

Tedi (Ok means river in Papua New Guinea) in Papua New Guinea on the border near Irian Jaya.

The South Africans and Indonesians pursued oil resources on Irian Jaya during the 1970s. Discovering oil-rich areas and then exploiting them is made more difficult first by the terrain and second by indigenous claims for compensation. Chevron, a U.S.-based company, had a pipeline damaged by the indigenous people over compensation for loss of communal lands and forests. Shell Oil Company ceased operations from 1983 to 1986 because of attacks by indigenous people.

Irian Jaya is nearly covered with what once was virgin forest, and now these forests are being heavily exploited. About 40% of the forests are in protected areas and World Heritage Sites; however, these designations apparently confer no special status. A variety of global multinationals are sharing the resources and neglecting native claims. Some 80% of the transmigration sites were carved from virgin tracts of forest (Secrett 1986). In effect, the reason we in the West are especially ignorant of the plight of the people of West Papua is that U.S. companies are exploiting these resources and enriching investors who want nothing more than to make a profit from their investments (Whittaker 1990). Traditional fishing stocks are being depleted by huge Japanese factory ships. Wildlife resources are being decimated by indiscriminate logging practices. Moreover, companies operating in Irian Jaya ignore the rights of the indigenous people and avoid compensating them for the loss of their forests, their wildlife, and the damage to their societies (Colchester 1986). These natural resources have been sustainably exploited by the indigenous people since humans occupied the island of New Guinea perhaps as long as 50,000 years ago. Now, the Western concept of "sustainable development" has replaced "indigenous sustainability." If the local people were given a choice, which would they choose?

INDIGENOUS SUSTAINABILITY

Between Australia and the island of New Guinea in the Torres Strait, indigenous seafaring people have plied a living for centuries (Nietschmann and Nietschmann 1981). The Torres Strait islanders have hunted dugongs and green turtles that are otherwise endangered elsewhere. The survival of the indigenous society is intimately linked to the hunting of these animals and ultimately to the animals' food supply. The islands in the Torres Strait are thinly populated by about 4500 people and minimally developed. Seagrasses and algae are plentiful in the warm shallow strait, and dugongs and sea turtles concentrate in well-known areas. A large tidal range opens and closes some hunting areas, and the dugongs frequently follow the tides, feeding on the flooded grasses during high tides. In some areas, dugongs have stripped the vegetation clean.

Four species of sea turtles are found, but only the green turtle is hunted regularly. However, the Torres Strait may be the most important green sea turtle sanctuary in the world. The ecology of the green turtle in the strait is well appreciated by the Torres Strait islanders. The native people have a detailed, consistent knowledge of the ecology of the animals they hunt and the physical processes governing their abundance and distribution. There are more than 80 terms for tides and tidal and water conditions.

Hunters focus on middle-age female dugongs and turtles that are said to taste better than other animals. These are also hardest to catch. Through the use of certain closely guarded charms, hunters can increase their chances of success. After a successful hunt, the butchering of the prey is ritualized. Choice cuts go to the hunter and his extended family. As is usual in hunting societies, a successful hunter always gives away meat because he knows that one day he will accept meat from another hunter. The rest of the meat is shared equally among families. The remains are always fed to the sharks that gather.

The Torres Strait islanders have minimized their interactions with the rest of Australia and Papua New Guinea. Many of their ancient beliefs and practices continue to be maintained. As long as they are able to hunt, the Torres Strait islanders will continue to live in harmony with the natural world.

EXERCISES

14.1 Find some remote areas in the world and elaborate on their environmental problems and wildlife issues. Try searching on the World Wide Web for information on the Indonesian states of Timor, Sulawesi, Sumatra, Bali, and Java.

14.2 What are the wildlife and natural resource issues in the newly independent states of the former Soviet Union? Is there a common theme they share?

14.3 Locate a reliable source for more information on recent developments in Irian Jaya. Occasionally, newspapers have some articles of interest. Irian Jaya has been notably unsuccessful in its efforts to become an independent country like Papua New Guinea. Political events often overwhelm wildlife issues.

14.4 Try searching around on the World Wide Web sites at CNN and the BBC news services for interesting wildlife issues or news from faraway places.

LITERATURE CITED

Allen, G.A. and N.J. Cross. 1982. *Rainbowfishes of Australia and Papua New Guinea.* Angus and Robertson, Sydney, Australia.

Archbold, R. and A.L. Rand 1940. *New Guinea Expedition.* Robert M. McBride and Company, New York.

Axelrod, D.I. and P.H. Raven. 1982. Paleobiography and origin of New Guinea flora. *in* Gressit, J.L. (Ed.). *Biogeography and Ecology of New Guinea,* Vol. 2. Dr. W. Junk, Publishers, The Hague.

Carcasson, R.H. 1977. *A Field-Guide to the Reef Fishes of Tropical Australia and the Indo-Pacific Region.* William Collins Sons, Glasgow, U.K.

Colchester, M. 1986. Banking on disaster: international support for transmigration. *The Ecologist* **16**(2/3):61–70.

Hardjono, J. 1991. The dimensions of Indonesia's environmental problems. *in* Hardjono, J. (Ed.). *Indonesia: Resources, Ecology, and Environment.* Oxford University Press, Oxford, U.K.

International Institute for Environment and Development/Government of Indonesia. 1985. A Review of Politics Affecting the Sustainable Development of Forest Lands in Indonesia. Jakarta, Java.

Leach, G.J. and P.L. Osborne. 1985. *Freshwater Plants of Papua New Guinea.* UPNG Press, Port Moresby, Papua New Guinea.

Monbiot, G. 1989. *Poisoned Arrows: An Investigative Journey Through Indonesia.* Michael Joseph Publishers, London.

Nietschmann, B. and J. Nietschmann. 1981. Good dugong, bad dugong: bad turtle, good turtle. *Natural History* **90**(5):54–63.

Osborne, R. 1985. *Indonesia's Secret War: The Guerrilla Struggle in Irian Jaya.* Allen & Unwin, Winchester, Massachusetts.

Perocz, R.G. 1989. *Conservation and Development in Irian Jaya.* E.J. Brill, Leiden, Germany.

Potter, L. 1991. Environmental and social aspects of timber exploitation in Kalimantan 1967–1989. *in* Hardjono, J. (Ed.). *Indonesia: Resources, Ecology, and Environment.* Oxford University Press, Oxford, U.K.

Sawhill, J.C. 1995. The Nature Conservancy and biodiversity: 1993 in review. *Nature Conservancy* **44**(1):5–9.

Secrett, C. 1986. The environmental impact of transmigration. *The Ecologist* **16**(2/3):77–88.

Steadman, D.W. 1995. Prehistoric extinctions of Pacific island birds: biodiversity meets zooarchaeology. *Science* **267**:1123–1131.

Whittaker, A. 1990. *West Papua: Plunder in Paradise.* Anti-Slavery Society, U.K.

HARVESTING
OF WILDLIFE

15

I n this chapter, the term "harvest" is used very loosely and is applied to any
type of removal of individuals from the wild state. Thus, we do not differentiate between live capture of parrots for the pet trade, for example, and
actual shooting of kangaroos for meat and skins. Throughout evolution, humans
have harvested wildlife species. Across the world, we can see a broad spectrum
of legal and illegal wildlife uses today. In undeveloped countries or countries
with undeveloped areas, we see subsistence hunting. At the opposite end of the
spectrum, we see wealthy hunters who pay large sums of money to shoot at
what may be little more than a captive animal on a game farm. Somewhere in
between these two worlds, we see the commercial hunters—some legal, some
illegal. In this chapter, a variety of aspects related to human harvest of wildlife
are explored, beginning with subsistence hunting and then proceeding to commercial and recreational hunting. The wildlife trade that is illegal is also examined and reveals that human culture can have a devastating effect on wildlife
populations.

Today, there are three central reasons for harvesting wildlife: the first is
simply for subsistence, the second is recreation, and the third is commercial/
financial. We differentiate between these three because their goals differ, and
this in turn may influence the population dynamics of the species that are
harvested. In principle, it may seem obvious enough that there is a fundamental
difference between hunting to live (subsistence hunters) and living to hunt
(recreational hunters). In reality, however, the distinction may be difficult to
discern. For the purpose of this discussion, subsistence hunters are defined as
hunters who must obtain wildlife meat in order to survive. Hunters in this

category would include, for example, nontribal humans who dwell in Amazonia or tribal humans in Africa or Southeast Asia.

SUBSISTENCE HUNTING: HUNTING TO LIVE

Imagine you are faced with the following problem. You live on the Great Plains of North America in the 1800s. You live in a village and you must live by hunting. Every day you must find food, and that means you must kill an animal. Moreover, it is bitterly cold six to eight months of every year, and animal skins are your only protection from the weather. You use these skins for clothing and to build your dwelling, since there is little structural vegetation for construction.

Native Americans in this region relied heavily on harvesting the American bison (Roe 1951). This was done via cooperative hunting. Cooperation gives humans a tremendous advantage in hunting. A group of humans could, for example, position themselves so as to drive a group of bison over a cliff. Some of the bison would die in the fall and others would suffer broken legs. The injured bison could be easily killed by slitting their throats with knives made from the bones of their ancestors.

When meat was available, Native Americans found ways to preserve it through a drying process. Thus, although the problem of finding food began anew every day, there were intermittent reprieves.

Weapons available to Native American were primitive before Europeans arrived. Nevertheless, the idea has been advanced that humans caused the extinction of a number of species of Pleistocene megafauna.

Now let's fast-forward to a village in the Amazon Basin in the 1990s. It is dawn and you are hungry. You emerge from your hut, made of vegetative material from the surrounding area, and it is pouring rain. In the Amazon Basin of South America, it rains frequently in some seasons. Your hut is in a small village. You have a "new" shotgun which you obtained by trading some artifacts to a passing miner. The shotgun is new only to you. It is in fact very old and partly rusted. You also have ten shotgun shells. Shotgun shells in the Amazon are very expensive and therefore very precious. Each one represents a meal—as long as you don't miss when you shoot. Your hunt for bush meat begins as soon as you leave the village.

Wildlife populations are scarce near the village, as those unwary animals were consumed long ago. Today, you know you must walk a great distance (perhaps several kilometers) to find an area where populations are large enough that your chance for success makes the effort worthwhile.

And what do you hope to find? The farther you travel, the farther you must transport the kill. Nevertheless, you hope for a large animal—one large enough to feed you for more than a day and still small enough that you can kill it with a single shot. (Remember, those shells are worth a fortune in the Amazon.)

In parts of the world, the daily problem of finding food for oneself and one's family has changed little from earlier times. Each day the problem must be solved anew. One way to partially offset this daily grind is to preserve the meat acquired in salt. Village huts are adequate, but there is no television, let alone a refrigerator. If clothes get too gamey, they must be cleaned so as not to betray one's presence to an animal (= a potential meal) with a sharp sense of smell. Clothes are cleaned by taking them to the river to wash them.

Solving the daily energy problems of oneself and one's family may mean finding something to trade for more shotgun shells or reliance on a more primitive means of killing, such as a bow and arrow, a blowpipe, or simply a sharp stick. Failure to make a kill may be offset by sharing food with a successful hunter from one's extended family in the village. (Hunters are expected to share their success.) Physical labor may also be traded for some food.

Every day is a struggle; life is very hard and is becoming more so every day. Consider the effects of deforestation on these populations. The forest is lost and so are the animals that live there. In place of the rain forest, which is often simply burned, grass is sown and cattle are raised on the grass. But the soil is not especially fertile and a lot of rain forest must be converted to rangeland to make it profitable. In the end, these cattle are slaughtered and their meat used in fast-food restaurants in North America. It is ironic that we pay so little for something that is so difficult to come by in some parts of the world.

Let's turn our attention to what kinds of species are harvested. We focus on Latin America because it is one of the last places on earth where subsistence hunting is an important way of life and because we have tremendous knowledge of the area through studies done by scientists at institutions such as the Center for Latin American Studies at the University of Florida.

In Amazonian Peru, "bush meat" constitutes 100% of the animal protein consumed by colonists. Among the Miskito Indians of Nicaragua, wildlife made up 98% of the meat consumed (Redford and Robinson 1991). In contrast, bush meat comprises less than 20% of the animal protein in the diets of colonists living along the transamerican highway in Brazil (Smith 1976).

If wildlife species are important to local peoples in Latin America, an interesting question involves which species are taken. In one study involving local people in Suriname, it was found that the people killed (for meat and skins) 27 species of mammals, 24 species of birds, 3 species of turtles, and 2 species of lizards (Redford and Robinson 1991). One might imagine that people take animals in proportion to their abundance, but this is too simplistic a view. Other important considerations involve cultural taboos. Mittermeier (1991) conducted in-depth interviews with local people in Suriname to determine their feelings about primate consumption. He found that some subsistence hunters avoided harvesting red-banded tamarins (*Saguinus midas*) or squirrel monkeys (*Saimiri sciureus*) due to local taboos because (1) the animals have sexual behavior too like that of humans, (2) the people believed that the meat would make them sick, (3) some species cradle their offspring like humans, and (4) the animals smelled bad (Mittermeier 1991).

Subsistence hunters may carefully pursue only certain species of mammals. In Suriname, for example, there are eight species of nonhuman primates that the local people hunt for meat and skins. Indeed, hunting for subsistence by local peoples has been identified as the most important factor in the disappearance of primates from Suriname (Mittermeier 1991).

Hunting habits and diets of local peoples are highly vulnerable to even minor development (Ayers et al. 1991). Thus, deforestation reduces population sizes, and roads bring in less knowledgeable hunters who may harvest previously unharvested species. Roads also may bring in supplies of canned meat from other parts of the world.

WILDLIFE FOR SALE

In Chapter 2, we learned that the caiman is a protected species. In Corumba, in southwestern Brazil, cowboys make a living herding cows and hunting caimans (Misch 1992). Although Brazil passed a law in 1967 protecting much of its wildlife from commercial hunting, the law is not enforced, which is not an uncommon occurrence. The cowboys shoot the caimans and sell them to local tanneries for around five dollars each. From there, the hides make their way to North America, Europe, and Asia. Estimates are that some 500,000 caimans are killed in the Pantanal region of Brazil each year. Scientists do not know if such harvests are sustainable.

Caimans are a small part of the illegal wildlife trade, however. Misch estimated the total value of wildlife sold to be from $5 to $8 billion annually. Most of the poaching is done by local people trying to make a better living. Although habitat loss is the primary threat to most of the world's species, trade in wildlife products can also wipe out a species. The passenger pigeon and the Carolina parakeet were two common North American species 100 years ago.

Both were driven to extinction by the wildlife trade. The Orinoco crocodile, the Javan and Sumatran tigers, and the black rhino are being driven to the same fate as a result of the wildlife trade.

Waste in the animal trade is staggering. Some 15 out of every 100 parrots imported into the United States die in transit. Among macaws, 30% die before they reach their owners. The dead birds are, of course, replaced by live birds from the wild. Although these losses seem high, they do not compare to those incurred by primates. When a young chimpanzee is taken from the wild, most of the adults must be killed first. Thus, for every chimp taken from the wild, some ten are killed. The Convention on International Trade in Endangered Species (CITES) (Chapter 1) is supposed to block import and export of endangered species and to regulate trade in threatened or potentially threatened species.

Thus, the treaty requires vigilant monitoring, which is proving to be an impossible task for many countries. One of the most notable successes of CITES has been the African elephant. Populations of elephants across Africa had plummeted to less than 600,000 in 1994. The international attention given elephants has raised consumer awareness and made the purchase of carved ivory, boots made of elephant skin, and wastepaper baskets made from an elephant's foot repugnant to most shoppers. CITES, however, has many loopholes that permit countries such as Zimbabwe, South Africa, Botswana, and Malawi to list "reservations" on Appendix I species such as elephants. Appendix II species can be traded provided wild populations are not compromised. But how are these populations monitored? Who verifies that the species is prospering? Some people even suggest that inclusion in the Appendix II list is an advertisement for poachers to collect now because tomorrow may be too late.

CITES agreements are difficult to trace, and no sanctions are placed on nations that violate the treaty. Vietnam, Myanmar, Cambodia, and Laos had not yet signed the treaty in 1996, and these are biologically rich nations. Once a product such as a tiger penis reaches Laos, anyone can purchase it and then attempt to ship it home.

As Misch points out, rangers in most parks are poorly paid and poorly equipped, and most parks are short-handed. It is far easier and safer to take a bride than to protect an animal when the poachers are heavily armed and determined. Is it reasonable to expect a guard who is paid five dollars a month to protect a rhinoceros worth $1000 in horn alone. Most often, guards are chosen from the local population and are resented because they have the highest paying jobs in the area. Moreover, the guards are charged with keeping their neighbors from making a living off the park's natural resources. Frequently, the guards are ostracized in their own villages.

COMMERCIAL HARVEST OF WILDLIFE IN NORTH AMERICA*

On Earth Day, April 22, 1996, the *Tampa Tribune* ran a story on a Waldo, Florida wildlife gift shop. The store sells snake skins to major boot manufacturers, but shoppers can buy many interesting and unusual products. For instance, python cummerbunds or sports jackets can be purchased, or even alligator back scratchers. Road-killed, stuffed bobcats, opossums, armadillos, and snakes are also available. Among the more exotic gifts are cobra-head belt buckles; rattlesnake belts, ties, and hatbands; and alligator boots. Certainly, animal rights activists actively campaign against such shops. However, although many of us are repulsed by these macabre gift shops, they serve as a constant reminder that humans continue to exploit wildlife and some people make a living doing it.

A large number of species are currently exploited commercially. The taxa involved range from sponges to mammals. In the United States, shellfish, sponges, jellyfish, and several species of fur-bearing mammals are commercially harvested. Historically, a number of species of waterfowl, upland gamebirds, and big game mammals once were commercially harvested in the United States. Some of these species are discussed below, but only after examining some of the tragedies of market hunting in the United States. Hopefully, a pattern will quickly become apparent: there is no safety in numbers.

Fur Industry

There are still six or seven chinchilla farms left in North America and only four buyers of the skins. As of 1993, there were 556 mink farms in the United States, down from some 2000 a few years ago; 57 of these farms raise foxes.

State	Number of mink farms
Utah	150
Wisconsin	114
Minnesota	72
Oregon	29
Washington	28
Idaho	27

---

* *International Wildlife Trade: Whose Business Is It?* by Sarah Fitzgerald (World Wildlife Fund, 1989) is recommended as supplemental reading.

Iowa	25
Pennsylvania	21
Illinois	15
New York	12
Ohio	11
South Dakota	7
Other	45

The Passenger Pigeon (*Ectopistes migratorius*)

When the first Europeans landed in what is now called North America, the passenger pigeon may have been the most abundant bird species (Schorger 1973). Early reports described flocks that blackened the sky and extended for miles. We will never know how many passenger pigeons there once were, but we do know how many there are today—none. Passenger pigeons were victimized by a combination of habitat destruction and overhunting. The last surviving passenger pigeon was a female named Martha; she died in the Cincinnati Zoo on September 1, 1914 (Greenway 1967).

One habit of the passenger pigeon no doubt left the species especially vulnerable to overharvesting: they were very gregarious. Passenger pigeons nested in great concentrations and roosted in enormous flocks. Schorger (1973) described the sad history of the species once Europeans arrived. The vast numbers were reduced by the mid 1800s, and only remnant populations persisted by the late 1800s. Market hunters could kill large numbers by setting out poles for the birds to roost on and then firing their shotguns down the poles. Hunters could also kill vast numbers by smoking their roosts with burning sulfur. The hunters would place little pots of sulfur around the roosts after nightfall. They would then light the sulfur and wait for the birds to drop to the ground. Some individuals were killed outright by the poisonous fumes, and the others were bludgeoned to death. Other techniques involved the use of "stool pigeons." A calling bird would be placed on a perch (i.e., a stool) in a large trap. Wild birds would be attracted to the trap and easily ambushed. Market hunters sold passenger pigeons by the thousands for only pennies. Now the remnants of this species can be seen only as study skins in trays in the bird collection at various museums of natural history.

Waterfowl

Humans interested in making a buck through killing wildlife are often far too ingenious for their quarry, as exemplified by the market hunters who discovered that smoking sulfur would bring roosting passenger pigeons to the ground. Waterfowlers were also rather ingenious. They invented the so-called "punt gun." A punt gun was a large bore shotgun mounted on the back of a small boat (i.e., a punt). The bore of the gun was much larger than what waterfowl hunters are legally restricted to today, and punt guns were, in fact, little more than cannons on the backs of these little boats (Baldassarre and Bolen 1994). The hunters could row up to a flock of unsuspecting waterfowl and fire away. Because the gun was mounted on the boat, the tremendous recoil would be absorbed by the waterway and not the hunter's shoulder. Waterfowl were slaughtered by the millions in this way. Some examples of the slaughter include more than 400 ducks and 450 geese sent to market in a single day by a market hunter in Louisiana, 122 wood ducks killed before 9:00 A.M. on the Mississippi River, and a group of market hunters who sent 1000 ducks and shorebirds to market per week (Baldassarre and Bolen 1994 and references therein).

Nevertheless, there is no example of a waterfowl species that was forced to extinction by the use of punt guns. Is it possible that market hunters could have continued to use punt guns and kill waterfowl without human-imposed legal limits? Probably not. The slaughter of waterfowl in North America likely was a motivating factor in establishing laws to protect the species. Today, the ducks, geese, and swans remain, but many populations are reduced. Without laws and law enforcement, many of these species no doubt would be gone.

There are examples of waterfowl extinctions that were likely caused by commercial hunting. The common eider (*Somateria mollissima*) population of Maine was reduced to a single nesting pair by 1907 (Greenway 1967), but the species recovered in Maine to some extent after it was protected. The Labrador duck (*Camptorhynchos labrodorius*), which apparently was never very common, nevertheless appeared in markets between 1850 and 1870 but was not cherished for its palatability (Greenway 1967).

COMMERCIAL HARVESTING OF WILDLIFE IN OTHER NATIONS

Kangaroos

Five species of kangaroos currently are harvested in Australia. The three most common species are red kangaroos (*Macropus rufus*), eastern grey kangaroos (*M. giganteous*), and western grey kangaroos (*M. fuligonosus*). It is generally believed that there are more kangaroos today than when Captain James Cook landed in Australia in 1770 (Fitzgerald 1989). When European colonists came to Australia, they cleared forests for agriculture. These activities apparently were not good for smaller species of kangaroos but seemed to be beneficial for larger species. Larger species were seen to be pests as early as the 1850s. Large species were not protected as recently as 50 years ago, but soon it became clear that the commercial harvest of these species had to be regulated. The skins (1 to 1.7 million skins per year between 1981 and 1986) are exported for leather, mostly to Southeast Asia and Europe, and the meat is made into pet food, although at one time it was sold for human consumption. In the early 1980s, more than 1000 tons of kangaroo meat was exported to Europe as "sausage." When undercover agents found that the meat could not pass health inspections, exports dropped to less than 50 tons in 1984. The meat is commonly contaminated with salmonella, in addition to dirt, vegetation, and the parasite *Dirofilaria roemeri* (Shepherd and Caughley 1987).

Commercial harvest of kangaroos is an important management tool because the five species included are often serious pests. State-sponsored shooters are too expensive and recreational shooters do not kill enough to control the populations (Shepherd and Caughley 1987).

Interestingly, the United States once was the largest importer of kangaroo products. However, following a public outcry involving certain endangered species in Australia, the market (meaning the demand) for kangaroo products dried up (Fitzgerald 1989).

Introduced Deer in New Zealand

Several species of deer (about ten) have been introduced into New Zealand (Daniel 1962). There are no native deer there. Some of the introduced species have become quite common, which has sparked a commercial trade in meat and hides. For the most part, the deer have been hunted on foot, but recently helicopters have been used. Some argue that the populations have since fallen by 75%. This hurt the commercial trade and represents another example of how technology can influence harvesting success.

European Hares in Argentina

European hares (*Lepus europeus*) were introduced into Argentina in the 1800s and have been quite successful. Now they are shot by licensed hunters, and the processed meat is exported to Europe. Between 1976 and 1980, an average of 11,800 tons of hare meat was exported from Argentina to Europe (Fujita and Calvo 1982).

Crocodilians and Sea Turtles

There are 23 species of crocodilians worldwide. In 1971, all 23 species were either declining in number or endangered. Today, seven species are still endangered, but the others have benefited from management. Because the skins of these species have high commercial value, private companies have invested in establishing "crocodile farms" around the world. These farms help by hatching eggs and also work to preserve the species in the wild. Other methods of conservation include carefully regulated hunting (as in Florida) and habitat preservation. This is an example of how commercial value can serve as an incentive to citizens to preserve species.

Management programs for sea turtles include the harvest of eggs of Olive Ridley sea turtles in Central America. Lagueux (1991) studied human harvest of sea turtle eggs in Honduras from 1982 through 1987. She found that nearly 100% of the Olive Ridley eggs layed in some areas were harvested, a figure that no population can sustain.

Sponges

Sponges were once commercially harvested along the west coast of Florida and in the Keys. In the 1890s, sponges were harvested and exported to Europe and were used domestically for surgeries. The industry in Key West began in the 1830s, and by the 1890s Key West was one of the four most important centers in the world. The other centers were the Bahamas (Nassau), Cuba, and Calaimo, Greece (Munroe, 1987).

Sponges are still commercially harvested along the west coast of Florida, in the vicinity of Tarpon Springs, but there is no more commercial sponge harvesting in the Keys. In the summer of 1995, sponges near Tarpon Springs began to suffer from an affliction of unknown origin that left their bodies brittle and unusable. This may be yet another impact of a recent red tide outbreak.

ILLEGAL TRADE

When discussing commercial uses of wildlife, it is important to keep in mind that there are both legal and illegal uses. It is sometimes difficult to say that a certain type of trade is illegal, since there may not be any legal basis for saying it is. One example is fishing on the high seas. Is France or Taiwan breaking any laws by overharvesting fish on the open oceans? Illegal uses include trafficking endangered species or their body parts. The trade becomes illegal when wildlife traffic is imported into a country against its laws. For the purpose of our discussion, we refer to any trade as being illegal if it violates known laws in the United States, which has some very strict laws.

What Drives the Illegal Wildlife Trade?

In many cases, people involved in illegal harvesting (poaching) can double their annual income with just a few kills (in some cases, one tusk of ivory). Bear gallbladders, tiger bones and penises, spotted cat skins, etc. are all highly valuable. The same is true for wild species captured for the pet trade.

One important point to consider is that the more abundant and common a species is, the less likely it is to be involved in illegal activities. Sadly, it is the rare species, those that can least afford it, that are victimized by human greed. As a species become rare, it becomes more valuable—a simple economic principle.

Examples of Illegal Commercial Use of Wildlife

Rhinoceroses

There are five species worldwide, and a variety of products are used, including meat, horn, penis, hide, blood, and urine. In India, one zoo sells rhinoceros urine for 44 cents per liter as a cure for asthma or sore throats. The penis of a rhino may sell for $600 and is used as an aphrodisiac in some cultures. In North Yemen, the horns are used for knife handles. Fitzgerald (1989) claims that there are now fewer than 11,000 rhinos of all species in the wild.

Elephants

The main product is ivory from the tusks. There are two species: African and Asian. Some isolated populations of Asian elephants (i.e., in Sri Lanka) do not have tusks. One major conservation concern is that there has been elevated inbreeding of Asian elephants in some areas because males have been disproportionately harvested for their ivory. Asian elephants are also used as beasts of burden. The biggest concern for Asian elephants is loss of habitat.

African elephants are seldom used as beasts of burden, but they have high-quality ivory. Between 1979 and 1989, the world population dropped from 1.3 million to 625,000, mostly due to illegal hunting (= poaching). Other factors responsible for the decline in population are habitat loss, drought, and disease.

RECREATIONAL OR SPORT HUNTING: LIVING TO HUNT

Eisler and Buckley asked an interesting question in *USA Today,* April 25, 1996: "Should the public dictate hunting policy that once was left to the state?" Their question, however, does not go back far enough. We learned in Chapter 1 that the federal government once dictated hunting policy and then granted the states the right to dictate that policy. The question that should be asked is, "Should the public dictate hunting policy that once was left to the federal government?"

SNOW LEOPARD ✴✴ WILD ASS

SPECIAL MONGOLIA HUNT

16 DAY ITINERARY US $7,000; OBSERVER US $3,000 INCLUDES EVERYTHING IN MONGOLIA, EXCEPT TROPHY FEES AS LISTED BELOW.

SPECIE	TROPHY FEE, IF TAKEN
SNOW LEOPARD✴ (PANTHERA UNCIA)	$13,000
WILD ASS✴ (EQUUS HEMIONUS)	1,970
ALSO AVAILABLE ON SAME HUNT:	
BLACKTAIL GAZELLE (GAZELLA SUBGUTTOROSA SUBGUTTOROSA)	750
LYNX	660
WOLF	200

✴BOTH THE SNOW LEOPARD AND WILD ASS ARE LISTED ON THE U.S.A. AND CITES LISTS, AS ENDANGERED (EVEN THOUGH NOT ENDANGERED IN MONGOLIA). THEREFORE, THEY CANNOT BE BROUGHT INTO THE U.S.A. WITHOUT SPECIAL PERMITS. PROBABLY ONLY MUSEUM PERMITS WILL BE CONSIDERED.

PERIOD OF HUNTS WILL TAKE PLACE MARCH AND APRIL OR 01 OCTOBER TO 15 NOVEMBER.

AREA TO BE HUNTED IS SOUTH GOBI. THE MONGOLIAN WILDLIFE OFFICIALS HAVE NOW DETERMINED A SURPLUS OF THE SNOW LEOPARD AND WILD ASS AND ARE ALLOWING **VERY FEW PERMITS** EACH YEAR.

CONFIRMATION WILL BE TAKEN ON A FIRST COME FIRST SERVED BASIS UPON RECEIPT OF 50% DEPOSIT.

FIGURE 15.1 This ad appeared in 1990. Mongolia has since signed CITES, and hunts like this are now a thing of the past.

A record number of states are putting hunting referenda before the voters, according to Eisler and Buckley. As always, the two ends of the continuum are obvious. On the far right is the National Rifle Association, and on the far left are the animal rights activists. The ballot questions vary widely with region.

In most of the modern world, hunting is no longer really a major means of feeding oneself, although fishing might play a major role in supplementing people's diets in parts of the United States (according to an article in *Florida Sportsman*).

Traditionally, species involved in recreational hunting have been divided into categories. One category includes big game species such as white-tailed and mule deer, elk, mountain sheep, mountain goats, javelinas, and the host of exotics in Texas (discussed in Chapter 16). Big game hunting outside of the United States is also appealing to many recreational hunters (see Figure 15.1). A second category includes small game species, both mammals (such as squirrels and rabbits) and birds. The birds may be either upland gamebirds or waterfowl. Upland gamebirds include species such as ring-necked pheasants, bobwhites, various species of quail and grouse, mourning doves and other columbiforms, and turkeys. Waterfowl includes species such as ducks, geese, and swans. There is a very important reason for this distinction between upland gamebirds and waterfowl. Upland gamebirds are typically residents in a state. Moreover, they also include exotic species such as the chukar, grey partridge, and ring-necked pheasant. Waterfowl, on the other hand, are largely migratory, and they cross several state and national borders in any given year. Management of upland species may be handled by individual states, but waterfowl require an interstate and international program.

One measure aimed at producing funds for waterfowl management is the Duck Stamp which all waterfowl hunters in the United States must acquire in addition to a small game license.

SPECIAL HUNTS

Alligators in Florida

Alligators were once hunted nearly to extinction, mostly for their skins but also for meat. Even today, the meat may sell for as much as $4 to $5 per pound. The skins are used for leather products and sell for $25 to $35 per linear foot.

Alligators are not only hunted in a special season (in Florida it has been the month of September since 1988) but are also raised on alligator farms. Louisiana has a large alligator farming industry and yields the greatest number of skins of any state.

In Florida, there is a lottery for permits to trap alligators. Florida residents pay $250 for a trapping permit, and nonresidents pay $1000. Each trapper is then assigned an area and has two weeks to remove as many as six alligators. In 1995, there were 573 hunters (selected by computer from 9000 applicants), and the harvest quota for 1995 was 3500. The Florida Game and Fresh Water Fish Commission claims that there are as many as 16,000 alligators in Lake Okeechobee alone; thus, the removal of 3500 from the entire state does not represent a high percentage.

Commercial use of alligators extends to the so-called nuisance alligators. They are taken by licensed trappers. See Figure 15.2 for an idea of the number taken.

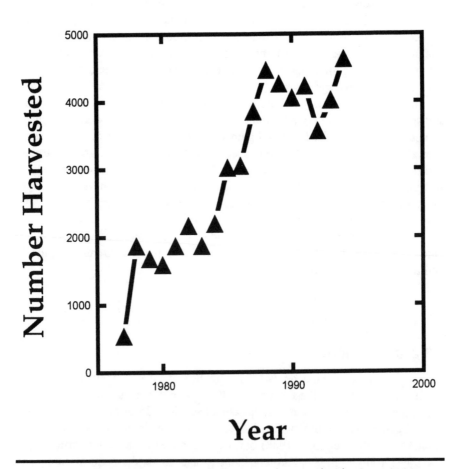

FIGURE 15.2   Number of nuisance alligators taken in Florida since 1980.

Rattlesnake Roundups

Across the southern states, rattlesnake roundups take place each year. One of the largest hunts is in Sweetwater, Texas. People collect snakes and bring them to a large barn on a specified day. Awards are given for the most snakes caught, the largest snake, and so on. The snakes are milked for their venom and then slaughtered for the meat and skins. The harvest is uncontrolled. Because the Sweetwater Round-up occurs in early March, when it is often still too cold for much rattlesnake activity, the hunters flush the snakes from their burrows mechanically with hooks or chemically by pouring gasoline down the burrows. Individuals of many other species are victims of the gasoline. In the southeastern United States, these other victims include indigo snakes (*Drymarchon corais*), gopher tortoises (*Gopherus polyhemus*), and possibly gopher frogs (*Rana capito*) and Florida mice (*Podomys floridanus*).

SUMMARY

Wildlife is harvested for subsistence in many parts of the world. As technology advances, the temptation to commercially harvest species increases. Commercial harvesting typically is not sustainable. Indeed, there are few examples, like the kangaroos in Australia, of species commercially harvested under tight controls where we see any inkling of sustainability.

Recreational hunting is practiced in many parts of world. A number of species are harvested, and this may be economically beneficial to those guiding the hunts. Recreational hunting is probably most popular in states with lower population densities. In states such as Florida, fewer than 2% of the population hunts.

EXERCISES

15.1 Identify three examples of bird species that are harvested for subsistence.

15.2 How would you characterize these species?

15.3 What is the most common reason for use of animal body parts in Asia?

15.4 Pick some states and/or countries and find out what it costs to hunt big game species there.

15.5 Give one example of an introduced species that is harvested commercially somewhere in the world (other than the ones listed in this chapter).

15.6   How many African elephants are there now? How many were there 20 years ago? Why has their population crashed?

15.7   Are hunting reserves the answer to preserving wildlife? If a local village can get $20,000 from a hunter willing to shoot a bull elephant, wouldn't that be a powerful incentive to raise more bull elephants?

LITERATURE CITED

Ayres, J.M., D. dM. Lima, E. dS. Martins, and J.L.K. Barreiros. 1991. On the track of the road: changes in subsistence hunting in a Brazilian Amazonian village. pp. 82–92 *in* Robinson, J.G. and K.H. Redford (Eds.). *Neotropical Wildlife Use and Conservation.* University of Chicago Press, Chicago.

Baldassarre, G.A. and E.G. Bolen. 1994. *Waterfowl Ecology and Management.* John Wiley & Sons, New York.

Daniel, M.J. 1962. Control of introduced deer in New Zealand. *Nature* **194**:527–528.

Fitzgerald, S. 1989. *International Wildlife Trade: Whose Business Is It?* World Wildlife Fund, Washington, D.C.

Fujita, H.O. and J.O. Calvo. 1982. Las exportaciones de productos y subproductos de la fauna silvestre en el quinquenio 1976/1980. *IDIA* **397/400**:1–26.

Greenway, J.C. 1967. *Extinct and Vanishing Birds of the World.* Dover Publications, New York.

Lagueux, C.J. 1991. Economic analysis of sea turtle eggs in a coastal community on the Pacific coast of Honduras. pp. 136–144 *in* Robinson, J.G. and K.H. Redford (Eds.). *Neotropical Wildlife Use and Conservation.* University of Chicago Press, Chicago.

Misch, A. 1992. Can wildlife traffic be stopped? *World Watch* **5**(5):26–33.

Mittermeier, R.A. 1991. Hunting and its effect on wild primate populations in Suriname. pp. 93–107 *in* Robinson, J.G. and K.H. Redford (Eds.). *Neotropical Wildlife Use and Conservation.* University of Chicago Press, Chicago.

Munroe, K. 1987. Sponge and spongers of the Florida reef. pp. 29–39 *in* Oppel, F. and T. Meisel (Eds.). *Tales of Old Florida.* Castle, Secaucus, New Jersey.

Redford, K.H. and J.G. Robinson. 1991. Subsistence and commercial uses of wildlife in Latin America. pp. 6–23 *in* Robinson, J.G. and K.H. Redford (Eds.). *Neotropical Wildlife Use and Conservation.* University of Chicago Press, Chicago.

Roe, F.G. 1951. *The North American Buffalo: A Critical Study of the Species in its Wild State.* University of Toronto Press, Toronto.

Schorger, A.W. 1973. *The Passenger Pigeon: Its Natural History and Extinction.* University of Oklahoma Press, Norman.

Shepherd, N. and G. Caughley. 1987. Options for management of kangaroos. pp. 188–219 *in* Caughley, G., N. Shepherd, and J. Short (Eds.). *Kangaroos: Their Ecology and Management in the Sheep Rangelands of Australia.* Cambridge University Press, Cambridge, U.K.

Smith, N.J.H. 1976. Utilization of game along Brazil's transamazon highway. *Acta Amazonica* **6**:455–466.

NONINDIGENOUS SPECIES AND SPECIES INTRODUCTIONS

16

All species that evolved in some region of the world are said to be *indigenous* to that region. When species that are indigenous to one region of the world are transported to another region, they are *nonindigenous* to the new region. Thus, nonindigenous species are those species that exist in parts of the world where they do not naturally occur. For instance, species that evolved in Europe, such as the house sparrow of North America, are considered to be nonindigenous to North America and indigenous to Europe. The term nonindigenous is relative in nature: every species is indigenous to some region; no species is truly distributed worldwide. However, only a subset of the world's species occur somewhere else as nonindigenous species.

A variety of terms have been employed to describe nonindigenous species. One term that is often used in nontechnical publications is *exotic* species. This term can be somewhat misleading because it may give the impression that the species is in some sense "glamorous" or at least from a glamorous place. But "glamorous" is in the eye of the beholder. House sparrows may not seem glamorous to some people, and many do not think of northern Europe as an especially glamorous part of the world. Therefore, even though exotic is a term that may be misleading, it is used so frequently that we may be stuck with it.

A second term that is often used is *introduced* species. This term carries the connotation that the species was actually introduced somewhere by humans. Some species are physically introduced elsewhere, but their descendants, if born in the new place, are themselves native to the new place, and to label them as being introduced may be confusing. One way to avoid confusion is to use the term *introduced* to refer to the species and not the individuals in the species. In any event, there is no doubt that many of the species that are nonindigenous found their way to the new regions through human introductions (e.g., Caum 1933, Long 1981, Lever 1987).

Another term that is occasionally used with nonindigenous species is *alien* (e.g., Mack 1986, Macdonald et al. 1986) species. We object to this term principally because it has a political rather than geographical or biogeographical meaning.

It is logical to discuss *feral* species at this point. Feral refers to species that have escaped domestication. These species do not have to be nonindigenous. In fact, house cats (*Felis catus*) may be feral yet native to parts of northern Europe. Across the world, feral species have caused a number of problems. Throughout the United States, feral hogs may harbor pseudo-rabies and infect domestic swine. Feral cats have had a devastating effect on native birds of small islands, such as those around New Zealand. Feral dogs may kill wildlife (such as deer) or livestock (sheep or cattle), and sometimes even humans.

The phenomenon of nonindigenous species played a role in Darwin's arguments against creationism. Darwin (1859) argued that one could not explain the absence of rabbits from Australian grasslands on the grounds that the grasslands "down under" could not support rabbits, because European rabbits (*Oryctolagus* or *Lepus*) were thriving there. Darwin also made the case that species in New Zealand, although well adapted to each other for co-existence, were being replaced by the advancing legions of nonindigenous species from Europe.

Indeed, Europeans traveling to the South Pacific and Indian Ocean introduced various types of mammals and birds onto small islands in the hope that the individuals released would generate progeny for later harvesting by future travelers to the islands. Captain Cook released cattle and hogs in Hawaii and elsewhere (Tomich 1986). This made good logistic sense to travelers whose journeys lasted for months or even years. By establishing food supplies in the form of harvestable populations of feral livestock on distant islands, these early traders could avoid transporting the feed and other supplies that livestock on a ship would need for voyages that might last years.

Throughout the world, nonindigenous species have become a hazard of immense proportion both for economic as well as ecological reasons. Species from virtually every taxonomic group have been introduced somewhere. A few examples are mentioned here to provide some insight into the scope of the problem. In terms of invertebrates, we can look to the waterways of the Great Lakes in the United States as they are being choked by introduced zebra mussels (*Dreissena polymorpha*). A nematode (pseudocoelomate) species (*Bursaphelenchus xylophilus*) has affected nearly 25% of Japan's 2.6 million hectares of pine forests. So far, at least ten million Japanese trees have been killed by this parasite which apparently was introduced from North America on diseased timber.

From the kingdom Protista, we see red tides caused by dinoflagellates. Red tides may have directly or indirectly led to the deaths of marine mammals in the North Atlantic (Anderson 1994) and manatees in the Gulf of Mexico. Many of the organisms that cause red tides have been transported throughout the world in the same way that marine invertebrates have been able to colonize distant shores: in ship ballast.

From the kingdom Fungi, a number of tragic examples are available. An introduced fungus (*Cryphonectria parasitica*) led to the virtual extinction of the American chestnut tree (*Castanea dentata*). Similarly, another fungus (*Ophiostoma ulmi*) was introduced into North America from Europe and led to the loss of the American elm (van Broembsen 1989).

Among plants, several species have also become severe pests where they have been introduced. For simplicity, we present examples of aquatic and terrestrial species. For terrestrial plants, there are major infestations of an Australian tree (*Melaleuca quinquiveria*) and a South American species (*Schinus terebinthifolius*) in south Florida (Ewel 1986). As for aquatic plants, *Hydrilla verticillata* has created severe problems in Florida waterways and the water milfoil has posed problems in the northeastern United States.

A number of vertebrates have also invaded new environments and posed problems of varying degrees. The gray squirrel from North America was introduced into the United Kingdom (Laycock 1966) and may have had a negative impact on the native red squirrel. Riders on the Texas range may today encounter large grazing mammals from three different continents (Africa, Asia, and Europe) (Mungall and Sheffield 1994), and indeed there may be more blackbuck antelope in Texas than in their native India. In south Florida, a diverse fauna of introduced reptiles and amphibians has been spawned through human releases (Wilson and Porras 1983). Finally, visitors to Kapiolani Park on the island of Oahu in Hawaii would have no trouble observing birds introduced from five continents (Pratt et al. 1987): northern cardinal and house finch (North America), red-crested cardinal (South America), common myna (Asia), yellow-fronted canaries and warbling silverbills (Africa), and barred doves (Australia).

THE ORIGIN OF INTRODUCED SPECIES

As we have seen, species from virtually every kingdom of living organisms now occur as nonindigenous species somewhere in the world. But if any species can be nonindigenous somewhere, we might ask: Where do nonindigenous species originate? We can ask this from a biogeographic perspective or from a human dimensions perspective. In the first case (biogeography), the question can be rephrased as: What part of the world do nonindigenous species come from? The answer is that nonindigenous species can come from anywhere in the world. There are, as mentioned above, species of birds from five continents (Asia, Australia, North America, South America, and Africa) now co-existing in the state of Hawaii. In Florida, one of the most serious nonindigenous species problems involves *Melaleuca*, which is indigenous to Australia.

From a human dimensions perspective, we might ask how the nonindigenous species get from one place to another. Are species introduced intentionally as a form of biological control (often the case with insects)? Do nonindigenous species sneak in with tropical fruit from Central America? Do pet owners simply release their pet parrots or alligators when they get bored with them? Are individuals of nonindigenous species released from roadside attractions during hurricanes? Do humans sometimes intentionally release individuals of nonindigenous species to establish populations for recreational or commercial hunting?

The answer to all of these questions is yes. We have already discussed the introductions made by early European visitors to distant lands. More recently, an organization in Hawaii called the Hui Manu (Hawaiian for Bird Club) existed solely for the purpose of buying birds to release in Hawaii, as there was a widespread perception that Hawaii had too few native birds (Berger 1981, Simberloff and Boecklen 1991). On Tahiti (Lockwood et al. 1993) and on Saint Helena (Brooke et al. 1995), humans released large numbers of individuals of several species, again because they were under the impression that the islands had too few native birds. (Tahiti has only three native perching birds, and Saint Helena has none).

Similarly, in New Zealand (Veltman et al. 1996), the Mascarene Islands (Simberloff 1992), and Australia (Long 1981), acclimatization societies existed solely for the purpose of establishing species that were nonindigenous to the region. These societies served the same function as the Hui Manu in Hawaii. In some cases, the intention of these societies was to liberate species that were thought to be potentially beneficial to humans in agriculture or other ways (Simberloff 1992), whereas in other cases the motivation was to modify the landscape of the new land to more nearly approximate the land from which the colonists came, as in New Zealand (Veltman et al. 1996).

SOME TAXA ARE MORE SUCCESSFUL THAN OTHERS

A reasonable question to ask in dealing with nonindigenous species is whether or not some taxa are more likely to become successfully established than others. For instance, we might wonder if mammals are superior (or inferior) as nonindigenous species when compared to lizards or birds.

There has been no comprehensive analysis aimed at addressing this question. Moreover, it may not be possible to ever answer this question at some levels. For example, it might be possible to compare birds from different families, but it may not be possible to compare birds (class Aves) to mammals (class Mammalia). The reason for this would simply be the scope of the comparison: it might be possible to gather adequate data for a sample of bird families but not for enough families of birds and mammals to make the comparison at the class level. Nevertheless, whether or not this question is answerable may be irrelevant. In any case, it is an interesting question, and it is reasonable to imagine that differences might exist in relative introduction success among various taxa. Faaborg (1977) made the argument that for a given body size, nonpasseriform (i.e., nonperching) birds might have higher resistance to extinction on islands than comparably sized passeriform (i.e., perching) birds for physiological reasons: nonpasseriforms have lower basal metabolic rates than passeriforms, thus reducing their food requirements for subsistence.

ENVIRONMENTAL CONDITIONS AND NONINDIGENOUS SPECIES

A number of factors may favor the success of nonindigenous species in a new land. The Office of Technology Assessment (1993) lists several factors that favor the success of nonindigenous species in Florida and Hawaii. To appreciate the diversity of species that have been introduced in Florida and Hawaii, vertebrate introductions in both states are summarized in Table 16.1 and nonvertebrate introductions in Florida are summarized in Table 16.2. First, there is the subtropical climate. A subtropical (Florida) or tropical (Hawaii) climate insulates the nonindigenous species to some extent from the hard cold

TABLE 16.1 Established Nonindigenous Vertebrate Species in Hawaii and Florida

	Number of species	
Taxa	Hawaii	Florida
Fish	?	19
Amphibians	4	3
Reptiles	14	22
Birds	>70	11
Mammals	18	17

After Office of Technology Assessment 1993.

weather so typical of much of the temperate zone. A second factor involves the large number of ports of entry. There are many places for nonindigenous species to enter these states. Both Hawaii and Florida have extensive pet trades. This trade may be tightly controlled for the majority of humans in both Hawaii and Florida through restricted entry at airports and seaports. However, Hawaii also has extensive military operations which might facilitate the entry of some species that would not pass customs from transport on a commercial airline. Some have blamed military personnel for the introduction of the two species of bulbul on the island of Oahu in Hawaii (Berger 1981).

Another factor is extensive habitat manipulation. Once native habitats have been altered and native species reduced in number, nonindigenous species may have better chances for successful establishment of a new population. In Hawaii, where many introduced species of plants now comprise new nonindigenous

TABLE 16.2 Nonvertebrate Nonindigenous Species in Florida

Taxa	Number of species
Plants	>975
Insects	271
Freshwater snails	6
Land snails	40

After Office of Technology Assessment 1993.

lowland plant communities, native species are no longer adapted to these lowland habitats because they have been so modified. Thus, in suburban areas of Oahu, for example, virtually all the birds one sees are nonindigenous. In south Florida, at least in the Miami area, this is not the case; a variety of native species occur alongside the nonindigenous species.

COSTS OF NONINDIGENOUS SPECIES

The diversity of species that may have high economic or ecological diversity is extremely broad. A list of species from different taxa introduced in Florida is presented in Table 16.3. The costs of introduced species may be paid in various types of currency. For instance, the costs could be assessed purely from a perspective of their economic impact on agriculture. Thus, the Weed Science Society of America (Office of Technology Assessment 1993) reported in 1992 that losses of 46 crops in all states but Alaska amounted to $4.1 billion annually, $2 to 3 billion of which could be attributed to nonindigenous species. Introduced weeds can lead not only to crop losses but can also harbor arthropod pests or produce toxins that are harmful to livestock or other plants.

An entirely separate economic concern involves loss of income from tourists. In Florida, it is widely held that introduced melaleuca trees have a negative effect on tourism (Diamond et al. 1991).

TABLE 16.3   Examples of High-Impact Nonindigenous Species in Florida[a]

Plants	Mammals
Melaleuca	Wild hogs
Schinus	Coyotes
Hydrilla	
Fish	*Birds*
Blue tilapia	Starling
Peacock bass	Monk parakeet
Invertebrates	*Insects*
Asiatic clam	Tiger mosquito

[a] Meaning high cost economically or ecologically.

After Office of Technology Assessment 1993.

In terms of economics, the tremendous financial commitment needed to combat or limit the spread of certain nonindigenous species must be considered. According to an Office of Technology Assessment (1993) report, the cost of removing introduced melaleuca trees in south Florida ranges from $500 to $2000 per acre, and in 1992 as many as 490,000 acres in Florida were infested. These estimates are for mechanical removal which involves physical uprooting. Other methods for removing melaleuca include herbicide applications. Schmitz (1994) reported that there were 703,000 acres of Brazilian pepper (another noxious weed) in Florida, as well as 373,000 acres of Australian pine. The cost of controlling a handful of nonindigenous plants just in highway rights-of-way exceeded $7 million in fiscal year 1993–94 (Caster 1994).

ECOLOGICAL IMPACTS

Several ecological effects involving nonindigenous species can occur. These effects include competition, predation and parasitism, disease transmission, and habitat alteration.

Competition, as previously discussed, is the interaction between populations where both species are negatively impacted. The negative impact may manifest itself either in reduced population growth rates or reduced population sizes where the competing species co-occur.

Examples of competition between nonindigenous and native species have been reported in Hawaiian forest birds (Mountainspring and Scott 1985) as well as populations of beach mice in Florida (Humphrey 1992). In both of these cases, the authors reported evidence that the native species appeared to be superior competitors in native habitats, but the nonindigenous species were able to continue to invade the native habitat to the eventual detriment of the native species. In the case of the Florida beach, the native habitat on coastal islands is being rapidly developed and hence lost, which creates additional habitat for the nonindigenous house mouse (*Mus musculus*). The interesting point here is that even if the nonindigenous species might normally be outcompeted because of human activities (i.e., loss of native habitat), the balance is tipped in favor of the nonindigenous species because of the enhanced opportunities to continuously reinvade from ever-expanding stretches of manipulated habitat. Mountainspring and Scott (1985) similarly argued that native forest birds in Hawaii may well be able to outcompete nonindigenous species in native habitats but that nonindigenous species at lower elevations were able to continuously reinvade these native (and higher elevation) habitats.

Predation is the interaction between two populations where one population is impacted negatively and the other positively. One particularly stunning example involves trout and grizzly bears in Yellowstone National Park. In the early 1990s, someone caught a lake trout (*Salvelinus namaycush*) in Lake Yellowstone (Kenworthy 1994). Lake trout are not native to Lake Yellowstone, where the only native species of trout is the cutthroat trout (*Onycorhynchus clarki*). Lake trout are much larger than cutthroat trout (lake trout can grow to over 40 pounds), and the problem is that lake trout may increase in number and start preying on the native trout.

There are countless other examples of introduced vertebrates that prey on the native wildlife. Atkinson (1977) presented evidence implicating introduced rats in the demise of native Hawaiian forest birds. Similar cases can be found regarding loss of birds and reptiles from islands following the introduction of cats (e.g., Fitzgerald 1985, Kirkpatrick and Rauzon 1986), but perhaps the most devastating case involves the brown tree snake and its impact on the native forest birds of Guam (Savidge 1987).

Guam is a small island in the Marianas archipelago. Jenkins (1983) described the distribution of the 11 native forest birds of Guam, noting that some species had suffered declines, and suggested a connection between *Boiga irregularis,* the brown tree snake, and the declines which began in the 1960s. Savidge (1987) conducted several tests of alternative hypotheses (see Table 16.4) for the decline of Guam's forest birds but concluded that the main factor was *B. irregularis.*

TABLE 16.4   Possible Forces in the Decline of Guam's Native Forest Birds

Force	Evaluation
Hunting	Populations have also declined on military lands where hunting is prohibited
Pesticides	Levels of pesticides in bodies of sampled animals were below those needed for adverse impact
Competition	Detailed field studies show that the only nonindigenous forest species uses different foods than native species
Habitat loss	Similar habitat loss on nearby islands has not led to comparable losses of forest birds
Disease	Native birds sampled for bacteria, viruses, and parasites were relatively free from any infestations as recently as 1986

Disease transmission is yet another possible impact of nonindigenous species on native species. Nonindigenous species can harbor diseases they are immune to but to which natives are vulnerable. For example, Warner worked on forest birds in Hawaii and found that native forest birds were absent from lowland forests possibly because of their susceptibility to avian malaria. Warner (1968) actually trapped native birds at high elevations and kept them in outdoor aviaries at lower elevations. These captives soon died from avian malaria. Warner reasoned that native species were able to persist at higher elevations because the introduced mosquitos that transmit malaria could not survive the low temperatures at higher elevations.

Nonindigenous species also may alter native habitats by destroying native vegetation. Perhaps the best example of this is wild hogs, which destroy vegetation by wallowing in the soil and thereby tearing up delicate root systems.

ECOLOGICAL AND ECONOMIC IMPACTS ARE NOT INDEPENDENT

It is important to consider that the breakdown of costs of nonindigenous species into economic versus ecological categories may seem convenient, but when any particular situation is thoroughly investigated, such a separation may often become inappropriate. In all likelihood, economics cannot be divorced completely from ecology because economic losses often result from ecological interactions. A nonindigenous plant species may compete with a crop species for water or nutrients, resulting in reduced crop production. Nonindigenous species may also be toxic to livestock or harbor introduced pests.

Thus, the problems caused by *Melaleuca* infestation in south Florida are both ecological and economic. Economically, the presence of *Melaleuca* trees requires increased maintenance costs for drainage conveyances. Ecologically, *Melaleuca* trees can compete with native species, and this may be especially serious in some ecosystems. Consider the case of coastal mangroves in Florida. Mangrove forests once stretched from Tampa Bay south across the Keys. In many areas, mangroves have been removed in the course of development, and today the total areal extent of mangroves in Florida may be as low as approximately 190,000 hectares (Odum and McIvor 1992). Are species from some parts of the world more likely to be successful or unsuccessful than species introduced from other regions?

Moulton and Pimm (1986) tested the hypothesis that perching birds (order Passeriformes) introduced into the Hawaiian Islands from different zoogeographic regions (see Chapter 7) might differ in their chances for success. The

TABLE 16.5 Outcomes of Passeriform Introductions in Hawaii Categorized by Zoogeographic Region

Region	Number of introductions
Palearctic	9
Ethiopian	10
Nearctic	6
Neotropical	7
Oriental	15
Australasian	2

reasoning behind this lies in the different competitive milieus in which the species evolved. In any case, no significant differences were found, although the numbers of species introduced from some of the zoogeographic regions (i.e., Australasian, Nearctic) were quite small (see Table 16.5).

SOME SPECIES SURVIVE AND OTHERS FAIL

Some species seem to be successful wherever they are introduced, whereas others never appear to succeed. This pattern of nearly always succeeding or failing was discussed in detail by Simberloff and Boecklen (1991). If this all-or-none pattern is a real phenomenon, it would represent a powerful tool for studying species introductions: one would be able to predict the fate of any introduction based only on its previous outcomes as an introduced species. Moulton (1993) argued that this pattern might be merely a sampling artifact. Thus, humans might stop releasing individuals of a certain species after just a few failed introductions of that species. If so, then species that appear to "always fail" might simply have not been provided sufficient opportunities to succeed somewhere as an introduced species.

Nevertheless, an all-or-none pattern might occur in some taxa but not others. Thus, hypothetically, it might appear in lizard species but not passeriform birds. The idea is very interesting, and hopefully scientists working on species other than birds will test for its presence.

Assuming for the moment that species vary in their chances for success depending upon the communities where they are released, several possible explanations emerge. First, some nonindigenous species may be released into what is essentially "enemy-free space." These species would have no natural controls (predators or competitors) and hence would be expected to proliferate. One example of this involves European hares and rabbits that were introduced into Australia and Argentina and soon took over huge areas of rangeland.

Finally, we must not overlook the amount of effort invested in any particular introduction. Gamebird introductions in the United States undoubtedly benefited from large numbers of individuals introduced and multiple introductions. Recently, Veltman et al. (1996) tested the hypothesis that species introduced in New Zealand in larger numbers and in greater frequency have had higher rates of success.

SOME REGIONS ARE MORE VULNERABLE TO INTRODUCTIONS THAN OTHERS

The great British ecologist Charles Elton argued in his classic book, *The Ecology of Invasions by Animals and Plants* (1958), that oceanic islands and crop monocultures were more vulnerable to invasions than were more complex ecosystems, such as those seen in forested or tropical areas. Elton's chief argument stemmed from the observation that in simpler ecosystems (i.e., those with fewer species), there may be a greater tendency for population fluctuations, and this may favor local extinctions, thus creating opportunities for invasions.

Birds

Historically, a large number of species introductions (birds and mammals) have occurred for the purpose of establishing populations for either commercial or recreational hunting. In the United States, perhaps the prime example of an introduced gamebird is the ring-necked pheasant (*Phasianus colchicus*). Ring-necked pheasants have been introduced in Hawaii as well as the continental United States (Long 1981). Other gamebird species that have been introduced successfully include the Hungarian or gray partridge (*Perdix perdix*), chukar partridge (*Alectoris graeca*) (Long 1981), and eight species of tinamous (South American) and francolin (African) species.

In other parts of the world, one example of an introduction for commercial purposes involves the ostrich, which was introduced into south Australia in the 1860s in the hope of establishing a feather trade. This population apparently expanded with influxes from ostrich farmers, who made additional releases following the collapse of the feather industry after the end of World War I (Long 1981).

Mammals

In the United States, one invasive mammal that was introduced to generate a commercial trade is the nutria (*Myocastor coypu*) (Bolen and Robinson 1995). The nutria has been released in the vicinity of Chesapeake Bay and now occurs throughout the eastern United States. Elton (1958) described the introduction of reindeer into Alaska, and volumes have been published on introduced and feral hogs in the United States.

Perhaps the most bizarre example of mammal introductions in the United States occurred in Texas, where a large number of species of ungulates (grazing herbivorous mammals) were introduced for hunting in confined areas. However, seven species have escaped and established wild populations. The species and their origins are listed in Table 16.6.

Notice that the table does not include introduced hogs, which are possibly the most widespread large introduced mammal in Texas today. There may be more blackbuck antelope in Texas than in their native India, and in 1988 there were an estimated 39,000 free-ranging axis deer in Texas. Despite the success of these few introductions, several other species that have the potential to establish wild free-ranging populations are still hunted in Texas on ranches.

Other examples of mammal introductions include wild pigs across the United States (Mayer and Brisbin 1991). As many as ten species of deer have been introduced into New Zealand (Daniel 1962), in part to establish herds for recreational hunting. Several of these species became very abundant and spawned a commercial trade, as noted earlier.

TABLE 16.6 Texas Nonindigenous Ungulates

Species	Native range
Axis deer	India
Nilgai antelope	India
Blackbuck	India
Aoudad	Africa
Mouflon	Europe
Sika deer	Asia
Fallow deer	Europe

From Mungall and Sheffield 1994.

Reindeer were introduced into South Georgia Island in the South Atlantic by Norwegian whalers to establish an alternative meat supply that would not require any husbandry and also possibly for recreational hunting (Leader-Williams 1988).

INTRODUCTIONS AND WILDLIFE MANAGEMENT OF ENDANGERED SPECIES

Following our discussion of introduced nonindigenous species, it is now appropriate to look at species introduction as a potential management tool. Intentional introductions have been termed "translocations" by Griffith et al. (1989). Across the original ranges of many species, there have been local extinctions or population declines of the proportion where the populations are thought to be unable to recover. Under these circumstances the forces that led to the declines may now have vanished and the habitat may still be adequate to support populations of the now missing or reduced species. In Florida, a glowing example involves the Florida panther. This subspecies of a once wide-ranging cat now occurs in numbers only west of the Mississippi River. A brewing controversy in Florida is whether or not cougars (as they are called in Texas) should be translocated to Florida to shore up the genetic diversity of the remnant population of 30 to 50 individuals (Alvarez 1993).

Elsewhere in the southeastern United States, the red wolf is being translocated to North Carolina (USFWS 1992). Red wolves (*Canis lupus*) are thought to have suffered from genetic swamping due to interbreeding with coyotes. Other examples of translocations for the sake of establishing companion or satellite populations for endangered species include several species of birds of prey (Cade 1984).

EXERCISES

16.1 Formulate a null hypothesis to test the notion that species from different families vary in their relative chances for introduction success.

16.2 Imagine how you could design a grand-scale experiment to test Elton's idea that communities with fewer species are more vulnerable to invasions than communities with many species.

16.3 Surf the World Wide Web for an example of an introduced wildlife population that is commercially harvested.

16.4 Surf the Web to find an example of techniques for controlling the spread of introduced species.

16.5 Find an example where wildlife biologists have used species introductions to restore populations of endangered or threatened species.

16.6 Find some examples of introduced insects from foreign countries. How do you suppose these species invaded North America?

16.7 Discuss the possibility that species from different taxa (phyla or kingdoms) differ in the severity of their potential impacts when introduced to new environments.

LITERATURE CITED

Alvarez, H. 1993. *Twilight of the Panther: Biology, Bureaucracy and Failure in an Endangered Species Program.* Myakka Publishing, Sarasota, Florida.

Anderson, D.M. 1994. Red tides. *Scientific American* August:62–68.

Atkinson, I.A.E. 1977. A reassessment of factors, particularly *Rattus rattus* (L.), that influenced the decline of endemic forest birds in Hawaii. *Pacific Science* 31:109–133.

Berger, A.J. 1981. *Hawaiian Birdlife,* 2nd edition. University Press of Hawaii, Honolulu, 260 pp.

Bolen, E.G. and W.L. Robinson. 1995. *Wildlife Ecology and Management,* 3rd edition. Prentice-Hall, Englewood Cliffs, New Jersey.

Brooke, R.K., J.L. Lockwood, and M.P. Moulton. 1995. Patterns of success in passeriform bird introductions on Saint Helena. *Oecologia* **103**:337–342.

Cade, T.J. 1984. Reintroduction as a method of conservation. pp. 72–84 *in* Senner, S.E., C.M. White, and J.R. Parrish (Eds.). *Raptor Research Report 5: Raptor Conservation in the Next 50 Years.* Proceedings of a conference held at Hawk Mountain Sanctuary, Kempton, Pennsylvania, October 14, 1984. Press Publishing, Provo, Utah.

Caster, J. 1994. Invasive alien species on DOT right-of-way managed land. pp. 197–205 *in* Schmitz, D.C. and T.C. Brown (Project Directors). An Assessment of Invasive Non-Indigenous Species in Florida's Public Lands. Florida Department of Environmental Protection, Tallahassee.

Caum, E.L. 1933. The exotic birds of Hawaii. *Occasional Papers of the Bernice P. Bishop Museum* **10**:1–55.

Daniel, M.J. 1962. Control of introduced deer in New Zealand. *Nature* **194**:527–528.

Darwin, C. 1859. *The Origin of Species by Means of Natural Selection,* Modern Library Reprint. Random House, New York.

Diamond, C., D. Davis, and D.C. Schmitz. 1991. Economic impact statement: the addition of *Melaleuca quinquiveria* to the Florida prohibited plant list. *in* Center, T.D. et al. (Eds.). Proceedings of the Symposium on Exotic Pest Plants, Technical Report NPS/NREVER/NRTR-9106. U.S. Department of the Interior/National Park Service, Washington, D.C.

Elton, C.S. 1958. *The Ecology of Invasions by Animals and Plants.* Methuen, London.

Ewel, J.J. 1986. Invasibility: lessons from South Florida. pp. 214–230 *in* Mooney, H.A. and J.A. Drake (Eds.). *Ecology of Biological Invasions of North America and Hawaii,* Ecological Studies 58. Springer-Verlag, New York.

Faaborg, J. 1977. Metabolic rates, resources, and the occurrence of nonpasserines in terrestrial avian communities. *The American Naturalist* **111**:903–916.

Fitzgerald, B.M. 1985. The cats of Herekopare Island, New Zealand: their history, ecology and effects of birdlife. *New Zealand Journal of Zoology* **12**:319–330.

Griffith, B., J.M. Scott, J.W. Carpenter, and C. Reed. 1989. Translocation as a species conservation tool: status and strategy. *Science* **245**:477–480.

Humphrey, S.R. 1992. Anastasia Island beach mouse: *Peromyscus poilionotus phasma.* pp. 94–102 *in* Humphrey, S.R. (Ed.). *Rare and Endangered Biota of Florida,* Vol. 1: Mammals. University Press of Florida, Gainesville.

Jenkins, J.M. 1983. The native forest birds of Guam. *Ornithological Monographs* **31**: 61 pp.

Kenworthy, T. 1994. It's a trout-eat-trout world out there. *The Washington Post National Weekly Edition* October 17–23.

Kirkpatrick, R.D. and M.J. Rauzon. 1986. Foods of feral cats (*Felis catus*) on Jarvis and Howland Islands, central Pacific Ocean. *Biotropica* **18**:72–75.

Laycock, G. 1966. *The Alien Animals.* Natural History Press, Garden City, New York, 240 pp.

Leader-Williams, N. 1988. *Reindeer on South Georgia: The Ecology of an Introduced Population.* Cambridge University Press, Cambridge, U.K.

Lever, C. 1987. *Naturalized Birds of the World.* Longman Scientific & Technical, Harlow, U.K.

Lockwood, J.L., M.P. Moulton, and S.K. Anderson. 1993. Morphological assortment and the assembly of communities of introduced passeriforms on oceanic islands: Oahu versus Tahiti. *American Naturalist* **141**:398–408.

Long, J.L. 1981. *Introduced Birds of the World.* David & Charles, London.

Macdonald, I.A.W., F.J. Kruger, and A.A. Ferrar. 1986. *The Ecology and Management of Biological Invasions in Southern Africa.* Oxford University Press, Cape Town, South Africa.

Mack, R.N. 1986. Alien plant invasion into the intermountain west: a case history. pp. 192–213 *in* Mooney, H.A. and J.A. Drake (Eds.). *Ecology of Biological Invasions of North America and Hawaii*, Ecological Studies 58. Springer-Verlag, New York.

Mayer, J.J. and I.L. Brisbin, Jr. 1991. *Wild Pigs in the United States: Their History, Comparative Morphology, and Current Status.* University of Georgia Press, Athens.

Moulton, M.P. 1993. The all-or-none pattern in introduced Hawaiian passeriforms: the role of competition sustained. *The American Naturalist* **141**:105–119.

Moulton, M.P. and S.L. Pimm. 1986. Species introductions to Hawaii. pp. 231–249 *in* Mooney, H.A. and J.A. Drake (Eds.). *Ecology of Biological Invasions of North America and Hawaii*, Ecological Studies 58. Springer-Verlag, New York.

Mountainspring, S. and J.M. Scott. 1985. Interspecific competition among Hawaiian forest birds. *Ecological Monographs* **55**:219–239.

Mungall, E.C. and W.J. Sheffield. 1994. *Exotics on the Range: The Texas Example.* Texas A&M University Press, College Station, 320 pp.

Odum, W.E. and C.C. McIvor. 1992. Mangroves. pp. 517–548 *in* Myers, R.L. and J.J. Ewel (Eds.). *Ecosystems of Florida.* University of Central Florida Press, Orlando.

Office of Technology Assessment. 1993. Harmful Non-Indigenous Species in the United States, OTA-F-565. Government Printing Office, Washington, D.C.

Pratt, H.D., P.L. Bruner, and D.G. Berrett. 1987. *A Field Guide to the Birds of Hawaii and the Tropical Pacific.* Princeton University Press, Princeton, New Jersey.

Savidge, J.A. 1987. Extinction of an island forest avifauna by an introduced snake. *Ecology* **68**:660–668.

Schmitz, D.C. 1994. The ecological impact of non-indigenous plants in Florida. pp. 10–28 *in* Schmitz, D.C. and T.C. Brown (Project Directors). An Assessment of Invasive Non-Indigenous Species in Florida's Public Lands. Florida Department of Environmental Protection, Tallahassee.

Simberloff, D. 1992. Extinction, survival, and effects of birds introduced to the Mascarenes. *Acta Ecologica* **13**:663–678.

Simberloff, D. and W. Boecklen. 1991. Patterns of extinction in the introduced Hawaiian avifauna: a reexamination of the role of competition. *The American Naturalist* **138**:300–327.

Tomich, P.Q. 1986. *Mammals in Hawaii*, 2nd edition. Bishop Museum Press, Honolulu, Hawaii.

USFWS. 1992. Report to Congress: Endangered and Threatened Species Recovery Program. U.S. Department of Agriculture, Fish and Wildlife Service, Washington, D.C.

van Broembsen, S.L. 1989. Invasions of natural ecosystems by plant pathogens. pp. 77–83 *in* Drake, J.A., H.A. Mooney, F. diCastri, R.H. Groves, F.J. Kruger, M. Rejmanek, and M. Williamson (Eds.). *Biological Invasions: A Global Perspective.* John Wiley & Sons, Chichester.

Veltman, C.J., S. Nee, and M.J. Crawley. 1996. Correlates of introduction success in exotic New Zealand birds. *The American Naturalist* **147**:542–557.

Warner, R.E. 1968. The role of introduced diseases in the extinction of the endemic Hawaiian avifauna. *Condor* **70**:101–120.

Wilson, L.D. and L. Porras. 1983. The ecological impact of man on the south Florida herpetofauna. *University of Kansas Museum of Natural History Special Publication* **9**:1–89.

NOVEL SOLUTIONS   17

The world's first national park was founded by the United States in 1876 when Yellowstone National Park was gazetted. Since then, many national parks in many countries have been established. The United Nations established a World Heritage Park designation, but this designation has failed to protect all such parks (see Figure 17.1). Parks so designated were meant to be the best of the best. Are national parks working today? Most people in the United States have visited a national park. Grand Canyon National Park receives 500,000 visitors a year. Great Smoky Mountains National Park receives 2.5 million people per year. Visitation is increasing. In Arches National Park in Utah, the campsites within the park are filled nightly during peak season. In Denali National Park in Alaska, visitors ride on buses because private vehicle traffic is highly regulated. The national park idea seems to work for people, so surely we can protect islands of biodiversity. The situation can be viewed in another way: if we can isolate wildlife issues in parks, maybe we can deal with them. However, for the flora and fauna of national parks, the idea that a boundary can save, preserve, and protect nature is nearly bankrupt.

Other attempts to minimize wildlife issues or prevent them altogether are more promising than national parks. The Man and the Biosphere program deals with wildlife and humans simultaneously. Humans and their activities are considered to be part of the greater landscape. Still other ways of conserving biodiversity and mitigating adverse impacts on wildlife are to ranch wildlife and to make room for wildlife by improving habitat. Private sector initiatives are also an important component of minimizing impacts on wildlife. Although each wildlife issue is ultimately unique, certain generalities can nevertheless be drawn from many examples around the world.

313

FIGURE 17.1   A saddlebill stork shades the water while hunting for fish in Akagera National Park, Rwanda. The park was destroyed by invading rebels in 1991.

NATIONAL PARKS

National parks and reserves will be the last refuge for many species, at least if current trends continue. Unfortunately, most parks are isolated and therefore do not permit genetic transfer between populations outside the boundaries of the park. The persistence of populations within parks and preserves is also not well understood; however, few argue that such reserves can sustain populations into the future. Newmark (1995) analyzed mammalian extinctions in several western North American national parks. Within the mammalian orders Lagomorpha (rabbits), Carnivora (carnivores), and Artiodactyla (hoofed animals), Newmark found that the number of extinctions exceeded the number of colonizations. While there were 7 colonizations of parks, there were 29 extinctions. For instance, in Bryce Canyon, Utah, white-tailed jackrabbits, red foxes, and spotted skunks have not been seen for ten years. At Crater Lake, Oregon, river otters, ermine, mink, and spotted skunks have been extirpated. The wolf has been lost from Mount Rainer, Manning Provincial Park, and Yellowstone National Park, although it has been reintroduced into Yellowstone. Pronghorn antelope and elk have disappeared from Mount Lassen in California, and the moose is gone from Manning Provincial Park in Canada.

Human activities and land use patterns near the national parks influence animal persistence patterns within the parks. For instance, if forested areas outside a heavily forested park are destroyed, the park is likely to become more like an island than a continental park. Animals within the park will most likely remain there and not venture beyond the boundaries. What Newmark's work shows is that species from rabbits and skunks to wolves and elk have difficulty persisting even in large parks and preserves. Thus, the presumption that parks and preserves will protect species is turning out to be more a dream than a reality, more a belief than a scientific fact.

Harris and Frederick (1990) noted that existing conservation strategies are inadequate to preserve the long-term biological diversity of a region. The Endangered Species Act is invoked when a species has suffered severe habitat loss and the population is reduced and declining. Harris and Frederick suggest that "old-growth forests must be conserved for many scientific, moral, and aesthetic reasons, only one of which involves an endangered species." The Endangered Species Act does not apply to habitats, but rather to species of plants and animals within those habitats. In an age of ecosystem management, there is no endangered habitat act.

MAN AND THE BIOSPHERE

The Action Plan for Biosphere Reserves was published in 1984 by the United Nations Environment Programme (UNEP) and the United Nations Educational, Scientific and Cultural Organization (UNESCO) (Nature and Resources 1984). Governments and international organizations were invited to undertake activities to improve and expand the international biosphere reserve network, to develop basic knowledge for conserving ecosystems and biological diversity, and to make biosphere reserves more effective in linking conservation and development in fulfilling the broad objectives of the Man and the Biosphere (MAB) program. MAB was initiated in 1971 to provide the information needed to solve practical problems in resource management. The United States has 44 biosphere reserves. Everglades National Park and Grand Canyon National Park are examples.

A minimum set of activities were recommended for implementation in each biosphere reserve:

1. Collection of a baseline inventory of flora and fauna and their uses
2. Preparation of a history of research done in the reserve
3. Establishment of research facilities and research programs
4. Establishment of training and education programs

5. Preparation of a management plan that addresses biosphere reserve functions

MAB research was directed at building an understanding of the structure and function of ecosystems and the effects of different types of human activity. It was an attempt to go beyond the idea of parks and reserves existing as islands within a human-dominated landscape. Key ingredients of MAB were the involvement of local people in research projects and establishing cooperative research projects with other researchers in the social, biological, and physical sciences.

One theme of the program was the conservation of natural areas and the genetic biodiversity they contained. The concept of a biosphere reserve was conceived to be a series of protected areas, linked through a coordinated international network that would demonstrate the value of conservation and its relationship with development. The first reserves were designated in 1976. In 1984, there were 243 reserves in 65 countries. Today, there are 328 biosphere reserves in 65 countries.

The Food and Agricultural Organization (FAO) was especially interested because biosphere reserves were *in situ* reservoirs of genetic resources, especially wild crop relatives, forest species, and ancestors and close relatives of domestic stocks. UNEP was interested in global monitoring using comparable methodologies and parameters. The International Union for Conservation of Nature and Natural Resources considered biosphere reserves to be a useful concept in regional planning because conservation was presumably linked with sustainable development.

The main characteristics of biosphere reserves were:

1. Protected areas of representative terrestrial and coastal environments that have been internationally recognized for their value in conservation and in providing the scientific knowledge, skills, and human values to support sustainable development.
2. United to form a worldwide network that facilitated information sharing relevant to conservation and management.
3. Representative examples of natural or minimally disturbed landscapes within one of the world's biogeographical provinces and as many of the following areas as possible:
   a. Centers of endemism and of genetic richness or unique natural features
   b. Areas of suitable experimental manipulation to develop, assess, and demonstrate the methods of sustainable development

    c. Examples of harmonious landscapes resulting from traditional patterns of land use

    d. Examples of modified or degraded landscapes that were suitable for restoration to natural or near-natural conditions

4. Biosphere reserves were large enough to be an effective conservation unit and have value for measurements of long-term changes in the biosphere.

5. Biosphere reserves provided opportunities for ecological research, education, and training.

6. There should be buffer zones surrounding the biosphere reserve.

7. There should exist effective long-term protection.

8. People should be considered part of a biosphere reserve.

9. Biosphere reserves were "harmonious marriages" of conservation and development.

10. Biosphere reserves were open systems with areas of undisturbed natural landscapes surrounded by areas of sympathetic and compatible use.

11. Because of their secure protection, large size, and the inclusion of areas free from significant human impact, biosphere reserves typically provide ideal sites for monitoring changes in the physical and biological components of the biosphere. Their protection and scientific mission make biosphere reserves particularly attractive sites for gathering scientific information. Scientists had more confidence that the integrity of their sites was respected and that collected data contributed to a growing data bank of increasing scientific significance.

12. In biosphere reserves, interdisciplinary research programs involving natural and social sciences were encouraged to develop models for sustainable conservation of a large natural region.

13. The international network provided a framework for comparative studies of similar problems in different parts of the world; for testing, standardizing, and transferring new methodologies; and for coordinating the development of information management systems.

14. Biosphere reserves served as important field centers for the education and training of scientists, resource managers, protected area administrators, visitors, and local people.

15. Biosphere reserve status provided a framework for improving cooperation at the local, regional, and international levels.

16. All biosphere reserves were part of the international network that provided a framework for communication within and among biogeographic regions. Cooperation involved sharing of technology and information,

and the development of coordinated monitoring and research projects, to provide better information on problems of common interest.
17. Biosphere reserves were to be used to:
    a. Collect background global monitoring of biological, chemical, and physical variables
    b. Carry out research in basic ecological processes that might be applied to management sciences
    c. Monitor the results and effectiveness of management
    d. Assemble traditional knowledge about the use of species and landscapes
    e. Make knowledge gained readily available

The biosphere program is alive today. Everglades National Park in Florida has become a focal point of restoration efforts of the U.S. government. Despite the designation of Everglades National Park as a World Heritage Site, man's management of the park has nearly destroyed it. Nevertheless, the MAB program continues to be a viable alternative to unmitigated exploitation.

TIGERS

In 1989, Ranthambore National Park in northern India was home to some 30 tigers. Although the park was a lush but dry forest, large herds of gaur, chital, and sambar; groups of langur monkeys; and birds thrived. Near a lake within the park, a female tiger named Noon hunted chital and sambar. Tigers are large and brightly colored; when the tiger walks, all animals take notice. When Noon walked boldly along the lakeshore, she uttered low growls at the hoof stamping and alarm calls of the chital. She could hardly be missed. She wandered off a short distance from the lake into the high grass, where she layed down to nap. The coming and going of the chital and sambar to drink did not disturb her. She awoke around 4:00 P.M., hungry for a meal. Carefully, bringing herself up to a crouch, she raised her head slightly to view her surroundings. Several chital were drinking from the lake. As the chital browsed on the tender shore grasses, Noon's muscles began to tense and ripple.

Sensing that the chital had no way to escape, Noon launched herself from her crouch and with leaps of 15 feet at a time closed the gap between herself and her prey in a few seconds. The confused chital scattered in all directions. One unfortunate chital headed into the lake. Noon powered her way through the water with sheer brute strength and caught the chital by the back of the neck. Her enormous paws wrapped around the chital's neck and her extended claws raked across the animal's back and neck, seeking a hold. Noon's jaw locked into the chital's throat and the struggle ended quickly. Partly swimming, partly walking, she dragged her prey ashore and cleaned herself. The chital carcass lasted four days.

In 1995, no tigers remained in Ranthambore. Surrounded by a landscape dominated by humans, with every green leaf within 10 feet of the ground eaten by goats, Ranthambore was invaded by villagers. India is one of only a few places where goats feed on the trees, so desperate are they for forage. The tigers were killed one by one. First, tigers in habitats within park areas frequented less often by tourists became victims. Slowly, tour drivers noticed that fewer tigers were being seen. Village woodcutters were seen more often in the park, collecting bundles of vegetation to feed their starving goats. One by one the tigers disappeared. Noon was one of the most photographed tigers in Ranthambore. Unfortunately, her status did not save her.

Now, an estimated 5000 wild tigers (*Pantera tigris*) remain in the wild. In years past, British hunters atop elephants could kill 20 tigers in a single hunt. Those days will never return. Private breeders in Thailand want the Thai Forestry Commission to allow them to raise tigers and sell them to Chinese medicinal companies. The Chinese believe that tiger bones, penises, and other body parts can cure anything from arthritis to impotence. Of course, there is no scientific evidence that tiger penises cure impotence, but perhaps if one believes that sleeping with a tiger penis under his pillow can cure his sexual ills, it will indeed work. Currently, wild tigers are illegally taken to supply part of the demand (see Chapter 3).

There is a worldwide ban on tiger products, and tigers are an endangered species under the Convention on International Trade in Endangered Species (CITES); hence international trade is forbidden. However, Thailand has a right to sell the Asian cats and their parts domestically. The director of Siracha Farm, Mr. Somphong Temsiriphong, has invested money in the hopes that the government of Thailand will approve his scheme to raise and sell tigers. He is now raising 35 tigers in Bangkok, where a whole dead tiger can be sold illegally for $10,000. He intends to breed as many tigers as possible to meet the local demand. The potential regional demand is enormous.

Somphong has a display case with, among other items, such valuable products as dried tiger penises that can sell for $4500. Other local breeders are ready to cash in as well. Breeders' practices are less than palatable for animal rights activists. Cubs are separated from their mothers as early as six months so that females can be made to produce more litters. Members of Thailand Wildlife Foundation say breeders are in it for the money. "What they want is to end up selling tiger steaks and penis soup for aphrodisiac purposes, and I just don't think animals should be used like this," said one member.

A government official said that tigers could be farmed as easily as pigs and that the legal supply would reduce prices and take pressure off wild tigers. The West, the official said, is too sentimental about animals. Opponents fear that trade in wild tigers could be more easily disguised and that the last of the world's remaining wild tigers could be wiped out. Thus, the wildlife issue here seems clear. Should raising endangered species legally for fun and profit be permitted? Could some of the profits be taxed and perhaps devoted to wild tiger protection and habitat restoration?

The free market is an incredibly powerful economic force. With tigers selling for $10,000 each, there is an enormous incentive to raise them domestically. When a fishery is a stake, the tragedy-of-the-commons takes over. Everyone thinks that since the resource is going to be depleted, they should get their share before someone else does. We must remember, however, that there is a lot of middle ground between unmitigated greed and the sustainable uses of natural resources. The most common bird in the world is the chicken (*Gallus gallus*). The reason this is so is because people all over the world eat chicken eggs and meat. Even their feathers are used to fill pillows. Chickens are relatively inexpensive almost everywhere people are found. One cannot help but wonder if the California condor (*Gymnogyps californianus*) would be facing extinction if people ate the meat and eggs of this beautiful bird.

On November 17, 1994, The Associated Press reported that Asian countries at a CITES meeting agreed to work toward elimination of tiger bone and rhinoceros horn used as traditional medicines. China, South Korea, and Thailand, the consuming countries, agreed to work with physicians and pharmaceutical companies to find alternative treatments.

Tiger bone was used to treat muscular problems, and rhino horn was used to reduce fever. Of course, the root problem is that 2000 years of traditional recorded medicine and belief, and not education and fact, led people to make their product decisions. These traditional cures have become increasing costly, and cost was no doubt a factor in bringing these countries to the bargaining table. Tiger bone sells for $75 to $155 a pound. Would any consumer know the difference between a vial of tiger bone and a vial of chicken bone? Rhino horn is outlandishly expensive, especially in China, where the average monthly wage is $29. Nevertheless, consumers seek minuscule amounts for treatments.

Japan was the third largest consumer of rhino horn medicines. When pharmaceutical companies discontinued use of the horn in the 1980s, consumption dropped. During that time, rhino populations dropped as well, from 70,000 in 1970 to 12,000 in 1995. Most of these are in pens or other facilities where they can be protected. Rhino horn is still used for dagger handles in Yemen.

BUTTERFLIES

Larry Orsak, director of the Christensen Research Institute in Papua New Guinea, considers selling insects such as butterflies a great way to preserve tropical rain forest. He suggests that "those who equate killing butterflies with destroying butterflies don't know much about butterflies, the tropics, or what strategies have gotten people in developing countries to save their forests. The fact is, buying tropical butterflies for your collection may be the best investment you ever made in tropical forest protection." How could this be? Perhaps insect ranching is the answer to insect conservation.

The government of Papua New Guinea set up the Insect Farming and Trading Agency (IFTA) in 1978. The agency purchases insects from local villagers and sells them to collectors around the world. Most of the insects are collected from the wild; however, the IFTA requires that common birdwing butterflies be bred by villagers. Many villagers now plant extra insect food plants and then catch and sell adult butterflies. Certainly, this is insect ranching for profit. In addition, not all butterflies are harvested, so the food plants serve to increase the available resources for all insects.

In the case of Papua New Guinea, raising and selling or collecting excess insects helps preserve wild populations. How sustainable is insect ranching? Insects generally have high reproductive rates. Obviously, they also have very high mortality rates. If more caterpillars could survive, there would be more butterflies. By collecting the caterpillars and bringing them home, villagers are increasing survival rates of the butterflies. However, caterpillars also serve as food to birds. Ultimately, by increasing the number of food plants, there will likely be an increase in the number of butterflies, and thus more can be harvested. Also, eggs can be placed on favored food plants and raised in glass containers. The emergent butterflies can be used as eggs layers or be harvested and sold.

Every legally exported Papua New Guinea lot of insects comes with an export permit. Each insect does not come with its own permit. If the lot contains birdwing butterflies (the world's largest butterflies), it must also have a CITES stamp. It is up to the buyer of the lot to then copy the permit or otherwise certify that such a permit is on file. If you are a serious collector of butterflies, your collection should certainly have a birdwing in it. Would you know the difference between a legitimate permit and a fraud? Would you be willing to risk a fine and possible jail sentence on a facsimile of a "legitimate" permit? If the "bugs" can be worked out, insect ranching might catch on.

PACIFIC SALMON

Salmon are amazing fish. After being born in the upreaches of a backwater stream, the young fry grow quickly on insect prey and then make their way to sea. Some four years later, they answer their biological clock and begin migrating back to their place of birth to spawn. The trip back is a hazardous one indeed. Presuming they have not been harvested at sea (most likely they have), the salmon head back toward the stream of their birth. Predatory seals know that the salmon are headed for freshwater streams. With a meal on the way, seals congregate in pools where rivers meet the sea. If enough salmon make the journey, the seals cannot eat all the bounty. However, when fewer salmon arrive, day after day the seals quickly attack and eat them.

A surviving salmon ceases eating when it reaches fresh water and begins to deteriorate and die. The most obvious change is its color, which turns a bright blood red. Many made-man and natural hazards lay in the salmon's path. Dams and waterfalls must be negotiated. It seems almost unbelievable that a salmon, or any fish for that matter, could possibly swim up a waterfall, but indeed salmon do. Salmon use natural pools to circle and then propel themselves upward, furiously swimming against the waterfall. Many times, they are washed back down where they again rest and gain strength. Once again, they propel themselves upward, swimming hard against the falls. Some propel themselves not upward but sideways and land hard against rocks and boulders. Some become trapped on land and are unable to struggle free. But the drive to spawn is a powerful one and the salmon are driven to answer this call. Many have survived a seal attack but are missing a fin or part of their tail. This severely impacts their ability to make the journey upstream, but they are compelled to try. Anyone who has stood by a waterfall and watched salmon struggle time and again to climb the falls will probably think twice before eating salmon, so incredible is their tenacity to spawn.

Fortunately, biologists know how to save the Pacific salmon populations because the biology of salmon has been studied for decades, and the causes of the decline are understood. Today, in some parts of Oregon and Washington, spawning salmon will find improved habitat in which to reproduce and die. More than any other factor, upstream habitat alteration and destruction have led to declining population numbers. Now, restoration efforts are underway to help improve these habitats. Many local and state governments are teaming with environmental groups, local volunteers, out-of-work loggers, and lumber companies to restore spawning grounds and fry habitat to more complex natural conditions the fish favor.

To reproduce, salmon require clean gravel beds, and hatchlings need a complex habitat to escape predation and feed successfully. Insects are the young fishes main prey, and the small fish must be able to hide and seize unsuspecting insects. In a more natural setting, fallen logs, boulders, bank overhangs, and shade trees provide an ideal habitat for both insects and fish. This complex structure also creates bottom ripples, uneven current patterns, and microhabitats which increase biological complexity. In other words, increased structural complexity leads to increased biological complexity. Increased biological complexity also supports and maintains increased structural complexity. Removing any component, such as a dead tree or a boulder or any of the insects, reduces complexity and therefore is detrimental to all elements of the system.

Previously, people removed dead logs in the mistaken belief that doing so would benefit fish. Indeed, as we now appreciate, these activities had just the opposite effect. By removing a log, environmental complexity was reduced. The local complex bottom topography of the streambed was changed from alternating ripples and pools to a uniform flat bottom. Fish hiding spots were taken away. The light patterns created by the log disappeared. Insects deserted. The bank overhang that had been held in place by grass roots and a reduced flow rate created by the log collapsed into the stream. Without the cool, shady overhang, the young fish had no place to hide.

Cutting logs along the stream not only took away the patchy light patterns but also released soil into the stream, choking spawning gravel beds. Insect diversity was reduced and more sun on the stream increased water temperatures, killing microorganisms. Long-term salmon production plummets when structural complexity decreases and requires three or four decades to recover. In an effort to jump-start the recovery process on the Upper Rogue River in Oregon, a restoration team brought in large tree trunks and anchored them in natural positions. Streambed complexity immediately began to improve. Pools and ripples developed and fish hiding places were created.

Downstream on the Rogue River, Savage Rapids Dam impedes or kills tens of thousands of migrating salmon yearly. The National Marine Fisheries Service estimates that some 45,000 more salmon and steelhead trout (20% of the population) would survive if the dam were completely removed. After a long struggle, Oregon residents decided the dam had to go. With the dam's imminent demise, restoration efforts are now underway. Certainly, the road to restoration will not be clear of obstacles. Agricultural interests fear losing hard-won irrigation rights. One question of interest that must be answered is just how far restoration efforts should proceed away from stream banks. The federal plan stipulates "a uniform zone equal to twice the height of the tallest streamside trees or 300 feet, whichever is greater"—sort of a one-size-fits-all approach to stream restoration. Nevertheless, restorers believe the cumulative impact will be great and the payoff rapid. To maintain public support and monitor restoration efforts, fish counts will be made each winter.

On March 30, 1994, the *Wall Street Journal* reported that a federal judge declared that the National Marine Fisheries Service, the U.S. Army Corps of Engineers, and other government agencies responsible for managing dams and reservoirs on the Snake and Columbia rivers had broken the law. The agencies, it seemed, had pushed through a dam-operating plan they knew would have killed millions of salmon.

PRIVATE SECTOR COOPERATION

Since habitat loss is usually the main, although not the only, problem behind a wildlife issue, acquisition of habitat is one means of protecting wildlife. However, habitat purchase is expensive and often impossible. Land use controls are also not acceptable to many landowners who feel that "big government" should not tell them what to do with their land. As a result, it is futile, almost impossible, to implement an extensive system of species-based land use controls (de Klemm 1993).

Private landowners should somehow be made more responsible for the management of their land to be consistent with species protection, while at the same time providing the necessary income a landowner expects.

Crested Caracara

Joan Morrison, University of Florida doctoral candidate, is carrying out an ecological study of the life history, nesting activity, habitat associations, and demographics of the crested caracara (*Caracara plancus*) (Figure 17.2) in cooperation with landowners in south-central Florida. The crested caracara was listed as threatened on July 6, 1987 under the Endangered Species Act (see Chapter 2).

As a cooperative effort between ranchers and scientists, the main focus of the research is to understand the biology of the crested caracara and document land management practices that are compatible with its survival. Morrison and the ranchers have forged a unique bond of trust, working together to increase awareness of the caracara among Floridians and to discuss how ranches can maintain sustainable, economically viable activities while also conserving native habitats and wildlife species.

The beginning of the year is when crested caracaras nest and raise young. In Florida, the breeding season can extend from September through June, although most of the population begins egg laying in January and February.

FIGURE 17.2 Crested caracara. The only population east of the Mississippi is found around Lake Okeechobee, Florida, where the species is listed as threatened.

Some young have already fledged by March. These early nesters may go on to produce another brood.

Because they nest in open habitat, caracaras are quite secretive during the nesting period. Adults do not spend much time at the nest except during incubation and while the chicks are very young. The yellow and brown pattern of the young provides effective camouflage, protecting them while the parents are away from the nest. Nest predators include crows, raccoons, and perhaps other raptors.

Crested caracaras reach the northern limits of their distribution in the southern United States. Populations occur in southeastern Texas, southwestern Arizona, and south-central Florida. Florida's population has been isolated since the last ice age. Crested caracaras also occur in Mexico and Cuba and in suitable

habitat throughout Central and South America. They prefer open, short grassland habitats with scattered trees for nesting. In Florida, they nest primarily in
palm trees.

Currently in Florida, crested caracaras are found primarily on privately
owned cattle ranches. Apparently, land management practices of the ranchers
keep the habitat in a condition suitable for caracaras. Nests as close together as
1 km have been found. Crested caracaras are diet generalists, feeding on a
variety of vertebrate prey as well as carrion. Unfortunately, the crested caracara
is threatened as its habitat falls victim to Florida's rapid urban and agricultural
development.

Unless the adults have a second brood, young caracaras may remain on the
territory for up to ten months, until the adults begin another breeding effort.
After they leave their natal territory, juvenile caracaras are nomadic, wandering
throughout the region. They often band together in groups of up to 30 individuals. If adults have a second brood, the young of the first brood are driven off
after only three months. Since young birds learn to forage from their parents,
perhaps there is a differential survival rate between young from the first brood
that spend only a short time with their parents versus young of the second
brood that spend eight months with the adults.

It is believed that caracaras, like eagles, do not breed until age three or four.
Radiotelemetry is only now beginning to provide information on survival, activities, and habitat selection of young, nonbreeding caracaras. Individuals
seem to be philopatric to a region of the study area not far from their natal
territory, and these juveniles are most often found on cattle ranches throughout
the region.

By leaving nesting trees such as palms in cattle pastures, local ranchers are
helping to save this unique bird of prey. Habitat destruction due to conversion
of cattle pastures into shopping malls, trailer parks, agriculture, and housing
developments continues to threaten the crested caracara's long-term existence
in Florida. With 13.7 million people in Florida and 892 people a day moving
into the state, habitat destruction will likely continue. Ranchers, however, have
found a way to allow the crested caracara to survive. How can ranchers be
compensated for their efforts?

In 1995, Georgia-Pacific Corporation, the largest U.S. forest products company, announced plans to protect red-cockaded woodpecker habitat on its production timberlands. Georgia-Pacific claims that some 300 to 400 red-cockaded
woodpeckers live on its land. The company announced plans to stop logging on
land that contains colonies of red-cockaded woodpeckers. Additionally, Georgia-Pacific will establish buffer areas around each colony, where timber will be
selectively harvested. No road building will take place where colonies exist.

Clearly, the private sector must steward its lands in a more ecologically responsible way. How can private companies be rewarded for protecting habitat for endangered species?

Ecotourism

Perhaps the most effective use of wildlife is ecotourism. The worldwide demand for travel to exotic places is increasing. Tourists interested in wildlife are willing to travel to remote places to get a glimpse of rare species. In Manu National Park in Peru, tourists are willing to pay more than $100 a night to see tropical birds and primates in a virgin lowland rain forest of the Peruvian Amazon. Tourist visits to these regions can be carefully controlled as well. Thus, core regions of the reserve can be carefully protected and can serve as population sources to other areas that are impacted by tourism. Areas can be placed on a rotation basis and allowed to recover.

Africa seems to be haunted by unstable governments, civil wars, droughts, extreme poverty, declining growth rates, and a rapidly increasing population. However, as the mountain gorilla project in Rwanda demonstrated, wildlife can be protected even under the most extreme conditions. The local guards in Rwanda performed admirably and went almost a year without salary. They protected the gorillas as best they could. Several of the guards lost family members to the war. Nevertheless, they protected the gorillas. There is real hope in Rwanda that the mountain gorillas can be saved and tourism will revive. In the past, gorilla tourism was the second largest source of hard currency for Rwanda. Unfortunately, very little money went back into the local community. Perhaps this will change under the new government.

Project SAFEGUARD in Alaska

Alaska covers 656,424 square miles; protecting wildlife against poachers is therefore a formidable task. In 1984, a private, nonprofit organization formed the Alaska Fish and Wildlife SAFEGUARD program to protect wildlife. SAFEGUARD pays money to anonymous citizens who report wildlife violations that lead to arrests or citations. Several examples cited on the SAFEGUARD Web page highlight the effectiveness of the program.

On April 1, 1991, three moose were poached and wasted in Kincaid Park in Anchorage. After extensive publicity, along with advertised rewards, a SAFEGUARD call resulted in the arrest and conviction of an individual. He was sentenced to 55 days in jail, lost all hunting and fishing privileges, was ordered to perform 100 hours of community service, and was fined $7500.

In 1991, SAFEGUARD received a call about a crab fishing vessel that was stealing other vessels' crabs and crab pots in the Bering Sea. Fish and Wildlife Protection obtained and served search warrants on the skipper. As a result, the skipper was charged and prosecuted on several misdemeanor and felony counts. He was fined $40,000, forfeited all crab pots in his possession, and his fishing privileges in Alaska were revoked. In addition, his million-dollar fishing vessel was forfeited to the state of Alaska.

In 1992, a report to SAFEGUARD indicated nine bottomfish trawlers were routinely fishing in the closed waters of Alaska near King Cove. This prompted the formation of a task force which included 40 state and U.S. enforcement agents. Over 1000 illegal fishing acts in Alaska waters were documented and 26 boats were targeted for prosecution. Just one company was responsible for the illegal taking of approximately 27 million pounds of fish valued at $5.4 million. The estimated criminal and civil settlements paid to the state of Alaska, resulting from this one SAFEGUARD case could exceed $15 million.

A call to SAFEGUARD resulted in the 1992 conviction of a lower Yukon fish processor for buying fish and not reporting the purchases to the Alaska Department of Fish and Game. The processor and fishermen who sold him the illegal product were fined nearly $1.5 million, and the judge ordered 23 vessels forfeited to the state of Alaska. These included fishing boats, tenders, and several large processing barges and ships.

SAFEGUARD received a complaint in 1993 that a man from Idaho had been buying Alaska resident licenses and tags for 11 years and that he had accumulated bear, moose, walrus, and musk ox trophies. After a lengthy joint investigation by Alaska Fish and Wildlife Protection, Idaho Fish and Game, and the U.S. Fish and Wildlife Service, the suspect was convicted of multiple hunting violations as well as falsifying license documents. The judge fined him $3000, sentenced him to 30 days in jail, revoked his hunting privileges, and ordered forfeiture of all game trophies related to the case.

Interestingly, records show that approximately 75% of callers refuse to accept a reward.

SUSTAINABLE DEVELOPMENT

Most of the earth's biodiversity is in the tropics. Therefore, it is very easy for northern Europeans and North Americans to suggest that wildlife everywhere should be protected. Isn't it curious that Europeans wiped out much of their native species at least 500 years ago? Europe was once heavily forested. Now, almost no forest remains. The United Kingdom had bear and moose—now there are none. It took a while longer to reach and nearly wipe out the buffalo of North America, but once the slaughter started, the end came quickly. Buffalo are only now recovering. Habitat change and loss in Europe and North America have been extensive. Still, logging companies yearn to finish off the old-growth timber of the Northwest and Alaska.

The richest nations on earth consume most of the earth's natural resources, particularly depletable resources. North America has a penchant for cheap fuel. The Japanese have an insatiable desire for rare and expensive wood products. The poorest nations generally are found in the tropics. The world's breadbaskets are in higher latitude countries. Thus, to suggest that the poorer countries on earth conserve their wildlife so that the rich nations can enjoy it is, to be generous, laughable. Why should Peruvian Indians living off the forest, as they have for thousands of years, not kill the last of this or that macaw for food? If it were not for the pet trade, there might be many more where the macaws came from. Why should an Eskimo avoid killing whales when the Japanese continue to eat whale meat?

Obviously, no nation can order another nation to conserve its wildlife or its natural resources. People everywhere want and deserve a better life for themselves and their families. Nor is it natural to assume that a nation will demand its citizens cease certain activities that have been a traditional way of life. The San peoples of the Kalahari have hunted wildlife for more than 100,000 years. And they would still be doing so today were it not for huge cattle ranches that have destroyed wildlife habitat over vast regions of southern Africa. The San are not responsible for the great loss of wildlife in southern Africa, any more than a South American forest dweller is responsible for the loss of macaws. Indeed, it is in the best interests of native peoples to ensure that no resource is consumed to extinction.

Early hunters of the post-glacial period may have hunted out the North American mammoth and the giant sloth. It is not true that native hunters have preserved every species. However, it was certainly in the best interests of native people to conserve their resources. The San people of the Kalahari Desert, for instance, eat only half of the berries on a bush and leave the remaining half for other species and for seed dispersal. Only highly efficient developed nations with modern factory ships could deplete the seas of fish, only commercial hunters could wipe out billions of passenger pigeons, and only demand for rhino horn could drive an ancient species to the brink of extinction.

Today, novel solutions are needed to address our wildlife issues. Earlier we discussed how the public of south Florida demanded an end to frog gigging. Within two days of the publication of a newspaper article educating the public about gigging in a national preserve, a public outcry ended the slaughter of frogs. What the public wants, the public gets! The novel solution to the frog gigging problem was not to call in legions of scientists but simply to educate the public to a potential problem.

What can be done about preserving biodiversity in the tropics? Can wildlife have economic as well as aesthetic value? How can aesthetic value be translated into economic value? Can humans live sustainably anywhere? Considering Easter Island, Mesopotamia, and Mesoamerica (Chapter 3), are humans even capable of living sustainably off our planet? Who must learn to live sustainably—the developed nations or the Third World nations?

The term "sustainable development" was introduced in a 1987 report entitled *Our Common Future* by the World Commission on Environment and Development of the United Nations. The commission defined sustainable development as "development that meets the needs of the present without compromising the ability of future generations to meet their own needs." Of course, meeting tomorrow's needs without meeting today's needs is irrelevant, so there is a natural priority, if only implicitly, attached to the definition. Beyond meeting basic human needs, most people agree that there is an economic meaning to the term "sustainable development."

Sustainable development was presumed to be "exploitation of resources" while ensuring "the ability of the biosphere to absorb the effects of human activities is consistent with future as well as present needs." Certainly, "sustainable development can be pursued more easily when population size is stabilized at a level consistent with the productive capacity of the ecosystem." At the United Nations Conference on Environment and Development in Rio de Janeiro in 1992, Agenda 21, with a target date of the middle of the 21st century, was proposed to allow earthlings to adjust their needs to the finite resources of the earth.

How is sustainable development achieved? Which economies are more sustainable? Is an economy built on large capital investments and cheap energy sources paid for in paper money sustainable? Or do we have to ensure that the Native Amerindian living in the Amazon can sustain their way of life through consumptive uses of wildlife into the future? In other words, which economy is more sustainable, especially when oil prices eventually climb to new heights? The effect of a tenfold increase in fuel prices on the developed world would be catastrophic, while the Amerindian would hardly notice the effect. Indeed, the concept of sustainable development is not an Amerindian idea; it is a rich nation idea brought about by the fear that other nations want what they have— access to capital, and cheap, nonrenewable resources. This concern has been brought about by increasing population densities, species extinctions, and loss of environmental quality.

In Robinson and Redford (1991), the question is asked, "Do we, as human beings, have the right to use wildlife for our own purposes and benefits, or do wild species have inalienable rights of their own?" If wildlife has no value, utilitarian or otherwise, then why should it be worth saving? If all people agreed that wildlife has no value, there would never be another wildlife issue.

Apparently, judging by the number of wildlife issues, some fraction of people think wildlife has value. This value might be aesthetic, scientific, spiritual, consumptive, or some other reason. For instance, you probably never will see a wild snow leopard and maybe you will never see one in a zoo, but you might be glad that such an animal as ghostlike as the wind exists in the high Himalayas. You may not know why hawk-moths exist, but you might understand the fact that because a hawk-moth's tongue is as long as its body, there is something special going on here. In fact, the hawk-moth pollinates certain plants. Without the hawk-moth, these plants could not reproduce.

Perhaps you are the kind of person who does not have to have an immediate reason to believe that everything is connected to everything else and that a creature's existence did not come about by chance alone. For instance, Emmons (1987) claims that jaguars, panthers, and ocelots eat prey in relation to its abundance in the environment. If one prey becomes more common, it is more likely to be eaten. If something is rare, it is less likely to end up as a meal. Thus, biodiversity is higher where these top carnivores knock back any species that becomes too common. The same might be true for birds of prey, seals in the sea, and sharks as well. It just might be that all top predators help maintain a healthy environment and increase diversity by their food habits. But if you did not understand this and you hunted jaguars and panthers to extinction because they are big cats and you think it is fun to shoot big cats, you might destroy biodiversity in the process of having your fun.

Wildlife has many uses to humankind, one of which goes well beyond the obvious uses suggested in Robinson and Redford (1991). Wildlife is important in maintaining a healthy environment because of the so-called ecosystem services, the work that it does for humans every day free of charge.

Think of insectivorous birds gleaning insects from trees. One famous ecological experiment compared the success of trees with and without services provided by insectivorous birds. In side-by-side experiments, some trees were covered with a mesh that let bugs in and kept birds out. Other trees were left alone. Net-covered trees failed to produce healthy leaves. Those leaves that opened were attacked by hordes of insect pests. Leaves of trees not covered by nets did fine, largely because birds consumed the leaf-eating insects. The birds performed a service—they ate insects. And they did it without sending us a bill.

If the birds were gone, our use of chemicals and pesticides would have to increase if we wanted to have trees.

There is no doubt that wildlife can be of economic value and can be sustainably harvested commercially. Alligator farms in Florida are doing a booming business in meat and hides. Wild alligator populations have responded to protection and there is now a limited hunting season on alligators. Where people depend on wildlife for food, the question is one of sustainably harvesting wildlife. Can wildlife be harvested sustainably to feed a family? How about two families? Can wild animals be harvested commercially?

Notice that we are not asking whether or not wildlife should be harvested. The fact of the matter is that across most of the world, people depend on bush meat to live. Perhaps people have replaced jaguars, panthers, lions, tigers, and leopards as the world's top predators.

South American Vicunas and Guanacos

Overhunting and habitat destruction continue to be the most severe and widespread human activities that threaten wildlife. In marginal lands, such as semi-arid and arid lands, human activities are especially detrimental. The high Andes of South America is important habitat for the South American vicuna (*Vicugna vicugna*) and the guanaco (*Lama guanicoe*). Both these animals have high economic potential for their wool; however, both have experienced dramatic population declines over the last century (Franklin and Fritz 1991).

Sustainable yield of wildlife products, especially commercially sustainable yields as compared to subsistence yields, is a difficult problem, especially in a semi-arid region where wildlife populations are scattered across a vast tractless region. Vicunas and guanacos could have a large economic impact if they could, in some way, be managed. The same is true for the other two members of the South American camelid family, the llama (*Lama glama*) and the alpaca (*L. pacos*). Vicunas produce "silky fine wool," followed by guanacos in terms of quality of wool. The llama is a beast of burden in South America, and the alpaca is a domestic wool producer. There is also a market for the meat and hides of these animals. Certainly, harvesting wild populations of these animals might be possible if their basic biology were understood. Can wild populations of these animals be harvested for their meat and hides and nondestructively for their wool—on a sustainable basis? Is it necessary to allow free-ranging populations to exist and harvest them carefully, or must a ranch be established for a sustained yield to be economically viable? The answers depend critically on knowing the animal's basic biology and ecology.

Green Iguanas

In many countries, slash-and-burn agricultural practices are the means by which land is converted from forest to pasture. Roughly 2 to 3 ha of forest is burned and cultivated by local people and used for 3 years, after which time the land is sold to a cattle rancher. The people move on to another patch of forest. Typically, beef cattle are raised for the export market and, because developed nations are willing to pay a higher price, local meat shortages develop. In some regions, armadillos, agouti, paca, iguanas, deer, and other small animals make up the meat people consume. Werner (1991) undertook research on green iguanas (*Iguana iguana*) as part of the Iguana Management Project sponsored by the Smithsonian Tropical Research Institute and the Pro Iguana Verde Foundation.

Iguana meat is a valuable protein source for rural people, and the eggs are considered aphrodisiacs and delicacies. In Panama, some 70% of the people would eat iguana if it was readily available. However, the iguana is considered endangered in many countries where it was once abundant. Once again, the wildlife issue is clear. Humans have overexploited the iguana so that now it is endangered. The solution is to sustainably manage iguana populations to increase their numbers and provide an inexpensive protein source for humans.

Iguanas are distributed from southern Mexico to Paraguay in South America. They are found on some islands as well. Iguanas are prolific vegetarians and live in a diversity of habitats from tropical to subtropical forests. Much is known about their breeding biology and ecology, and managing wild populations of iguanas is considered difficult. Ranching iguanas, however, might be a viable alternative, but experience shows that captive management of reptiles is "not easy." Werner (1991) claims that populations of iguanas can be made artificially high if their food supply can be maintained at a constant level. Artificial nests can be built, and trees favored by iguanas can be planted. All these management practices are predicated on creating and maintaining artificially high populations so that harvests can be sustained at particular levels.

Howler Monkey Sanctuary

The black howler monkey (*Alouatta pigra*) is known in north-central Belize as the baboon. The baboon is locally abundant and is not hunted by the local people. The Community Baboon Sanctuary in Belize was established on private lands where small-scale cattle ranching and subsistence farming were taking place. Horwich and Lyon (1995) described a "community-based plan" that paralleled the Man and the Biosphere program. Land management plans were jointly developed with local stakeholders because these people were the most knowledgeable about both local conditions and the baboon's requirements.

A tourism program was set up for baboon monkey viewing, and a community education program was established in the form of a museum exhibiting important ecological, conservation, and cultural themes. There is also an ecotourist education program to describe the entire project to tourists interested in visiting the sanctuary. So successful was the program that two other sanctuaries have been started—a sea turtle program to protect beaches where the turtles nest and a manatee community reserve that offers tourism and multiple use of nearby forests. These projects are community based and locally fine-tuned. They offer a substantial improvement to the declaration of national parks as the last refuges of our wildlife.

New Initiatives

Common species of wildlife throughout the United States are declining. Even species we take for granted are diminishing in number because of loss of habitat. More than 89% of all Americans participate in outdoor activities. Americans, it seems, have a love affair with the outdoors and with wildlife. More than 31 million people photographed wildlife in 1991. Between 1980 and 1990, the number of Americans who took wildlife-watching trips increased 63%. More than 76.5 million Americans watch wildlife, 35.6 million fish, and 14.1 million hunt. A proposal that will hopefully be introduced before the U.S. Congress in 1996 calls for a small tax to be levied on recreational products to support state-based wildlife conservation, education, and recreation. The Wildlife Diversity Funding Initiative started by the International Association of Fish and Wildlife Agencies might provide as much as $350 million annually to support conservation. More than 500 well-known companies and 700 conservation, outdoor education, and recreation groups support the proposal.

Previous support programs have been successful. Populations of many species of duck, turkey, pronghorn antelope, and striped bass among others have increased through such programs.

Animal Rights Activists and Endangered Species

The piping plover (*Charadrius melodus*) is endangered. Only 14 nesting pairs of piping plovers were found at the Monomoy National Wildlife Refuge near Chatham, Massachusetts in 1996. According to the U.S. Fish and Wildlife Service, over 900 nested there in 1966. In 1996, however, about 5700 great black-backed gulls (*Larus marinus*) and herring gulls (*L. argentatus*) were breeding in the refuge, whereas no gulls could be found in 1961. Gulls are predatory and will readily eat the young of other birds. On May 19, 1996, The Associated Press reported that the U.S. Fish and Wildlife Service planned to poison the gulls to protect the piping plover and other birds. The gulls now number "in the tens of thousands."

Poison-laced margarine on white bread was placed in the nests of 5700 breeding gulls. Gulls seem to do well wherever humans do well. Large numbers of gulls are seen at garbage dumps and refuse stations. There is little doubt the gulls have increased in number as a result of their association with humans. Animal rights activists, having lost a court appeal to halt the poisonings, placed tuna and charcoal filter sandwiches in 2400 gull nests in an attempt to save them from being poisoned.

The Endangered Species Act obligates the federal government to act within its power to protected listed species. Greater black-backed and herring gulls need no form of similar protection. There is little doubt that the larger and more aggressive gulls would eat the young piping plovers and drive away the adults. Indeed, the result is already clear: without constant vigilance, there will be no piping plovers.

On May 20, 1996, 400 dead gulls were found. The poison was only partially successful. Obviously, this action must be continued. The issue here is quite simple and was decided by the courts. In a democracy, a solution rarely pleases both sides.

THE NEXT 50 YEARS

In the end, humans will have to decide whether they want to live with wildlife or without it. While so much has been lost, ecotourism to exotic places is the fastest growing segment of the tourism industry. People need wild places and wildlife, and both are becoming increasingly rare and expensive.

As Mathews (1994) pointed out, the next 50 years of human existence will probably be the most important in human history. For the first time, humans have the power and technology to alter vast areas of the planet. The population will swell to ten billion people by 2040, and economic output will grow about ninefold. Energy consumption and waste production will continue to grow. Nearly three-fourths of the earth's present population uses as much energy as the other quarter. These fractions will grow closer as other nations develop. Humans will require even more of the earth's primary production to exist. Yet, human understanding and appreciation of ecology are lagging behind our technological prowess. Humans wield powerful machinery and capital, but we lack a fundamental understanding of the consequences of our actions. In many cases, Humpty Dumpty cannot be put back together again.

Wildlife becomes an issue when humans try to live outside nature. Human agricultural schemes attempt to defy nature; dams are built to tame rivers, swamps are drained to bring more land into production, parks are created to "preserve nature," trees are harvested in the name of progress, and fossil fuels are used with abandon to power the "modern" society. Species introductions are altering ecological relationships that evolved through millions of years. Increasingly often, we read, see, or hear about natural disasters. Indeed, the very process that created and maintained our beautiful forests is seen by humans as a destroyer of forests. But humans have prevented fires for so long that the accumulation of debris on the forest floor is indeed a disaster waiting to happen. In our infinite wisdom to protect our forests, we have condemned them to destruction.

The reason the fire in Yellowstone National Park during the summer of 1988 was such a "disaster" is not because the fire was too big but because the park is too small and humans have suppressed fires for too long. We rarely hear that fire in Yosemite National Park acts to increase diversity or a fire in the Great Smokies acted to increase the health of the forest, or a river flooded and fertile silt was spread over 100,000 ha, resulting in one million new cottonwood seedlings springing forth from the floodplain. Instead, it's always something like "a flood destroyed a mobile home park." Human free-water schemes are almost always disasters. Dams are ultimately failures because of their long-term, and unforeseen, deleterious effects.

Many problems arise because of government subsidies. Schemes that are not possible for whatever reason become possible because of a subsidy. Thus, there should be no more government subsidies. There should be no more grazing on public lands, no more harvesting of timber on public lands, no more sugar subsidies, no more dams, no more water projects, no more animal damage control. Habitat destruction must be stopped now, today. Eradication of nonnative species, including those introduced for sport hunting, should begin at once. Without government subsidies, private initiatives that preserve habitat and permit living in harmony with nature will become profitable ventures. Humans must live with nature as part of nature and not apart from nature. Most recreationists would gladly pay modest access fees for use of public forests, especially if they did not see clearcuts or cattle. Increased fees for the national parks would allow land connecting the parks to be purchased. More land, not less, should be put into the public sector. Massive habitat restoration projects, supported by businesses, should begin at once. Many private landowners have already decided to preserve natural habitat remnants. These efforts must be encouraged through tax reductions and other incentives. Grants for public education programs must be made available. Community assistance grants to support wildlife programs in grammar schools across the country would act to increase awareness of wildlife and habitat issues. There must be a new ethic of responsibility toward wildlife and habitat.

Living with nature and realizing that nature most often acts to benefit species increases human quality of life. Quality of life means living closer to nature, not further from it. People everywhere have already lost enough. Most do not accept that enough is enough. Many think enough has been too much. Now they want it back.

EXERCISES

17.1 Visit the Crested Caracara Conservation Project Web page. What incentives do private property landowners have to protect threatened or endangered species?

17.2 The red-cockaded woodpecker (*Picoides borealis*) is endangered. Recently, several forest product companies have established landmark conservation partnerships to help protect the bird's habitat. Do a Web search to learn more about the red-cockaded woodpecker. What makes this bird unique, and why is it important that it be protected?

17.3 Private property owners object to "big government" telling them how to manage their property. Wildlife does not belong to the property owner, however. Since protecting habitat is important, how can government help small private landowners to do so?

17.4 Steelhead trout are amazing fish. Unlike salmon, they return to the sea after spawning. Find out more about steelhead trout in the library or on the Web.

17.5 Use a World Wide Web search engine to locate any interesting approaches to conservation.

17.6 Make a list of the national parks, their areas, and the number of species in each national park.

17.7 Make a list of the World Heritage Parks, their areas, and locations. How many of them are in the tropics? Make use of the library and the World Wide Web.

17.8 Ranchers in Florida are providing excellent habitat for crested cara-caras, as well as Florida panthers and black bears. In the Rocky Mountains, ranchers provide habitat for deer and elk. Perhaps tax incentives would encourage more landowners to preserve habitat for more species. What other incentives might ranchers receive? Present such a proposal to your state representatives. What the public wants, the public gets.

17.9 Do a search on "sustainable development" and decide what "sustain-able" and "development" mean. Is this term an oxymoron?

17.10 Do a search on "fragmented forest" and summarize what happens to biodiversity when forests are continually fragmented. Isn't it time we started reconnecting forests?

17.11 What species are currently harvested commercially? Can wild animals be sustainably harvested? Read Part 4, Wildlife Farming and Ranch-ing, in Robinson and Redford (1991) and update their examples using the World Wide Web.

17.12 In 1991, Werner's research was "in progress." What has happened to iguana ranching since then?

17.13 Create a SAFEGUARD program for your state. What are the essential ingredients of such a program?

17.14 Organize a campaign to restore a critical wildlife habitat in your state. How can you get people interested?

LITERATURE CITED

de Klemm, C. 1993. *Biological Diversity Conservation and the Law.* IUCN, Gland, Switzerland.

Emmons, L.H. 1987. Comparative feeding ecology of felids in a neotropical rainforest. *Behavioral Ecology and Sociobiology* **20**:271–283.

Franklin, W.L. and M.A. Fritz. 1991. Sustained harvesting of Patagonia guanaco: is it possible or too late? pp. 317–336 *in* Robinson, J.G. and K.H. Redford (Eds.). *Neotropical Wildlife Use and Conservation.* University of Chicago Press, Chicago.

Harris, L.D. and Frederick, P.C. 1990. The role of the Endangered Species Act in the conservation of biological diversity. pp. 99–117 *in* Cairns, J. and T. Crawford (Eds.). *An Assessment: Integrated Environmental Management.* Lewis Publishers, Chelsea, Michigan.

Horwich, R.H. and J. Lyon. 1995. Multilevel conservation and education at the community baboon sanctuary, Belize. pp. 235–253 *in* Jacobson, S.K. (Ed.). *Conserving Wildlife*. Columbia University Press, New York.

Mathews, J. 1994. Hard lessons from the death of the Aral Sea. *St. Petersburg Times* October 19.

Nature and Resources. 1984. *UNESCO* **20**(4):1–12.

Newmark, W.D. 1995. Extinction of mammal populations in western North America national parks. *Conservation Biology* **9**(3):512–526.

Robinson, J.G. and K.H. Redford (Eds.). 1991. *Neotropical Wildlife Use and Conservation*. University of Chicago Press, Chicago.

Werner, D.I. 1991. The rational use of green iguanas. pp. 181–201 *in* Robinson, J.G. and K.H. Redford (Eds.). *Neotropical Wildlife Use and Conservation*. University of Chicago Press, Chicago.

INDEX